The Policy Game

The Policy Game

How Special Interests and Ideologues Are Stealing America

PETER NAVARRO

LEXINGTON BOOKS

D.C. Heath and Company • Lexington, Massachusetts • Toronto

Library of Congress Cataloging-in-Publication Data

Navarro, Peter.
  The policy game.

  Reprint. Originally published: New York : Wiley, c1984.
  Bibliography: p.
  Includes index.
  1. Pressure groups—United States.   2. Conservatism—
United States.   3. Liberalism—United States.   4. United
States—Economic policy—1981–   5. United
States—Politics and government—1981–
I. Title.
JK1118.N38   1986   332.4′3′0973   86-15214
ISBN 0-669-14112-7 (pbk. : alk. paper)

Published simultaneously in Canada
Printed in the United States of America
International Standard Book Number: 0-669-14112-7
Library of Congress Catalog Card Number 86-15214

The paper used in this publication meets the minimum
requirements of American National Standard for
Information Sciences—Permanence of Paper for Printed
Library Materials, ANSI Z39.48-1984.

86 87 88 89 90 8 7 6 5 4 3 2 1

to the memory of

Al
and
Lyda Green

Acknowledgments

This book is written for everyone interested in, angry about, or puzzled by the far-reaching economic consequences of American politics. It is a guide to understanding how both greedy special interests and well-intentioned—but at times misguided—ideologues are leading America down a dangerous path towards austerity, divisiveness, and ultimately, needless decline. It is also a guide to an alternative prosperous future, one in which public information, economic pragmatism, and political activism can triumph.

At the Harvard Business School, I would like to thank Professor George C. Lodge, whose analysis of American conservatism and liberalism spawned the "logic of ideology" developed here. Within the Harvard Economics Department, I especially want to thank Professor Joseph P. Kalt, whose pioneering research on the role of special interests and ideology in American politics provided both the inspiration and analytical framework for this book.

Celia Shneider carefully shepherded the manuscript's multiple revisions through the word processor while Jeffrey Zax, Ron Greenberg, Joseph DeManche, William Mogel, and John Slavin provided timely critiques of its early drafts. I am especially grateful to Menzie David Chinn and Louise Sheiner who not only provided considerable research skills but excellent editorial ones as well.

Finally, I must give thanks to two very special people. Professor Alan Lebowitz of Tufts University introduced me many years ago to the art and craft of writing; for his support, encouragement, and pearls of writing wisdom, I am eternally indebted. Wynne Cougill has served as editor, critic, and close friend throughout my writing career; following that tradition, she has carefully edited every letter and word of the many drafts of this book. Without her help, this book literally would not exist.

Peter Navarro

Cambridge, Massachusetts
July 1984

Introduction

Every time our government plays the policy game, some of us win and some of us lose: The federal government slaps a quota on Japanese car imports, and the auto industry gains at the expense of consumers, who pay higher prices for a more limited selection of cars. State legislators in the Southwest vote to raise severance taxes on coal, and their states gain revenues while Midwest and Northeast consumers spend more for electricity. A city council imposes rent controls, and tenants rejoice at frozen rents while landlords watch their property values plunge.

Who gains and who loses in these federal, state, and local policy arenas is rarely an accident. More often than not, the distributional consequences of "public policies" are the intended result of the private interests which have been instrumental in their design, passage, and implementation. Thus, the term *public policy*, which suggests government action designed to promote the general welfare, is often a misnomer. This lofty but misleading term imbues American democracy with much of its aura of goodness while it disguises the real nature of the policy game.

Unfortunately, the private use of public policy does more than merely benefit some interest groups at the expense of others. In most cases, there is also a net loss to our nation so that the public interest is almost always harmed. The litany of counterproductive public policies promoted by special interests is a long and familiar one.

For example, the systematic suppression of free trade through tariffs, quotas, trigger prices, and other import restrictions has protected the profits of a small core of domestic industries, but at the same time has made the shoes on our feet more expensive, the autos we drive less fuel efficient, and the color televisions we buy less reliable. This protectionist umbrella has also weakened the nation's productive capacity by deterring the investment in new factories and advanced technology that is necessary to compete in world markets.

Similarly, a plethora of agricultural price supports has enriched a small group of primarily large corporate farmers at the expense of taxpayers, consumers, and small farmers. But these supports have also institutionalized inflationary pressures—pressures that are packaged with every loaf of bread, every bag of sugar, every quart of milk, every pack of cigarettes, and every jar of peanut butter we buy.

Despite the obvious role of special interests, the policy game is more than just a struggle among them to capture the powers of government for their own gain. To a large extent, the outcome of the policy game also represents the resolution of a battle of beliefs in which the spoils of victory go to the standard bearers of a particular ideology. In this country, the "ideology wars" are typically waged between liberals and conservatives, with each camp having a diverse set of competing principles at stake.

For example, conservatives see the road to economic prosperity as one paved with free market efficiency, but liberals often prefer to regulate markets on the grounds that the economic system will operate more fairly with the helping hand of government. Likewise, the liberal commitment to the "welfare state" rests on a conception that the responsibility of good government is to provide people with the basic human needs of food, clothing, and shelter, while the conservative's preference for a "minimal state" rests on the competing belief that the best government is that which intrudes least.

Despite the undeniably good intentions of both liberals and conservatives, the effects of ideological struggle on the public interest can be every bit as damaging as special interest politics. There is, for example, increasing evidence suggesting that many welfare policies, which have been designed and implemented by liberals since the beginnings of the New Deal, have actually created a permanent "welfare caste." Its hard-core "beneficiaries" are now trapped in a far-from-gilded welfare cage that has destroyed individual self-respect, the incentive to work, and the ability to raise a family with true economic security. These policies have in effect relegated large masses of the "deserving poor" to exile in urban ghettos and rural backwaters and to a permanent low rung on the economic ladder.

At the same time, while the conservative push for deregulation in such industries as the airlines and banking has on the whole benefited the economy, their equally zealous pursuit of deregulation in industries like the railroads (where the economic rationale for free markets is much less cogent) has established, or threatens to establish, bastions of monopoly power. Particularly in the West, railroads wielding such power have not only greatly profited at the expense of energy consumers, but have also braked the development of western coal reserves. This, in turn, has slowed the transition from foreign oil to domestic coal and increased U.S. dependence on foreign energy sources.

Similarly, while subsidies like those for farm products wreak havoc with the economy, there are compelling economic and national security arguments that the nation would be better off subsidizing such activities as synfuels development, mass transit, and public education. Yet conservatives, blinded by the light of their own faith, perennially lump such "good" subsidies into an overly full bag of "bad" ones.

America has reached a point in its history where it cannot grow and prosper while buffeted by the well-meaning but often devastating consequences of misguided ideology. Nor can it any longer afford the increasingly debilitating effects of the private use of the public interest. Together, greedy special interests and misguided ideologues have dragged our once affluent society down the dark corridors of a new era of economic austerity. Now the primary fact of American life is that the nation's gross national product—our economic pie—is no longer growing as fast as it once did. The slack, the fat, and the abundance that were once the hallmarks of American society are gone; in turn, the fierce political battles over the shares of that shrinking economic pie have intensified.

Fortunately, this new era of economic austerity is not unalterable; contrary to the laments of one well-known economist, we do not live in a "zero-sum society,"[1] where what one person wins another must necessarily lose. The size of America's economic pie is, in fact, *variable*, and it can resume its healthy growth if we as a nation and an electorate learn to play the policy game better.

Government by and for special interests must give way to government in the public interest, a government that is unencumbered by wasteful subsidies, scandalous pork barrels, and prodigal industries prospering under the protective shelter of legislative largess. At the same time, our ideological society must give way to the pragmatic society. We must eschew blind faith in favor of the more precise compass of sound economics, the lodestar that will guide us fastest and farthest on our journey toward national growth and prosperity.

To accomplish these changes, we as citizens, taxpayers, and voters must learn to play the policy game better. To achieve this goal, we first must become aware of the broad scope of America's economic, political, and social problems. We then must be both willing and able to participate as a responsible electorate in finding and forging solutions that will make us all better off.

The willingness to participate must stem from the realization that the effects of the policy game are never confined simply to the special interests or ideologues who appear to be its major players. The policy game spills over into all our lives by interfering with the nation's growth, prosperity, and health; any "miscues" mean there is less abundance for all of us to share.

The ability to participate must stem from an understanding of who the players are, what they seek, and how the game works. This book is intended to provide a framework for that participation. The ultimate goal is to better understand and control the myriad political forces that affect our lives so that we can replace our current economic austerity with a new prosperity.

Contents

The Policy Game

Part 1

The Politics of the
Policy Game

In Chapter 1, the central conceptual tool of this book, the "capture-ideology" framework, is introduced. The application of this framework to probe the politics of any given issue is then illustrated in Chapter 2's rent control policy game.

1

Who Owns the Government

HOW SPECIAL INTERESTS AND IDEOLOGUES CAPTURE PUBLIC POLICY

The question of whether the American government serves the public interest or merely private interests lies bubbling at the core of a debate that has raged without resolution since James Madison first warned of the "mischief of factions" at the dawning of our nation. On the pessimistic side of the aisle are the "realists," who insist that the policy game is played exclusively by powerful special interests for their own gain. On the optimistic side are the "idealists," who argue with equal conviction that while it may not consistently succeed, American government always at least attempts to advance some broad conception of the public good or national interest.

Despite the compelling arguments advanced by each camp, this debate rests on an overly simplistic and false dichotomy that obscures the real and more complex nature of the policy game. Like so many questions that have two plausible but apparently contradictory answers, both answers are partly correct. The wisdom that both private interests and the public interest are likely to matter in any given policy game is embodied in the capture-ideology framework, which is the central conceptual tool of this book. This framework provides us with a way of integrating the hitherto competing private and public interest interpretations of the policy game into a complementary and more comprehensive view of American politics and economics.

I. THE PRIVATE INTEREST MODELS

The purpose of legislation . . . is to take from those who have less political
clout and give to those who have more.[1]

BRUCE GARDNER

The private interest models of American government are Machiavel-
lian in nature. They portray the policy game as a battle among competing
special interests who seek to control the government's unique coercive
power to tax and transfer wealth.

Of these approaches, the *monolith* model provides the simplest, and
perhaps the most cynical, vision of special interest politics. The Marxian
version of this model depicts the policy game as an exercise in class
exploitation whereby a ruling minority of bourgeois "monopoly capitalists" use the nation's economic and political machinery to dominate and
oppress the working class.[2] In a similar vein, the muckraking school,
most fully developed in recent decades by Ralph Nader and his "raid-
ers," has described the American government as a corporate state whose
major function is the protection of big business.[3]

The hallmark of both the Marxian and muckraking indictments is a
heavy reliance on a small number of heroes and villains and a smaller
number of plots. Black-hatted big business, in bed with big government,
seeks to gobble up natural resources, ravage the environment, and exploit
consumers, while the military-industrial complex and its henchmen at
the Pentagon and Central Intelligence Agency conspire to take over the
world (or at least make it safe for American merchants). Only the White
Knights of consumer advocacy, environmental protection, world peace,
and nuclear disarmament stand between these relentless forces of greed
and Armageddon.

Despite their journalistic appeal, neither the Marxian model nor the
"world according to Nader" describes the American political economy
very well. For instance, there is ample evidence that the monoliths fin-
gered by muckrakers are not monolithic at all: The many segments and
sectors of big business often squabble among themselves. For example,
within "Big Oil" alone, producers oppose refiners on price controls,
small refiners battle large refiners, and the national independent oil companies regularly attack the large multinationals. It also is now commonly

acknowledged that bigger businesses in America rarely wield political power in any proportion to their size and assets in a country where populism still runs strong. Nor are consumers monolithic, with their goals, preferences, and interests frequently diverging along regional, income, and other lines. Higher income consumers are, for example, more likely to support government regulations such as mandatory seat belts than are lower-income consumers, who would prefer a less expensive, albeit less safe, car.

By the same token, while the Marxist vision may bring sharp focus to the feudal landlord-peasant societies of the Third World or the rigid class structures of nineteenth-century Europe, it falls far short of mirroring the fluid multiclass, and predominantly middle-class, reality of America.

Accordingly, the political scientist's *pluralist* model provides a more realistic and elaborate vision of the rich diversity of special interests that cut across American social, economic, and political lines. This model rests on James Madison's presumption that America is comprised of literally thousands of interest groups and that these groups are the major, indeed the only, driving force in American politics.

The primary virtue of pluralism is that it allows us to see the full breadth and depth of interest group activity, ranging from the large farm, labor, professional, and business lobbies to the more microscopic world of Gray Panthers, garden clubs, church groups, and antiabortionists. Moreover, pluralism recognizes the many subdivisions within these groups and the inevitable intragroup conflict arising from these subdivisions.

Thus the "farm bloc" is not portrayed monolithically as a united front. Rather, it is seen as a loose and uneasy coalition whose members sometimes back a common cause but more often fight among themselves: Butter churners seek to tax margarine producers, corn farmers attempt to raise corn prices while hog farmers fight to lower them, and dairy farmers squabble with food processors and distributors over cartel-like marketing orders.

Unfortunately, despite its virtues of diversity and depth, the pluralist model likewise has a major flaw. According to pluralism's founder, Arthur Bentley, the political system's fierce struggle among competing private interests is, paradoxically, always supposed to promote the public interest.[4] This counterintuitive but fortuitous outcome is supposed to occur through a natural "balance wheel":[5] Whenever one set of special interests becomes too powerful, other groups will spontaneously rise up and organize so that "the larger, more nearly general interest would usually tend to defeat the smaller, narrow special interests."[6]

Today, as a cadre of "antipluralists" have graphically illustrated,[7] this faith in the ability of countervailing interest groups to organize and offset the power of narrow special interests is misplaced. Indeed, the converse generally is true, particularly for large groups with diffuse interests like consumers, the poor, or the general public. As Harvard professor Thomas McCraw has lamented, "unorganized, or as in the case of the poor, unorganizable," these groups have "stayed out in the cold, away from the American banquet."[8]

Fortunately, the *capture* model provides us with a more sophisticated, and ultimately more satisfactory, paradigm of special interest politics. It retains pluralism's rich portrayal of the special interest players in the policy game but departs from pluralism's roseate and unrealistic conclusion that special interests serve the public interest.

While economists generally take credit for formalizing the capture model, its lineage may be traced to several historians, most notably Gabriel Kolko. Kolko's dark chronicle of the nineteenth-century genesis of the Interstate Commerce Commission (ICC) devastatingly depicts that agency as the creation and willing creature of a monopolistic railroad industry out to feather its nest behind the panoply of rate and route regulation.[9]

In 1971, Nobel laureate George Stigler generalized Kolko's damning case study. From behind the free market walls of the "Chicago School," Stigler argued that ostensibly public policies such as subsidies, tariffs, price controls, and entry restrictions are merely manifestations of the ability of private interests to use the government's unique authority to coerce. In this capture context, the purpose of the policy game is to redistribute wealth to whichever special interests are powerful enough to seize the government's helm.[10] This capture model, expanded and refined by a host of economists following in Stigler's wake, serves as the first building block and private interest component of our capture-ideology framework; conceptually it allows for the possibility that private interest motives can indeed determine "public policy."

II. THE PUBLIC INTEREST MODELS

The public interest models are Panglossian in nature, portraying the policy game as a gallant contest among well-meaning altruists who use the powers of government for the greater good of the citizenry.

Perhaps the simplest and most sanctimonious of these is the *Constitutional* model. The combined legacy of the legal and political science professions, most of us have already been exposed to it as part of the obligatory high school civics course. Associated with it is the grandiose rhetoric that often bounces off the walls of congressional chambers and high school classrooms (and usually off the ears of those seated).

The model asserts that the American government exists to preserve a system of law and order as set forth in the Constitution. The hallmark of this model is its extremely broad, indeed vague, definition of the public interest. The model itself provides nothing more than general guidelines for policymakers to follow once the courts or the Congress invoke the Constitutional contract.

A second model, that of *market failure,* is the proud child of economists. It portrays the government as a benevolent *deus ex machina,* that owes its existence, legitimacy, and powers to imperfections in the free market. In this view, the policy game is played to correct these imperfections or "market failures."*

The model rests on Adam Smith's insight that under the conditions of pure and perfect competition, the "invisible hand" of the free market will guide the economy to its most prosperous outcome in the sense that the most goods and services will be produced from the available resources. However, when one or more of the conditions of perfect competition are not met (e.g., when monopoly is present), the invisible hand becomes crippled and the attractive property of free market efficiency disappears. At this point, it becomes necessary for the "visible foot" of government to assist the market's invisible hand by correcting for its failures and imperfections. Through such an action, the public interest

---

*The list of failures and imperfections that can afflict the free market includes the obvious problems of monopoly and oligopoly as well as more subtle problems associated with "public goods" such as national defense, roads and bridges, and "externalities" like air pollution.[11]

is served because a more efficient allocation of the nation's resources is obtained.

Still a third model is an offshoot of this market failure approach. The *government failure* model accepts the basic premise that the policy game is played to promote the public interest. But it blames the bureaucratic machinery or players in that game for sometimes bungling their efforts to meet that goal. In doing so, the government failure model adds an important dimension to the policy game: It raises the possibility that government in general, or well-meaning ideologues in particular, may intend to serve the public interest, but despite their good intentions, fail to do so. This insight forces us to focus not only on how a policy decision is made, as we shall do in examining its politics, but also to take a closer look at the economic results of that decision, particularly within the context of the actions of well-meaning ideologues.

Given the many garden varieties of public interest models—of which the above are but a sample—it would seem to be a confusing task to sort out just which model might help explain the existence of a particular public policy. Fortunately, the newest *ideological* model of the public interest provides a useful unifying shorthand for the other models. In doing so, it forms the second half of the capture-ideology framework.[12]

An individual's ideology can be most simply described as a set of beliefs and values about how the world should be. In the arenas of the policy game, these beliefs and values translate into a set of principles on which one's policy choices are based. These principles, which form the basis for ideological action, may be fleshed out within the context of America's two dominant ideologies, conservatism and liberalism (the subject of Part 3 of this book).

For example, American conservatives embrace the principle of *free markets* and policies like deregulation because they believe that adhering to such a system will result in maximum economic efficiency and therefore the greatest prosperity for society to share. In contrast, liberals prefer *regulated markets* in many cases because they believe that an essentially good market system can be made to operate even better, resulting in a more efficient and fair system through prudent government planning.

Despite this ideological conflict over principles (e.g., free versus regulated markets), the policy preferences of a conservative to deregulate and of a liberal to regulate nonetheless can both be regarded as essentially altruistic because they reflect concern over making America a better place to live. From this broad perspective, pure ideological principles are synonymous with the individual's conception of what would serve the public interest; the actions taken in the policy arena to fulfill that vision of the world may likewise be equated with altruistic or public-interested behavior.

From this definition of ideology and prescription for ideological action, we can easily see how American conservatism and liberalism can serve as a shorthand for the various public interest models. Suppose, for example, we ascribe to a Constitutional model view of the policy game. Both conservatives and liberals will agree that the right to due process, as guaranteed by the Constitution's Fifth Amendment, includes the accused's right to a fair and speedy trial and, if convicted, to protection from cruel and unusual punishment. However, conservatives and liberals are likely to disagree sharply over how to translate those general guarantees into specific public policies.

On the one hand, the liberal is likely to support Supreme Court decisions like *Miranda* v. *Arizona* and *Escobedo* v. *Illinois*, which guarantee the right of the accused to remain silent upon arrest and to have a lawyer present during interrogation. On the other hand, the conservative is more apt to see these legal safeguards as "loopholes" that not only allow guilty individuals to escape justice but, in doing so, also undermine the whole Constitutional system of law and order. By the same token, the liberal might see capital punishment as constituting cruel and unusual punishment, while the conservative sees it as an unfortunate but fair and necessary deterrent to acts of violent crime. But despite their ideological disagreements over the policy implications of the model, it is clear that both conservatives and liberals are acting on their own conception of the public interest.

Suppose we take a market failure view of the policy game instead. Both conservatives and liberals may agree that imperfect competition exists in markets such as those for housing, automobiles, or computers. However, they are likely to disagree sharply over the amount of harm such imperfect competition is likely to do as well as over any policy prescriptions proposed to correct such failures.

For example, the liberal might view an urban apartment market such as that in New York or Los Angeles as hopelessly noncompetitive and, to avoid monopolistic rent gouging by landlords, argue for regulation in the form of rent controls. The conservative, on the other hand, might see the same apartment market as flawed but nonetheless functioning, and, rather than truncate the property rights of landlords through rent restrictions, argue for market-type incentives such as tax breaks or subsidies for new apartment construction to improve competition.

The point, then, is that public-interested behavior, like beauty, is in the eyes of the beholder. It is directly contingent on one's ideology. Thus diametrically opposite policy choices such as the regulation and deregulation responses of liberals versus conservatives can both be legitimately regarded as actions intended to promote the public interest. At the same time, American conservatism and liberalism can serve as a useful shorthand for various public interest motives.

Accordingly, we can plug this ideological proxy in as the second half of the capture-ideology framework. To illustrate how to adopt this framework as a way of thinking about and assessing the politics of any given issue, let's use it in the next chapter to examine the causes and consequences of a specific policy game, rent control. In doing so, we will see that who wins and loses in the political arena has important economic consequences that make policy reforms desirable.

2

Vanishing Apartments

THE RENT CONTROL POLICY GAME

On a wall outside the Harvard Housing Office in Cambridge, Massachusetts, an anonymous street sage has inscribed the following Day-Glo painted message:

> HELL is looking for an apartment in Cambridge
>
> HEAVEN is finding one under rent control

Anyone who has had to look for rental housing in a rent-controlled community will detect more than a kernel of truth in this graffiti: Such a search can involve hellish weeks, and sometimes months, of combing want ads, pounding the pavement, and finding a busy signal on the lines of landlords already besieged with callers seeking their coveted units. But for the chosen few whose search ends successfully, the payoff is heavenly: A lease on a rent-controlled apartment entitles the lucky bearer to accommodations that are 30 to 60 percent cheaper per month than an identical unit in the uncontrolled part of the market.

Between this heaven and hell lurk important questions, not just for policymakers, but for all of us here on earth who will ever have to hunt for a new place to live or worry about being displaced from where we now call home. For example, do rent controls create a tight housing market in which it is impossible to find a place to live, or does a tight housing market create opportunities for unfair profiteering and in so doing create a need for controls? Similarly, are rents high in the absence of controls because renegade landlords and speculators rapaciously gouge tenants, or do these higher market rents merely reflect inflationary pressures bearing down on all of life's necessities, from food and clothing to transportation? And does rent control really work; does it fulfill the goals proclaimed by many of its proponents, for example, protecting the health and welfare of the poor, elderly, and handicapped?

Finding the answers to these and other questions raised in this chapter is all the more important because rent control is one of the most popular policy games sweeping the country. Indeed, during the last decade, such major cities as Los Angeles, San Francisco, Washington, D.C., and Boston have all adopted controls, as have some nine states and over 200 local communities from Santa Monica, California to Cambridge, Massachusetts.[1]

Let's examine this policy game, then, through the lens of the capture-ideology framework, to see if it can be played better. The basic format for this examination is the same one we will use for all of our case studies.

A brief history and background discussion will set the stage for probing the politics of the issue within the context of private interest capture and public-interested ideological motives. The economics of the issue are then evaluated to see what greedy special interests and possibly misguided ideologues have wrought. After assessing the damage, the case study concludes with a discussion of policy reforms—the ways to play the particular policy game better.

I. HISTORY AND BACKGROUND

While the last decade saw a literal explosion of rent controls across the country, the rent control movement is hardly new. In fact, various forms of this policy game have been played in America for the better part of this century.

The first generation of controls surfaced in response to emergency housing shortages created by World War I. Initially, these emergency controls were "limited to servicemen and their families and to workers engaged in the production of war material."[2] But by the end of World War I, controls were extended in many areas to the total housing market as a means to curtail pervasive rent profiteering.

While controls in most communities were gradually abandoned after the armistice, World War II created a second emergency housing shortage and controls were reimposed. These controls were initially concentrated in service-related areas such as military installations, Atlantic and Pacific ports, and major inland defense production cities; but enabling legislation designated the entire country as eligible for controls and marked their first use on a national scale.[3]

During the war and immediate postwar period, a number of states, including Connecticut, Illinois, Maryland, Minnesota, and New Jersey passed "standby" rent control legislation to become effective when federal controls lapsed. These statutes went into effect in 1950; but by the mid-1950s, New York was the only state that still retained controls.

All remained quiet on the rent control front for the better part of the next two decades until the Nixon administration shattered the peace in 1971 with its wage, price, and rent freeze. Like previous federal rent control measures, the Nixon freeze was a temporary one directed at a general (albeit peacetime) national emergency, namely, runaway inflation.

However, both prior to and in the wake of the Nixon freeze, many states and communities were seeking to impose controls of a much different nature. These "second generation" controls were not temporary and absolute freezes related to a general emergency, but longer-term peacetime economic controls that allowed for regulated rent increases, but left wages and prices alone.

Today, many of the conditions that precipitated this 1970s rent control movement persist. Mortgage interest rates remain stubbornly high and volatile, while the price of a single-family home or a condominium continues to escalate beyond the reach of more and more middle- and lower-income Americans. At the same time, the already tight rental housing market is being further squeezed by a persistent stagnation in the construction of new apartment units.

Given these pressures, one must wonder whether the wave of peacetime rent controls that broke over the U.S. housing market in the 1970s will be followed by another, perhaps larger, tidal wave of controls in the 1980s. If so, what will be the political causes and economic consequences? The capture-ideology framework will help us to answer that question within the context of the rent control experience in a city that has been at the vanguard of the new rent control movement: Cambridge, Massachusetts.

On August 31, 1970, a year before the Nixon freeze, Massachusetts passed a state enabling act giving cities and towns with over 50,000 inhabitants the right to enact local rent control ordinances.[4] A scant 14 days later, on a 7–2 vote by its city council, Cambridge became one of the first communities to adopt controls.

The Cambridge experience is used as a microcosm of the national rent control phenomenon because it provides a classic example of the second generation of rent regulations, which are designed to be more adaptive to both overall and local economic conditions. If the major problems typically associated with rent control persist under this more innovative system, then the indictment of rent control ritually laid down by most economists will be all the more damning. On the other hand, if the Cambridge system alleviates most or all of these problems, it may indicate the path to a useful policy system.

II. THE POLITICS OF RENT CONTROL

A.   The Public Interest View

On the surface, rent control in Cambridge appears to be a classic embodiment of a government policy made in the public interest. In declaring a "housing emergency," the Cambridge Rent Control Enabling Act artfully puts forth public interest arguments heavily suggestive of both the Constitutional and market failure models (discussed in Chapter 1). Drawing on several court decisions from the 1920s,[5] the act asserts the Constitutional right of the government to intervene in the housing market to prevent "serious threats to the public health, safety, and general welfare," while the source of those threats is identified as a "substantial and increasing shortage of rental housing accommodations" created by the failure of the housing market to produce an adequate supply of rental units.

Both this market failure and the nature of these threats to the public welfare shed considerable light on the ideological principles implicit in the rent control debate. For example, the alleged failure of the free apartment market to provide sufficient housing at affordable prices is the fount from which flow all liberal arguments for rent control. The nature of this failure is imperfect (and therefore, unfair) competition, a problem tied to a number of characteristics peculiar to apartment units. Among the 14 that housing analyst Monica Lett lists are durability and long construction time, lack of sufficient information among tenants and landlords, and "market segmentation" (e.g., by neighborhood, size of units, and such), which reduces the substitutability of one unit for another.[6] When these market imperfections are combined with conditions like those that have periodically plagued the economy over the last decade—high interest rates, inflated construction costs, and community-imposed constraints on growth—the frequent result is a housing shortage during which tenants are vulnerable to rent-gouging.

Liberals in Cambridge have used precisely this argument first to enact and later to perpetuate the rent control system. These advocates cite Cambridge's extremely low vacancy rate as evidence of a housing shortage, a rate that typically hovers below 3 percent and makes Cambridge one of the tightest apartment markets in America.[7] One major reason for this tightness is the heavy demand for living space by the large numbers of students and other transients who regularly flock to this intellectual and cultural mecca. At the same time, since the late 1960s, young professionals have increasingly begun to spurn suburban living for the more gentrified urban existence of Cambridge, while on the supply side, dense building patterns and zoning regulations curbing growth mean that space for new construction in Cambridge has become more limited.

According to rent control proponents, it is primarily these conditions that set the stage for a rapid rise in Cambridge rents during the late 1960s and early 1970. At that time, rent control was justified on the basis of several ideological arguments related to the effects of market failure.

The first was that controls were needed to prevent an undesirable and inequitable redistribution of income from tenants to landlords as a result of rent gouging. To liberals, profits garnered from shortages are "unearned" in the sense that they are the result, not of the sweat from any landlord's brow, but of the failure of market supply to meet demand. Accordingly, the government—in this case the Cambridge City Council—has the right to limit the property rights of landlords through rent controls to prevent such a redistribution. (Conservative critics, of course, regard such a truncation as mere confiscation of landlord property.)

At the same time, it was argued that the poor and elderly were most threatened by profiteering landlords (inevitably portrayed as affluent property owners). Implicit in this characterization was a second important function of rent control: a more even distribution of income achieved through the subsidization of lower-income tenants by higher-income landlords.

The last, but in Cambridge hardly the least, important ideological argument for rent control centers on the liberal concept of the community and the role of government in preserving that community. Besides a large student and transient population that clusters around the Harvard and MIT campuses and an influx of young professionals who have found living in Cambridge increasingly attractive, the city is also populated by diverse economic and ethnic groups. Large pockets of blacks, Irish, Italians, and Portuguese, and a significant elderly population generally comprise the lower end of the city's income spectrum. The heavy apartment demand by the student-transient-professional troika creates a Hobson's choice for these ethnic and economic groups in the absence of rent control: pay up or move out.

More often than not, the "move out" option means the displacement of lower- and middle-income families, who are forced from their homes by the invisible and impersonal hand of the market. This, in turn, means that the cohesive family fabric and colorful, cultural diversity of the community—viewed as an intrinsic good—is replaced by a more homogeneous and unstable population of wealthy (often single) professionals and students from upper income families. To liberals, this is not only economic discrimination, but it also creates great hardship for those displaced, particularly the elderly, for whom the burden of relocation is often the most heavy.

Thus, through the lens of ideology, liberals in Cambridge appear to have imposed and sustained rent controls on the basis of an altruistic judgment that the income redistribution, displacement, and community effects generated by the failure of the apartment market are inequitable and undesirable. Therefore, they must be corrected.

B. The Private Interest View: Tenant Capture

Despite these compelling public interest arguments, an equally strong case can be made that special interests are responsible for rent control. Indeed, when viewed through the capture lens, we seem to have a classic case: a large voting majority of tenants has seized control of the Cambridge City Council and used its power to impose confiscatory controls

on a small minority of landlords, many of whom live outside the city
and don't vote in its elections.

In this characterization, the liberal case for rent control reduces to a
rhetorical cloak for tenant interests who, with the aid of city councillors
dressed in liberal clothing, have commandeered policy in their own
behalf. In the same vein, the legal language of the enabling legislation
declaring an emergency and warning of threats to the public welfare may
be interpreted as mere boiler plate inserted by special interests to meet
the requirements of past court decisions regarding the constitutionality
of imposing rent controls.[8]

For those who believe that dollars translate into votes, the sheer magnitude of the redistribution involved in rent control lends support to the
capture hypothesis. Consider that market rents run from 30 to 60 percent
above controlled levels on the 18,000-plus rent controlled units in Cambridge and that the average controlled rent is roughly $275. This means
that controls redistribute from $18 to $36 million dollars annually from
landlords to tenants and that the average tenant captures an annual
benefit of from $1,000 to $2,000. Public interest arguments notwithstanding, such a "reward" provides tenants with a great incentive to play the
rent control game to their advantage.

An analysis of the strategy and tactics of the major players in the rent
control game—tenants, landlords, and political entrepreneurs—provides
further clues regarding capture.

**1.   Indirect or Grass-Roots Lobbying: The Mother's Milk of Lo-
cal Politics.**   The hallmark of local politics is indirect lobbying; and in
Cambridge, the rent control issue has been the single most effective
grass-roots organizing tool for politicians seeking a seat on the city council. While rent control was a somewhat peripheral political issue when
the city first instituted it in 1970, it has since played a major role in
every biennial city council election. While the capture theory implies
that the importance of rent control as an election issue is related to the
high distributional stakes involved, its singular prominence in Cambridge elections is ultimately attributable to the ability of skillful political
entrepreneurs working closely with major tenant organizations to rally
tenant interests around the rent control flag.

The major tenants' organizations in Cambridge include the Alliance
of Cambridge Tenants, the Harvard Tenants Union, the Cambridge Ten-

ants Organization, the Word of Tenants Association, and the unlikely sounding Simplex Steering Committee. These organizations have banded together into the powerful Cambridge Rent Control Coalition, which claims a membership of over 10,000. However, most of the activities pursued by the coalition are performed by a small core of activists who regularly appear at city council meetings and rent control board hearings.[9] This pattern of a large interest group bloc led by a small activist elite is fairly typical of modern grass-roots political movements.

However, these tenant organizations have not played the most prominent role in making rent control an issue; rather, it is the Cambridge Civic Association (CCA), a political organization dedicated primarily to placing its slate of candidates in positions of power in the Cambridge government, from the school board to the city council.

A major plank of this avowedly liberal organization's platform has been the maintenance of rent controls. Since the imposition of these controls, it has successfully maintained four seats on the nine-seat council and, through a *coalition* with a fifth "independent" councillor,[10] it has always been able to maintain a majority vote. An analysis of the campaign strategy and tactics of the CCA's leading rent control advocate, Councillor David Sullivan, illustrates both the simplicity and power of local grass-roots lobbying.

Sullivan, like all councillors, resides in Cambridge and, like some, lives in a rent-controlled apartment. Since 1975, he has campaigned for election and reelection throughout the year (as opposed to just near election time) by patiently and methodically knocking on the doors of Cambridge residents and explaining his positions. For such a "Johnny Appleseed" tactic, Sullivan incurs virtually no campaign costs other than shoe leather and time. His approach is very effective since in a city of Cambridge's size, it is possible to talk to virtually every resident during an election year cycle.

Moreover, Cambridge's unique system of "proportional voting" makes such a grass-roots tactic particularly potent. Under that system, it is theoretically possible to win a seat on the council by receiving less than 10 percent of the votes. Thus, if a candidate in Cambridge can nail down the strong support of only 2,500 people, he can win an election in which roughly 25,000 people vote.

At the same time, Sullivan has skillfully cultivated members of the press on such local papers as the *Cambridge Express* and *Cambridge*

Chronicle as well as the *Boston Globe* and, like the CCA, regularly "makes news" for his rent control stance. In doing so, he has made extremely effective use of a basic tool of the politician's trade: propaganda. For in espousing controls, Sullivan's liberal (or to critics, "leftist") rhetoric is laced with the naked power language that Ralph Nader and his disciples have used so effectively: Landlords are ripping off tenants, powerful lobbies are blocking the will of the people, and developers are raping the Cambridge landscape. (When a rent control opponent was appointed to be the landlord representative on the Cambridge Rent Board, Sullivan unceremoniously dubbed the woman the "James Watt of Cambridge" in an attempt to paint her as a pawn of the developers.)[11] Sullivan's campaign tactics and rhetoric graphically illustrate the power of *single issue* politics in the American democratic system: running on an unadorned platform of the preservation of rent control, Sullivan has managed to hold his seat through several elections.

From this grass-roots look at the behavior of local politicians, the real picture of capture that one must paint is not one of large numbers of tenants gathering in big auditoriums to plot the exploitation of landlords. Rather, it is more plausible that Cambridge politicians have been highly successful in mobilizing ordinarily weak and disorganized tenant interests into a solid voting bloc that regularly returns the CCA slate to power to look after tenant interests. In this effort, the rent control issue has proved to be the lightning rod of support.

2. Strategies and Tactics of the Other Major Players. For their part, the opponents of rent control in Cambridge—primarily landlords who incur rent losses and real estate brokers who must cope with a more stagnant and lower-valued housing market—have been singularly unsuccessful at mounting a counterattack. Working through organizations like the Cambridge Chamber of Commerce and the Cambridge Property Owners, these perennial losers in the rent control game have been unable to elect their own candidates to oust the CCA. One reason, of course, is that they are numerically smaller and therefore do not have the votes to mobilize.

But another reason is that, at the local level, the strategies and tactics employed by rent control opponents are not very potent when compared to the type of grass-roots lobbying that pro–rent control forces have used so effectively. For example, dollar lobbying via campaign contributions is largely ineffective because local campaigns simply do not cost that much to run. In fact, the average total contributions to successful city councillor candidates usually only run to around $8,000, and the primary campaign expenses are low-budget items such as leaflets, bumper stickers, and buttons. Moreover, since all campaign contributions must be reported, there is a real danger that large contributions from landlord interests, if uncovered, would be a major political liability. Further, even if a candidate is bankrolled sufficiently to launch an ad campaign in the local press, that tactic pales in comparison to the shoestring budget, in-the-trenches door-knocking of an indefatigable campaigner like Sullivan. Thus it is hardly surprising that the voices of landlords are often lost in the wilderness.

C.   The Politics of Rent Control: A Statistical Test

So which is it in the Cambridge housing market: capture by tenants looking after their own private interests or well-intentioned liberals altruistically intervening in the apartment market for the public interest? One of the virtues of the capture-ideology framework is that it can actually give us a statistically measurable answer to this question. The test, which has been developed by a small cadre of economists and political scientists, involves a simple four-step procedure.[12]

The first step is to frame the politics of an issue in terms of a specific *policy choice*, typically some type of legislative or constituent vote. In this case, we can examine the politics of rent control by analyzing the voting patterns of the Cambridge electorate in choosing a pro–rent control city council. This vote (the policy choice) represents the "dependent variable" in a political equation that can be explained statistically by a number of "independent" or "explanatory" variables representing special interests and ideology.

The second step distinguishes the major special interests by using some measure of their economic stakes in, or their political power to determine, the outcome of the policy choice. In this particular policy game, tenants in rent-controlled apartments represent the major special interest beneficiaries of rent control (at least in the short run);* the polit-

---

*As the next section on the economics of rent control will explain, most of the benefits of rent control to tenants are eroded over time.

ical power of tenants of rent-controlled apartments can be measured by the percentage of rent-controlled housing in each of Cambridge's 55 voting precincts.

The third step adds some measure of ideology as a final explanatory variable to the political equation. When we examine congressional voting patterns in the case studies on farm policy and defense spending, we can simply recruit one of several existing ideological ratings for congressmen such as those prepared by the liberal Americans for Democratic Action. In this case, we must be more creative and infer the ideology of Cambridge's voting electorate by examining their voting behavior on arguably pure ideological referenda such as capital punishment or a nuclear freeze, with either a no vote for capital punishment or a yes vote for a nuclear freeze indicating a liberal viewpoint.

The fourth and final step is to plug the data of this political equation into the computer's "black box" and instruct it to use an appropriate procedure (e.g., regression analysis) to statistically relate the policy choice or dependent variable to the explanatory variables. Such a test provides us with a set of results that actually rank each of the various special interest and ideological players according to their relative importance in determining the outcome of the particular policy game.[13]

Applying this technique to the politics of rent control, we find strong support for the basic premise of the capture-ideology framework that both private and public interest motives are likely to matter on any given policy issue. According to the test,* ideology is the single most important influence on Cambridge voters in their selection of a pro–rent control city council. However, as testimony to the power of the capture theory, the statistical importance of tenants in rent-controlled housing is almost as great. Accordingly, we can conclude that capture and ideology motives play roughly equal roles in the politics of Cambridge rent control.

This capture cum ideology conclusion is further bolstered by an examination of the campaign contributions to a number of the major candidates for city council. For example, to raise money for his rather modest financial campaign, the leading rent control candidate, David Sullivan, received numerous small contributions from rent-controlled apartment tenants. However, a numerically smaller category of contributors, upper-

---

*As with all case studies that follow, the complete statistical results are reported in Appendix A.

income liberals living in large single-family houses, actually accounted for much more of the dollar total, while landlords gave virtually no money to Sullivan. At the other end of the spectrum, Councillor Walter Sullivan, an outspoken opponent of rent control, raised over 35 percent of his Cambridge contributions from landlords and less than 3 percent from tenant interests.[14]

Thus the politics of rent control appear to indicate that liberals in Cambridge have successfully formed a coalition with tenant interests to impose rent controls at the expense of landlords and ideological conservatives. The next step in using the capture-ideology framework for constructive policy change is to find out what implications these politics have for the economic welfare of the players in the game. We do this now within the context of two important questions about the economic effects of rent control: Do the benefits to private interest tenants in rent-controlled units justify the costs imposed by the system and are the public interest goals of liberals actually well-served by rent control?

III. THE ECONOMICS OF RENT CONTROL

. . . the introduction and continuance of rent control/restriction/regulation has done much more harm than good in rental housing markets—let alone the economy at large—by perpetuating shortages, encouraging immobility, swamping consumer preferences, fostering dilapidation of housing stocks and eroding production incentives, distorting land use patterns and the allocation of scarce resources, and all in the name of distributive justice it has manifestly failed to achieve because at best it has been related only randomly to the needs and individual income circumstances of households.[15]

F. G. PENNANCE

The preceding quote from a Scottish economist commenting on the experience of rent controls in the United States, France, England, Sweden, and Austria reflects a rare consensus in the economics profession: Rent control creates many more problems than it solves. Table 2.1 lists the panoply of these "primary" and "secondary" problems. Let's see which of them may apply to our Cambridge microcosm.

TABLE 2.1.   THE GENERAL ECONOMIC COSTS OF RENT CONTROL

Primary Effects
   Reduced supply of rental housing
   Deterioration of existing housing stock
   Erosion of the community's property tax base

Secondary Effects
   Administrative costs
   Tenant immobility (the "lock-in effect") and associated unemployment
   Increased energy consumption
   Discrimination and abuses of tenants

A.   Primary Economic Effects

The traditional argument that rent control *reduces the supply of rental housing* is based on the simple notion that real estate developers are motivated by profit; because rent control reduces the profitability of an apartment building, it reduces the rate at which such buildings will be constructed. Instead, developers choose to build decontrolled new homes, condominiums, office buildings, or simply not build at all, investing their funds elsewhere.

Rent control advocates rebut this argument by pointing out that virtually every rent control law (including Cambridge's) exempts new rental housing from controls. But in this game of charge and countercharge, rent control critics reply that these exemptions hardly solve the problem:

> It is not apparent that even blanket exemption encourages new construction since the housing industry is often fearful that the exemption may be withdrawn at a later date. In this regard, New York City provides an example. After exempting all units constructed after February 1, 1947 in its original rent control law, twenty-three years later, the city imposed rent stabilization regulations on these structures.[16]

Despite this controversy, the data appear to be generally consistent with the idea that controls reduce construction. For example, in England, where controls have been in effect for over 60 years, rental housing has shrunk from 61 percent to less than 15 percent of the country's total housing. Similarly, New York has seen both the total number of its units and percentage of renters shrink, as has the District of Columbia, which now has 8,000 fewer rental units and has experienced a sharp decline in the issuance of multifamily building permits since controls were imposed.[17]

In Cambridge, however, the problem is not so much a lack of new construction but rather a landlord shift to condominium conversions. Indeed, as befits a modern system of rent control, condo conversions represent a modern source of rental housing loss. In the absence of restrictions, the conversion option provides landlords with a relatively easy and convenient form of escape from rent controls. This "landlord's loophole"[18] is also very lucrative, as condominium conversion provides landlords with a selling price as much as double that of simply selling their property as a controlled rental unit.

Currently, Cambridge has very strict controls on condominium conversion. But before this loophole was closed, roughly 10 percent of the city's rent-controlled housing stock was converted to condominiums and moved out from under the ordinance's grasp.[19] As a result, the percent of renter-occupied private units has shrunk from 75 in 1970, to 72 in 1975, to 66 in 1980.[20]

Today, however, the condo ban is under even greater siege than the rent control law itself. Ironically, much of the pressure comes from tenants in rent-controlled buildings who feel they are being unfairly denied the right to buy their units.[21] Thus, if the condo ban is repealed (or overturned in a case pending in the courts), the city can expect an even further reduction of its rent-controlled stock.

As a final note, it is worth mentioning that rent control also creates an incentive to demolish rental buildings prematurely—either legally or through arson—and build uncontrolled dwellings in their place. Economist Stephen Cheung has vividly illustrated this phenomenon using Hong Kong's experience with rent controls in the 1920s,[22] but we need not go as far away as that for evidence. In Cambridge, for example, there have been a number of "forced demolitions" through fires, some of suspicious origins. In place of these burned-out shells have arisen condominiums.

The second and perhaps most indisputable problem with rent control is that it leads to the *deterioration of existing apartment units*. When operations and maintenance (O&M) expenses rise with inflation, the landlord typically has three options: raise rents, decrease or defer expenses, or sell out and reinvest in something more lucrative. Rent control places an obvious limit on the first option and discourages the third because it depresses the selling price of a controlled building. Typically, the landlord is left with the second option and the result is an "O&M squeeze" in which he skimps on these expenses in order to preserve his net operating income.

While the short-term effects of deferred O&M may be slight, there is an avalanche of evidence that "the long-term effects can be disastrous."[23] For example, in separate studies of New York's "30-year rent control emergency," economists John Moorhouse and George Sternlieb found that controlled units had less maintenance, were of lower quality, and had more deterioration than uncontrolled units.[24] Joel Brenner and Herbert Franklin draw a similar conclusion about controls in England and France,[25] while in a case study of Boston, Monica Lett estimated that landlords spent almost $50 per year less on maintenance alone for controlled buildings.[26]

In the most comprehensive study of Cambridge to date, Professor Herman Leonard of Harvard found corroborating evidence of the O&M squeeze. Because the Cambridge system makes rent adjustments on the basis of historical data and because there are delays involved in granting adjustments, inflation is allowed to erode the value of rent increases. As a result, landlords receive "only 70 to 75 percent of the amount designated by the Rent Control Board as 'fair' "[27] which, in Leonard's words, constitutes a "dramatic squeeze" on the landlord's operating margin.[28] According to Leonard, this and other flaws in Cambridge's system translate into less upkeep, lower quality, and faster deterioration of the city's rent-controlled stock.

The third problem with rent control, *erosion of the community tax base*, is perhaps the most crucial, but often, the least understood issue in the rent control controversy. But the logic of this effect is simple: Rent controls lower the rental income of a piece of property, and this in turn lowers the market value of the property, since that value is nothing more than the capitalized value of the rent stream. Because tax assessments are based on the property's market value, the amount of taxes the owner pays shrinks with the reduction in rents.

For example, suppose that in a given community landlords pay taxes roughly equal to 20 percent of their rental income. Thus, for every dollar that controls lower rents, the taxing authority foregoes 20¢. For an apartment valued at $250 per month with a rent ceiling of $200 per month, the difference in annual rents is $600, and the taxes foregone by the community equal $120 dollars annually.[29]

Again, the general evidence of the existence and magnitude of this loss is incontrovertible. For example, Elizabeth Roistacher estimates that controls in New York City have cost a whopping $115 million annually in foregone taxes.[30] In Cambridge, Leonard found the actual tax loss to be considerable—$5 to $10 million per year, a figure that constitutes 10 to 20 percent of Cambridge's $50 million property tax base.[31]

This loss in tax revenues is in turn reflected either in a higher tax burden for home owners and tenants in the noncontrolled segment of the apartment market or a reduction in municipal services, or both. Given that: (1) the cost of municipal services is rising, (2) "backlash" votes like Proposition 13 in California and Proposition 2½ in Massachusetts have restricted property tax increases, and (3) the property tax is the single largest source of revenue in virtually all local communities, this erosion of the tax base is potentially devastating to cities' efforts to balance their budgets. At the same time, it represents a hidden drain on city coffers that far exceeds the city's reported expenditures on running its rent control system.

B. Secondary Economic Effects

Besides the primary economic costs relating to the supply and quality of the housing stock and the size of the community tax base, rent control can also generate a number of generally acknowledged secondary costs.

The first such cost is that of *supporting the bureaucracy that administers rent controls.* In Cambridge, for example, the annual budget for the city's rent control board and related rent control activities runs to about $700,000.[32] That means it costs taxpayers about $40 in regulatory costs for each of the roughly 18,000 apartment units under control. These regulatory costs—small on the Richter scale of economic impacts—are, however, merely the tip of the iceberg regarding treasury costs since, as we have seen, the $700,000 budgetary allocation constitutes a small fraction of the $5 to 10 million in lost property tax revenues.

A second, potentially more serious cost can be traced to the *immobilization of tenants* that rent control induces. Because of the rental "bargain" that tenants in controlled units enjoy and because controls can make it difficult to find similarly priced accommodations elsewhere, there is a tendency for tenants to stay put.

In their study of the Los Angeles experience, Rand researchers found a clear "trend toward declining mobility of renter households" under rent control, as measured by the percentage of renters moving annually.[33] Similarly, drawing on the Austrian experience, F. A. Hayek reports that Vienna's tram traffic doubled between 1913 and 1928, primarily because of inhibited mobility due to rent control.[34]

One consequence of this "lock-in effect" is increased unemployment as workers are less willing to commute longer distances to find and hold jobs. Similarly, there is less flexibility and job switching in the labor force; as a result, labor resources are distributed less effectively because workers are less responsive to wage signals in the job market.

Despite evidence of this "lock-in effect" elsewhere, it is doubtful that Cambridge suffers very seriously from this particular malady. In fact, Leonard reports a fairly rapid turnover in Cambridge, even in controlled units. But, as we shall see below, this high turnover rate is a double-edged sword: While minimizing "lock-in," it helps to thwart one of the stated goals of rent control, that is, preservation of a diverse community.

Another secondary effect is an *increase in energy consumption*. This inefficiency results from two factors. First, to the extent the "lock-in effect" leads to longer commutes, workers consume more gasoline. Second, and perhaps more relevant to Cambridge, the city's rent control mechanism provides little incentive for landlords to conserve fuel because of a "dollar-for-dollar" clause that allows landlords to pass any increase in fuel expenses directly through to tenants. Such pass-through clauses exacerbate a problem that is endemic to rental property in general since renters are typically charged for heat as part of their rent. This gives the renter little incentive to conserve and the landlords little incentive to install conservation devices. "Rent controls exacerbate this problem by formally mandating pass-throughs."[35]

The final, not inconsequential, secondary cost of rent control is that, ironically, it provides landlords with an *expanded opportunity to discriminate* among precisely those kinds of tenants—ethnic and racial groups, families, and people of low income—that it was designed to protect. In particular, when landlords are not able to discriminate among tenants on the basis of price, they are likely to choose tenants more to their liking from the long line of potential renters queuing up for their bargain apartments. Those likely to be discriminated against include not only ethnic and racial groups (e.g., Italians or blacks), but also families with children and lower-income, less credit-worthy tenants. As an example of this form of discrimination in Cambridge, Jeffrey Stearns has noted that "due to the high demand for housing in the city, landlords prefer and are able to rent their units to higher-income tenants not receiving public subsidies."[36]

This excess demand and queuing for rent control units also creates what economists call "non-price rationing" abuses. As Charles Baird has noted:

> If the explicit rent on a dwelling unit is kept below what the supply and demand would generate in an unregulated market, the landlord and tenants may agree that in order for a tenant to get occupancy, a large non-refundable key deposit, cleaning deposit, or security deposit must be paid; they might agree that the tenants will pay for maintenance and repairs; they might agree that the tenants will purchase the secondhand furniture in the apartment for new furniture prices; or they might agree that each tenant will simply make an unrecorded cash payment to the landlord.[37]

Proof of such abuses is necessarily anecdotal but, in Cambridge, as elsewhere in rent-controlled communities, anecdotes abound.[38]

In summary, rent controls typically impose a number of both primary and secondary economic costs on communities that adopt them. From the universe of these costs, it appears that Cambridge suffers in some degree from almost all of these symptoms. Housing supply and quality appear to have been reduced, while the tax base has been significantly eroded. At the same time that the city incurs relatively small administrative costs to run the system, there is indirect evidence that rent controls have also led to some discrimination, abuses of tenants, and possibly, increased energy consumption, primarily of fuel oil (New England's primary heating fuel).

The remaining questions are whether the benefits of rent control compensate for this diverse array of economic costs and in conferring those benefits, are the ideologically oriented, public interest goals of rent control achieved? The answer to both these questions appears to be no. Let us see why.

C.   The Benefits and Goals of Rent Control

Indisputably, the largest benefit of rent control accrues to tenants in the form of *rent reductions*. As already noted, the average Cambridge market rents are 30 to 60 percent higher than controlled rents, which average about $275 per month. Thus the typical tenant in a rent-controlled unit saves about $1,000 to $2,000 a year, which can constitute a substantial fraction of an individual's or family's income in the low and moderate ranges. However, having given rent control its major due, several additional considerations that diminish the size of this ostensible benefit must be taken into account.

First, while this rent reduction is pure gravy to tenants in the short run, much or all of the gain is eroded over the long run by the reduction in housing services that is caused by the O&M squeeze discussed earlier. To the extent that landlords cut back on O&M and allow their property to deteriorate, the quality and flow of housing services to tenants are reduced: Heat may be lowered and supplied more erratically, halls may be swept less frequently, the exteriors may be allowed to chip and peel, the plumbing may drip and leak, and there may be an increase in roaches or mice infestations as exterminator visits are reduced.

Thus, although tenants may *pay less* for their rent-controlled apartment, over time, the regulated landlord *provides less*. That means in order to calculate the net benefits of rent controls to tenants, one must subtract this "deterioration effect" from the gross rent reduction. For example, in their analysis of Los Angeles, Rand researchers found that a 3.5 percent rent reduction from controls was partially offset by a 2.2 percent deterioration, for a net rent benefit of only 1.3 percent to tenants.[39] The point is that "rent control confers fewer benefits than the rent reductions would imply upon naive examination."[40]

But even if the gain is smaller than it appears, tenants are still winners in the rent control policy game, right? Well, not exactly. The proper answer to that question is that while some tenants win, other tenants unquestionably lose. Consider the Cambridge housing stock. Rent control covers only about 50 percent of the total rental market. While rent control unquestionably reduces rents to tenants in rent-controlled units, it actually *increases* rents to tenants in uncontrolled units.

First, recall that in Cambridge, rent control means that landlords of rent-controlled buildings pay $5 to $10 million less in property taxes because of the lower assessed values of their properties. If the city does not raise this revenue elsewhere, then everyone in Cambridge—tenants, landlords, home owners—shares this loss in the form of reduced city services. However, to the extent that the city raises taxes on uncontrolled property to offset the loss, the tax burden is shifted not only to single-family homeowners, but also to tenants in the uncontrolled market. These tenants must bear part or all of the increase in the tax because landlords of uncontrolled apartments will pass it through to them in the form of higher rents.

At the same time, to the extent that controls reduce housing supply, excess demand drives up rents in the only sector rents can rise—the uncontrolled sector. Thus prospective tenants not only pay more but also find their search for housing much more difficult and time-consuming than it otherwise would be.

What we have then is a situation in which, at best, only *half* of the tenants in Cambridge benefit from rent reductions while the other half, as well as those waiting in the wings to move into the community, actually suffer from higher rents and a harder search.

The next logical question, which also relates to the avowed ideological goals of rent control, is whether there is something special about this preferred group of rent-controlled tenants that warrants this discriminatory treatment by the rent control system. Surprisingly, the answer is *no.* In examining the composition of tenants in the controlled versus uncontrolled sector, both Kirk McClure[41] and Leonard found the two groups to be very similar in terms of distribution of income as well as the distribution of the elderly, students, professionals, and families.[42] In other words, the poor, the elderly, and families—the three major groups targeted for benefits by rent control—were no more likely to be found in controlled than uncontrolled units.

This finding not only raises a disturbing question of equity—why does one group of tenants gain at the expense of another virtually identical group—but also casts doubt on the ability of rent control to meet its two major ideologically-motivated public interest goals, that is, income redistribution and the preservation of the community.

While the capture theory suggests that the rent reductions achieved by controls go to line the pockets of politically powerful but not necessarily poor tenants in controlled housing, the public interest theories justify this redistribution on the assumption that poor tenants receive this transfer of wealth from "rich" landlords.

As a general proposition, this Robin Hood characterization of rent control is simply wrong; Richard Ault points out, for example, that there is no body of evidence indicating that tenants have significantly lower incomes than landlords.[43] At the same time, there is a good bit of both systematic and anecdotal evidence to suggest that landlords are sometimes worse off than their tenants.

But the redistributive effects can be analyzed more precisely in terms of a "targeting efficiency": what percentage of "deserving" households in the low and moderate income range actually occupy rent-controlled housing? As a general rule, the targeting efficiency of rent control and therefore its ability to help low income groups is very poor.

For example, in Los Angeles, only 48 percent of the households under rent control were occupied by low-income tenants,[44] while the remaining 52 percent were occupied by the middle- and upper-income brackets. In Cambridge, the targeting of rent control benefits is even worse. Only 35 percent of the tenants in controlled units had incomes of $10,000 or less, while 17 percent or *almost one-fifth of the tenants had incomes over $25,000.*[45]

Thus, both as a program to redistribute income to the poor and as a means of specifically helping the elderly and families, the Cambridge rent control system is an extremely blunt and ineffective tool. Rather than targeting those groups of tenants the city has said it wants to protect, it merely provides assistance to a broad range of households: some rich, some poor, some elderly, and some students and professionals.

While this finding may put a knowing smirk on the faces of those cynics who cry "tenant capture," it cannot gladden the heart of any well-intentioned liberal who believes that controls only help the poor, elderly, and families. But the news for ideologically motivated rent control supporters is just a bit worse.

In Cambridge, the broad public interest goal of preserving a heterogeneous, culturally colorful, and cohesive community translates simply into maintaining the share of housing units occupied by the more preferred groups. However, in attempting to attain that goal through rent control, the city has started out with one big strike against it because, as surveys indicate, "elderly, family, and low-income households . . . are less likely to occupy controlled units than other Cambridge households."[46]

Strike two comes in the form of the aforementioned high turnover rate in Cambridge apartments: Despite the apparent bargain in rent-controlled units, most such units are vacated and then rerented at least once every five years, while virtually all turn over once in a decade. At the time of that turnover, there is no guarantee that landlords will choose a new tenant from among the groups preferred by the city. In fact, one might expect just the opposite for several reasons.

For one thing, members of the preferred group, such as families and the elderly, are numerically smaller than others waiting in the queue of prospective tenants, so simple odds work against this choice. Moreover, landlords are more likely to exercise the aforementioned expanded opportunity that rent control offers by discriminating precisely against those groups the city wants to protect: Lower income individuals are often viewed as less credit-worthy, families with children create more "wear and tear" on unit interiors, the elderly are often shunned for fear they will be impossible to evict in the event of nonpayment of rent, and blacks and Chicanos are less likely to win the favor of some white landlords who can choose a young and wealthy white professional instead.

Given these dynamics and the pressures bearing down on Cambridge from the heavy influx of the student-transient-professional troika, it should not be surprising that apartment occupancy *trends* between the 1970 census (the year controls were first imposed) and the 1980 census indicate that rent control has failed miserably in its attempt to protect the community from broad-sweeping demographic changes. The number of families occupying rent-controlled units has fallen a dramatic 50 percent, while both the total number of students and fraction of student households has nearly doubled, so that where students were once roughly one out of ten occupants, they are now roughly one out of five. At the same time, while the fraction of elderly households has suffered only a modest decline over the decade (falling from 18 to 15 percent), the number of professional households has doubled, so that while students and professionals once occupied only one-sixth of the controlled units, they now occupy about one-third.[47]

In uncovering these trends, Professor Leonard calls strike three by concluding that "while rent controls may perhaps be able to insulate *individual households* from market forces to some degree, controls do not appear to be able to insulate the community from evolutionary changes."[48]

IV. POLICY REFORMS

For communities which have or are considering rent control, the general policy prescription that emerges from the Cambridge experience is straightforward: Abandon controls and seek more effective and efficient policies to achieve the range of public interest goals that rent regulation seeks to attain.

Indeed, from the vantage point of the public interest, it does not appear prudent for liberals concerned with equitable income redistribution and community preservation to join with rent-controlled tenants in a voting coalition to sustain controls. Nor, from the vantage point of tenant capture, does it appear to be in the interests of tenants in the relatively large, uncontrolled apartment market to join in that coalition either.

However, how such a general policy prescription will be administered will necessarily depend on the ideological bias of the particular community, for inevitably there will be controversy over both the range of goals pursued and the policy approach. For example, both liberals and conservatives may agree that the goal of alleviating a housing shortage and attendant high, exploitative rents is desirable. But liberals may lean more toward a public housing program to alleviate that shortage, whereas conservatives may favor stimulating the private market through tax incentives or developing or "unfettering" that market through rezoning that allows more growth and bigger buildings.

At the same time, liberals and conservatives are likely to disagree sharply over the need for, and scope of, income redistribution to the poor as well as the desirability of any expansion of local government powers to protect certain members of the community (e.g., the elderly) at the expense of property owners. Accordingly, where liberals might favor an income assistance program (such as housing subsidies) to the poor in lieu of controls, conservatives might view such a policy as being just as onerous as controls, even if such subsidies were more effective in targeting benefits.

Having acknowledged these inevitable ideological obstacles to a consensus over both goals and policy within any community, let us see, in an illustrative way, how our general policy prescription of "abandon controls, adopt other policies" would play out in a predominantly liberal community like Cambridge—keeping in mind that a more conservative community might adopt a different mix of goals and policies.

A.   Decontrol

One of the many problems rent controls create is how to abandon them without an enormous "rent shock" to tenants, for the longer control is in place, the larger the gap between market and controlled rents.

Among the major cities that have removed controls in recent times—Boston, Los Angeles, Washington, D.C.—the preferred method seems to be *vacancy decontrol.** Under this policy option, rent control remains in effect until the tenant(s) who occupied the units at the time they were decontrolled elect to move out.

The primary virtue of this approach is that decontrol occurs gradually; most policymakers find this type of transition politically more palatable than simply taking the lid off pent-up rents all at once. However, one unfortunate side effect is that vacancy decontrol amplifies the lock-in effect, as some tenants are apt to cling even more tenaciously to their rental bargain. Moreover, if the vacancy decontrol rule doesn't have strong sanctions against subletting, the controlled units are simply passed along to friends or, for a fee, from the new to the old tenants when the old tenant moves out.

Thus, in considering decontrol, Cambridge might instead try another option, *phased decontrol.* Under this option, which is similar to the gradual lifting of oil and natural gas price controls, controlled rents would be allowed to rise, say over a two- or three-year period, to market levels. Such a phase-in would both moderate rent shock and mute the lock-in effect. It would also give the city time to implement other policies to alleviate Cambridge's chronic housing shortage.

B.   Alleviating the Housing Shortage

Conventional wisdom has it that local communities like Cambridge have little influence over the pace of new apartment construction, which is primarily dependent on more macroeconomic factors like interest rates and the general health of the economy. While there is a good bit of truth to that argument, nonetheless, there remains considerable scope for local government action.

---

*The removal of controls in these cities was in large part due to the recognition of many of the adverse economic effects created by controls (as discussed in Section III).

First and foremost, a community can stimulate apartment construction by entering into ironclad convenants with apartment developers that at no future time will new buildings ever be subject to controls. Such covenants would be particularly important in Cambridge, where the threat of future controls hangs like a pall over developers' plans.

At the same time, cities like Cambridge can finance the construction of more public housing for their low and moderate income population, a step that would also help preserve the existing character of the community. Similarly, it is possible to change zoning laws to allocate more land to apartment construction and to allow larger buildings. While such rezoning may be less palatable to those within the "limits to growth" wing of Cambridge's liberal contingent, pondering such a policy shift nonetheless would reflect an acknowledgment of the inevitable trade-off between housing space and a limit to growth.

C. Income Redistribution

Assuming a public interest consensus in Cambridge that some redistribution of income from predominantly middle- and upper-income groups to those of lower income is desirable, there are a number of well-acknowledged policy devices that target such redistribution far more effectively and efficiently than rent control.

The most administratively simple device would be *cash subsidies* to the preferred groups. For example, households with incomes below a certain level (say, $10,000) would receive monthly cash supplements to finance their housing needs.

Another alternative would be a "rent stamp" voucher system similar to the federal food stamp program. While this approach is administratively more cumbersome, it (according to critics, "paternalistically") removes the obvious danger that cash rent subsidies would be "misspent" on cigarettes, liquor, drugs, and the like.

Obviously, either of these approaches would entail a much more direct drain on city coffers than rent control. But these direct costs would be far less than the indirect costs of current controls while the benefits would actually reach their intended beneficiaries. Moreover, acknowledging these costs in the city budget would allow the degree of the desired redistribution to occur within the context of a known price tag. Thus a better balance between the city's fiscal capabilities and its desire for redistribution might be struck.

D. Preserving the Existing Character
of the Community

The abject failure of rent control to insulate the city's preferred ethnic, economic, and family groups from the broad changes occurring in Cambridge bodes ill for policymakers attempting to stem the student-professional-transient tide of displacement. Nonetheless, several of the options previously discussed within the context of achieving other goals offer some protection. For example, more public housing dedicated to the elderly or families would guarantee these groups a share in the city's space. Similarly, a cash subsidy or rent stamp program would allow lower-income groups to compete on a more equal footing with affluent groups, while measures taken to alleviate housing shortages would achieve a similar result by moderating the rate of rent increases.

E. Conclusions

Obviously, the details of any decontrol and expanded housing assistance program would require painstaking months of planning, and the policies set forth here are merely suggestive. There would also have to be considerable debate within the community in order to forge a consensus on the desirability and scope of various parts of the program, many of which are heavily value-laden.

But in the final analysis, any ideological debate over issues like the size of the public housing sector or the amount of desired redistribution should not obscure the incontrovertible fact that in communities that have rent control, such regulation has not solved the problem; accordingly, there should at least be a consensus that such a system is not in either the liberal's or conservative's conception of the public interest.

Part 2

America's Special Interests

In this part, we delve more deeply into the world of America's special interests. Chapter 3 examines *who* the major interest groups are, while the protectionist policy game presented in Chapter 4 illustrates how, on any given issue, some subset of these groups becomes active in the policy debate. Chapter 5 then examines the *strategies* and *tactics* of the special interests, while Chapter 6 illustrates how these strategies and tactics are put into practice by the major interest groups in the farm policy game.

3

The Greedmongers

WHO THE SPECIAL INTERESTS ARE

The term "special interests" invariably conjures up an image much like that popularized by the nineteenth-century cartoonist Thomas Nast: fat-fingered, pot-bellied, cigar-smoking lobbyists descending on Washington to buy Congress. In the mind's eye, these nefarious ambassadors of greed prowl the smoke-filled corridors of power with moneybags slung heavily over their shoulders plying politicians with bribes, booze, and blondes in exchange for subsidies, tax breaks, and other special favors for which the taxpayer ultimately picks up the tab.

Such an image is outdated, however, on several accounts. For one, the modern version of Nast's political buccaneer is more likely to be sleek and urbane, stylishly clad in pinstripes (or, at worst, polyester). Rather than relying on such an unsubtle device as a bribe, he tends to offer information, persuasion, and campaign contributions to weave his web of influence.

More important, the Nastian caricature projects a far too narrow image of who the special interests are. Properly construed, they encompass not only the standard villains of the policy process—big business, big labor, the farm lobby, and others of their ilk—but also the far more numerous factions, from environmentalists and antiabortionists to Gray Panther grandmothers. The thousands of interest groups that populate the American political landscape can be discussed within the context of three broad categories, which are outlined in Table 3.1.

TABLE 3.1.   WHO THE SPECIAL
INTERESTS ARE

  I. Private interest lobbies
      A. Business
      B. Labor
      C. Farm
      D. Professional
      E. Government
      F. Foreign
 II. Noneconomic Lobbies
      A. Public interest
      B. Single issue
      C. Ideological
      D. Religious and ethnic
      E. Universities and research organizations
III. Geographic and Demographic Lobbies
      A. Locality
      B. Age
      C. Sex
      D. Socioeconomic

I.   THE PRIVATE INTEREST LOBBIES

The private interest lobbies are characterized by their rather single-minded pursuit of economic enrichment through the manipulation of public policy. This category includes the "big four" of the business, labor, farm, and professional lobbies. Also included in this list are the government lobby, which has seen its membership and power rise proportionally with the explosion in government spending over the last two decades, and the foreign lobby, which not only sends foreign agents to our shores, but also often hires the best and brightest of our deposed politicians to peddle its influence.

A.   The Business Lobby

The three biggest guns of the business lobby are the Chamber of Commerce (CC), the National Association of Manufacturers (NAM), and the Business Roundtable (BR). The national Chamber, headquartered in Washington, is a federation of thousands of local chambers, through which it is able to wield tremendous grass-roots power, while the NAM draws its membership from industry groups, and the BR is an elite, secretive organization whose members include the chief executive officers of many of the Fortune 500 corporations.

Together, these three "umbrella organizations" spend millions of dollars each year to promote the broad interests of the business community. Typically, those interests are cloaked in the conservative rhetoric of "preserving the free market." But as befits a special interest group, when an intervention in the market is favorable to them (a protective tariff, for instance), these groups will often support it.

Despite their common business bond, these organizations do, however, sometimes find it difficult to agree on issues. For example, the Chamber, which represents both small and large businesses, will occasionally endorse policies that the NAM, with its primarily large corporate constituency, may vehemently oppose. Because of this inability of the umbrella business groups to always speak with a single voice, the business lobby is also organized at the industry level.

Trade associations are by far the most common form of industry-specific organizations. They provide information and services to their members, set industry standards, and last, but hardly least, they lobby. More than 1,500 of these trade associations are headquartered in Washington. Their ranks include such giants as the American Iron and Steel Institute, with a membership of 2,600 companies and a budget of $10 million and the American Bankers Association, with a membership of 13,254 banks and a budget of $20 million as well as smaller associations like the Soy Protein Council and the Sugar Association, which have as few as 15 members.

While the trade association is better able to serve industry-specific needs than are umbrella organizations such as the NAM and the CC, it is still too blunt a tool to meet all of the needs of all of its members, for even within an industry, there are numerous disagreements over public policy.

The National Coal Association (NCA), for example, has been mute on many of the provisions of the Clean Air Act, even though these provisions have an enormous impact on coal production. The reason is that the NCA contains both low-sulphur, Western coal producers and high-sulphur, Eastern coal producers. Because some provisions of the act discriminate against low-sulphur coal (as did the "scrubber law"), it was impossible for the NCA to speak for all its members, even though enactment of the law meant an overall drop in coal production.

Similarly, the American Petroleum Institute represents both small and large oil producers (who frequently disagree on matters such as special tax breaks to small independent producers) as well as refiners and distributors (who, unlike petroleum producers, are likely to support price and allocation controls on petroleum production).

Accordingly, many corporations also find it useful to field their own lobbying team. Such teams typically consist of one or more people who are registered lobbyists, a backup public relations department, and legal or consulting firms (so-called Washington representatives) that provide auxiliary lobbying services. The budgets for corporate lobbying teams range from several million dollars for some Fortune 500 companies to less than $100,000 for smaller firms.

B. The Labor Lobby

Like its bête noire, the business lobby, the labor lobby is multilayered, with the American Federation of Labor–Congress of Industrial Organizations (AFL–CIO) sitting atop the pyramid of labor power.

The AFL–CIO's roots stretch back to 1886, when its first component, the AFL, was founded after the demise of the Knights of Labor. Drawing primarily on the trade and craft unions for its membership and led by the legendary Samuel Gompers, the AFL practiced a philosophy of "business unionism," which accepted the prevailing capitalist structure of the economy and sought only to improve the wages and working conditions of its members through such tactics as the strike and the boycott. The increasing industrialization of America during the early part of the twentieth century, coupled with an apparent decline in the power of the AFL, created a need for an alternate form of labor organization based not on craft, but on industry. In response, the Congress of Industrial Organizations was formed in 1938.

Recognizing their mutual interest, the AFL and CIO merged in 1955; today, the AFL–CIO is the voice of big labor. The only major union which is not a member of this umbrella organization is the Teamsters, who were expelled in 1957 for corrupt practices. (The United Auto Workers withdrew in 1968 citing philosophical differences but have since returned to the fold.) Each year, the AFL–CIO reports spending more than one million dollars on registered lobbyists alone.[1]

As the AFL–CIO corresponds to the larger business lobbies, the labor lobby's many unions are analogous to (and often the answer to) the business lobby's trade associations. Today, virtually every American industry is unionized (even if all segments of an industry are not). In fact, there are over 260 separate unions, at least 50 of which maintain separate lobbying offices in Washington.

Through close contact via newsletters, pamphlets, meetings, and bulletins, these unions can readily mobilize their rank and file membership. A potent grass-roots lobbying force, they can exert tremendous pressure at both the congressional district and the state levels, and for large unions like the Teamsters and United Auto Workers, at the federal level as well.

C. The Farm Lobby

The farm lobby likewise has its umbrella organizations. The oldest is the National Grange, which happens to have a higher proportion of older farmers (as opposed to young and commercial farmers) in its membership. The largest is the American Farm Bureau Federation (AFBF). A third group, the National Farm Union (NFU), although organized nationally, draws primarily on the Great Plains states for its membership. And a fourth group, the National Farm Organization, specializes in collective bargaining.

These groups are frequently at odds with each other. For example, the AFBF "has expressed a free-market ideology since the 1940s, forsaking its original commitment to subsidies," while the more liberal NFU is "an advocate of more extensive support, with a zealous enthusiasm for 100 percent parity."[2] (These issues and differences will be discussed in more detail in Chapter 6.)

Analogous to the business lobby's trade associations and the labor lobby's unions, the farm lobby is also organized along a host of crop- and commodity-specific lines. These groups, numbering in the hundreds, provide a virtual "soup to nuts" representation of farm producers, from the Southwestern Peanut Growers Association and National Wool Growers Association to the United Egg Producers and the National Shrimp Congress.

While these groups serve their members with information, marketing expertise, and other nonpolitical functions, they are also tailor-made for lobbying. Indeed, the crop and commodity lobbyists are much more prevalent and powerful than the umbrella groups because the highly fragmented nature of the farm market and its decentralized political structure make it hard for the umbrella groups to reach a consensus. In contrast, the crop and commodity groups can focus sharply on specific issues related to their products, such as price supports.

Other segments of the farm lobby include the thousands of cooperatives and the hundreds of "middlemen" associations which represent the various food processing, distributing, and merchandising interests. These latter groups introduce a further divisive element into the farm lobby.

For example, the National Turkey Federation and the National Broiler Council typically oppose target prices for grain since such producer-supported programs drive up the price of poultry feed; and, contrary to milk producer's goals, both the International Association of Ice Cream Manufacturers and the Chocolate Manufacturers of America seek to keep dairy price supports low because milk and cream are key ingredients in their products.

D. The Professional Lobby

Completing the list of the traditional big four private interests is an imposing array of professional groups that can muster formidable financial and analytic resources from their typically well-heeled ranks.

Perhaps the two best-known of these groups in the professional lobby are the American Medical Association (AMA) and American Bar Association (ABA). Others include the business-oriented National Association of Real Estate Boards and the National Education Association while accountants, engineers, architects, pharmacists, optometrists, and morticians all have their own organizations to represent their interests.

The hallmark of these groups is their ability to link professional acceptance and competence to membership in their organizations. They do this directly by regulating entry into the profession and by setting professional standards. They also do this indirectly by publishing journals, reports, and newsletters. These publications not only provide information, but also serve as an important vehicle for their members to gain recognition. The ABA, for example, draws much of its force from the fact that it helps to regulate entry into the law profession: One must "pass the bar" to join, while the AMA helps to regulate professional entry through its medical school accreditation procedures and its *AMA Journal*.

Besides being a paradigm of the sometimes immense power of the professional lobbying groups, the AMA offers a good example of how the leadership of a lobbying organization sometimes pushes for its own political agenda rather than for the wishes of an often too silent majority of its members. Perhaps the best illustration of this is the trench warfare that the AMA waged against Medicare-type programs. From the dawn of the Truman administration to a striking victory in the Kennedy administration and through to a crushing defeat during the Johnson administration, the AMA ritually portrayed health care for the elderly as "socialized medicine" and vigorously opposed Medicare and other such programs. Yet many doctors were uneasy, not only with the often tawdry tactics and propaganda the AMA used, but also with the fervor of its opposition.

E.   The Government Lobby

While it may seem peculiar to categorize the government as a special interest, anyone who has played the policy game on such issues as revenue sharing, budget cutbacks, and welfare programs is well aware that the government is not only the target of special interest pressure, but also one of its biggest instigators. We can conceptualize government interests as a lobby in three ways.

First, the various *vertical* branches of government—local, state, and federal—lobby each other. For example, the cities, counties, and states have a number of powerful and well-organized groups that lobby under the banner of public interest groups or PIGs (an acronym that one wag has found particularly apt because of their "insatiable desire for federal funds").[3] These PIGs include the Council of State Governors, the National Governors' Conference, the National Association of Counties, the International City Management Association, the National League of Cities, and the U.S. Conference of Mayors. All these groups have Washington offices, employ over 200 lobbyists, and spend over $5 million a year on lobbying activities. In addition, many states have their own lobbying apparatus; California alone maintains 35 people full-time in its numerous lobbying units.[4]

Thus, when Ronald Reagan introduced his "New Federalism" plan, which was designed to give state and local governments greater responsibility in administering and paying for government programs, it drew storms of protest from state and local groups such as the National Council of Mayors and the National Conference of State Legislatures.

Second, the various *horizontal* branches of government—administrative, legislative, and judicial—try to influence one another. For example, the president lobbies Congress to ensure passage of the administration's budget, the Department of Energy fights with the Department of Commerce over who should oversee oil leasing, and so on. Similarly, department secretaries, agency heads, and other federal executives all actively lobby Congress to increase their budgets and to authorize their programs, while the White House has over 10 congressional liaison officers who represent the interests of the president.

Third, government *employees* themselves have a vested interest in maintaining and expanding government programs and expenditures. Accordingly, organizations like the National Federation of Federal Employees, representing federal government employees, also have stridently opposed budget cutbacks proposed by Ronald Reagan, while fiscal crises in cities like Boston and New York, which have led to layoffs of police, firemen, and other city workers, have been hotly and at times violently protested by unions and other organizations representing government workers.

F. The Foreign Lobby

The foreign lobby rounds out our list of the private interest lobbies. It consists of the many foreign governments that use both official and unofficial "Washington representatives" to promote their interests in American policy.

The archetypical foreign special interest of the 1950s was the infamous sugar lobby. Scrambling for their share of U.S. sugar market quotas, countries like Cuba, then under Batista's leadership, and the Dominican Republic, then under Trujillo, poured millions of dollars into lobbying campaigns. During the 1950s and 1960s and particularly during the Nixon–Kennedy presidential campaign, the Nationalist China lobby similarly crossed swords with politicians and government agencies to protect Taiwan from the threat of liberalized policies toward mainland China. In the 1970s, infamous Korean lobbyist Tong Sun Park sought to mute congressional criticism of Korea's military dictatorship.

Today, the foreign lobby continues in this long tradition; it has been particularly successful in enlisting prominent Washington figures (usually deposed politicians) to carry its message into the corridors of power. For example, the Arab lobby has had former Secretary of State Clark Clifford and former Vice President Spiro Agnew on its payroll. This lobby has sought partly to counterbalance the mighty Israeli lobby (which consists of 34 separate organizations) and partly to advance goals unrelated to the Arab–Israeli conflict, such as petroleum market controls. Other active foreign lobbies include the China External Trade Development Council and the Japan External Trade Organization.

II. THE NONECONOMIC LOBBIES

The second category of special interests includes the so-called public interest and various "single issue" groups as well as scores of religious and ethnic groups, equally numerous universities and research "think tanks," and various ideological organizations. Harmon Zeigler and Wayne Peak have dubbed these groups "noneconomic"; they are distinguishable from the private interest groups not so much by the policies they demand from the political system, but rather, by the goals and values on which their memberships are based. Presumably more altruistic, these groups focus less on their direct material benefit and more on the general welfare of themselves and society.[5]

A. The Public Interest Lobby

The public interest groups, which lobby "for the people," include consumer organizations such as Congress Watch and Common Cause, environmental groups such as the Natural Resources Defense Council, civil rights groups such as the American Civil Liberties Union, peace groups such as the Friends Peace Committee, and population control groups such as the Council on Population and Environment.

Their moniker notwithstanding, considerable controversy exists over whether these groups truly serve the public interest. As political scientist Jeffrey Berry has argued:

> The lobbying activity of public interest groups is no more legitimate than that of their private interest counterparts. . . . Critics and opponents of public interest groups have often pointed out that these organizations frequently have goals that place the comfort and well-being of a minority over that of a majority. For example, most people probably prefer the

convenience of cars and highways, despite the air pollution they cause, to mass transit and bicycles. Yet this will never deter environmentalists, who see clean air as an absolute necessity, regardless of the changes that must be made.[6]

Regardless of whether public interest groups truly serve the public interest, they are readily distinguishable from the private interest lobbies by several important characteristics.

First and foremost, these interest groups typically pursue *collective* goals, such as clean air, an end to world hunger, or nuclear disarmament. None of these goals materially benefit their members (but may well psychologically).

Second, and a characteristic that has added fuel to the public interest group fire, these groups are typically *oligarchical* in structure. That is, the rank-and-file membership is often led by an activist elite of political entrepreneurs such as Ralph Nader of Public Citizen fame and Fred Wertheimer and John Gardner of Common Cause. Each group's leadership determines policy for a financially contributing, but often nonparticipatory, membership; in fact, as many as one-third of the public interest groups have no dues-paying members at all.[7] They are financed through third parties such as private foundations and, to a large extent, by the federal government. This lack of a dues-paying membership participating in the determination of the groups' goals and actions has had some interesting legal ramifications. U.S. District Court Judge John Sirica, for one, has prevented these groups from filing lawsuits in many circumstances, ruling that "only a democratically organized group with dues-paying members and elected officers would have a legitimate right to sue."[8]

For the purposes of this book, the public interest groups will be treated as special interests, their nomenclature notwithstanding. For while these groups typically pursue more altruistic goals than their private interest counterparts, each represents only a subset (albeit an often large one) of the American polity and invariably there are other groups that oppose their goals.

B. The Single-Issue Groups

The recent rise in power of the public interest groups has also been accompanied by an equally impressive ascendency of the so-called single-issue groups. The hallmark of these groups is their dogged allegiance to one issue (e.g., busing, abortion, gun control, or school prayer) and their willingness to support or oppose (often ruthlessly) politicians and government officials solely on the basis of their stance on that particular issue.

One of the oldest, and unquestionably one of the most powerful, single issue groups is the National Rifle Association (NRA), which has zealously defended the right to bear arms against almost perennial legislative efforts to impose gun control. Despite public opinion polls that show that a majority of Americans favor some kind of gun control, Congress has consistently defeated such efforts in large part because of the power of the NRA. Other well-known single-issue groups include the National Right to Life while less renowned of the hundreds of these groups that have swarmed onto Capitol Hill during the last several decades are the American League to Abolish Capital Punishment and the Infant Formula Action Coalition.

Critics of these groups claim that they wreak havoc with a democratic majoritarian system and describe them as a divisive and fractious force. Anecdotes abound of good liberals who support welfare programs, aid to farmers, and the union shop but find themselves out of office because they fail to support the right to abortion. Otherwise good conservatives voting for government spending cuts, anti-Communist foreign policy, and deregulation likewise have felt the whiplash of the single-issue groups for failing to support school prayer or oppose busing.

But defenders of the single-issue group phenomenon describe these organizations as the ultimate expression of a pluralistic society, with each group speaking in a loud and clear voice for its interests. Regardless of these disparate views, there is an ironclad consensus that the single-issue groups are a force to be reckoned with in the policy game, particularly when it comes to social issues.

C. The Ideological Groups

Each shade of the ideological spectrum—conservative, liberal, far Right, far Left, and sometimes just far out—has organizations to represent it.[9]

The oldest and best-known liberal pressure group is the Americans for Democratic Action (ADA). Founded in 1946, the ADA operates on an annual budget of $800,000. Its principal activities include the preparation of research materials, the publication of periodicals and newsletters, and the compilation of congressional voting records (ratings we will put to extensive use in several of our cases). The ADA's conservative counterpart, which performs many similar functions (including their own compilation of voting records) is the Americans for Constitutional Action (ACA). Like the ADA, the ACA is headquartered in Washington, D.C. Its annual budget is $125,000.

Coexisting with these mainstream ideological groups are a wide variety of organizations representing other shades of the ideological spectrum. Far Right extremist groups include the well-funded John Birch Society and the infamous American Nazi party, while, despite a sharp drop in membership since the New Left's heyday during Vietnam, organizations such as the American Socialist Party and the American Communist Party represent the Far Left.

D. The Religious and Ethnic Lobbies

The diverse religious and ethnic groups represent yet another potent force in American pressure politics, particularly when social and civil rights issues are involved.

In the religious orb, the major American denominations—Catholic, Protestant, Jewish, and Mormon—all maintain well-staffed Washington offices to coordinate their lobbying activities. The powerful U.S. Catholic Conference, for example, spends $1 million a year on indirect and direct lobbying, while the American Jewish Congress, the spearhead of the so-called Jewish lobby, likewise pours out millions each year to influence various branches of the government.

These groups also share several characteristics with the more secular public interest organizations: Often they are oligarchical in structure, and an elite clergy typically leads the congregation without necessarily reflecting the church members' policy preferences. At the same time, their goals—religious freedom, an end to discrimination, aid to the poor—typically benefit not only members of that sect, but many outside the group as well. (Notable exceptions exist, however; the Catholic church's self-interested support for tuition tax credits for its parochial school system is one.)

The church lobby has played an important role in a number of major policy battles, one of its most successful being the civil rights legislation that it helped pass in 1964. In that battle, one of the staunchest opponents of the civil rights bill, Senator Richard B. Russell of Georgia, learned an important lesson about the power of the church lobby, which steamrolled Russell's attempts at filibuster. Licking his wounds, the senior senator from the Peach State trenchantly observed that the strongest tools available to religious groups are not legal arguments and sophisticated political analysis, but rather, the ability to pronounce moral judgments on political action. More recently, the Mormon and Baptist churches have used such moral suasion to help defeat the Equal Rights Amendment (as discussed in Chapter 10).

But the church lobby does not necessarily confine itself to social issues. Jewish and Arab groups exert perhaps the most widespread influence on policymaking. Because of the connection between Arab oil and the security of both America and Israel, these groups have found themselves involved in issues ranging from price controls on natural gas and oil to the level of defense spending and foreign military aid to the Middle East. Similarly, the Catholic church has played a leading role in the nuclear freeze movement.

In the ethnic sphere, melting pot America has spawned hundreds of political organizations that represent the many races, colors, and creeds that comprise the U.S. population. Perhaps the most powerful of these ethnic groups on the national scene are those representing black Americans. Washington-officed organizations such as the National Association for the Advancement of Colored People (NAACP), which draws a high proportion of its members from the black upper classes, and the more militant, grass-roots-oriented Congress of Racial Equality are but two of a score or more of groups that have consistently pressed the American system—sometimes with great success, other times with deep frustration—to open wider our economic, political, and social doors to blacks.

Similarly, the "Irish machine" in Massachusetts, the Polish and German coalitions in Milwaukee, and the Hispanic organizations in many cities of the Sun Belt are but a few examples of ethnic groups that have played key roles in controlling state and local governments.

E. Universities and Research Organizations

As with the government lobby, it may come as a surprise that the nation's universities and research organizations frequently engage in the bruising battles of the policy game. But on such issues as aid to public education and student loans, research and development funding, and tax law changes, this "brain lobby" has few equals in the lobbying arena. Indeed, the prestige of American universities and their highly articulate presidents and professors make academia a force to be reckoned with on issues that encroach on its territory.

For example, during the Reagan administration's campaign to cut student loans, private university interests, led by Harvard University President Derek Bok, converged on Capitol Hill to testify on the dire consequences of such a cutback: not only would it threaten the financial viability of many universities, but it would also do serious damage to the development of the nation's most precious resource, its people. As a result of this pressure, the student loan program has remained largely intact.

Similarly, research organizations such as the liberal-oriented Brookings Institution and its conservative counterpart, the American Enterprise Institute, exert significant intellectual pressure on the policy process. In grinding out research reports, holding conferences, and publishing journals, these think tanks provide important theoretical ammunition and opinions for public policy debate.

Even more specific in their impact on policy are the consulting and quasi-consulting organizations whose fortunes tend to rise or fall with increases or decreases in the federal budget or specific program expenditures. For example, the prestigious nonprofit RAND and MITRE corporations have much to say about the size and character of defense appropriations, while a whole slew of profit-making private consulting firms regularly shape policies ranging from transportation and energy to welfare and the environment.

III.   THE GEOGRAPHIC AND DEMOGRAPHIC LOBBIES

The third and final major category of America's special interests includes those lobbies that represent geographic and demographic interests.

For example, *regional conflict* has been an enduring part of the American heritage. In the 1800s, the North and South fought first in the Congress and later on the battlefield over slavery and such related issues as industrial tariffs. Today, the energy-poor Frost Belt and energy-rich

Sun Belt are in constant battle over natural gas price deregulation and the right of an energy-producing state to impose severance taxes, which raise the price of energy to consuming states.

Similarly, differences among rural and urban America and the continually growing suburbs often put these three geographic divisions at loggerheads with each other. Urban dwellers typically favor large government subsidies to mass transit and have sought to finance such systems through highway and gasoline taxes. But residents of rural areas, who generally must drive greater distances, oppose such taxes and often the systems themselves. Suburbanites, on yet another hand, would prefer tax policies and government expenditures that facilitate the growth of their own area's infrastructure—malls, bus lines, and the like. Such disparities have given rise to groups representing geographic interests such as the Council for Rural Housing and Development, the Western Regional Council, and the Midwest-Northeast Coalition.

Age is also playing an increasingly important role in special interest politics. A case in point is the issue of Social Security, where the primary combatants have been aging and retired workers about to receive or now receiving Social Security benefits and the young workers who must finance an increasingly large share of old-age benefits. The Gray Panthers, the American Association of Retired Persons, and the United States Student Association have been formed primarily to represent particular age groups.

At the same time, *sex* and, increasingly, *sexual preference*, provide important divisions in the American polity. Women's groups—which have existed since the days of Carrie Nation and before—have organized to break down the barriers to hitherto closed parts of society, from corporate executive positions to men's bars, while gay activists are playing an increasingly powerful role in politics, particularly in pockets of the country—San Francisco, Miami Beach, New York—where the gay community is concentrated. (e.g., The Gay Public Health Workers Caucus speaks up for its members.)

Economic and social class provide a final delineation of demographic special interests. While there are few if any organizations that overtly promote the interests of the rich, both the poor and the middle class have their own lobbies to seek special favors. The National Community Action Foundation represents people with low incomes, and the United Organization of Taxpayers represents the members of the middle class.

Besides this battle along broad economic lines, there are also more specific economic conflicts such as that between landlord and tenant, which was demonstrated in Chapter 2's case on rent control.

In summary, the special interest players in the policy game are many and varied—a fact that has led James Deakin to remark wryly:

> There is an association, union, society, league, conference, institute, organization, federation, chamber, foundation, congress, order, brotherhood, company, corporation, bureau, mutual, cooperative, committee, council, plan, trusteeship, movement, district, assembly, club, board, service or tribe for every human need, desire, motive, ambition, goal, aim, drive, affiliation, occupation, industry, interest, incentive, fear, anxiety, greed, compulsion, frustration, hate, spirit, reform and cussedness in the United States.[10]

On any given issue, some *subset* of the long list of players presented above will be actively involved in the policy debate. This last point will be highlighted in Chapter 4.

4

The Coming of the Second Great Depression

THE PROTECTIONIST POLICY GAME

Young man, tariffs are the whole of politics. Study them.[1]

Advice of a senior senator to a freshman colleague

As the blistery winds of foreign competition blow across the U.S. economy, a host of domestic industries can be seen scurrying for the shelter of a protectionist trade policy. From shoes, textiles, and electronics to more basic industries like autos, steel, and machine tools and even to the esoterica of clothespins and bicycles, we are witnessing the steady buildup of a variety of trade barriers. Indeed, at no time since the days of the Great Depression has America taken such a sharp turn towards protectionism.

The clear danger of this trend is an all-out global trade war; for when one country excludes others from its markets, the other countries inevitably retaliate with their own trade barriers. And as history has painfully taught, once protectionist wars begin, the likely result is a deadly and well-nigh unstoppable downward spiral by the entire world economy.

If the world is, in fact, sucked into this spiral, enormous gains from trade will be sacrificed. While such a sacrifice might save some jobs in the sheltered domestic industries, it will destroy as many or more in other home industries, particularly those that rely heavily on export trade. At the same time, consumers will pay tens of billions of dollars more in higher prices for a much more limited selection of goods. Sacrificed, too, on the altar of protectionism will be the very heart of an international world order that since World War II has successfully channeled the aggressive struggle among nations for world resources and markets into a peaceful economic competition rather than a confrontational political or military one.

Is there any way to avoid this protectionist spiral and its potentially disastrous consequences? This chapter examines that question with the help of the capture-ideology framework.

I. BACKGROUND AND HISTORY

While many people tend to associate America with a free-trade philosophy, the fact is that this nation has a long, and at times rather sordid history of protectionism that dates all the way back to the American Revolution.

In 1791, the founding father of American protectionism, Alexander Hamilton, published his ode to trade barriers, *The Report on Manufacturers*, setting forth what has come to be known as the "infant industry" argument.[2] According to Hamilton, an industry learns how to be efficient by doing. But without the protection of trade barriers, America's fledgling industries would never go through this process because older, more mature manufacturers like the English would consistently outcompete the American "infants." Thus trade barriers would be necessary if the country wanted to foster an industrial base.

Hamilton's argument initially met with only a lukewarm response. However, the War of 1812 exposed America's weak industrial underbelly, as it was subjected to a humiliating series of embargos, economic sanctions, and boycotts that nearly brought the young nation to its knees. In the wake of this near disaster, America took Hamilton's advice to heart, and for the next 120 years, his protectionist argument became the basis of our trade policy.

The first wave of trade barriers spanned the years 1816 to 1934 and saw as its high water mark the infamous Smoot–Hawley Tariffs of 1930. This legislation assigned specific tariff schedules to over 20,000 items and the average rate on dutiable imports rose to over 50 percent.

These tariffs are often credited with pushing the world economy over a precipice and into the depths of the Great Depression.[3] For in retaliation to Smoot–Hawley, some 26 other major trading nations erected their own restrictions and controls while England abandoned free trade altogether.[4] In a span of a few short years, U.S. exports fell from $5.2 billion to $1.7 billion while imports fell from $4.4 billion to $1.5 billion. As the world's factories grew colder and darker and the jobless lines grew longer, world trade dropped from $34 billion to $12 billion.[5]

By 1934, the contributions of Smoot–Hawley and retaliatory policies to the Great Depression were fully acknowledged. This acknowledgment, in turn, led to an important power shift in American politics, as the primary responsibility for trade policy shifted from a tariff-minded Congress to a more free-trade oriented, and less politically vulnerable, executive branch. An important sign of this shift was passage of the Reciprocal Trade Act of 1934, the first product of an internationalist approach to trade and the brainchild of FDR's Secretary of State Cordell Hull. Yet it wasn't until World War II, which established the military and economic preeminence of the United States that the act was implemented to secure negotiations on a free-trade order.

In this context, the Bretton Woods Agreement, established by the Western allies in the wake of World War II, attempted to establish a set of "rules of the game" to avoid a replay of the disastrous 1930s. The General Agreement on Tariffs and Trade (GATT) was one of its major planks. The GATT, which remains the centerpiece of international trade relations today, established a framework under which nations could come together to negotiate reductions in trade barriers, especially tariffs.

While the GATT framework has been responsible for more than an eightfold reduction in the level of world tariffs since its inception, initially this progress was rather slow. A primary reason was that America continued to resist a free-trade philosophy in the postwar period, despite the efforts of the conservative Eisenhower administration to promote free trade. The problem was America's own prosperity in that decade: Business, labor, and consumer interests were all basking in the glow of steadily rising profits and wages and stable prices.

In the 1960s, however, the nation's industrial base was established as the most modern and powerful in the world, and America's captains of industry had less fear that they would be outcompeted. At the same time, as the economy began to stall under Ike's economic policies, these same captains began to look for expanded foreign markets that would pave the way for a whole new decade of prosperity and higher profits.[6] The problem, however, was getting other nations—long accustomed to American protectionism—to open their markets. This problem was especially acute in Western Europe where the European Economic Community (or "Common Market") had begun to assert itself; through protectionism, it had the potential to curtail one-third of existing U.S. trade.

To solve this problem, the Kennedy administration played its free-trade card; using America's own trade barriers as bargaining chips, U.S. negotiators proposed immediate and drastic reductions in tariffs. After prolonged (and, at times, theatrical) negotiations, the Kennedy round of GATT talks ended with one of the most sweeping reductions in tariffs ever recorded, its cuts averaging around 35 percent.[7]

This reduction of trade barriers provided a tremendous spur to both the U.S. and world economies. As the American economy opened its markets, total import–export trade doubled from 6 to 12 percent of national income. Ironically, however, the very success of America's new free-trade philosophy planted the seeds of a "new protectionism." While export industries flourished, import-sensitive industries such as textiles and steel began to feel additional competitive pressures. As a result, labor interests became much more sensitive to foreign competition; while the AFL–CIO still at least nominally supported free trade in 1968, in 1970 it openly announced its support for protectionist measures. At the same time, business interests hurt by imports began to beat the drums for protectionism even as they filed complaint after complaint before the U.S. International Trade Commission,* citing dumping (selling below cost) and unfair competition under the rules of the GATT.

---

*The International Trade Commission (formerly the U.S. Tariff Commission) is the U.S. agency established to rule on petitions by domestic producers hurt by imports.

While there was some truth in these cries of unfair competition, it was also true that under the shelter of protectionism, many of these import-beleaguered industries had become bloated, inbred, and stagnant. High executive salaries and union wages, coupled with a sluggish rate of investment and modernization, had left capital-intensive industries such as steel and shipbuilding vulnerable to more efficient competitors like Japan and Germany which had undergone "forced modernization" through the decimation of their industrial base during World War II. At the same time, countries like Singapore, South Korea, Taiwan, and Hong Kong—the so-called Gang of Four in international trade—could draw on large pools of cheap labor and thereby threaten labor-intensive American textile, electronics, and shoe manufacturers.

By 1970, the sun had already begun to set on America's budding free trade philosophy. Today, as the trickle of foreign textiles, shoes, bicycles, TV's, autos, and steel have turned into a flood, cries for the reimposition of import restrictions have risen to a crescendo. These cries have left us knee-deep in a new protectionism characterized not only by the standard methods of erecting trade barriers, tariffs, and quotas, but also by a variety of much more subtle (but no less effective) nontariff distortions. For example, both direct and indirect subsidies such as tax breaks on research and development, loan guarantees, and the provision of insurance for exporters have become important weapons to defend the import-beleaguered industries or to boost the competitive advantage of America's export industries.[8]

Similarly, there is a whole new arsenal of ostensibly "voluntary" export restraints and "temporary" import quotas. According to William Cline of the Institute for International Economics, "nearly a third of the U.S. import market is covered by these non-tariff barriers or NTBs."[9] In a very real sense, it is these NTBs that are potentially the most dangerous and virulent of the protectionist weapons, precisely because they hide behind the empty rhetorical guise of "voluntary" and "temporary." As experience has shown, however, there is little that is voluntary about the Japanese agreeing—under extreme U.S. coercion—to reduce their auto imports or about Brazil reducing its sales of cheap steel. Nor have such voluntary agreements proved to be very temporary: Many have been renewed and have become an integral part of the protectionist landscape.

II.   THE POLITICS OF PROTECTIONISM

A.   The Capture Theory

The history of the American tariff records the triumph of special interests over the general welfare.[10]

HENRY J. TASCA

Through the lens of the "monolithic" version of the capture model, the politics of protectionism are simple enough: a coterie of business and labor interests has commandeered American trade policy for its own private benefit—protecting high profits and wages at the expense of consumers.

As our first chapter warned, however, such a monolithic view of America's special interests is likely to be too simplistic. Indeed, as Chapter 3 just illustrated, the alleged monoliths of American politics—from Big Business and Big Labor to the farm bloc—are not monolithic at all but rather fragmented and often fractious. This point is illustrated in the following discussion, which introduces a very rich and diverse "pluralistic" set of players in the protectionist policy game; these players are listed in Table 4.1.

1.   Business Interests.   From Table 4.1, it is clear that many import-beleaguered industries and their suppliers stand to benefit from protectionism.* However, it is equally clear that no united business front can exist when a large number of export-dependent domestic industries and their suppliers are threatened by restrictions in foreign markets brought about in retaliation to American protectionism

On the side of protectionism, there are those import-beleaguered industries under heavy attack from foreign competition. These include autos, steel, machine tools, electronics, shoes, dairy, textiles, apparel, motorcycles and bicycles, tires, and watches. At the same time, import competition seriously threatens the production levels and profits of a large number of suppliers to the beleaguered industries. For example, the rubber, plastic, and aluminum industries all are heavily dependent on a

---

*As will be explained in Section III on the economics of protectionism, any benefits from trade barriers are likely to be only *short run*.

TABLE 4.1.   MAJOR PLAYERS IN THE PROTECTIONIST POLICY GAME

Supporters of Protectionism	Opponents of Protectionism
1. Import-beleaguered domestic industries: Autos Steel and machine tools Electronics (TVs, radios, hand calculators, etc.) Shoes Dairy Textiles and apparel Motorcycles, bicycles Tires Watches Uranium	1. Export-dependent domestic industries: Agricultural products Aircraft Construction and related machinery Telecommunications equipment Electric power machinery Precision instruments Computers Pharmaceuticals Photographic supplies
2. Supplier industries to import-beleaguered domestic industries: Rubber Plastics Aluminum Coal Iron Ore Shoe and textile machinery Fasteners	2. Supplier industries to export-beleaguered domestic and service-related industries: Fertilizer, seeds Farm machinery Precious and semi-precious metals Insurance companies Cargo companies
3. Labor interests in import nexus: The industries listed above in 1 and 2	3. Labor interests in export nexus: The industries listed above in 1 and 2
4. Segments of the government lobby: Department of Commerce Department of Labor	4. Segments of the government lobby: Department of State Council of Economic Advisors Department of Treasury
	5. The foreign lobby
	6. Consumers: Retail Retail outlets "Linkage industries"

steady stream of Ford, General Motors, and Chrysler products rolling off American assembly lines just as the coal and iron ore industries thrive on U.S. steel production.

However, a large number of other domestic industries depend heavily on the sale of exports to America's trading partners. Because protectionism at home invites a retaliatory protectionism abroad, these export industries vehemently oppose the erection of any domestic trade barriers. These export-dependent industries include agricultural products, aircraft, construction and electric power machinery, telecommunications equipment, precision instruments, computers, pharmaceuticals, and photographic supplies.

At the same time, these export-dependent industries have their own web of supplier industries whose interests lie in a free-trade order. Farmers, for example, buy seeds, fertilizers, and farm machinery, while completing this export-dependent nexus are a number of additional industries that thrive on a healthy flow of import–export trade: air and sea cargo companies, insurance companies that underwrite cargos, and service industries at ports of entry and exit that handle cargo.

Further fracturing the monolithic picture is the fact that many import-beleaguered industries are exporters as well. For example, both the auto and machine tool industries do a brisk export business, but protectionist devices threaten their foreign markets even as they shelter domestic markets. Moreover, many American industries have substantial capacity abroad so that certain kinds of protectionism—such as domestic content legislation for the auto industry—can turn against them. At the same time, many industries supply both import-beleaguered *and* export-dependent industries, as the aluminum industry does for autos and airplanes and as the steel industry does for autos and construction machinery.

This divergence of pro- and antiprotectionist interests within the business community not only helps debunk the myth of a monolithic Big Business but also helps us illustrate another point of Chapter 3, that umbrella organizations are often ineffectual at lobbying because they are rarely able to speak with one voice.

In this case, the two biggest umbrella organizations of business interests, the Chamber of Commerce and the National Association of Manufacturers, are fairly quiet on tariff issues, even when certain industries under their umbrellas are suffering. The reason is that the umbrella groups also encompass those portions of the business sector that depend on exports. Hence any consensus is very difficult.

2. Labor Interests. Just as we have import-beleaguered versus export-dependent industries, there are also workers in these industries on different sides of the protectionist aisle. Accordingly, we can expect workers in the import-beleaguered industries along with workers in supplier industries to support protectionism while workers in the export-dependent nexus oppose protectionism.

This obvious crack in the Big Labor monolith too often becomes obscured. One major reason is that the largest and most powerful labor umbrella group, the AFL–CIO, has been far more effective in taking a position in strong support of protectionism than its business sector counterparts.

Why? It's a matter of simple arithmetic. Whereas the memberships of the Chamber of Commerce and the National Association of Manufacturers are split fairly equally among pro- and antiprotectionist factions, a large bloc of the AFL–CIO's membership is drawn from the import-beleaguered industries such as auto, steel, and rubber while antiprotectionist unions in the AFL–CIO such as the International Longshoremens' Association constitute a small minority.[11] Moreover, farmers, who constitute a potentially strong antiprotectionist force, aren't even in the AFL–CIO. The same is true of many of the workers in the high tech export-dependent industries, many of whom are simply not unionized. Their voice is lost amidst the more vocal chants of organized labor in the smokestack industries.

3. The Government Lobby. The constant battle between the Congress and the president over control of trade policy, coupled with the infighting among various agencies whose turf includes budget and trade issues, reflects the same divisiveness found in the business and labor communities.

Historically, the Department of Commerce, which has a mandate to take care of the business community and which has many former business people in its key positions, has been the most outspoken agency in defense of protectionism.[12] To a lesser extent, the same has been true of the Department of Labor. Lending support to these agencies in the executive branch have been congressional representatives from districts with a large percentage of import-beleaguered business and labor interests.

On the other hand, the Department of State historically has sought to maintain stable relationships with our trading-partner allies and sees a wave of protectionism rocking the boats of diplomacy.[13] Similarly, the Council of Economic Advisers and the Treasury Department worry about protectionism within the context of financial stability, economic growth, and related issues such as the balance of trade, balance of payments, and the dollar's exchange rate.*

Other federal entities are often caught in the crossfire of pro- and antiprotectionist forces. For example, the U.S. Trade Representative's office, which is responsible for negotiating trade issues with our trading partners, generally seeks to promote free trade. But it has also been one of the major actors responsible for forcing countries like Japan and Brazil to adopt those so-called voluntary and temporary restraints.

4. The Foreign Lobby. Not surprisingly, we find that the myriad and largely uncoordinated components of the foreign lobby are generally saying the same thing; that is, they are opposed to protectionism.

For example, the Japanese Automobile Manufacturers' Association is a fixture at congressional hearings and debates over measures to restrict Japanese auto imports. Through its publications and an aggressive public relations campaign, it has, in coalition with U.S. auto dealers who sell imports, worked to defeat such restrictions.

However, not all firms importing to the U.S. are foreign-owned. As early as the 1950s, the Venezuelan Chamber of Commerce (of American-owned businesses) spoke out against the oil import quotas then being considered. Thus, American business overseas has also opposed protectionism. The same is true for many American-based multinational companies which, despite pressures from imports on their factories at home, sometimes decide they have more to lose in their factories abroad by supporting protectionism. A case in point—which is brought out in the following statistical analysis—is General Motors, which has opposed

---

*While tariffs and other trade barriers might bolster these balances in the short run, most economists and policy analysts believe that protectionism ultimately worsens the balances.

domestic content legislation for autos in part because it has a large number of subsidiaries and parts manufacturing plants abroad.

5. Consumers. The biggest losers in the protectionist policy game are consumers. Even here, however, "consumers" do not constitute a monolith, for there are several different consumer categories.

Bearing the greatest burden of protectionism are American retail shoppers who pay over $70 billion annually in higher prices (and reduced consumption) for products ranging from autos, bicycles, and color TVs, to shoes, shirts, and cutlery.[14] Indeed, protection of the U.S. auto industry has raised the price of a foreign car by as much as $1900 while apparel, textile, and footwear quotas alone cost over $5 billion a year.[15]

A wide range of commercial and industrial consumers likewise share the protectionist burden. At the commercial level, higher wholesale prices for the shirts, shoes, or Toyotas that go on retail outlets' display shelves and into their showrooms cut into profit margins. In a similar fashion, a number of key "linkage industries" are hurt because they have to buy the products of protected industries to use in their production process.

A classic case is offered by the linkage of the apparel industry to the textile industry, which is in turn linked to the wool and cotton industries.[16] Beginning in the 1930s, the U.S. government instituted a series of programs that, for the next several decades, supported the price of domestic wool and cotton and restricted foreign imports of raw materials. As a result, by the 1950s, U.S. textile manufacturers found themselves producing at a sizable cost disadvantage relative to foreign textile producers. As textile imports rose, so, too, did the clamor for protection. In 1957, restrictions were finally imposed and, in 1973, the Multi-Fiber Agreement between the U.S. and 17 other textile-producing countries made such restrictions a permanent part of the textile market landscape.

In the meantime, as the price of U.S. textiles rose with these import restrictions, U.S. apparel manufacturers in turn began to find themselves at a cost disadvantage relative to foreign apparel manufacturers. By the mid-1960s, the apparel industry was drowning in a flood of foreign imports and, like the textile industry, saw a fall in jobs, profits, and market share. Other such linkage industries include appliances, machine tools, autos, and drilling equipment, all of which are linked to steel.

Despite the large costs of protectionism borne by consumers, it would be a mistake, however, to believe that they wield anything close to the amount of lobbying influence exhibited by the protectionist forces in business and labor. The roots of this asymmetry of political power may be traced to a problem that plagues any broad-based diffuse interest, not only consumers, but also such groups as taxpayers, the poor, and the elderly.

In particular, the special interest beneficiaries of a public policy typically enjoy very concentrated benefits. In the case of protectionism, a relatively small number of firms and workers enjoy relatively large shares of the billions of dollars in increased profits and wages that trade barriers bring. This *concentration of benefits,* in turn, provides great incentives for the protected industries and their workers to organize and lobby for trade barriers.

In contrast, while consumers have to bear the multibillion dollar burden of protectionism (or other policies such as the farm subsidies discussed in Chapter 6), the costs are spread out over hundreds of millions of people in the form of a few cents or dollars more spent on a protected product. Hence this *diffusion of costs* provides the perennial losers in the policy games with much less incentive to organize.[17]

This problem is further compounded by the fact that most consumers don't even have an awareness of or any accurate information on just how high their costs are. Thus, not surprisingly, the voices of consumers—particularly retail consumers—have tended to become lost in the protectionist shuffle.*

B.   The Public Interest View

As the capture-ideology framework suggests, there are likely to be equally plausible public interest ideological arguments for and against protectionism. For example, in its modern version, the "infant industry" argument has matured (along with America's industrial base) into a "commanding heights" rationale. To wit, certain industries such as autos and steel must be protected because in time of war, their factories would

---

*As former chairman of the Council of Economic Advisers Murray Weidenbaum has observed, protectionism "is a means by which small and well-organized groups use the political process to their advantage at the expense of the mass of consumers."[18]

become a vital part of defense production. In a rare convergence, this commanding heights argument can be heard coming from both conservatives and liberals. Such˚ is not the case, however, for two additional ideological issues which are much more at the forefront of today's public interest debate over protectionism.*

The first revolves around the conservative–liberal split over a free market versus a regulated and planned economy. To the conservative, the key to both American and world prosperity—and peace—lies in keeping world markets free of protectionist fetters and the resultant economic distortions. Only in such a free-trade order will the potential gains from trade be realized and will the American economic pie grow the fastest. At the same time, the conservative believes that only through exposure to world competition will our domestic industries produce efficiently and undertake the investments necessary to innovate and modernize. Without such market pressures, our growth will slow and our economy will stagnate.

The liberal, on the other hand, seriously questions whether anything close to a free world market can exist. In a world where foreign governments such as "Japan, Inc." now allegedly subsidize their export industries, American faith in the free market will first result in the impoverishment of our import-beleaguered industries and then of the nation itself. Accordingly, a more prudent approach in this modern world of rampant protectionism is to fight fire with fire: counter subsidies and the like with regulated and planned trade agreements in the form of quotas, voluntary export restraints, orderly marketing agreements, and provisions such as domestic content legislation that force foreign manufacturers to set up shop in the U.S. At the same time, the liberal sees little to be gained in the realm of efficiency from the spur of unfair competition because it deprives our import-beleaguered industries of both the profits and the incentives to invest and grow.

---

*Historically, conservatives and liberals have flipflopped on the free-trade issue. Until World War II (and to a certain extent through the 1960s), American conservatives tended to be isolationist, showing little interest in free trade. Liberals, on the other hand, particularly during the Roosevelt and Kennedy years, saw free trade as the cornerstone to their more internationalist approach to foreign policy. Today, conservatives lead the charge for free trade and liberals tend to favor protectionism. As the following discussion indicates, this reversal is rooted in the ascendancy of several principles in the conservative and liberal ideologies.

These contrasting visions of the benefits and costs from a protectionist versus a free-trade order, in turn, set the stage for a second ideological dispute.

To the conservative, a free-trade order in which markets, not the government, sets prices and quantities dovetails nicely with the conservative preference for a "minimal state" in which the role of government—and the budget and taxes to fund it—are kept to a minimum. In such a free-trade order, buyers and sellers are not only free to choose from the widest selection of lowest-priced products but are also protected from any omnipotent state intruding in their lives or bank accounts.

In contrast, the liberal believes that the government has a responsibility to solve the severe social problems that a free-trade order creates, primarily high unemployment and disruptions in communities built around the import-beleaguered industries (e.g., the steel towns or Detroit's motor city). From this "welfare state" perspective, protectionism becomes a safety net for workers in the vulnerable industries. In the mild version of this argument, this "safety net" is often portrayed as "short run" protection: a steel tariff or a voluntary import restraint on autos will be temporary until domestic manufacturers have had a chance to modernize and become competitive. But very often, these "temporary" restrictions become a permanent part of the trade policy landscape. Regardless of the longevity of these restrictions, protectionism can be thought of as a jobs program or an income assistance program—one that is merely administered in a less than direct way.

C. The Politics of Protectionism: A Statistical Test

To measure the relative importance of private and public interest motives in the politics of protectionism, the capture-ideology framework was used to examine congressional voting on a piece of legislation that epitomizes the new protectionism, Domestic Content Legislation or DCL. In its various forms, DCL requires that all autos sold in the U.S. contain a certain percentage of American labor and American-made parts (in some bills, as much as 90 percent).[19] If an automaker (foreign or domestic) does not meet this percentage, the federal government can set a ceiling on the amount of cars that the firm can sell in the U.S.

In effect, DCL offers a form of job protection to workers in the domestic auto industry and its linkage industries (e.g., steel, rubber, glass, and parts manufacturing). At the same time, it helps to protect automakers' profits to the extent that it excludes imports through the above-mentioned ceiling.

However, DCL also threatens the profits of automakers to the extent that it forces them to purchase or manufacture American parts rather than purchasing foreign parts, which are often cheaper, or manufacturing such parts in foreign subsidiaries. DCL similarly poses a longer-term threat to automakers that rely heavily on export sales because it raises prices and invites retaliation. Accordingly, we might expect General Motors to be less enthusiastic about DCL than, say, the Chrysler Corporation, because GM relies more on export sales than Chrysler.

According to the capture theory, labor interests in the DCL-protected auto and auto-dependent industries would support DCL, while the support of domestic automakers would fall as their reliance on foreign parts and foreign markets rises. Likewise, business and labor interests in the export-dependent nexus (from computer manufacturers to cargo handlers) would oppose DCL for fear of retaliation and because of reduced import–export traffic. Joining these export-dependent industries as anti-protectionist forces would be consumers, foreign auto dealers, and foreign auto manufacturers.

In the public interest view of protectionism, ideological liberals would support DCL as an important regulatory response to unfair foreign competition and as a jobs and income assistance program to American workers, while free market and minimal state conservatives would generally oppose it.

Using the approach described in Chapter 2, a number of measures were constructed to reflect the degree of economic or political influence the special interests players in the DCL game are likely to exert on a congressman's voting behavior. For example, the political influence of labor interests in the auto and auto-dependent industries was measured by the number of jobs in those industries that are at stake in a congressman's district (as a fraction of total district employment). Similarly, their economic influence was measured by the extent of their "dollar lobbying," that is, by campaign contributions to each congressman from two important pro-protectionist political action committees (PACs), those of the United Auto Workers and the AFL–CIO. Such economic influence is more mobile in the sense that a labor PAC can support any representative, even those with no auto or auto-dependent workers in their districts.

The power of domestic automakers was measured by the PAC contributions that each congressman received from General Motors, Ford, Chrysler, and American Motors, while any potential "logrolling" help from other import-beleaguered industries (shoes, apparel, TV and radio, and motorcycles and bicycles) was measured by the number of jobs at stake in these industries within each congressional district.*

On the antiprotectionist side, a similar set of "jobs at stake" and other measures was constructed to reflect the political and economic influence of the export-dependent nexus and consumers.†

Besides representing the various special interests, the capture-ideology framework also requires that some measure of a congressman's ideology be included in the explanatory measures. One such measure that has been frequently used during the scholarly development of the capture-ideology framework is the liberalness ratings that the Americans for Democratic Action regularly give to senators and congressmen on the basis of their voting record on a selected sample of ADA-endorsed legislation.[20]

For example, well-known liberal luminaries such as Ted Kennedy, Gary Hart, and Richard Ottinger regularly score at or near the purely liberal 100 mark, while staunch conservatives like Jesse Helms, Paul Laxalt, and Barry Goldwater wind up in the teens, tens, or close to zero on the ADA scale. Following the lines of previous research, ADA ratings were used here to reflect each congressman's ideology.

These special interest and ideology measures of pro- and antiprotectionist sentiment were fed into the computer and a common statistical procedure was used to determine the relative influence of each on congressional voting on DCL.

In a world of "pure capture," congressmen from districts with substantial industrial capacity and employment in the auto, auto-dependent industries, and logrolling import-beleaguered industries should vote for DCL regardless of their ideology. So, too, should congressmen receiving significant UAW or AFL–CIO PAC contributions. On the other hand,

---

*As explained in more detail in chapters 5 and 6, logrolling means that an interest group, say shoe interests, will vote for DCL with the expectation that auto interests will support a protectionist shoe bill.
†No suitable measures could be found for either the government or foreign lobbies and their influence must remain conjectural.

TABLE 4.2. RANKED SPECIAL INTEREST
AND IDEOLOGY MEASURES IN THE
PROTECTIONIST POLICY GAME

Rank[a]

1. Ideology (+)
2. Steelworker jobs at stake (+)
3. United Auto Workers' PAC contributions (+)
4. Logrolling import-beleaguered industries (+)
5. Autoworker jobs at stake (+)
6. Chrysler PAC contributions (+)
7. Auto consumers (−)
8. General Motors PAC contributions (−)
9. Ford PAC contributions (+)
10. AMC PAC contributions (−)
11. Export-dependent industries (−)
12. AFL–CIO PAC contributions (+)

[a]Rank is by the test results reported in Appendix A. A (+) indicates support for DCL, while a (−) indicates opposition.

congressmen representing the export-dependent districts or receiving large foreign lobby PAC contributions should vote against it.

Conversely, in a world of "pure ideology," congressmen with high ADA liberalness ratings should vote for DCL regardless of the number of farmers, longshoremen, or auto import car dealers in their districts and irrespective of any foreign lobby PAC largess directed at them. Conservative congressmen with low ADA ratings should in turn oppose DCL, regardless of the number of automakers, steel mills, or glass factories in their districts and in spite of any pro-DCL PAC contributions.

The test results, presented in Table 4.2, confirm the basic insight of the capture-ideology framework: Neither capture nor ideology alone can completely explain the politics of DCL and the new protectionism. This table ranks each of the measures of special interests and ideology in order of its statistical importance in explaining congressional voting on DCL.*

From the table, it appears that ideology is the single most important predictor of a congressman's vote on DCL; according to the test, its effect

---

*This ordering is based on the procedure described in Chapter 2. The full statistical results are presented in Appendix A.

is more than *twice* that of any other special interest variable. This statistical conclusion is reinforced by some rather interesting observations about the purity of voting behavior among some of the House of Representatives' leading ideologues.

In the realm of pure liberalism, Congressmen Norman Mineta of California and Al Swift of Washington regularly score in the 80s on the ADA's 0–100 liberalness rating scale, while Barbara Kennelly of Connecticut and Bruce Vento of Minnesota score in the 90s. True to their ideology, all have consistently voted for DCL despite the presence of a significant export-dependent constituency. For example, almost one-fourth of the employment in Mineta's Silicon Valley constituency is in computers and high tech goods while Kennelly's Hartford district is a major center for United Technologies, which makes a large share of the world's jet engines.[21]

On the other end of the spectrum, conservatives such as Daniel Crane of Illinois, Guy Vander Jagt of Michigan, and Michael Oxley and the late John Ashbrook of Ohio regularly score near zero on the ADA liberalness voting scale. True to their ideology, they have consistently opposed DCL despite the fact that jobs in the auto and steel industries constitute a significant fraction of total employment in their districts.

Despite the significance of ideology, the results in Table 4.2 suggest that both business and labor constituencies along with PAC contributions also play statistically important roles. The percentage of steelworkers in a district, for example, is the second most important determinant of a congressman's vote, while close behind are the United Auto Workers' PAC and the auto worker jobs at stake measures, in third and fifth place respectively. Again, we can uncover some rather marked deviations in ideological voting patterns that bolster the statistical finding that some congressmen have indeed been captured by special interests.

In the realm of constituency pressure, the most striking example of capture is offered by William Broomfield of Michigan who regularly scores in the low teens on the ADA liberalness test. However, with over 40 percent of the jobs in his Detroit-Pontiac district in the auto industry, Broomfield has consistently voted against his ideology and for DCL. Under similar constituency pressures, Gene Snyder of Kentucky, with a low ADA rating but over 10 percent of the jobs in his district auto-dependent, has likewise gone against his conservative grain to support DCL.

Nor are conservatives the only ones susceptible to capture. Liberal Congressmen Matthew McHugh of New York and Michael Lowry of Washington frequently score a perfect 100 on the ADA liberalness test. But both have consistently voted against DCL, no doubt because a significant fraction of the employment in their districts is in export-dependent industries.[22]

In the realm of PAC contributions and economic influence, there are likewise instances of capture voting. Congressmen Ronnie G. Flippo of Alabama, Ike Skelton of Missouri, and Charles Wilson of Texas, for instance, all boast solid conservative credentials, and with little or no pro-DCL interests in their districts, one would expect them to oppose DCL.[23] Yet, over the last three electoral cycles, each of these congressmen has received more than $4,000 from the United Auto Workers PAC and each has consistently supported DCL, a fact strongly suggestive of "PAC power."

Besides confirming the importance of both ideology and special interests in the new protectionism, the results of Table 4.2 also lend support to several additional points made in this chapter.

First, there appears to be a powerful logrolling "protectionist coalition." This is indicated by the fact that the measure of the non-auto-dependent but import-beleaguered industries ranks fourth in explanatory power. This means that the apparel, footwear, TV–radio, and motorcycle and bicycle industries are supporting protectionism in the auto industry no doubt as a quid pro quo for similar support for trade barriers in their own respective industries.

Second, the PAC power of automakers appears to have at least a moderate influence on congressional voting but, as indicated in the table, the *direction* of influence among the PACs is mixed. According to the test, both GM, which relies considerably on foreign parts and export sales, and American Motors, which is partially owned by the French automaker Renault, appear to oppose DCL. Chrysler, on the other hand, which has relatively less dependence on sales abroad, seems to support DCL along with Ford, which sees DCL as "a signal" to the import competition that the United States is not going to surrender its markets.[24]

A third point supported by the statistical results is that umbrella organizations tend to be much less potent political forces than more industry-specific groups. This is seen in the fact that while both the UAW and AFL-CIO support DCL, their PAC contributions have remarkably different impacts on congressional voting. While the industry-specific UAW PAC is the third most important predictor of congressional voting, the umbrella AFL-CIO PAC finishes dead last in the test and is of dubious statistical importance.

Finally, the seventh-place finish for consumers supports the observation that such broad-based groups, which bear substantial but very diffused costs from public policies, wield very little political clout when they are up against a small coalition of special interests.

In summary, the politics of the new protectionism suggest that while public-interested ideological behavior has played an important role in the formation of U.S. trade policy, protectionism is also very much a special interest policy game. In the next section, the economic and distributional consequences of this policy game are examined to see what well-intentioned ideologues and selfish special interests have wrought.

III. THE ECONOMICS OF PROTECTIONISM

Underlying the economics of protectionism are two important distinctions that are crucial to understanding the high costs of restraining free trade.

The first is between *short-* and *longer-*term effects. In the rent control policy game, we saw that while tenants benefited in the short run from rent reductions, over time, much of the benefit was eroded by market forces such as the "O&M squeeze" on landlords that led to apartment deterioration. Here, too, time will erode most, indeed perhaps all, of the short-run gains from protectionism.

The second distinction is between real *resource costs* and redistributional *transfer payments*. Typically, any government policy that redistributes income includes both a transfer payment and a resource cost component. The transfer payment consists of the flow of income from the losers in the policy game to the winners; for example, with rent control, income flows from landlords to tenants. Real resource costs also arise because such redistributional transfers typically distort market price signals. These distortions in turn reduce the ability or "efficiency" of the economy to produce. The result is a real reduction in the size of the American economic pie and an overall loss of wealth for the nation. This loss can come in many forms; with rent control, it is too few

TABLE 4.3.   SHORT-VERSUS LONGER-RUN EFFECTS OF
PROTECTIONISM

A.   Short-Run Effects
  1.   Higher consumer prices for a more limited selection of goods
  2.   More jobs and higher profits in protected industry
  3.   Increased government revenues from customs duties
  4.   A "deadweight loss" to society (i.e., a misallocation of resources)

B.   Longer-Run Effects
  1.   Fewer jobs and lower profits in export-dependent nexus (and possible net drop in total employment)
  2.   Reduced rate of investment, innovation, and growth
  3.   National security benefits in the form of protectionism for defense-related industries
  4.   National security costs in the form of destabilizing the international economic order

apartments constructed and an accelerated deterioration of the existing apartment stock.

Table 4.3 lists the short- and longer-run effects of protectionism, which are discussed below within the context of real resource costs versus transfer payments.*

A.   Short-Run Effects

1.   Higher Consumer Prices for a More Limited Selection of Goods.   In the absence of trade barriers, goods ranging from autos and apparel to shoes and televisions are imported into America precisely because they are offered to consumers at lower prices (or higher quality) than if U.S. producers manufactured them. However, when a device such as a tariff is imposed, the importer must pay a duty to the U.S. government to sell his product. This, in effect, raises the importer's costs and forces the importer to raise his price by all or part of the duty. U.S. producers can then raise their prices, which hitherto were lowered by

---

*For illustrative purposes, these effects are shown for the most common form of protectionism, the tariff. Other forms of protectionism lead to different magnitudes of these effects. For example, a production subsidy results in a smaller efficiency loss to society than a tariff.[25]

import competition. Similarly, when a quota is slapped on, the supply of imported goods is reduced. Consumers must then vie for a reduced supply of, say, Toyotas and Datsuns, and both Japanese manufacturers and their U.S. dealers are able to raise their prices.

To see why consumers pay higher prices for a more limited selection of goods, consider the case of voluntary export restraints adopted by the Japanese (under the duress of the U.S. Congress). Under restraints that set limits on Japanese imports, there are over one and a half million fewer Datsuns, Toyotas, and Mazdas to compete with the American menu of Chevettes, Vegas, Sunbirds, and Pintos.[26] Besides reducing the choice of styles and colors, in some cases the price of the imported car in short supply has gone up and out of the range of a consumer's budget for a compact. More subtly, because import restraints limit the *number* rather than the *dollar value* of imports, in an attempt to maximize their profits, Japanese automakers have shifted their line of exports to America from low-priced, fuel-efficient, no-frill compacts to higher-priced luxury models heavily laden with accessories—cars that are often too expensive for the average American buyer.

2. More Jobs and Higher Profits in the Protected Industries. The major benefit of protectionism is to increase employment and raise total profits in the protected industry and its suppliers. Profits increase because domestic producers sell more of the protected good at higher prices while jobs and total wages paid to labor increase with the expansion of output. For example, estimates of the increase in jobs that DCL would provide for the auto industry range from 60,000 by the Department of Commerce to almost a million by the United Auto Workers' research department.*[27]

These benefits come, of course, at the expense of consumers, for a large part of the price hikes borne by consumers represents an implicit subsidy to domestic producers and workers. Accordingly, these benefits may be looked on merely as a redistributive transfer payment, and whether such a transfer is in the public interest is an interesting question.

The most commonly invoked public interest argument in support of such transfers is that they will result in a more equal, and therefore more

---

*The gap between these estimates aptly illustrates a point that will be made in Chapter 5 that in the battles of "research and counterresearch," one must always take into account the source of an estimate.

fair, redistribution of income by taking from the richer and giving to the poorer. For this argument in equity to hold here, consumers of the protected good would have to be, on average, wealthier than both the stockholders and workers in the protected industry.

Given that the median income of corporate stockholders is $29,000 and the median income of all Americans is $19,000, it is clear that any protectionist transfer from consumers to stockholders can only further skew the income distribution.[28] For labor interests, the case is somewhat less clear-cut. In industries such as textiles, shoes, and apparel the average annual income ranges well below the median, at $10,000 to $12,000.[29] Here a case can be made that some of the redistributive transfer goes in the direction of greater equality. However, for other protected industries such as autos and steel, the average worker income ranges from $24,000 to $27,000, well above the median income for American consumers.[30] Accordingly, such transfers appear to be less in the public interest and more a subtle way for powerful and organized special interests to gain at the expense of weaker, more diffuse consumer interests.

3.   Increased Government Revenues.   While consumers pay higher prices to enrich business and labor interests in the protected industries, part of these price hikes also represent a transfer payment to the federal government. Each year, Uncle Sam collects almost $10 billion in customs duties; consumers share the burden of these taxes with foreign importers.[31]

4.   The "Deadweight Loss" to Society.   Despite the fact that protectionism transfers income from consumers to business, labor, and the government, it is not a zero sum game. As alluded to earlier, these transfer payments create a real resource cost in the form of what economists call an efficiency or "deadweight loss" to society. This deadweight loss has two components.

The first is a "producer's cost." Under the protectionist umbrella, otherwise inefficient domestic producers enter the market and divert valuable resources away from important uses in order to manufacture protected goods. As a result, the nation's resources are devoted to producing too much of a protected good (e.g., autos or shoes) and, more important, too few other goods that we produce more efficiently, such as computers or houses.

The second is a "consumer's cost." Because trade barriers raise the price of the protected good, consumers buy fewer units than they otherwise would. This means they not only pay high prices for what they do buy but are also denied the satisfaction they would have enjoyed with increased consumption of the good. This foregone satisfaction likewise represents a real loss to society.

Estimates of the deadweight loss to society of protectionism range from 0.11 to one percent of the GNP.[32] While these numbers may seem small, in a $3.2 trillion economy, they translate into an annual cost to the nation of billions of dollars each year.

By way of summary, Table 4.4 catalogues the total costs to consumers of protectionism from the transfer payments to business, labor, and government interests that are made in the form of higher prices and from the deadweight loss that protectionism creates.

As shown in the table, tariffs on textiles and apparel boost consumer costs by a staggering $14.9 billion while quantitative restrictions add another $3.4 billion. Iron and steel and machinery tariffs and quotas likewise total $5.7 billion. Michael Munger of Washington University has calculated the total tariff bill to be a staggering $56 billion while quantitative restrictions add another $14 billion.[33] While much of these costs to consumers represent a direct gain to the protected interests, the

TABLE 4.4.   THE COSTS OF PROTECTIONISM TO CONSUMERS
FOR SELECTED GOODS

Selected Goods	Consumer Costs of Tariffs (millions of dollars)	Consumer Costs of Quantitative Restrictions (millions of dollars)
Apparel, textiles	14,955	3,416
Chemicals	829	—
Coffee	—	720
Copper	1,589	—
Footwear	1,037	1,634
Iron and steel	4,047	1,706
Machinery	10,970	—
Sugar	1,742	1,000

Source: Michael C. Munger. "The Costs of Protectionism: Estimates of the Hidden Tax of Trade Restraint." (St. Louis, Missouri: Center for the Study of American Business, Working Paper Number 80, July 1983). Estimates compiled by Munger are from a variety of sources including the Federal Trade Commission, International Trade Commission, Council on Wage and Price Stability, and the Brookings Institution.

same cannot be said for most of the long-term effects, which make *everyone* a loser.

B.   Longer-Run Effects

1.   Fewer Jobs and Lower Profits.   In the short run, the industries hurt by protectionism are primarily those that assist in the importation and distribution of the restricted goods. For example, quotas on foreign autos immediately mean fewer jobs for longshoremen and lower profits for Honda and Toyota dealers. While these negative employment and profit effects are important, they are small compared to the longer-run potential losses in other sectors of the economy.

To understand what is at stake in the protectionist wars, it is useful to know that roughly 80 percent of all new jobs created in the United States between 1977 and 1980 were due to increased exports. At the same time, between 1981 and 1983, a million jobs were lost due to a deterioration of trade.[34] Moreover, the Census Bureau reports that almost 5 million American jobs depend on the export of goods and related services.[35]

American protectionism threatens employment and profits in the export-dependent nexus because it invites retaliation from our trading partners. For example, the ongoing battle over European steel imports and subsequent trade restrictions have in turn provoked the European Economic Community (EEC) countries to threaten restrictions on American agricultural products, aircraft, and machine tools. Similarly, the U.S. recently imposed unilateral trade restrictions on Chinese textiles and China retaliated with bans on U.S. cotton, soybeans, and chemical fibers. Such stories abound in today's protectionist climate. The protectionist threat to U.S. employment and profits doesn't stop with these simple and direct retaliatory effects, however. More subtle forces also threaten American workers and firms outside the export-dependent nexus.

One such force is the "ripple effect" on linkage industries that use protected goods in their production process. This ripple effect begins in a price rise for the protected good, this price rise is transmitted to the linkage industry as a cost increase, the cost increase in turn drives the price of the linked good up, consumers buy less of the good because of the high price, and, finally, both jobs and profits fall in the linked industry.

A classic case of this ripple effect was already offered by events in the cotton, wool, textile and apparel industries. The ripple effects of protectionism likewise can be graphically illustrated in the auto and steel industries. In the early 1970s, the steel industry successfully lobbied for "trigger prices" and voluntary export restraints to protect its dwindling U.S. markets.* As a result, the U.S. auto industry was forced to buy steel priced over 30 percent above what European and Japanese automakers were paying. With steel comprising a large fraction of the cost of materials to build an auto, this protectionist price hike further widened the gap—initially opened by lower labor costs abroad—between the cost of producing a car in the U.S. and a car in Europe or Japan. Protectionism in the steel industry thus helped set the stage for Detroit's subsequent and dramatic drubbing in both domestic and foreign markets, a beating that has cut employment in the U.S. auto industry by over 25 percent.[37]

Still a second subtle protectionist force is the "end run" strategy which has been successfully adopted by many foreign competitors confronted by U.S. trade barriers. A case in point is the misfortune that has befallen U.S. manufacturers of *specialty steel* as a result of the protection of basic commodity steel.† Before commodity steel was protected, specialty steel was relatively immune to foreign competition, largely because of the technological edge enjoyed by U.S. specialty steel manufacturers. However, with the imposition of restrictions on basic steel, foreign manufacturers shifted to specialty steel production; today, specialty steel has joined the ranks of the import-beleaguered industries suffering from fewer jobs and lower profits—and those clamoring for protection. Similarly, Korea and Taiwan have recently gotten around restrictions on importing shoes by switching from leather to rubber in certain parts of their shoes.[38]

From these direct and indirect effects, it is clear that over time, the major benefits of protectionism—more jobs and higher profits—are largely and perhaps completely offset by a reduction in jobs and profits in export and linkage industries and in those industries vulnerable to the "end run." Therefore, the argument that protectionism serves as a jobs and income assistance program must be discounted.

---

*During the 1950s, the U.S. produced almost 50 percent of the world's basic commodity steel. Today, it produces only 16 percent of the world total and has lost almost 20 percent of its domestic market to foreign producers.[36]

†Specialty steel includes stainless and alloy tool steels while basic commodity steel includes sheet and hot-rolled bar steels.

2. Reduced Investment, Innovation, and Growth. Reductions in the rate of investment, innovation, and growth in the economy occur primarily within—but are not limited to—the protected industries. This effect stems from two major sources.

The first is what economists call "managerial slack."[39] As the monopolist grows complacent in the quiet life of no competition, so too do executives who have their short-run profits assured by the protectionist umbrella. This complacency in turn affects a whole range of operating and management decisions.

For example, there is less pressure on executives to invest in cost-cutting plant modernization or methods to boost labor productivity. Nor is there as much incentive to negotiate at the bargaining table to hold labor costs down, while executives themselves are likely to boost their own wages, rationalizing such hikes by the profits that protectionism—not their own shrewd management—engendered.

At the same time, protectionism means fewer incentives to invest in research and development to keep one jump ahead of import competition. The result is an increase in the production costs of the protected good to levels higher than they otherwise would be under the spur of competition. These higher costs constitute a "technical inefficiency" which is every bit as real a resource cost to the nation as the allocative inefficiency of deadweight loss. Economists like Harvard's Harvey Leibenstein have estimated that the costs of technical inefficiency are likely to be every bit as big or bigger than those of the deadweight loss.[40]

The second source is that under certain circumstances, protectionism can create incentives for firms to diversify out of the protected industry. In this case, the profits generated by protectionism are not ploughed back into plant modernization or expansion, but are rebated to shareholders or diverted to nonrelated industries where expected profits are higher.

This sober little lesson in diversification strategy is one that the U.S. steel industry has sordidly taught the nation.* Since the imposition of protectionism in the 1970s, its aggressive movement out of steel production has left a wake of closed plants, unemployed workers, and a dying, not a revitalized, industry. For example, U.S. Steel shut down 13 of its plants in 1979, invested in a shopping center in the Pittsburgh suburbs,

---

*The problem is not with diversification per se but using protectionist profits to diversify—rather than modernize as promised.

and announced plans to build chemical facilities in Houston. More recently, it used most of its $2.5 billion cash reserve to purchase the Marathon Oil Company. Similarly, National Steel has bought three large savings and loans companies for $6.9 billion, Republic Steel has diversified into the insurance business and "Armco has diversified itself so extensively . . . that it has now dropped the word 'steel' from its corporate title."[41]

3. National Security Benefits and Costs. On the benefit side, protectionism within certain basic industries like autos, steel, and electronics helps to create and sustain an industrial base that, in times of war or national peril, can be shifted to defense purposes. However, this national security argument—and the existence of any benefits resulting from protecting these industries—can legitimately be called into question for several reasons.

First, the existence of any sizable benefits rests on the assumption that import competition in our defense-related industries would not only reduce the size of these industries but also shrink them to the point where they would be too small to support our defense needs. The threshold of danger is a matter of some dispute. How big, after all, do our auto, steel, or electronics industries have to be to keep our borders safe? In spite of this uncertainty, few analysts would argue that import competition is likely to push a nation with as large and mature an industrial base as ours anywhere close to that threshold.

Second, it is highly possible that our defense capability might actually be enhanced—not damaged—by import competition. Without the umbrella of protectionism, our defense-related industries would be forced to operate at lowest cost, engage in more research and development, aggressively innovate to stay one step ahead of the competition, and modernize their plants at a faster pace. Thus, while import competition might shrink these industries, they would be leaner, tougher, more efficient, and more modern and in all likelihood outperform a bigger and inefficient (protected) version of those same industries.

On the national security cost side, the major effect of protectionism is to threaten the stability of the international economic order through a global trade war. While it is difficult to quantify the costs of such a destabilization, it is all too easy to borrow from the lessons of the infamous Smoot–Hawley tariffs and the Great Depression to construct a trade war scenario that ends in another catastrophic economic collapse and possibly, world war.

Suppose that America continues to raise its protectionist barriers. "Temporary" voluntary export restraints on Japanese and European autos and steel become permanent; orderly marketing agreements for textiles and apparel are forced on Korea, Taiwan, and China; quotas are imposed on Brazilian steel, Mexican agricultural produce, and Argentinian beef; and restrictions are placed on the importation of Australian uranium.

Japan, in turn, raises its trade barriers on American soybeans, oranges, beef, and telecommunications equipment; the EEC responds with a flat boycott of American agricultural goods and aircraft; Korea, Taiwan and China turn to Japan for their high tech and machine tool needs; Mexico reduces its U.S. petroleum exports and raises its prices; Brazil and Argentina look toward both the EEC and Japan for their imports of machinery and chemicals, and Australia restricts its importation of U.S. electrical goods.

This first wave of protectionism and retaliation reduces employment within all the export industries of the "belligerents" in this budding trade war. As employment and purchasing power shrink, so too does consumer demand *within* each country's borders. As production ratchets down, a robust free-trade economy begins to slow into a protectionist recessionary one. In a "multiplier effect," this recession squeezes protected industries even more, while hitherto unprotected industries who feel the recessionary pinch begin to clamor for their own protection. At the same time, the export-dependent industries pressure their governments for subsidies to offset higher tariffs in world markets.

Meanwhile, the export-dependent economics of developing countries like Argentina, Brazil, and Mexico begin to stagnate as the industrialized nations further raise the barriers to their markets. This stagnation, in turn, makes it increasingly difficult for the Third World countries to pay off their considerable foreign debt—almost half of which is held by American banks.[42] At the same time, this stagnation further reduces the demand for U.S. and European exports, almost one-third of which find outlets in the Third World.[43] As the economies of the developed nations contract still further, the commercial banks step in and agree to restructure the debt but only if the debtor nations accept austerity measures as a quid pro quo. These measures, however, fuel already growing political pressures on the governments in power.

Amidst this climate, another wave of tariffs and countertariffs, quotas and counterquotas follows. The EEC breaks off altogether from trade with the United States—and the NATO alliance—and forms its own trading zone. World output and employment ratchets down another notch and then, yet another notch, as the income of workers and therefore, the purchasing power of consumers, falls further. With these ripple and multiplier effects, recession sinks deeper into the morass of depression.

Brazil is the first to default on its loans, but Argentina, Mexico, Chile, and others soon follow suit. Bank America, Chase Manhattan, Citibank, and several more of the New York megabanks are left holding over $100 billion in bad debts. With these defaulted loans constituting over 150 percent of total bank equity, the megabanks totter on the brink of collapse. To prevent this collapse and a domino effect through the smaller institutions tied to the megabanks, the federal government (i.e., taxpayers) is forced to step in and underwrite the massive megabank liabilities.[44] While this bailout saves the domestic banking system, the budget deficit soars along with the price of gold, and world financial markets totally dry up—along with the hopes of any further economic development in the Third World.

At the same time, growing joblessness further fuels pressures in both the developed and developing nations. Japan turns its back on the U.S. and its European allies, who refuse to buy its goods, and enters into a Pan Asian military and trading pact with the Soviet Union and China, uniting Japanese technology and capital with Soviet raw materials and Chinese labor. Right-wing military coups topple the governments of Brazil and Argentina, while Mexico swings sharply to the left and tensions at the U.S. border rise to the boiling point over immigration and trade policies. Increasingly, protectionist America is left out in an isolationist cold.

In such a world, even if war does not follow—as it once did in an uncomfortably similar scenario on the heels of the first Great Depression—the nation can only be far worse off both economically and militarily after a world trade war. Such a scenario is, of course, alarmist—but it is intended to be. As history has taught us before, it is sometimes necessary to sound the alarm if we are to avert disaster. What, then, can be done to avoid the substantial short- and longer-term costs of protectionism?

IV. POLICY REFORMS

With trade barriers steadily rising even as the community of developed and developing nations become increasingly interlinked in a global economy, the future direction of trade policy promises to be a perennial issue in American politics, particularly during election years.

The economics of protectionism clearly indicate that the best trade policy is one that resumes the process begun after World War II—but aborted in recent years—of steadily lowering trade barriers through international cooperative efforts. However, the politics of protectionism indicate equally clearly that protectionist pressures can be averted only if additional measures are taken to offset the asymmetrical power of special interests in the protected industries. At the same time, any successful reform of trade policy requires addressing the legitimate ideological arguments that have been put forth in defense of protectionism.

To curb the power of special interests, the most effective spur to free trade would be increased political organization and opposition by those numerically-superior interests most adversely affected by protectionism: consumers and business and labor interests in the export-dependent nexus. Such opposition will result only if these groups—particularly consumers—are better informed about the costs of protectionism. Towards this end, the federal government might increase its sponsorship of public information programs about trade policy issues, including disseminating information on the adverse effects of various trade barriers.

At the same time, Congress might adopt a device like the environmental impact statement, which has been successful in alerting and informing the public about possible effects on the environment of new laws, regulations, or projects. Requiring a "protectionist impact assessment" to accompany any new proposed trade restrictions would go a long way toward bringing the often hidden effects of protectionism out into the sunshine.

One must not be so naive as to assume, however, that even perfectly informed consumers will rise up to defeat the forces of protectionism. As the earlier discussion of the dynamics of consumer apathy illustrated, there are very good reasons why special interests in the protected industries are likely to be far more effective in the policy trenches. Accordingly, several additional measures must be adopted to help insulate the public interest from private interest pressures.

First, the primary responsibility for the administration of trade policy should remain with the executive branch rather than the Congress because congressmen are very vulnerable to short-run political pressure—particularly those with a preponderance of protectionist interests in their districts and those who are forced to depend on PAC contributions for their reelection campaigns. In contrast, presidents serve a much broader constituency and are therefore more likely (but alas, not guaranteed) to favor the national interest over more narrow special interests. The same is true of bureaucrats within the executive branch who don't have to face an angry electorate every two, four, or six years. Accordingly, the nation should support its president in resisting any efforts by the Congress to reassert its primacy over trade policy. It is also in the interests of Congress to forego this power because congressmen can counter constituency pressures with the legitimate argument that they are helpless in the matter.

In a similar fashion, America must reaffirm its support for the GATT as the final arbiter of international trade disputes. An unwavering American commitment to both the letter and spirit of the GATT agreement would provide the president, his trade representatives, and his administrators with the same escape from domestic protectionist pressures as the removal of trade policy from the congressional arena does for congressmen. To wit, the issue would be out of their hands.

In addressing the public interest arguments advanced by both liberals and conservatives in defense of protectionism, it is perhaps most important to deal with the argument of "unfair competition." Without question, such unfair competition is very prevalent: Foreign governments now routinely subsidize their industries along virtually the entire chain of production and distribution, from research and development grants and investment tax credits to export loans, loan guarantees, and insurance against risk. For America to turn a blind eye to such practices and simply open its markets would be to invite a drowning of the economy in dumped and subsidized goods.

While there is little disagreement that unfair competition exists, there is however, considerable debate over how to deal with it. One path (which America is fairly well along) is to retaliate with a combination of protectionism and a latticework of countervailing subsidies to both import-beleaguered and export industries. For export industries, the idea is to create a set of "national champions" that can go out and do battle with the Japan, Incs., German Ministries of Technology, and French Foreign

Trade Banks of this world. This path, however, runs a grave risk of sparking a trade war, precisely because retaliation is one of its principal features. At the same time, the merger of industry and government around the globe threatens to ossify the free-market forces that yield such great gains from trade while destroying the smaller businesses responsible for so much of our innovation and economic growth.

There is another path, however: America can take the lead in making the GATT a more fair and effective international organization, one that has both the authority to settle world trade disputes and, more important, the power to enforce them. To take this path, several loopholes in the GATT must be closed, and America must take better advantage of the protections that the GATT currently offers.

The first loophole allows devices such as "orderly marketing agreement" to exist. Under the current GATT rules, such bilateral agreements are legal because they are "voluntary" arrangements. However, in most cases, such nontariff barriers are simply thinly disguised ways of avoiding the spirit, if not the letter, of the GATT.

In a similar vein, the GATT's authority only extends to ruling on the legitimacy of foreign government practices to use subsidies and other neomercantilist devices to promote export trade or to protect their import-beleaguered industries. While there is a fine line between a prudent industrial policy designed to stimulate economic growth and a neo-mercantilist one which is designed to do so by "beggaring thy neighbor," the clear tendency of many nations today is to stray on the neo-mercantilist side of that line. Giving the GATT power to police such policies would go a long way toward forcing the 88 trading nations that subscribe to the GATT to play by the rules. This, in turn, would require continued U.S. negotiations to "close the loopholes."

But we need not rely solely on GATT to prevent unfair competition. Under the GATT's existing rules, several clauses allow domestic industries hurt by unfair competition to petition for retaliatory actions. For example, an industry hurt by the "dumping" of foreign goods can petition the U.S. International Trade Commission (ITC) for restrictions on the offending imports. For this complaint process to be effective in deterring foreign governments from risking unfair competition, it must, however, be both swift and sure. Thus the federal bureaucracy should streamline its processing of such complaints, reducing the adjudicatory period from its current protracted span.

The second ideological issue that must be addressed is the desirability of protectionism as a jobs program or form of income redistribution. From the economic analysis, the message should be clear: Protectionism fails miserably on both counts. Accordingly, other ways must be found to cushion the effects of import competition on labor markets and to meet the full employment goal of both conservatives and liberals.

One possible way is already authorized under the Trade Adjustment Act of 1974. This act provides for unemployment benefits that pay up to 70 percent of lost wages if workers can demonstrate that they lost their jobs due to import competition. More important, the act provides workers with job retraining, as well as job-search and relocation assistance. However, for this legislation to be truly effective several improvements are mandatory.

First, the act only provides benefits to workers *directly* affected by import competition, while it completely ignores the network of supplier industries that suffer ripple effects. Thus an auto worker is eligible for such benefits, but not a worker in a factory making components for autos. An extension of benefits to this supplier network is both fair and politically astute because it would help diffuse protectionist pressures from labor interests.

Second, the benefits available under the act are more skewed toward unemployment compensation than job retraining and relocation. This has the unfortunate side effect of keeping workers in declining industries rather than easing them into other opportunities in the growing sectors. It also is a waste of federal money when worker layoffs are due to cyclical downturns in the economy (as they sometimes are in the auto and steel industries) rather than to any permanent downward decline (such as that experienced in the textile and leather industries).

The solution is to focus federal funds more on job retraining, job-search, and relocation assistance. That means raising the meager allowance currently offered under the act.[45] More broadly, it means the federal government should attempt to forecast where job shortages are likely to be and structure its retraining programs—which are at present fairly ineffectual—accordingly. Strengthening this and other such programs would do far more to address the long-run effects of import competition than any short-run "Band-Aid" protectionism.

In considering such an escalation of federal aid to workers in the import-beleaguered industries, it should be pointed out—if for no other reason than to quell conservative cries of additional strains on the federal budget—that the U.S. is the only country among the industrialized nations with no comprehensive retraining program. Such a program, while not totally eliminating the cost of adjustment, would greatly reduce the social and psychological costs and political pressures of such an adjustment.

At the same time, the cost of such a program to the American public as *taxpayers* would be far less than the costs of protectionism to the American public as *consumers*. Indeed, the Council on Wage and Price Stability calculates that it costs American consumers $81,000 per year for each textile job protected, $62,000 for each steelworker protected, and $110,000 for each job protected in the U.S. footwear industry.[46]

As a means of income assistance, the economics of protectionism also have demonstrated that it does not make the income distribution more equal and fair. Any simple arguments of equity made in defense of protectionism should be discounted as private interest arguments cloaked in public interest rhetoric.

Finally, the "national defense" issue is always an emotionally charged and therefore highly potent argument for protectionism. However, defense-related arguments for a strong industrial base must be tempered by a realistic appraisal of our defense needs. For example, to argue that we need to protect the auto industry so that it can remain large enough to produce 7 million vehicles a year is pushing the security argument too far, particularly in a nuclear age where the likelihood of a prolonged conventional world war appears to be very small.

We must likewise realistically appraise the national self-sufficiency arguments for protectionism which have typically been voiced in the debate over the "de-industrialization of America." In that debate, we are offered a bleak vision of a high tech world landscape populated by great masses of unemployed workers stranded in the rubble of dying smokestack industries.

However, as the economic analysis indicated, the choice is not between preserving smokestack industries or relying on high tech wonderlands. Rather, it is between a protected but inefficient and declining industrial base versus a more innovative industrial sector that, under the spur of import competition, can and does invest in the rapid technological developments that promise a prosperous merger of the two worlds.

5

How They Get What They Want

STRATEGIES AND TACTICS OF
THE SPECIAL INTERESTS

In the first two policy games, we have seen that price regulation in the form of rent control and protectionism in the form of domestic content legislation are two powerful government policies that can benefit special interests. Other ways for special interests to "score" in the policy game include government subsidies (as illustrated in Chapter 6 on farm policy), favorable regulation (as illustrated in Chapter 8 on electric utilities), government grants and contracts (as illustrated in Chapter 11 on defense policy), and special tax breaks. Table 5.1 outlines six basic *strategies* and 13 major *tactics* that special interests have at their disposal to achieve these various "public policy" goals.

I. DIRECT LOBBYING

You can't use tact with a Congressman. A Congressman is a hog. You must take a stick and hit him on the snout.[1]

A MEMBER OF THE GRANT CABINET
QUOTED BY HENRY ADAMS

91

TABLE 5.1.   STRATEGIES AND TACTICS
OF SPECIAL INTERESTS

    I. Direct Lobbying
        A. Personal communications, presentations, and contact
        B. Presentation of research results
   II. Indirect Lobbying
        A. Direct or "pressure mail"
        B. Public relations campaigns
        C. Public criticism
  III. Dollar Lobbying
        A. Campaign contributions
        B. In-kind contributions and support services
   IV. Questionable Payments
        A. Direct bribery
        B. Indirect bribery
    V. Questionable Practices
        A. Deception, distortion, and lying
        B. Litigation, inundation, and delay
        C. Cooptation
   VI. Coalition Building
        A. Legislative logrolling

Direct lobbying involves various forms of direct contact for the purpose of influencing policymakers and their staffs. In their efforts at persuasion, most lobbyists regard *personal communications*—whether by phone, face-to-face encounters, or personal memos—as the most effective tactic to get their message across.[2] The advantage of such a direct encounter is that it permits the lobbyist to confront the policymaker one on one; when lobbyists prepare their cases well and argue them effectively, such direct communication is most persuasive.

The *presentation of research results* is a similarly effective direct lobbying tool.[3] Accordingly, many interest groups employ their own research staffs—so-called fact factories—to generate information and analyses that will bolster their claims during a policy debate.

For example, the Chamber of Commerce employs a small army of economists, lawyers, engineers, and scientists to grind out policy analyses that range from evaluating the negative effects on business investment of a proposed corporate tax increase to the dangers of wage and price controls on the economy. Alternatively, many interest groups hire academics and consultants to perform research, either as a substitute for or adjunct to their own research departments. These "hired guns" often testify at hearings and regulatory proceedings to publicize their results and promote their benefactors' causes.

What is perhaps most interesting (and, to some, most disturbing) about the use of research as a tactic of influence is that very often, two competing interest groups (such as business and labor) will start with the same set of facts and wind up with analyses that illustrate diametrically opposite conclusions. On this phenomenon, Jacob Viner has ruefully observed, "I am impressed by the extent to which vested interests and going institutions seem to have the power to generate ideas congruent with themselves."[4]

A case in point is the "research and counterresearch" over whether coal-burning power plants cause acid rain. Utility industry analysts have steadfastly refused to acknowledge any causal link, while researchers representing environmental groups and the scientific community claim that the same data overwhelmingly point to coal-fired power plants as a major source of acid rain.

II. INDIRECT OR GRASS-ROOTS LOBBYING

Public sentiment is everything. With public sentiment nothing can fail. Without it nothing can succeed. Consequently, he who molds public sentiment goes deeper than he who enacts statutes or pronounces decisions. He makes statutes and decisions possible or impossible.[5]

ABRAHAM LINCOLN

Indirect or grass-roots lobbying is a very powerful tool of persuasion, particularly with congressional representatives who have large concentrations of special interests in their districts. This strategy involves mobilizing third parties to exert pressure on policymakers: Corporate executives call their employees to arms, union leaders recruit the rank and file, public interest groups issue alerts to their memberships, and so on.

Direct or *"pressure" mail* is the most popular, although by most accounts, the least effective, grass-roots lobbying tactic. At the federal level, the White House and Capitol Hill are bombarded each year by literally millions of letters. The White House alone receives 10,000 to 20,000 letters every day. A small portion of this mail is handwritten and expresses the genuine concerns of individual citizens. It is generally read closely by staff and is usually answered, sometimes by the policymaker himself.

Most pressure mail, however, has its origin in the higher echelons of special interest groups. Just as corporations make regular mailings to their stockholders telling them when and what to write to policymakers about impending legislation, corporate executives regularly recruit employees to get involved in the policy game on behalf of the company. Richard Berman offers insight into the way this works:

> In order to generate interest in the program, we tie the individual's and the company's fortunes together. The whole picture comes into focus for the employee: as the company's profits grow, there are increasing opportunities for the individual. Where there are cost pressures on the company, the availability of employee gains diminishes. We stress that involvement in the governmental process is important to our future as a company and our futures as individuals.[6]

Similarly, an umbrella labor organization like the AFL-CIO can mobilize its 50 state organizations and 740 local units to rally more than 100 unions and a 14-million-plus membership, while the godfather of grass-roots lobbying, the Chamber of Commerce, can summon its network of 1,200 local congressional action committees. When pressure is needed, that network responds by inundating members of Congress with letters, telegrams, and phone calls.

But the pressure mail tactic is hardly confined to the economic special interests. A public interest organization like the League of Women Voters can readily mobilize its 160,000 members to deluge Capitol Hill with letters and wires while Common Cause devotes 70 percent of its annual budget to such grass-roots tactics as the mailing of newsletters and alerts to its members.

Of this "third party"-initiated pressure mail, the most ubiquitous—and perhaps the least read—is that which has been "manufactured." In this age of computerized mailing lists, word processors, and high speed printers, many interest groups have developed sophisticated pressure "mail shops" that can fire off barrages of seemingly personalized letters.

These strident epistles explain, cajole, and sometimes threaten policy-makers with a loss of support.

For example, during the 1980 debate over the Panama Canal Treaty, Richard Viguerie, head of the National Conservative Political Action Committee and perhaps the most notorious of the pressure mail producers, claimed responsibility for sending Congress 2.5 million letters opposing the treaty. Senator Howard Baker alone got more than 1,000 letters opposing the treaty, but his own polls in Tennessee showed that 60 percent of his constituents *favored* the treaty—which he voted for. Similarly, the National Rifle Association can produce up to 14 million letters in a matter of days; these letters roll off its printing presses and are mailed to members ready to sign and send off.

The public relations campaign is a second major tactic of grass-roots lobbying. Its purpose is to create a favorable image of the sponsoring special interest and its policy pursuits.

For example, business lobbies strive to create images of industry as the lifeblood of the economy and downplay the polluting by-products of industrial production, while conservationist groups typically trumpet the virtues of an undeveloped and pristine environment and minimize the negative effects that the attainment of that goal may have on jobs and economic growth.

The "advocacy ad," which involves special interest sponsorship of a newspaper ad or a TV or radio slot, is an important public relations device to project such images. A no doubt readily recognizable example of this technique is that of Mobil Oil's highly visible (and, to some, highly abrasive) series of "op-ed"-like articles on topics ranging from whale oil to OPEC. Appearing alongside columnists in newspapers like *The New York Times*, these paid advertisements have presented Mobil as an aggressive champion of free market capitalism.

A less direct form of advocacy advertising is the preparation of anonymous "canned editorials." Groups ranging from the Chamber of Commerce to the American Booksellers Association regularly prepare such editorials to express their point of view and then circulate them throughout the nation's newspaper network. Because of staff limitations or because their staffs sympathize with the views expressed, many newspapers reprint these editorials free of charge and very often without attribution, as if the papers' editors wrote them.

Such groups also write op-ed articles and letters to the editor, which are often published at arm's length by third parties, presumably without the taint of the advocacy group's bias and sometimes even without the awareness of the supposed author. An account of how one such article wound up in the *Washington Post* indicates how special interest ghost writers can remain hidden. The article, warning of the dangers of a nuclear power moratorium, appeared under the byline of a well-known congressman. While the congressman was under the impression that his legislative aide had prepared it, it had actually been provided to that aide by a pro-industry lobbying group. The aide was happy to take credit for it, the lobbying group was delighted to let him, and the congressman was proud of "his article."[7]

Other forms of public relations propaganda include such items as those friendly folders one finds in one's monthly bills extolling the virtues of, say, the phone company, American Express, or the local department store as well as personal appearances by interest group spokespersons and the "free use" of self-produced movies and radio programs.

Convention speeches, press conferences, and the opinion pages of newspapers, magazines, and interest group journals are typical staging platforms for a third tactic of indirect lobbying, *public criticism*. A spokesperson for the AFL-CIO may blast the president for his labor and welfare policies in a speech at the union's annual convention, as Lane Kirkland has often done during Ronald Reagan's presidency; a consumer advocate may hold a press conference to excoriate the Federal Trade Commission for its "anti-consumer" bias, as Ralph Nader did during James Miller's tenure as chairman; or the defense minister of Israel may go on the offensive against "Arabists" in the U.S. government in an op-ed piece in *The New York Times*, as Ariel Sharon did during the Israeli invasion of Lebanon.

Sometimes the purpose of these public criticism missiles is to "flush out" a policymaker's position: After being accused of forsaking a special interest, the policymaker is expected to respond with a denial and show of support for the group. At other times the purpose is to confront, or even embarrass, policymakers in the public eye. Such attacks are predicated on the policymaker's sensitivity to the resultant pressure, as revealed in the remarks of one Common Cause lobbyist who insisted that "criticizing members of Congress is an effective weapon. . . . To expose a person in his or her district or state is to strike a sensitive nerve."[8]

A more militant variation on this public criticism theme is the mass political demonstration. From a single file of 20 activists pacing the sidewalk in front of the White House demanding justice for Moslems in the Philippines or several hundred tractors circling Capitol Hill in protest of falling wheat prices to tens of thousands of antiwar marchers descending on Washington to show opposition to U.S. military involvement abroad, political demonstrations are an integral part of interst group pressure. At times such demonstrations have borne great success: Civil rights demonstrators succeeded in moving the Congress forward to passage of the 1964 Civil Rights Act, and the antiwar movement's chants penetrated the walls of the Nixon White House to influence the policies created there. But demonstrations in other situations also have proved futile, as the anarchic ghetto riots of the 1960s and the bloody student demonstrations at the 1968 Democratic convention attest.

III.   DOLLAR LOBBYING

An honest politician is one who, when bought, stays bought.[9]

SIMON CAMERON,
LINCOLN'S SECRETARY OF WAR

"Dollar lobbying" refers to the use of cash and other financial support to influence policy. With this type of lobbying strategy, we begin a descent into the darker, ethically more cloudy realms of the policy game.

Campaign contributions represent the most obvious form of dollar lobbying; each year, special interest groups contribute billions of dollars to the candidates of their choice. The common notion about these campaign contributions is that they "buy" votes; unfortunately, this characterization has sometimes proven accurate.

One notorious example has bubbled up out of the murky depths of Watergate. Just after the ITT corporation contributed $400,000 to the Republican National Convention, Attorney General John Mitchell, who was also Richard Nixon's campaign manager, authorized the Justice Department to drop its attempt to make ITT give up its $2 billion Hartford Insurance Company. ITT in turn agreed to divest itself of other firms worth $1 billion. A confidential memo from ITT lobbyist Dita Beard confirms that the Nixon administration let ITT off the hook.[10]

According to most political observers, such tawdry episodes are, however, the exception rather than the rule. These observers argue that the real purpose of campaign contributions is not to buy votes, but rather, to gain access to the policy game: Dollars open hitherto closed doors and blocked lines of communication. Fred Wertheimer of Common Cause has described how dollars serve as the key to the influence kingdom: "It's not a question of buying votes, it's a question of relationships that get built, obligations and dependencies that get established."[11] Out of these relationships, obligations, and dependencies and through early access to the policy process, the contributing special interests are able to shape agendas, legislation, and, ultimately, policy outcomes.

The legalization of political action committees in 1971 and subsequent legislation limiting the amount an individual can contribute to campaigns have led to a proliferation of campaign contributions by special interests. In the decade of "PAC-mania," the number of PACs has swelled from 516 in 1974 to over 3000 today. PACs now provide more than 25 percent of all campaign contributions.

Surprisingly, when special interests give money, they are, as a rule, blind to both party and ideology. They typically target contributions quite narrowly at legislators who represent the districts and states where they do business, regardless of whether they are conservatives or liberals, Republicans or Democrats. They also are likely to shower money on members of legislative committees that focus on their problems. Thus a policymaker in Michigan might be the beneficiary of funds from Middle Atlantic auto parts manufacturers, and a congressman from New York City might find himself on the receiving end of a substantial contribution from a farm group simply because he serves on the House Agricultural Committee.

Despite the growing magnitude of campaign contributions, they are but the tip of a much larger iceberg of dollar lobbying that consists of a dizzying array of *support services* and *in-kind contributions*. The essence of these services and contributions is the provision of resources that policymakers would otherwise have to buy, often at great expense.

Perhaps the most influential of the support services is the drafting and preparation of legislation and regulations. According to some lobbyists, fully half of all Congressional bills are written in whole or in part by pressure groups or their high-priced Washington lawyers. As a result, some interest groups actually become extensions of policymakers' often inadequate staffs.

Mark Green and Andrew Buchsbaum, for example, have documented how the Business Roundtable used its staff to draft pieces of important legislation: "Roundtable-retained lawyers worked with the minority subcommittee on Education and Labor in the House to produce Rep. John Ehrelenborn's Employee Bill of Rights, a pro-business 'reform' of labor law based on a previous Roundtable report. The Roundtable authored eight of the bill's nine provisions."[12]

Special interests also furnish policymakers with a wide array of other written materials that range from issue papers, research reports, and membership lists to speeches, articles, and answers to correspondence by "paid volunteers." The list of services and contributions does not stop here, however. Many pressure groups also provide such election and re-election boosters as survey research and free opinion surveys; underwritten mailings, campaign work, and get-out-the-vote assistance (e.g., busing the elderly to the polls); and free transportation in the lobbyist's limousine or the corporation's jet.

The dollar value of these services and contributions is difficult to estimate because it is in no way monitored—a fact that should surprise and sober any would-be reformer of the lobbying process who naively thinks that capping campaign contributions will quash policymakers' susceptibility to influence. But at least the tactics of dollar lobbying are aboveboard. The next two lobbying strategies, questionable payments and questionable practices, do not possess this characteristic.

IV.   QUESTIONABLE PAYMENTS

Corporate philanthropy can be a big weapon in the battle for men's minds.[13]

D. CRAIG YESSE, LOCTITE CORPORATION

The strategy of questionable payments encompasses both direct and indirect attempts by special interests to exchange dollars for influence. *Direct bribery* is its most obvious form, one that is undeniably both unethical and illegal.

While most observers of the political scene regard the direct bribe as an infrequent occurrence, from time immemorial policymakers have been caught with their hands in the till—to the dismay of a trusting public and the delight of newspaper sales managers.

A classic case occurred during the Eisenhower administration when an overenthusiastic natural gas lobbyist delivered a $2,500 cash "campaign contribution" to a key senator just before an important vote on natural gas legislation. Rather than spend the money, the angry senator dumped it out of the paper bag it was delivered in onto the Senate floor as he announced the bribery attempt. (The bill passed, but Ike vetoed it because of the bribe.)

More recently, in the infamous "Abscam affair," the age of videotape and hidden cameras gave us feature-length documentaries of several congressmen caught, *flagrante delicto*, receiving bales of crisp, fresh bills from FBI agents disguised as Arab lobbyists in exchange for the promise of influence.

Despite these well-publicized episodes, it is doubtful that direct bribery is a prevalent practice. One reason is that the courts have not been particularly kind to recipients, as ex-convicts like Bobby Baker and the once Honorable Harrison Williams can attest. But the most important curb on direct bribery is the greater ease and legality of bribing policymakers indirectly.

Of the numerous and often nefarious methods of *indirect bribery*, a favorite form is the lecture fee or honorarium: As payment for a speech or brief appearance, a senator, cabinet officer, regulator, or White House staffer can receive several thousand dollars or more. While the presentation is in some cases worth the high price paid, it is also true that part or most of the fee is often an indirect method of transferring funds.

A second popular pressure group gambit is to put a policymaker on a large consulting or legal retainer. Again, while some of the recipients may actually earn these fees, in many instances, they are simply special interests' IOUs on access to the influence process. (One example where a special interest apparently called in its IOU is provided by Kentucky Representative Gene Snyder. In 1972, Snyder received $110,000 in lawyers' fees for closing a real estate deal for a utility; three years later, Snyder attached a special interest amendment to a House bill that aided that same utility.)[14]

A third, even more questionable, tactic of indirect bribery is giving policymakers easy access to highly profitable business ventures. The business deal payoff is particularly unethical when the investment in question is tied directly to the policymaker's decision process, when, for example, a congressman finds himself with several thousand shares of a small oil company and then must vote on a special exemption that will net that company millions.

Finally, more pervasive and often no less squalid, there are the gifts— free entertainment, sexual favors, and trips—that comprise the oft-cited troika of booze, blondes, and bribes. Many corporations send legislators and their staffs Christmas and other holiday gifts, while one corporation is reputed to send each member of Congress a birthday gift. The entertainment hustle runs the gamut from big cocktail parties and black-tie dinners to intimate luxury-suite gatherings while the "junket payoff" can transport willing policymakers—often under the guise of government business—to hunting lodges, golf links, and exotic spots around the globe.

V. QUESTIONABLE PRACTICES

Never give false statistics, but be selective with statistics that will support arguments for increased spending. If we want more ships, indicate that a potential enemy has more ships than the United States. Don't mention that U.S. ships are larger or have greater firepower. Or, talk about inferior troop strength in NATO—only 20 divisions compared to 100 Warsaw Pact divisions. Don't mention that a Russian troop division is about one-fifth the size of a U.S. troop division, or that an American division's firepower is greater than the firepower of five Russian divisions.[15]

> AN ANONYMOUS
> DEFENSE DEPARTMENT BUREAUCRAT

Like questionable payments, the strategy of questionable practices spans the ethical and legal spectrums and ranges from outright lying and preemptive litigation to outright cooptation.

According to conventional wisdom, outright lying is a rarity since the uncovered lie invariably damages a lobbyist's credibility and threatens access to the halls of influence. However, this wisdom ignores the myriad ways that special interests can stack the "truth" in their favor through more subtle techniques of *deception* and *distortion*.

One common means of distortion besides the ubiquitous juggling of facts and figures is the loading of the assumptions underpinning an analysis that generates those facts and figures. For example, in determining how the deregulation of natural gas prices would affect producers and consumers, assumptions must be made about how fast oil prices will rise over time and whether gas prices will rise to the price of oil in the absence of controls. Researchers for a consumer group that opposes deregulation may choose to assume that oil prices will rise very quickly over time and that gas prices will rise immediately to parity with oil. On the other hand, the analysts of pro-deregulation producers might instead assume a lower rate of escalation of oil prices and less or no linkage of gas prices to oil. The results of the two groups' studies are likely to deviate from each other by billions of dollars, with the consumer group's report showing devastating consequences for consumers and the producer's document showing only mild ones.

A second distortion is the "error of omission." In explaining the benefits of a special tax exemption for his group, for example, a lobbyist may cite a major piece of research that predicts strong investment as a response to that tax break, but neglect to mention that the report (or an equally reputable one) also predicted a substantial loss of tax revenues that would make the policy ultimately counterproductive. In the same vein, quoting objective sources out of context is an all too frequent occurrence, while the selective use of statistics—as illustrated in our opening quote in this section—is a similar gambit.

Finally, there are the "fearmongers," interest groups that thrive on propaganda and sometimes slander—mudslinging that is literally designed to "scare up" support for the group through its imagery and symbols. In American politics, no symbol is more frequently invoked to fight off a policy than the specter of socialism. "This symbol, made famous by its repeated use by the American Medical Association, has become almost standard operating procedure of nearly all organizations whose objectives can, without a thoroughly implausible stretching of the imagination, be associated with free enterprise."[16] The following vintage quote from the *AMA News* illustrates this point:

> *The Socialist Party in the United States has launched a nationwide campaign for socialized medicine in America and has made it clear it supports President Kennedy's proposal for health and medical care through*

the Social Security program to bring full-blown socialized medicine to this country. . . . The Socialists intend to use socialized medicine as the springboard to reach that bigger prize—full socialism in the United States.[17]

Besides these methods of distortion, policymakers must also contend with various kinds of deception. One such form is simple obfuscation. According to AFL–CIO's chief lobbyist: "Obfuscation is as time-honored a method of nondisclosure as silence. Significant facts tend to be buried in voluminous compilations of trivia."[18] The Watergate burglars put another form, the "dirty trick," into the lexicon of American politics.* But a gentler deception, no doubt more prevalent than dirty tricks, is the use of "front organizations" to spread an interest group's gospel. For example, a group like the American Bar Association often enlists banks and insurance companies to deliver its message, and some lobbying groups actually recruit and finance seemingly independent organizations to speak for them. As one railroad public relations specialist has described this practice: "Of course we release some stories under direct attribution, but they will be of less propaganda value than those we can generate from motorists, property owners, tax payers, farmers, or women's groups."[20]

While *litigation* can be both an important counterforce to interest group pressure and a public interest tool, it must also be included as a questionable practice when its purpose is mere delay. For example, a large corporation can play "procedural chess" with the courts to stave off the Justice Department's efforts to enforce existing antitrust laws. The longer it delays divesting itself of its monopoly power through appeals and various other legal steps, the longer it reaps the benefits of its monopoly. The cavalier and calculating way this procedural-delay gambit

---

*Sam J. Ervin, Jr. describes one of these pranks:

In March 1972, members of Nixon's staff had a counterfeit letter, falsely purporting to be the composition of the "Senator Ed Muskie Staff" sent to Florida voters three days before the primary. This letter, written on stationery of Muskie's campaign organization, charged that one of Muskie's major opponents, Senator Jackson, had previously fathered an illegitimate child and been arrested on homosexual charges. It further claimed that Senator Humphrey, another of Muskie's opponents, had been arrested in Washington on a drunken driving charge while in the company of a well-known call girl hired by a lobbyist to entertain him.[19]

sometimes is played is evident in the following boast of Washington lawyer Bruce Bromley:

> *Now I was born, I think, to be a protractor. . . . I quickly realized in my early days at the bar that I could take the simplest antitrust case that Judge Hansen (Antitrust Division chief) could think of and protract it for the defense almost to infinity. . . . If you will look at that record (United States v. Bethlehem Steel) you will see immediately the Bromley protractor touch in the third line. Promptly after the answer was filed I served quite a comprehensive set of interrogatories on the Government. I said to myself, "That'll tie brother Hansen up for a while," and I went about other business.*[21]

Inundation likewise is an effective means of delaying litigation. In essence a "legal filibuster," inundation entails submitting vast quantities of information to the courts. Essential information gets lost in a sea of extraneous data, and the justice system's resources are severely strained. Riding the crest of its computer technology, juggernaut IBM used precisely this technique to submit to the courts several million pages of "information," which it delivered literally by the trailerload during an antitrust case brought against it by the Justice Department. The case was finally dropped after years of legal sparring, in large part because the court had neither the time nor the resources to wade through IBM's flood of documents.

Cooptation is a final questionable practice. It occurs when special interests provide lucrative jobs to former policymakers and their staffs, in order to buy immediate access to the political arena. For this reason, we observe a high incidence of deposed congressmen working for the special interests that once so ardently wooed them.* Former public interest representatives turned high-paid special interest "Washington representatives" include such liberal luminaries as former senators and presidential candidates Edmund Muskie and Birch Bayh. Muskie represents Arab and other foreign interests while Bayh was last seen trying to rescue client Georgia Pacific from a multi-million-dollar price-fixing case, to the dismay of his one-time liberal supporters. Similarly, former representatives Tom Railsback and James Corman lobby for the Motion Picture Association and Nissan Motors, respectively. Says Corman of his

---

*Former congressional aide Larry King has irreverently dubbed congressmen turned lobbyists as the species "lameduck emeritus."

once lofty ideals: "When you're in public office you have the privilege of representing the public interest. When you work for a law firm, you represent your client."[22]

Another favorite candidate for cooptation is the academic or intellectual who is an expert in the field of policy that a special interest is attempting to influence. Lured by fees that often dwarf their regular salaries, many professors become paid consultants to special interests, testifying at congressional and regulatory proceedings and performing requested research. While some maintain their objectivity (despite obvious pressures to provide more favorable "facts" for the interest group benefactor), others simply do not. A particularly distasteful example of the cooptation of the medical profession has been documented by Green and Buchsbaum:

> . . . two years after the first round of hearings, it was discovered that all doctors and professionals who had publicly criticized the surgeon general's report had been solicited by the Tobacco Institute. Their testimony had apparently been typed on the same typewriter, and most had been paid large fees by the institute. This surprised the Senate Commerce Committee, which had assumed that the professional opinions they had heard were unsullied by any financial ties to business.[23]

Moreover, even if the experts fail to generate favorable arguments for a policy, the special interest gains by eliminating a potential opponent.

VI.   COALITION BUILDING

A final lobbying strategy is coalition building. Often interest group coalitions need nothing more than tradition and broad common goals to bind them; labor and farm groups, for instance, typically find themselves allied with one another on most issues. But one also observes coalitions in which natural enemies enter into seemingly unnatural alliances; typically, a common political objective brings these "strange bedfellows" together, despite their remarkably different goals.

A case in point is the so-called unholy alliance that was forged between environmental groups and the United Mine Workers (UMW) to create pressure for several amendments to the Clean Air Act.[24] The goal of these amendments (the "scrubber" and "prevention of significant deterioration" clauses) was to reduce the mining and burning of low-sulfur surface coal. The environmentalists supported the amendments because they saw them as one way of stopping strip mining and air pollution in the "pristine West" while the UMW saw the amendments as a jobs bill that would protect the higher-sulfur underground mines of the Midwest and East (where the UMW has the bulk of its membership) from Western competition.

Legislative logrolling is typically a significant feature of any successful coalition building. This tactic is most prevalent when interest groups do not have a common goal, but need added support in order to get a share of the political pie. Thus, in the legislative arena where logrolling is most frequently observed, labor interests might agree to support a consumer protection bill that will have little direct impact on them if consumer groups will lend their support to a labor bill authorizing on-site picketing. Similarly, the tobacco lobby might push the Congress to vote for peanut, wheat, and milk price supports in exchange for similar support for tobacco subsidies from the farm coalition.

VII. CONCLUSIONS

We see, then, that there is a wide range of lobbying strategies and tactics to choose from. Typically, a special interest group will choose some subset of these strategies and tactics to achieve its goals. The actual mix will depend both on the *kind* of interest group it is and the *type* of policy it seeks.

For example, a coterie of small oil refiners seeking a special subsidy may rely on the direct lobbying of individual congressmen and their staffs outside the spotlight of public opinion as the best way to encourage the passage of legislation with such a narrow focus. In contrast, a public interest group concerned, say, with establishing a new consumer protection agency will rely much more heavily on grass-roots lobbying to arouse public opinion, bombarding its members with "news alerts" so that they, in turn, will inundate the Congress and White House with favorable "pressure mail."

In the following chapter on farm subsidies, let's see how a discussion of the strategies and tactics of the special interests can further boost the power of our capture-ideology framework in explaining the politics of the policy game.

6

Between Feast and Famine

THE FARM POLICY GAME

The American farmer, living on his own land, remains our
ideal of self-reliance and of spiritual balance—the source
from which the reservoirs of the Nation's strength are
constantly renewed. It is from the men and women of our
farms living close to the soil that this Nation, like the Greek
giant Antaeus, touches Mother Earth and rises with
strength renewed a hundredfold.[1]

Franklin Roosevelt

While American farm products
regularly pile up in government storage bins literally bursting at their
seams, American farmers—the most productive in world history—are
going broke. For even as the federal government spends over $4 billion a
year in farm subsidies,[2] each year, over 800 farms are foreclosed and
thousands more farmers voluntarily shut down their farms.[3] Clearly,
something is wrong.

This paradox of American farm policy is not a new phenomenon.
Since the days of the Great Depression, the "farm problem"[4] of chronic
overabundance, low food prices and farm incomes, and loss of farm

population* has plagued farmers. But while the farm problem has been with us for over 60 years, it remains an open question as to whether American farm policy has worked to solve or to exacerbate that problem.

1. HISTORY AND BACKGROUND

The eminent agricultural economist Luther Tweeten has described American farm policy as a lurching roller coaster of reactions to various crises. In the early 1900s, American farmers enjoyed unusual prosperity, primarily because of the food and commodity demands generated by World War I. However, the armistice brought the collapse of foreign demand as European farmers returned to their farms and greatly expanded their agricultural output. The ensuing postwar slump brought great hardship, as farm prices decreased by more than 40 percent between 1919 and 1922.[6]

The farm problem then, as now, was a crisis of abundance sharply punctuated by periodic weather-induced crop failures. Throughout the 1920s, farmers continued to produce food in such great quantities that farm prices, and therefore farm incomes, remained at perilously low levels. The onset of the Great Depression wreaked further havoc, and finally, the droughts of the early 1930s pushed the American farmer over the financial brink and set the stage for New Deal farm legislation.

As he did with so many of today's federal programs, President Franklin D. Roosevelt laid the foundation of modern farm policy with his signing of the Agricultural Adjustment Acts of 1933 and 1938, and the associated acts of 1936 and 1937. Today, that foundation still rests on the acts' two major pillars: price supports and supply controls.[7]

Price supports were designed to guarantee farmers some minimum level of income necessary to sustain a reasonable standard of living. They do so by setting a "floor" or support price for farmers' crops or commodities, even if the market price falls below that floor. For example, suppose the support level is set at $1.50 per bushel for wheat, but the market

---

*The number of farmers has dwindled from 25 percent of the population in 1930 to less than 3 percent today, while the number of farms has fallen from 6.2 million to 2.5 million.[5]

price is $1.30. Through the support system, the government makes up the difference.

Of course, then as now, maintaining price supports above market levels has the undesirable effect of overstimulating production; the resultant surpluses perversely push market prices even further below support prices. For this reason, FDR's original acts also established *supply controls* as a necessary adjunct to supports. The controls included in the acts ranged from "plowing every third row under" to destroying part of the surpluses. The idea was first to raise prices artificially through price supports to boost farm income and then eventually reduce supply through controls to ensure that the market price rose above support levels. Hence controls would eventually obviate the need for the support system's drain on the treasury—or so it was thought.

With the onset of World War II and the need to feed not only America but also her allies, national concern shifted abruptly to preventing shortages and inflation. As demand rose, efforts were made to put a *ceiling* on prices, a somewhat ironic goal given the previous anxiety about price floors. The ceiling that was finally implemented allowed significant price increases, despite the best efforts of President Roosevelt. Resistance to lower ceilings arose from fears of a postwar replay of the 1920 debacle. To allay these anxieties, the president recommended that the Congress consider price support programs for ". . . whatever period is necessary after the end of the war."[8] The beginnings were thus set for the postwar era of bursting grain bins and depressed farm income.

After the war these high and fixed price supports remained in effect and, predictably, surpluses began to mount. Postwar aid to U.S. allies via the Marshall Plan helped to diminish these surpluses in the early postwar period, as did the Korean Conflict. But by 1952 surplus stocks began to accumulate rapidly.

Supply controls were reimplemented in 1956, and passage of the Agricultural Act of 1956 incorporated a "soil bank" to remove acreage from production over the long term. The act established an "acreage reserve" whereby farmers could receive compensation for setting land aside and authorized "conservation reserve" payments to farmers converting their land to specified conservation practices. However, as discussed in more detail later, technological advances in agriculture outstripped supply controls; spurred by high price supports, farmers managed to evade controls and continued to overproduce.

The failure of farm policy to control surpluses and reduce the drain on the federal treasury during the 1950s was particularly vexing to President Eisenhower, who desperately tried to reform or eliminate the support-supply control programs. For his efforts, the Republican party suffered a devastating defeat in the off-year congressional election of 1958, primarily because of farm interests, who were angry with Ike's attempts at "reforms."[9] Out of frustration, Ike lashed back, decrying the use of "federal subsidies to create millionaires . . . under programs ostensibly devised to protect the little farmer."[10] And in a stinging special message to Congress in January 1959, Ike insisted that neither the price support nor the supply control programs worked. Discontent with Republican farm policy only served to lose the party votes, however, as John F. Kennedy was able to garner support from farm interests, support that helped him greatly in his 1960 "squeaker" victory over Nixon.

The latest stage in farm policy points toward a more "market oriented"[11] approach, which began with the 1973 attempts of the Nixon administration to eliminate the support framework. In its stead, Agriculture Secretary Earl Butz proposed a heightened emphasis on *supply controls* through such mechanisms as set-asides. Agricultural interests and their predominantly liberal Democratic allies in the Congress, however, had other ideas. Rather than a phaseout of support prices, they proposed the compromise of "target prices." The ensuing battle over "parity" versus "target" pricing, which has continued into the 1980s, is interesting not only because of the different economic implications of the two systems, but also because, in large part, they reflect the divergent philosophies of liberals and conservatives.

The *parity formula*, which first surfaced in FDR's landmark Agricultural Acts, is a rather byzantine device with the primary goal of providing farmers with a "fair" level of real income. According to the enabling legislation, that fair, or parity, income equal the same amount (or some percentage) of the real income that farmers earned during the aforementioned period of farm prosperity from 1910 to 1914. Under the parity formula, the support price of an agricultural product is set so that the farmer earns enough income to cover all his production expenses and still has the purchasing power to buy enough goods and services to sustain a standard of living comparable to that in the base period.[12] Thus, as long as the parity price remains above the market price, it represents a subsidy to farmers.

The parity formula by and large reflects the goals of farmers,[13] and the philosophy of liberals, who see the formula as a means of ensuring the farmer an equitable level of income. As C. M. Hardin has observed, "Parity is much more than a ratio of prices received to prices paid—it is 'simple economic justice.' It is an economic right turned into a political obligation."[14] (One wag has satirized this "right" by changing the three biblical virtues to "Faith, Hope, and Parity."[15])

As an income-based formula, parity prices bear no obvious relationship to market prices. According to conservative critics, this has led to huge farm surpluses, bursting storage bins, and an unwarranted bonanza for certain farm interests. One reason cited is that the fixed parity price does not fall as surpluses rise. But the most important reason is that the parity price support system has typically been administered through the use of "nonrecourse loans": Specifically, a farmer is allowed to borrow on his or her crop or commodity at the parity support price (also called the loan rate). If the market price is above the parity price, the farmer repays the loan and sells his crop or commodity at the market price. However, if the market price is below the loan rate, the farmer simply gives the crop or commodity to the government as payment for the loan and the government then puts it in storage. It is this part of the parity mechanism that has periodically resulted in bloated government storage silos.

As an alternative to the parity/nonrecourse loan scheme, there is the more market-based "target price-deficiency payment" approach favored by conservatives. The DOA secretary sets annual target prices on the basis not only of the income needs of farmers, but also on projections of supply and demand for the coming year and the size of existing surpluses. If a shortage is forecast (e.g., because of a corn blight), the target price for corn is set higher to stimulate production. If large surpluses are anticipated (e.g., after a bumper corn crop), the target price is set lower to reduce the stimulus. If the market price falls short of this target, the government provides a deficiency payment equal to the difference between the target and market prices.*

In its pure form, the target pricing-deficiency payment system involves neither the massive provision of government credit nor the purchases of

---

*For example, if the average market price of wheat is $2.25 per bushel during the year and the target price is $2.90 per bushel, a farmer who raises 3,000 bushels will be paid by the government a total of $1,950 [3000 × (2.90-2.25)].[16] On the other hand, if the market price for the crop or commodity is above the target price (as it was for cotton in 1982), no support is required.

large surpluses that the parity/nonrecourse loan approach entails. At the same time, support levels are more flexible and responsive to the market conditions of supply and demand.

Despite the efforts of the Nixon and subsequent administrations to replace the pure parity/nonrecourse loan approach with the pure target price-deficiency payment scheme (preferably at low rates), Congress has refused to surrender completely either the parity formula or its authority to set support levels. Today, as a result of both bitter battles and political compromise, the price support system is a hybrid of the two approaches. Table 6.1 describes this hybridization of price supports now in effect for major crops and commodities. From the table, it is clear that wheat and feed grains, and rice and upland cotton have moved the furthest toward a market orientation. Peanut, soybean, sugar, tobacco, and the especially costly dairy programs retain much of their original forms.

A number of possible outcomes can occur under this hybrid system, with different ramifications for the public interest. First, and least likely, the market price may be above both the target price *and* the support rate. In this "best case," the farmer sells his crop on the open market and the government makes neither a deficiency payment nor a purchase for storage. Everyone is happy.

TABLE 6.1.   MAJOR CROP AND COMMODITY PRICE
SUPPORT PROGRAMS

Crop or Commodity	Supports Calculated by Parity[a]	Targets	Supports
Dairy	X		X
Wheat		X	X
Feed grains		X	X
Rice		X	X
Cotton		X	X
Peanuts			X
Soybeans			X
Sugar	X		X
Tobacco			X

Source: U.S. Department of Agriculture, Economic Research Service. *Provisions of the Agriculture and Food Act of 1981* (Staff report AGES 811228). Washington, D.C.: DoC/NTIS, January 1982.

[a]Lower and/or upper bounds set by parity calculations for nonrecourse loan rates.

Second, and more likely, the market price may be *between* the higher target price and the lower support rate. In this case, the farmer again sells his crop on the market, but the government also provides him with a deficiency payment equal to the difference between the target and market prices.*

Finally, and most likely, the market price may be below *both* the target price and the support rate. In this case, the farmer is twice blessed while the government is hit by a double whammy: The farmer bypasses the market and instead gives the government his crop (i.e., he defaults) at the support rate. In addition, the government must also provide a deficiency payment over and above the support rate equal to the difference between that rate and the target price.

Now if you have had difficulty following the preceding permutations and possibilities, you are in good company. As Bruce Gardner has remarked: ". . . one could read the entire substantial compilation of farm-commodity legislation in law today, and at the end have only the foggiest notion of what is actually being done in farm policy."[17] But the bottom line is that even with this hybridization, America still has a farm policy that overstimulates production through supports and drains the treasury through the large-scale provision of subsidies at the same time that it hurts many farmers.

Let's examine the politics of farm policy through the lens of our capture-ideology framework to try to understand why this seemingly perverse result has persisted over five decades. In doing so, we also will see how a supplementary discussion of the strategies and tactics of the various players in the farm policy game helps shed further light on the private use of the public interest.

II.   THE POLITICS OF AMERICAN FARM POLICY

A.   Private Interest Capture

According to the capture model, the farm policy game is a distributional fight between farmers and farm suppliers seeking government subsidies

---

*There are limitations on the deficiency payments. For most crops, it is $50,000.

and taxpayers, consumers, and farm product middlemen who are forced to finance these subsidies.

On the surface, this view seems to fit farm policy like a glove. The federal government annually transfers billions of dollars to farmers through its price support programs while taxpayers pick up the tab. At the same time, when controls successfully restrict supply and thereby bolster prices, middlemen (food processors and distributors) pay farmers more for their crops and commodities, and consumers ultimately pay higher prices in supermarkets and restaurants.

Probing behind this broad distributional struggle, a close examination of the players in the farm policy game, coupled with an analysis of some of the strategies and tactics discussed in the preceding chapter, reveal mounting evidence that a powerful "farm bloc," as political scientists have dubbed it,[18] has captured the government.

1. Who Makes Up the Farm Lobby. Atop the pyramid of farm power are four umbrella organizations: The American Farm Bureau Federation, the National Grange, the National Farmers Union, and the National Farmers Organization. Interestingly, these groups are more often at odds with each other than working in concert to promote any "monolithic" farm interest. The primary reason is that each organization represents a definable subgroup of farmers whose goals are not always in concert.

The Farm Bureau is a rather conservative organization with strong ties to the Republican party and a high proportion of large commercial farmers in its membership. Since World War II, "it has advocated the progressive removal of production controls and the reduction of price supports . . ."[19] On the other hand, the National Farmers Union ". . . claims to be the spokesman for the 'family farmer.' It has favored high price supports and rigid controls, accused the Farm Bureau of working on behalf of processors, and has allied itself with liberal bureaucrats and sometimes labor unions . . ."[20]

Because of the divisiveness among general farm organizations, it is not surprising that the real power of the farm lobby lies in its far more numerous individual crop and commodity organizations. From the American Soybean Association to the United Egg Producers, these groups number in the hundreds, their budgets stretch into the millions of dollars, and virtually all of the major organizations maintain lobbying offices in Washington.

Augmenting these professional lobbying groups are numerous PACs. They include large, well-funded PACs such as Dairymen, Inc. and the National Cotton Council of America to lesser-budgeted PACs such as the Florida Sugar Cane League and the Pear Growers for Responsible Government.

A third major force in the farm lobby are the steadily growing farm cooperatives and agribusiness corporations, which, with the consolidation of small farms, have increasingly come to dominate farm production, sales, and distribution. The farm cooperatives are voluntary associations of producers that attempt to organize marketing arrangements in a region. Several of them have become rather large political and economic forces in and of themselves (the dairy coops, for example).

The agribusiness firms include manufacturers of farm inputs like herbicides, pesticides, and fertilizers; producers of heavy equipment for soil preparation, planting, tilling, fertilizing, and harvesting; and makers of farm appliances, feed supplements, and the like. In addition, there are farm output firms that store, transport, sell, package, distribute, and export farm products. The agribusiness groups have a clear interest in any government programs that stimulate farm production, which in turn creates a demand for their products.

A fourth major force that has often worked to promote farm interests is the government lobby's Department of Agriculture, which has more than 15 "clientele agencies"* that administer various farm programs.[21] As Wesley McCune has observed, "more than any other federal agency, the DOA has been the major protagonist for farm interests."[22] Literally thousands of bureaucrats within its honeycombs depend on a large federal budget appropriation for the programs they administer, and, not surprisingly, they have fought hard to maintain and expand their share of the budget.

For example, the Agricultural Stablization and Conservation Service (ASCS), which administers many of the price support and supply con-

---

*This term refers to agencies within the government that have historically acted to promote the interests of their constituents. The Departments of Agriculture, Defense, and Labor are often accused of being subservient to their clientele: the farm bloc, the defense industry, and Big Labor, respectively.

trol programs, employs over 2,300 people and has a budget of $400 million. This figure is misleadingly small since ASCS has at its disposal the resources of the Commodity Credit Corporation (CCC), with a budget of over $17 billion.[23] It is an active participant in the making of farm policy, both on Capitol Hill and within the administration.

A final building block of the farm lobby is what has been dubbed the "research establishment." As Alex McCalla has described it, this establishment "is a morass of loosely related, sometimes complementary, sometimes competitive, organizations. . . . Its magnitude, in recent years, is approaching a $2 billion a year enterprise, about 50 percent public and 50 percent private."[24] Its members include the numerous public land-grant colleges and private universities that spend almost $800 million per year on agricultural research; various federal research agencies, such as the National Academy of Science, which devote almost $400 million per year to agricultural research; and private firms like the Stanford Research Institute and Batelle that spend another $50 to $100 million per year.[25]

The research establishment's stake in price support and supply control programs is precisely these millions of dollars that both federal and state governments expend to determine how best to administer the programs, to measure their costs and benefits, and to figure out ways to reform the programs.

2. Strategy and Tactics of the Farm Lobby.   Historically, *direct lobbying* has been an extremely effective strategy for farm interests. The tactics of personal communication and presentation are put to frequent use on Capitol Hill, particularly at the various clientele agencies within the DOA. Farm lobbyists regularly testify at congressional hearings, while the research departments of the various umbrella and crop and commodity organizations grind out a constant stream of policy analyses that bolster their political goals and demands.

At the same time, the farm lobby has historically been extremely successful in placing congressmen from farm states on key agricultural committees and subcommittees. This was particularly true during the heyday of price support legislation before 1970 when the seniority system was still in effect. For example, when high price supports were the law of the land during the late 1940s and 1950s, the Chairmen of the House Agricultural Committee were Clifford R. Hope of wheat-state Kansas and Harold D. Cooley of tobacco-state North Carolina, and a majority of the seats on the committee were held by farm-state congressmen.[26] A similar situation existed in the Senate, which helps to explain why President Eisenhower was so ineffective in reforming the price support system.

Today, the seniority system has gone the way of all flesh, but farm state congressmen continue to dominate these committees. The Chairman of the Senate Agriculture, Nutrition and Forestry Committee is the voice of peanut- and tobacco-producing North Carolina, Jesse Helms, while 15 of the 18 committee members come from farm states. In the House, a similar situation exists, where "Kika" de la Garza from Texas is chairman of the Agriculture Committee, and 31 of the 40 members are from farm states.

Similarly, the farm lobby has had great success at planting its supporters in key positions in agencies like the DOA. The DOA secretary has traditionally been a farmer, and Democrats (e.g., Orville Freeman under Kennedy and Johnson, and Bob Bergland under Carter) have generally favored the price support program. (Republicans like Ezra Taft Benson under Eisenhower and Earl Butz under Nixon hardly pleased the farm lobby, however.) Likewise, the upper and middle echelons of the DOA are dotted with sympathizers appointed with the help of the farm lobby. For instance, during the Reagan administration, Deputy Secretary Richard E. Lyng was a former president of the American Meat Institute (as well as CCC director under Nixon), while C. W. McMillan, assistant secretary of marketing and transportation services, was at one time a vice-president of the National Cattlemen's Association.

The farm lobby has been somewhat less effective and more erratic in its use of *indirect lobbying* techniques. The problem appears to be with the farmers themselves, who, as Ed Edwin has portrayed them, are apolitical and "phlegmatic when times are good" and only "vociferous after adversities."[27]

Despite the farmers' often apathetic behavior, once mobilized the farm vote can be a powerful grass-roots persuader to politicians, who, as students of history, are mindful of the numerous elections that the farm vote has helped to sway. Prominent examples of this swing-vote effect include Truman's 1948 upset of Dewey when the former carried much of the traditionally Republican Midwest,[28] Kennedy's aforementioned narrow victory over Nixon, and more recently, the off-year 1982 election where a number of Reaganite congressmen in the farm belt were deposed.[29]

In recent years, as the number of farmers has continued to shrink, one major offsetting factor has been the explosive growth in farm PACs.* Accordingly, the strategy of *dollar lobbying* has come to play a pivotal role in preserving the farm bloc's power. Through their PACs, both the umbrella and crop and commodity lobbying groups provide policymakers with a variety of in-kind services such as campaign assistance and free surveys. But the staple of dollar lobbying is still campaign contributions, and these flow in the millions from farm PAC coffers. For example, in documenting "Ag-PAC" contributions to the 97th Congress, Common Cause reported such large sums as $17,950 to Senate majority leader Howard Baker and $21,550 to farm state Senator Alan Cranston of California, while most contributions fell in the $5000 to 10,000 range.[30]

Perhaps the most fiscally promiscuous of the farm PACs are those representing the "most firmly established of all farm organizations,"[31] the formidable dairy lobby. Consider the following boast (cited in a *Wall Street Journal* article) of a milk lobbyist:

> *Associated Milk Producers, Inc., a dairy-farmer cooperative with just 33,000 members, controls one of the richest of all PACs. AMPI gave $1.1 million this 1982 election, and then issued a news release saying 92% of the candidates it backed were elected. "The great majority of U.S. Congressional districts have no significant milk production," AMPI said. But "dairy farmers have proved that they can make substantial impact nationwide on the decision-making process."*[32]

The dairy lobby's past contributions to presidential candidates illustrate not only the effectiveness of dollar lobbying, but also how it is sometimes indistinguishable from the strategy of questionable payments and the tactic of bribery. In 1971, the Nixon White House revised a ruling by its own DOA and increased dairy supports by $300 million a year. A $400,000 campaign contribution to reelect Nixon followed shortly. In a case more suggestive of nefarious activity, Special Watergate Prosecutor Archibald Cox uncovered a letter from the dairy lobby to President Nixon suggesting that a $2 million campaign contribution could be had if import quotas on certain dairy products were imposed. As Edwin

---

*PACs are discussed in Chapter 5 in the general discussion of dollar lobbying.

reports, Nixon set quotas on ice cream, certain chocolate products, animal feeds containing milk derivatives, and low-fat cheeses two weeks later. This was followed by his order to raise the government support price for milk by 27¢ for a hundred pounds.[33]

While these strategies and tactics help to explain at least part of the political power wielded by the farm lobby, they do not fully explain how it has managed to garner political support on Capitol Hill in far greater proportion than its small numbers. Farmers, after all, comprise less than 3 percent of the population. In the House, the number of representatives from districts in which over 20 percent or more of the population live on farms has dwindled from 251 of the 435 seats in 1928, to about 30 today.[34]

One answer lies in the fact that the small number of farm representatives in the House has no parallel in the Senate, where representation is based on geography rather than population. But another answer to the power of the farm bloc is a final strategy, that of coalition building and the associated tactic of logrolling. While the recent assaults of the Reagan administration have created stresses and cracks within the farm bloc, diverse farming interests in the different farm states historically have cooperated to get individual pieces of the farm program—peanut, milk, wheat, corn, rice, and tobacco supports—passed as part of an overall farm bill. For example, congressmen from tobacco state North Carolina will vote favorably on wheat and dairy price supports with the expectation that congressmen from Kansas and Wisconsin will in turn vote favorably on tobacco.

Nor is this behavior limited to politicians from the big agricultural states. As McCune has observed: "The notion that the farm bloc is a group of willful Western and Southern congressmen is a fallacy. When a legislative crisis impends it is the votes of congressmen from Eastern and Northern states, who also have rural constituents, that put the farm bloc over to its accustomed victory."[35]

But perhaps the most important logrollers are the "food stamp" congressmen who represent inner-city districts where welfare is as much a way of life to the urban poor as price supports are to rural farmers. As Hyde H. Murray has observed, there is an alliance "between farm and nonfarm groups, associating a generous food stamp program with high farm supports in a log-rolling operation."[36] This farm belt–food stamp coalition played its first major role in 1964 when Southern and Midwestern Democrats made a deal with urban Democrats who wanted a food stamp bill and won passage of legislation that subsidized cotton mills and maintained high wheat price supports.[37] The farm lobby likewise has sometimes drawn Big Labor into a coalition. For example, when farm interests agreed to limit state discretion on right-to-work laws, this helped to garner labor's vote for passage of the Food and Agriculture Act of 1965.[38]

3. The Farm Lobby's Opponents. For their part, the apparent victims of high price supports—consumers, taxpayers, and food middlemen—have not been able, at least in the past, to muster either the organization or the political muscle to defeat the farm bloc. Their ineffectiveness is not surprising. A small number of farmers enjoy massive and very concentrated federal benefits, providing them with great incentive to organize. But the costs of these farm programs are diffused over virtually the entire population of taxpayers and consumers so that a few more dollars at tax time and a few more cents on the weekly grocery bill provide little impetus for an organized counterattack.* Nonetheless, as the social costs of farm programs to consumers and taxpayers continue to rise, so too does opposition.

As noted public interest group analyst Jeffrey Berry has observed, organizations like the Center for Science in the Public Interest and the Community Nutrition Service have begun to represent consumer interests more aggressively on Capitol Hill. Like elements of the farm lobby, these groups practice both direct and indirect lobbying strategies, calling on congressmen, testifying, and publishing research and newsletters to alert their members to possible adverse legislation. However, these groups are no match for the farm bloc in the realm of dollar lobbying and, like most public interest groups, contribute very little to political candidates.

The same cannot be said for the farm middlemen and the large bulk of commercial consumers and food processors, who have become increasingly militant. In recent years, groups representing restaurants, food processors, and candy and dessert manufacturers have entered the political arena to challenge the high price supports that drive up their costs and cut into their profit margins. One noted example of this new coun-

---

*Recall that this was also the situation with protectionism. (See Chapter 4.)

tervailing force is provided by the lobbying of Pizza Hut, which relies heavily on dairy products to produce its pizzas. In 1981 it fought the dairy lobby's efforts to raise dairy price supports and restrict the importation of casein, a milk derivative often used in the making of pizza cheese. In testimony on Capitol Hill and through an aggressive public relations campaign, Pizza Hut led a successful challenge against the restrictions, which would have raised the chain's costs substantially.[39]

4. Conclusions about Simple Capture. Despite occasional signs of backlash against the farm lobby, the preceding description of it (and its associated strategies and tactics) provides a fairly convincing picture that this policy game appears to be the creation of farm lobbyists who have captured the government. Holding taxpayers and consumers hostage, they enjoy high price supports and supply controls to enrich themselves.

There are, however, some disquieting statistics that throw this slightly too neat picture out of focus. For one, despite the billions of dollars of support that farmers receive each year, average farm income continues to be depressed, and rural poverty remains an endemic and epidemic problem in our country. Farm bankruptcies continue to occur at a fast pace and the farm population continues to shrink. Finally, as we shall see, the majority of farmers don't really enjoy most of the benefits of farm programs. These signs all suggest that there is something more than simple capture going on and that ideological considerations may also play a role.

B. The Public Interest View

The liberal argument for comprehensive intervention in the farm market begins with the presumption that, left to its own devices, a free market in farm goods simply won't work. The nature of this market failure is a chronic boom and bust cycle in which farmers first overproduce, depress farm prices and income, and drive some of their lot out of business. Then, as production is cut back (or bad weather or pests strike unexpectedly), farmers underproduce, create shortages, and make food prices and inflation skyrocket. Thus, rather than producing an adequate supply of food and fiber at affordable and stable prices, a free market leads to volatile prices and chronic gluts and shortages, a situation in which both consumers and farmers are worse off.

Conservatives don't necessarily dispute the instability of the free farm market. Rather, the ideological disagreement lies in the approach taken to correct the failure. While liberals often favor the planning approach of high, fixed price supports calibrated on the income yardstick of parity for farmers, conservatives favor more market-oriented measures such as target pricing based on market forces.

At the same time, conservatives generally prefer that the secretary of agriculture rather than Congress implement measures such as setting price support levels. This republican preference (in the ideological, not the party sense)* rests on the premise that the secretary is both better informed and, as an appointed rather than an elected official, less exposed to political pressure than the typical congressman. Accordingly, he is more likely to take actions in the public interest than Congress, which is more vulnerable to the "democratic rabble" of farm interests.

Liberals also view the support-supply control program as a means to redistribute income more equitably between the rural poor and the rest of the nation. To liberals, a free farm market would tend to depress farm prices and incomes, which would only further distort an already unequal, and therefore inequitable, distribution of income. Price supports premised on the income-based measure of parity are particularly important to the liberal in effecting the desired redistribution.

However, conservatives reject this rather large redistribution of income from taxpayers and consumers to the farm community on the grounds that it is a subtle and unacceptable assault on property rights and a dangerous expansion of the welfare state. Target pricing (or the abolition of price supports) is more in keeping with the conservative's minimal state.

The third strand of the ideological split over farm policy revolves around one of America's most sacred of cows, the family farm. From the days of Thomas Jefferson, the liberal has assigned the nation's small family farm an important role in lending stability, decency, dignity, and industriousness to the American character.[40] To the liberal, the tendency of the free farm market to put the family farmer out of business thus

---

*The republican preferences of conservatives are discussed in more detail in the Chapter 9 analysis of traditional conservatism versus modern liberalism.

weakens the national fabric, a weakening that price supports help to brake, if not prevent.

While the conservative may also recognize the value of a strong family farm community and mourn the passing of the family farm, he is mindful that the building block of that community is the individual farmer. And he fears that massive government "welfare" in the form of high price supports will weaken the backbone and good judgment of that rugged individual.

At the same time, his view of the modern farmer is far less pastoral than his Jeffersonian counterpart: Where the liberal sees a traditional tower of strength in the sunburned farmer riding a tractor, the conservative sees a more modern "captain of industry" directing mechanized combines from an air-conditioned, computerized control room. To the conservative, the larger and more modern the farm, the lower the cost of production and the higher the yield. He sees this as a necessary market evolution in a world of explosive population growth, where the shift from a small cohesive farm community to more efficient and productive corporate farms is essential to feed a hungry world.

C. The Politics of Farm Policy: A Statistical Test

In assessing the politics of farm policy, the capture-ideology framework was used to examine Senate voting on the two largest price support programs, grain (including wheat, corn, feed grains, and rice) and dairy.[41] Following our standard approach, a number of measures were constructed to reflect the degree of economic or political influence that the major special interest players in the farm policy game are likely to exert on a senator's voting behavior.

For example, the political clout of grain and dairy farmers was measured by the value of these commodities relative to a state's total personal income, with a high value denoting a grain or dairy state. At the same time, the economic influence or "dollar lobbying" of grain and dairy interests was reflected in a variable measuring their PAC contributions.

Similarly, the power of the food stamp lobby was reflected in state per-capita food stamp expenditures while a "logrolling" variable reflecting a state's dependence on agricultural output *other than* grain or dairy was included to see whether sugar, tobacco, peanut, and other farming interests voted as a bloc on individual pieces of the total farm price support system.

Besides these special interest measures, the ideology of each senator was measured by his or her rating (on a 0–100 scale) by the liberal Americans for Democratic Action, with a high ADA rating indicating a liberal and a low ADA rating indicating a conservative.

These special interest and ideology measures were fed into a computer and a common statistical procedure was used to determine their relative importance in influencing senate voting on grain and dairy price supports.

In a world of pure ideology in which U.S. senators act to promote their conception of the public interest, we would expect conservative senators to consistently vote against grain and dairy price supports, regardless of the number of grain or dairy farmers in their states and irrespective of any campaign contribution from farm PACs. We would likewise expect liberal senators to vote for grain and dairy price supports even if grain and dairy production in their states is low and even if they do not receive any dollar lobbying inducements from farm PACs.

But in a world of pure private interest politics, we should observe conservative senators from grain or dairy states captured by their constituencies consistently voting for grain or dairy price supports while evidence of "PAC capture" will likewise be indicated if conservative senators with large grain or dairy PAC contributions vote for supports. (This evidence will be all the more damning if the senator comes from a nonfarm state.)

TABLE 6.2.   THE INFLUENCE OF SPECIAL INTERESTS AND
IDEOLOGY IN THE FARM POLICY GAME[a]

Voting for Grain Subsidies	Voting for Dairy Price Supports
Rank	*Rank*
1. Ideology	1. Ideology
2. Grain producers	2. Milk producers
3. The food stamp lobby	3. The food stamp lobby
4. Grain PACs	4. Logrolling farm interests
5. Logrolling farm interests	5. Dairy PACs

[a]Ideally, measures of consumer, food middlemen, taxpayer, research establishment, and government lobby interests should also have been included in the test. However, in this particular case, there was insufficient data to represent these interests and their influence must remain conjectural.

The results of the test, presented in Table 6.2, rank each of the various measures of special interests and ideology by their statistical importance* and illustrate that both ideology *and* special interests play important roles in the determination of farm policy.

From the table, it appears that ideology is the most important predictor of a senator's vote on both grain and dairy supports; according to the test, its influence is roughly twice that of the next important measure. This statistical conclusion is reinforced by some rather interesting observations about some of the senate's leading conservatives and liberals.

For example, in the votes examined, liberals like Colorado's Gary Hart and Michigan's Carl Levin consistently voted with their ideology and for dairy supports despite low dairy output in their states and low dairy PAC contributions; conservatives similarly insulated from dairy lobby pressures like Arizona's Barry Goldwater, Texan John Tower, and Wyoming's Alan Simpson and Malcolm Wallop regularly opposed them.

The *real* test of "pure ideology" comes, however, when conservatives find themselves serving a farm constituency or taking large farm PAC dollars. In these circumstances, perhaps the most striking example of ideological purity is found in the voting behavior of conservative senators from the epicenter of the nation's grain belt. Idaho's James McClure and Steve Symms, Iowa's Roger Jepsen and Charles Grassley, and Kansas's Bob Dole all regularly score in the teens or below on the ADA rating scale. Despite the heavy reliance of their states on grain production, each consistently voted the conservative position, that is, against grain price supports.

This ideological behavior is, however, in sharp contrast to the voting patterns of four other conservative senators apparently captured by their grain belt constituencies. Indeed, while South Dakota's James Abdnor and Larry Pressler, North Dakota's Mark Andrews, and Nebraska's Edward Zorinsky all have solid conservative credentials, each, with a large grain producer constituency, consistently voted *for* grain supports.[42]

Evidence of constituency capture is likewise apparent in dairy voting. With a large dairy farm constituency complementing their grain farm interests, the South Dakota "conservative" contingent of Abdnor and Pressler can again be seen voting for price supports. An even more

*The full results are provided in Appendix A.

striking example of abandoned ideology is evident in dairy-rich Wisconsin where ultraconservative Robert Kasten regularly pulls down ADA ratings close to zero but consistently votes for dairy supports. Thus it is hardly surprising that the second most important predictors of senate voting for grain and dairy supports are the measures of grain and dairy producers.

Whither PAC power? At least in the case of farm policy, senators do seem somewhat more resistant to PAC capture and dollar lobbying. This is evidenced by the rather weak performance of both the grain and, perhaps surprisingly, the dairy PAC measures. But again, observation of senatorial behavior reinforces this conclusion: Both Senate Majority Leader Howard Baker of Tennessee and Utah's Jake Garn, for example, were on the receiving end of considerable farm PAC money (particularly from the well-heeled dairy PACs) but these funds didn't seem to have altered their conservative propensity to reject supports. In a contrast that helps, however, to explain the weak statistical influence of the PACs, conservative senators like Rudy Boschwitz of Minnesota and the aforementioned Pressler of South Dakota not only have a significant dairy farmer constituency but they have also been the beneficiaries of substantial dairy PAC contributions: Both consistently voted for dairy supports.*

As a final comment on the politics of farm policy, the results in Table 6.2 seem to confirm two additional points made in this chapter. One is that in both the grain and dairy votes, the food stamp lobby places a respectable third in explanatory importance, suggesting that food stamp interests have indeed entered into a coalition with farm producers. Similarly, the performance of the logrolling measure suggests, albeit weakly, that farm interests tend to vote for each other's separate support programs.

In summary, the politics of farm policy provide us with a picture similar to the one painted for protectionism: While public interested ideological behavior has played an important role, farm price supports are also very much a special interest policy game. In the next section, we examine the economic consequences of this political reality.

---

*Over the last three electoral cycles, Boschwitz received roughly $12,000 from the dairy PACs while Pressler received approximately $16,000. Since the newly elected Pressler was present for only one of these cycles, this amount is particularly large.

III.   THE ECONOMICS OF FARM POLICY

A.   The Costs of Current Farm Policy

The *costs to taxpayers* that result from current farm policy are the most obvious and readily calculable. Each year, the support-supply control program transfers anywhere from $4 billion to, more recently, $18 billion to farmers through direct payments and nonrecourse loan provisions.[43] Another $51 million is spent by the government to administer the program, while the storage, handling, and transport of surpluses generated by price supports costs another $376 million.[44]

The *costs to consumers* arise from the effects the support-supply control program has on crop and commodity prices. To the extent that supply controls actually reduce the quantities of marketed crops and commodities available, the prices that consumers pay rise through the laws of supply and demand. Various economists over the past decade, including Charles Schultze, D. Gale Johnson, and Bruce Gardner, have estimated these consumer costs at about $5 billion annually.[45]

The *costs to the nation* arise in three major areas. The first involves the general allocative and technical inefficiencies that result from distorting price signals. An *allocative inefficiency* arises when price supports are set above market prices and thereby provide farmers with incentives to produce *more* than the market will bear. If supply controls are inadequate, as they have historically been, the inevitable result is huge farm surpluses. In the most literal sense, these sitting surpluses are a nonproductive deadweight loss of billions of dollars to the nation's economy.*

A *technical inefficiency* arises when high price supports make it profitable for farmers to increase their capital investments in fertilizers, pesticides, and farm machinery and when land rationing stimulates technological developments to boost yields through such breakthroughs as new seed varieties. The result is that farmers adopt far more capital-intensive and technologically advanced production processes than they would have in the absence of federal programs, and the nation winds up with too much investment in the farm sector and too little investment in the nonfarm economy.[46] To understand the costs of this technical ineffi-

*The concept of deadweight loss was explained in Chapter 4.

ciency, simply imagine what the nonfarm economy could have produced—more factories, jobs, goods, and services—if it had taken that portion of the invested farm capital that has generated the huge surplus of farm goods and used it instead for more productive purposes.

A second cost to the nation of farm programs involves *erosion* and *depletion* of one of America's greatest treasures, its incredibly rich soil. Agricultural experts estimate that our topsoil is being eroded at the rate of six billion tons per year,[47] a pace far faster than the earth's natural ability to regenerate topsoil. To the extent price supports result in overproduction, soil depletion occurs at a faster pace. At the same time, the supply-control system encourages both depletion and erosion because it locks farmers into producing only one major crop, year in and year out, on the same land. This "monoculture syndrome" is particularly evident in the corn belt where erosion has been severe, but it also affects farmers of other soil-depleting crops such as tobacco. In the absence of price supports, farmers would respond more to the market by planting different crops; for example, if the outlook for soybeans was good, some cornfields might be diverted to soybean production.

A final cost to the nation involves a *reduction in farm exports* and resultant *inflation*. Each year, farm goods account for about 16 percent of all our exports and, as the single largest source of foreign exchange, are worth over $44 billion.[48] As such, they are an important way for the nation to reduce its balance of payments deficit. However, to the extent that support-supply control programs drive up prices, and other countries sell their farm products more cheaply than the U.S., our exports are reduced. If our balance of payments is then in deficit (a result of importing more than we export), there is greater downward pressure on the dollar, which can in turn generate inflation.

B. The Benefits of Current Farm Policy

Given these substantial costs, one would expect that the farmers would reap substantial benefits. Surprisingly, this is not the case; only a small segment of farm interests—mainly large, upper-income farmers and landlords—actually gain from the programs, while the majority of farmers are at best untouched and at worst deeply hurt. Moreover, the support programs do not further the liberal goals of preserving the family farm and creating a more equitable distribution of income. In fact, they have speeded the exodus of farm labor and the demise of the family farm. Let's see how this works.

1. The Level of Farm Income.   While billions of dollars in gross benefits are transferred to the farm sector each year, as much as half of these subsidies are dissipated before they ever reach the farmer. One reason benefits are dissipated is that farmers must actually forego production, and therefore income, to be eligible for subsidies. Thus part of the subsidies don't represent *additional* income, but rather, *replacement* income for the production foregone.[49] But the biggest part of the dissipation problem is that most of the benefits of government subsidies are "capitalized" into the value of the land.[50]

Although the capitalization concept is a tricky one, it is crucial in understanding some of the more perverse effects that farm programs generate. In a nutshell, the capitalization of farm subsidies refers to the increase in land values that results from these government programs. The difference in land values with and without programs arises because under federal programs, the crop or commodity grown on that land will fetch a higher price. Consequently, farmers or landlords bid more for the right to own and use that land.

For example, suppose you own 50 acres of prime farmland in North Carolina, and its market value is $5,000 per acre in the absence of any federal acreage allotment permitting you to grow tobacco. Now suppose instead that you had a tobacco allotment that allowed you to grow the leaf without breaking the law. Because of the opportunity to grow part of the limited supply of tobacco, the value of your land could be as much as $2,000 more per acre.[51]

The capitalization phenomenon is in large part reflected in the dramatic increase in the price of farmland since the 1950s. Between 1953 and 1971, the acreage value of farm real estate rose 142 percent.[52] From 1973 to 1978, alone, this figure more than doubled.[53] The capitalization phenomenon in turn has important long-term effects on a number of the liberal's goals for farm policy.

First, because over two-fifths of the nation's crop acreage is farmed by renters, tenant farmers don't benefit at all from the subsidies. Instead, they merely pay their landlords higher rent to reflect the increase in land values. The result is that government subsidies may make the ownership of farmland profitable, but farming is not necessarily so.

Second, the capitalization of land values actually reduces the number of family farms because it increases their ownership "startup" costs. As economist Howard Hjort has argued, the hyperinflation of farmland values makes it difficult for the young farmer to get a start. Instead, the capitalization phenomenon lends itself more to corporate and landlord farming, both of which run contrary to liberal goals.[54]

Finally, the capitalization phenomenon creates a vicious upward spiral: to the extent that the value of government subsidies is imputed to land, future farmers bear higher costs and will therefore need higher prices to remain solvent.[55] Thus, while capitalization creates "a windfall for those who own land when the capitalization takes place . . . it raises production costs for subsequent owners."[56]

2.   The Distribution of Farm Subsidies.   Ironically, the distribution of benefits that remains after dissipation is skewed towards large, upper-income farmers. This inequitable redistribution can be demonstrated in a number of ways.

Looking at the *size* of the government payment, economist D. Gale Johnson has found that payments are most unequally distributed under the cotton program, where only 2.6 percent of the farms receive 38 percent of the benefits of support programs. Similarly, under the feed grain program (corn, sorghum), 10.8 percent of the farms receive 42.4 percent of the payments, while with the wheat program, 4 percent of the farms receive 32 percent of the payments.[57]

Alternatively, comparing payments on the basis of farm sales, Johnson likewise found that the 8.8 percent of farms with sales of $40,000 or more receive 34.5 percent of the direct government subsidies, while 59.3 percent of payments go to the 21.5 percent of farm operators with sales of $20,000 or more (the income of these farms is well above the national average).[58]

Moreover, farm programs do not equitably transfer income from high-income urban consumers and taxpayers to low-income small farmers.[59] Rather, as both Luther Tweeten and Charles Schultze have illustrated, "there is a redistribution of income from lower income people, in general—not just farm people, but throughout society—to high-income farms through commodity programs via price and tax increases brought about by these programs."[60]

3.   The Effect on Farm Labor.   While price support programs have contributed to the demise of the family farm through the capitalization effect on land values, the supply control programs have likewise speeded up the exodus of labor from the farm community through their effect on the production process. As discussed earlier, the rationing of land through supply control restrictions, coupled with high price supports, has encouraged the rapid introduction of more capital-intensive new seed varieties, fertilizers, insecticides, herbicides, and mechanical methods of production. These technological changes have caused a sharp reduction in both the numbers of farms and farmers. As economic simulations of the farm economy with and without these controls clearly indicate: "There would have been more labor in agriculture with a free market than with the government programs, price supports and supply controls that were in effect."[61]

4. Short- Versus Long-Run Price Effects. As a final perverse effect of current policy on farmers, it is worthwhile to examine the controversy over the short- versus long-run price effects of these programs. Recall that in measuring the costs to consumers of farm programs, it was found that the support programs raised prices, at least in the *short* run. However, economists are in some disagreement as to whether these programs actually prop up prices (and therefore farm income) over the *long* run. In fact, many argue that the current policies do not raise, but ironically actually reduce, long-run farm prices and income.

To understand this depressive effect on farm prices and income, we need only remember that one of the major effects of the support program has been to stimulate overinvestment, and as a result overproduction, in the farm sector. The burden of this overcapacity and attendant surpluses on farm markets translates into chronically depressed farm prices that the support programs only partially offset. In fact, economists Frederick Nelson and Willard Cochrane have found strong support for this effect.[62]

IV. POLICY REFORMS

The price support and supply control programs that dominate U.S. farm policy appear to have imposed substantially greater costs on taxpayers, consumers, and the nation than the benefits that are received by farmers. Further, roughly half of the gross payments to farmers are dissipated, while many of the remaining benefits show up not as higher income to farmers but as higher land values and rents for farm landlords (the "capitalization effect"). This capitalization phenomenon in turn works contrary to the liberal goal of preserving the family farm and instead encourages more corporate and landlord farming.

At the same time, government subsidies do not benefit the broad farm community proportionally, but instead are skewed toward a small subset of large, upper-income farmers. Moreover, part of the burden of net redistribution to these wealthier farmers is borne by lower-income taxpayers and consumers so that the liberal goal of a more equitable distribution of income is again thwarted.

Finally, the support programs appear to have accelerated the exodus of farm labor by encouraging more capital-intensive agricultural methods, while they may also have actually reduced long-run farm prices and incomes.

The inevitable conclusion one can draw from this survey is that the only real winners in the farm policy game are a small number of large, primarily corporate farmers and farm landlords. The rest of the farm community appears to lose along with taxpayers, consumers, and the nation, as do liberals who have clung to current farm policies. But how do we play this policy game better so that there are more winners?

A.   Price Support Reforms

Because it has been demonstrated since the 1930s that high price supports based on the parity income standard simply don't work, the evolution to more market-oriented supports, which began with target pricing in the Agriculture and Consumer Protection Act of 1973, should continue. Following the intent of this act, the price support level should be flexible, linked to market prices, and should not rise too far above market prices. Moreover, as surpluses rise, the support level should fall. While this type of price support system will foster a more efficient farm sector, it does not solve the perennial questions of equity and redistribution that farm programs are meant to address.

With regard to equity, the crucial political problem is for farmers and ideological interests to agree on a "fair" level of farm income. Once this is decided, a better way to ensure that farmers receive that level of income than price supports would be a system of *direct cash payments*. In fact, an income standard based on the difference between farmers' market income and that fair income level was actually proposed in 1949 by then-Secretary of Agriculture Charles Brannan, but its "giveaway" nature met with nonpartisan derision and it was rejected.[63] Today, however, many farm groups, policymakers, and economists believe that providing cash directly to farmers would be cheaper than paying that money indirectly through farm programs.

Similarly, should it be deemed desirable to redistribute income to the rural poor, this can be done more effectively through a *negative income tax* or some other general income maintenance program. This would ensure that farmers received the income without overstimulating the production process.

B. Supply Control Reforms

With any supply control program, the incentive to overcapitalize is perhaps unavoidable. However, more market-oriented price supports should mute this stimulus. At the same time, more cost-effective and strict methods of removing acreage from production can be pursued.

One such reform would be to *remove the geographical restrictions* from current supply controls. Under present policy, acreage is removed uniformly across the nation, regardless of the relative productivity of the land. A more efficient way to do this, which would both lower the cost per acre to the government of reducing production (and help with the problem of erosion), would be to choose the land to be retired in areas where, because of lower yields or high transportation costs, that land is less economically productive. The gains to be realized from such a reform are considerable. According to economists Ashok Chowdhury and Earl O. Heady, it could save over a billion dollars a year and cut government costs for land diversion by more than half.[64]

A similar reform would be to use a *sealed bid* system to achieve land diversion. This would allow the government "to discriminate among bids, paying only the amount necessary to retire land from production and selecting those bids that remove most production per program dollar."[65]

C. The Decapitalization Obstacle

While the preceding reforms would make the nation better off, one of the major political obstacles to such reforms is that they threaten to make the owners of farm land suddenly worse off through a "decapitalization effect." Recalling that most of the benefits of farm programs are capitalized into land values, it follows that any reduction in these benefits would result in a substantial reduction (decapitalization) of land values. For example, J. L. Hedrick found that abandoning tobacco programs would reduce the rental value of tobacco land by 85 percent,[66] while D. Gale Johnson concluded that eliminating "all forms of protection to U.S. agriculture will result in a reduction in land values of 30–50 billion dollars."[67]

Obviously, then, this decapitalization effect is an important political consideration which, at least in the past, has been "an excuse or a rationalization for continuing the farm programs whether or not any basis exists."[68] Thus, in the name of both equity and political pragmatism, one additional policy measure to accompany these reforms would be for the federal government to provide farmers a *one-time lump sum payment* equal to the loss in land value that reforming current policy would entail. While such payments would involve a significant one-time cost to the treasury, nonetheless, they would be far less than the cumulative costs now imposed annually on the nation.

D.   Whither the Family Farm?

The issue of preserving the family farm will not be resolved here. But it is clear that current policy does not further, and indeed takes us farther from, that goal. It is equally clear that even in the absence of present farm policy, an exploding world population and an accelerating technology have made the large corporate farm the wave of the future. When assessing whether we can afford the luxury of the family farm, we might keep in mind the following analogy offered by Glenn L. Johnson:

> For a long while, people in this country worried about the replacement of the family-operated "pop and mom" grocery stores by chain stores. However, pop and mom were finally replaced (although not entirely) for the most part by supermarket workers and managers. Since we cannot see how the moral fiber and other aspects of American society were damaged by this transition, we cannot conclude, a priori, that American society would necessarily be damaged by a restructuring of our agricultural society to put agricultural production in the hands of input suppliers or processors, distributors, or corporate owners.[69]

E. Conclusions

The above analysis illustrates that we can indeed play the farm policy game far better, and our capture-ideology framework provides us once again with a lever for constructive change.

The obvious losers in this game—food consumers and taxpayers—must become more sensitized to the billions of dollars that farm programs are costing. In turn, they must express their dissatisfaction more vocally, both through individual actions like letters to congressmen and through collective action such as greater participation in (or financial support of) consumer and taxpayer groups.

At the same time, the subtle losers in this game—small farmers, the rural poor, and ideological liberals—must realize that current policy is perversely working against their welfare and goals. Such an acknowledgment will deprive the small group of corporate farmers of the political support they desperately need to continue feathering their own nests at the expense of the nation.

Part 3

America's Ideologies

$\mathbf{W}$hile America may harbor its share of fascists and reactionaries on the Right and radicals and revolutionaries on the Left, the two dominant American ideologies are conservatism and liberalism. In this part, we take a closer look at the eight contrasting principles of these two ideologies within the context of a demonstrable "logic of ideology."

Chapter 7 introduces this logic and indicates why it is useful to make a conceptual distinction between the three strands of modern conservatism: "libertarian," "traditionalist," and "fusionist". The three principles of libertarian conservatism are then contrasted with three essentially mirror-image principles of modern liberalism. Chapter 8 highlights several of these principles in a case on electric utility regulation.

In a similar fashion, Chapter 9 contrasts the four principles of traditional (or "Burkean") conservatism with liberalism while Chapter 10 applies several of these principles in a case on the Equal Rights Amendment.

Finally, Chapter 11's defense policy game highlights the eighth "fusionist" principle, which separates conservatives and liberals at the same time that it has united libertarian and traditional conservatives.

7

The Logic of Ideology

LIBERTARIAN CONSERVATISM VERSUS MODERN LIBERALISM

I. THE LOGIC OF IDEOLOGY

The logic of ideology is a three-link chain that begins in a set of values as well as certain assumptions and beliefs about the nature of people and their roles in society. From these values, beliefs, and assumptions follow a set of eight principles that form the core of the conservative-liberal debate. Out of these principles emerges the final link in the chains of liberalism and conservatism: different preferences about what the outcome of the policy game should be.

For example, the high value that the conservative puts on individual liberty, coupled with his* belief that Big Government is the single greatest threat to liberty, contribute to his preference for a "minimal state" in which the functions and size of government are severely limited. This minimal state principle, in turn, is reflected in a wide range of policy preferences, ranging from across-the-board budget cuts to the targeted elimination of specific programs.

In contrast, the high value the liberal places on community, coupled with his belief that good government has the responsibility of making

---

*My apologies for relying heavily on the convenient "his" and "he" as proxies for his/her and he/she in Chapters 7 and 9.

sure that everyone has a job, food, clothing, and shelter, contribute to his preference for a "welfare state."* This welfare state principle crystallizes in liberal support for policies ranging from general budget increases for social spending to the maintenance and expansion of programs like food stamps and Medicare.

For most people, this logic of ideology has long been internalized and lies submerged in the subconscious. As a result, the major emphasis in the conservative-liberal debate is the last link in the chain of logic, policy choices. However, by exposing the roots of modern conservatism and liberalism, it is possible to gain not only a better understanding of the sense—and at times the nonsense—of the two competing doctrines, but also a more clear rationale for how relying on either one of these ideologies will lead, as their adherents promise, to the "good society."

Before presenting this logic of ideology, however, we should confront a major confusion that has historically surrounded the use—and occasional abuse—of the conservative and liberal labels. This confusion arises because the term liberal once was associated with a number of principles that are today generally recognized as conservative.

Specifically, "classical" or "Manchester" liberalism, which was the prevailing ideology in both eighteenth-century England and nineteenth-century America, placed its highest value on individual freedom and saw a system of free markets, inviolable property rights, and limited government as the best means of assuring that freedom. These Manchester liberal principles have since been embraced by what is now called the "libertarian" wing of modern conservatism. This accounts for the tendency of many libertarian conservatives such as Milton Friedman and Friedrich Hayek to refer to themselves as liberals, rather than what they apparently regard as the pejorative "conservative."

In addition to libertarian conservatism there also is a "traditional" conservatism that has its roots in the nineteenth-century philosophy of Sir Edmund Burke of England. This traditional or Burkean brand of conservatism stresses such factors as the stabilizing role of institutions like the family and the church, the wisdom and importance of tradi-

---

*The term "welfare state" should not be interpreted to mean an entire nation is "on the dole." Rather, the term is used to describe a typically non-Communist egalitarian state that substantially intervenes in economic and social affairs to provide economic security for its citizens.[1]

TABLE 7.1.   THE EIGHT MAJOR PRINCIPLES OF THE
CONSERVATIVE–LIBERAL DEBATE

Conservatism	Liberalism
1. Free-market economy	Regulated and planned economy
2. Property rights	Redistribution
3. Minimal state	Welfare state
4. Traditionalism	Experimentalism
5. Law and order	Due process
6. Republicanism	Democratism
7. States' rights	Federalism
8. Nationalistic anti- Communism	International globalism

tions in protecting the "delicate fabric" of society, and the need for law and order.

Table 7.1 lists the eight principles of the conservative–liberal debate.* Of those in the left-hand column comprising modern conservatism, the first three—a free-market economy, property rights, and the minimal state—are loosely clustered around libertarian conservatism. The four following principles—traditionalism, law and order, republicanism, and states' rights—are more closely identified (but again loosely) with traditional or Burkean conservatism.

The degree to which the two types of conservatism value each of these first seven principles has created considerable tension within the conservative movement.[2] For example, the libertarian conservative's commitment to a minimal government often clashes head-on with the traditional conservative's longing for law and order, while the traditional conservative's reverence for institutions makes him a bit less fearful of Big Government than his libertarian cousin.

It is the eighth principle in the conservative catechism, nationalistic anti-Communism, which has been credited by many scholars as being the catalyst for the "fusion" of the two conservatisms. The fusionist argument is that there has always been more kinship than contradiction between libertarian and traditional conservatism and with the coming of

*My thanks to George Lodge whose book *The New American Ideology* (New York: Alfred A. Knopf, 1975) suggested organizing the conservative–liberal debate around a set of contrasting principles.

the Cold War in the 1950s, the jointly perceived "Communist threat" was sufficient to unite the two wings in a common defense of their collective principles.[3]

Whether or not the two conservatisms have been truly reconciled, it is clear that *modern* conservatives take from both wings in evincing their principles. For instance, Barry Goldwater has railed against the dangers of Big Government at the same time that he has supported large increases in the government budget for defense spending. Similarly, Ronald Reagan has called on both the libertarian's free market to solve economic problems and the traditionalist's family and church to help mitigate social problems, while William Buckley, who has been called the epitome of the fusionist, has warned against the dangers of the "Leviathan state" in the same breath that he has concluded we would "have to acquiesce in the big government required to defeat Communism."[4]

It is this eclecticism that explains many of the inconsistencies and occasional waffling of modern conservatives on issues like abortion, no-knock laws, and the draft, where libertarian laissez-faire clashes with the traditionalist's family, neighborhood, and defense needs. But despite these inconsistencies, here we accept the fusionist argument that while both the libertarian and traditional wings of conservatism are different enough to identify, they have enough affinity for one another (and enough antithesis with liberalism) so that it is both useful and possible to group the two ideological factions under a common banner and contrast them with modern liberalism.

II. LIBERTARIAN CONSERVATISM VERSUS MODERN LIBERALISM

In our previous chapters on rent control, protectionism, and farm policy, one or more of the first three principles of the conservative–liberal split lay embedded in the public interest arguments over these policies. For example, the conservative's free-market preferences helped lead him to oppose rent controls, protective tariffs, and farm price supports, while the liberal's commitment to a more equal distribution of income helped lead him to support these policies. Here, we take a more systematic look at the logic of these three principles—a free market versus a regulated and planned economy, property rights versus redistribution, and the minimal versus welfare state—and their more general policy implications.

A. A Free Market Versus a Regulated and Planned Economy

In the economic arena, America's ideology wars begin—and often end—with the fierce battle over a free market versus a regulated and planned economy.

1. The Conservative Free Market Economy.

Laissez-faire *should be the general practice: every departure from it, unless required by some great good, is a certain evil.*[5]

JOHN STUART MILL

The conservative's free-market preference begins in his belief in "consumer sovereignty," that each individual is the best judge of his needs and is capable of expressing his preferences in the marketplace. Like his intellectual forefather Adam Smith, the conservative also puts great faith in the market's "invisible hand" to meet consumers' needs with the widest possible choices. He sees this invisible hand channeling the aggressive and competitive behavior of selfish buyers and sellers into a happy and harmonious result for society: Through "natural laws" like supply equals demand, this invisible hand guides America's scarce resources into their best possible uses. The unfettered economy responds by producing the most goods and services possible. This *efficient* outcome is the primary benefit of the free market and it follows that any attempt to interfere with this miraculous process—by tampering with prices or imposing unnecessary regulations—can only reduce this efficiency and prosperity.

At the same time, the conservative emphatically rejects the notion that human reason is sufficiently powerful to comprehend and manipulate the economy. Accordingly, it is better to submit to the impersonal forces of the market than to rely on any authoritarian planning system that would come in its place. It likewise follows that the free market is the best economic system to keep Americans free. This "free markets, free men" assumption is embodied in an oft-quoted passage by the dean of free market economists, Milton Friedman:

> No one who buys bread knows whether the wheat from which it was made was grown by a Communist or a Republican, by a Constitutionalist or a Fascist, or, for that matter, by a Negro or a White. This illustrates how an impersonal market separates economic activities from political views and protects men from being discriminated against in their economic activities for reasons that are irrelevant to their productivity—whether these reasons are associated with their views or their color.[6]

Implicit in this free-market faith are two important additional assumptions. The first is that the American economy approximates the workings of the free market; if it could be made even more competitive through fewer regulations and less planning, it would function even better. Second, if left alone, the free market will "self-correct" when problems like unemployment or inflation arise. For example, when there is unemployment in a free market, wages should fall. This, in turn, will lower the costs of goods and people will buy more of them. This stimulus to production results in more jobs and eliminates unemployment.

2. The Liberal Regulated and Planned Economy.

Where is the free-enterprise system? I am trying to find it. Is it the oil oligopoly, protected by import quotas? The shared monopolies in consumer products? The securities market, that bastion of capitalism operating on fixed commissions and now provided with socialized insurance?[7]

RALPH NADER

The liberal's counterpoint preference for a more regulated and planned economy likewise follows logically; but it is a logic rooted in a set of values, beliefs, and assumptions that essentially are a mirror image of the conservative's.

For example, rather than a sovereign consumer, the liberal sees the big corporations dictating what consumers want through persuasive advertising campaigns and the exercise of their monopoly power. The result is an exploitation of the consumer and a collateral inefficiency as billions of dollars are poured into mindless gimmicks, wasteful promotions, and such dubious pursuits as designing sleeker car fins.

At the same time, the liberal is far more skeptical of the alleged benefits of the free-market system and the assumption that the American economy approximates the workings of a free market. As counterpoint to the conservative's characterization of an America bustling with atomistic, hotly competing entrepreneurs, the liberal offers a vision of corporations working in collusion with one another. From this perspective, it follows that the more visible foot of government regulation and planning will be far more effective in promoting efficiency than any blind faith in an invisible hand crippled by oligopolies and monopolies.

The liberal likewise rejects the assertion that the free market is self-correcting: The problems of inflation, unemployment, and lagging productivity won't simply melt away under the competitive heat of market forces. Indeed, in the absence of government planning, he believes that the American economic machinery will suffer recurrent breakdowns—the booms and busts of the business cycle that alternatively bring inflation and recession and, in recent times, one on top of the other. At the same time, the liberal has an abiding faith in the powers of man's reason to not only comprehend but also to solve the economic problems that plague the American economy. As witness to that, he points to the Great Depression and a recovery that was achieved only through the active intervention of the government.

Moreover, the liberal is quick to observe that in the absence of regulations, the free market not only provides ample goods and services, but also ample "bads" in the form of air pollution, hazardous products, dangerous workplaces, and toxic wastes. The existence of these bads—Appalachian coal slag heaps, Los Angeles smog, thalidomide babies—make various regulations necessary to force the business sector to accept the responsibilities—which it would otherwise shirk—of protecting the environment, consumers, and workers.

Finally, the liberal sees the wealth in America as overly concentrated. This creates, in effect, an unfair "monopoly power," which the rich can exert over the poor and which the big corporations can exert over small businesses. Thus, Milton Friedman notwithstanding, there is no personal freedom to be gained from the opportunity to buy from or compete with the corporate giants like Exxon and IBM that dominate the American economy. True individual freedom must entail government regulations, planning, and control of the economy, both to offset the power of the large corporations and to eliminate the monopoly power of the wealthy over the poor.

   3. Free-Market–Regulation Policy Games. In the policy arena, this conflict over free versus regulated markets surfaces primarily in disputes over economic issues. At the microeconomic level where myriad business interests compete, the liberal favors a wide range of "social" regulations, including those governing environmental pollution, auto safety, consumer protection, and ingredient labeling; the conservative is concerned, of course, with reducing such regulations. In this regard, the liberal must fight a constant rear-guard action against a largely conservative-inspired deregulation movement aimed at dismantling traditional regulatory agencies such as those governing railroads, trucks, airlines, and utilities and eliminating specific regulations (e.g., natural gas price controls) and, as we saw in our first three policy games, rent controls, protective tariffs, and farm subsidies.

   At the macroeconomic level, where the problems of inflation and unemployment must be resolved, the liberal supports stimulative government spending ("Keynesian pump-priming") to fight recessions, public works and jobs programs to reduce unemployment, and general wage, price, and credit controls to curb extreme inflation. In contrast, the conservative sees *less* government spending as the cure for macroeconomic ills. If less spending means smaller budget deficits, more resources and credit will be available to the private sector at lower cost. The result will be a renewed private sector investment in new capacity and the creation of new jobs which will be more productive and longer lasting than any "make work" public works programs. At the same time, reduced government spending helps cool inflationary pressures far better than any mechanical controls.

B. Property Rights Versus Redistribution

A second major battle in the ideology wars is fought over the sanctity of property rights versus the need for government redistribution.

1.   The Conservative Commitment to Property Rights.

The great and chief end of men's uniting into commonwealth and putting themselves under government is the preservation of their property.[8]

JOHN LOCKE

The conservative regards the unlimited right to hold property* as the sacred anchor of the American system: Individuals should be allowed to accumulate and use property without restriction so long as they do not hurt anyone or interfere with someone else's property rights. Any attempt by the government to limit or truncate property rights through redistributive taxation, nationalization, or other means is a flagrant violation of individual rights and constitutes nothing short of confiscation.

The conservative's commitment to inviolable property rights begins in his embrace of the philosopher John Locke's notion that people's property is the result of hard work, applied skill, unusual talent, or a combination of these factors and that each person is entitled to the "fruits of his labor." He regards this entitlement as sacrosanct and "one of the foremost precepts of natural law."[9]

The conservative also presupposes a natural and inherent inequality among individuals and believes that the acquisition of property is an important way to mark these differences. Thus an unequal distribution is part of the natural order of things. Accordingly, while the conservative has an unwavering commitment to the equal opportunity of every individual to compete in the economic system, he does not believe that any individual should be guaranteed an actual equality or "equality of result" through redistribution.

More important than these considerations, however, is the conservative's belief that inviolable property rights are essential both for individual freedom and economic prosperity. To the conservative, it is impossible to be free without property because true freedom can never be enjoyed by anyone who must rely on other people or agencies, especially the government, for food and shelter. At the same time, the conservative sees the taking of property for redistributive purposes as a "pun-

---

*"Property" is meant to encompass not only land but all forms of wealth and income such as stocks, bonds, cars, cash, etc.

ishment for success" that destroys the major incentive for productive work. In the modern "supply-side economics" version of this assumption, the logical result is less production in the overall economy and fewer goods and services for all to share.

2.   The Liberal Commitment to Redistribution.

Our community is an association of persons—of human beings—not a partnership founded on property.[10]

DAVID BUEL, JR.

While the modern liberal likewise respects property rights, he also sees government redistribution as sometimes necessary to protect and promote more basic human rights. Such redistribution is not "confiscation," but a legitimate function of government, which is imbued by the requirements of social justice with a responsibility to provide a more equitable—and in this case a more egalitarian—distribution of income.

The liberal's commitment to redistribution begins in a markedly different interpretation of Locke's "fruits of labor" doctrine. Indeed, Locke himself warned that no individual should be allowed to own more property than he can use. According to this "spoilage principle," any surplus should be available for the government to redistribute.

The liberal likewise rejects the conservative notion of any "natural inequality" and instead sees people as inherently equal. To the liberal, the apparent inequalities among individuals arise out of the different social, political, and economic circumstances in which people are forced to develop. Redistributive government policies are a moral and just way to compensate for these "accidents of birth." As a practical matter, the liberal also believes that a failure to address these inequalities through redistribution will only lead to crime and social unrest.

Nor does private property constitute the guarantor of freedom that conservatives purport. To the extent that unlimited property rights and the resultant overaccumulation of property by the few exclude many Americans from their just share of the nation's economic pie, they also exclude them from exercising their social and political rights. In this regard, the concentration of wealth in the hands of the rich is a far greater infringement on individual freedom than government redistribution.

Finally, while the liberal may acknowledge that redistribution may have some effect on incentives to produce, he also believes that in the American economy, such redistribution occurs on a moderate enough scale so that its effects are too small to have any significant impact on our overall economic growth. Thus supply-side economics rightly crashes on the shoals of social justice.

3. Property Rights–Redistribution Policy Games. The first significant policy dispute over property rights versus redistribution occurred when, riding a wave of populist sentiment, the first peacetime income tax was imposed in 1894. When the Sixteenth Amendment to the Constitution was passed in 1913 to make the progressive income tax legal, conservatives decried it as conferring upon Congress the power to confiscate all of the income from private property, while liberals hailed the amendment as a great victory for social justice.

Today this battle continues primarily around tax issues. While the liberal seeks to maintain, and perhaps increase, both the progressivity of the personal income tax and corporate tax rates, the conservative pushes for a "flat" or proportional personal income tax and the total abolition of the corporate tax. But the conservative is well aware of the political obstacles to such Draconian reforms and therefore also embraces a number of indirect policies to vitiate the tax system.

For example, preferential treatment of capital gains and interest income, "indexing" tax rates to inflation, and lowering the cap on the marginal tax rate (e.g., by reducing it from 70 to 50 percent as was done during the Reagan administration) reduce the progressivity of the personal income tax just as effectively as conservative-endorsed policies such as accelerated depreciation and investment tax credits lower the effective corporate tax rate.

Such loopholes, of course, inflame liberals, who see behind the supply-side rhetoric inspiring such "reforms" an unacceptable "trickle down" approach where the poor have to wait for the crumbs to fall from the tables of the rich. Nor does the indexing of income tax rates have much appeal to liberals since indexing prevents "bracket creep," a phenomenon that leads to a more progressive tax.

Besides these tax issues, there are a number of other redistributive policies over which conservatives and liberals regularly lock horns. For example, besides interfering with the efficiency of the free market, the conservative sees liberal policies such as rent control and natural gas price controls as disguised but unacceptable means of redistributing income from the holders of property (landlords and gas well owners) to consumers (tenants and gas users).

More obliquely, this debate also is embedded in the dispute over affirmative action programs such as minority hiring and school admission quotas, programs that the conservative regards as reverse discrimination, but which liberals regard as an essential way of helping the disadvantaged rise to economic, as well as social and political, parity with others.

III.   THE MINIMAL VERSUS THE WELFARE STATE

The ongoing debate over the appropriate size and role of government constitutes a third major battle between American conservatives and liberals.

> *A government big enough to give you everything you want is a government big enough to take from you everything you have.*[11]

> RICHARD NIXON

1.   The Conservative's Minimal State.   The conservative seeks to limit the role of government to three basic areas: national defense, preserving law and order, and administering justice. The cornerstone of the "minimal state" is the high value the conservative places on individual liberty and a collateral belief that "throughout history, government has been the chief instrument for thwarting man's liberty."[12] Big Government's threat to liberty arises out of its unique powers such as taxation, conscription, censorship, and surveillance. Because of his generally pessimistic presumptions about man's tendencies to be corrupted by power, the conservative fears that as government grows, it invariably must usurp more and more of man's liberty in all spheres—economic, political, and social. The only way to avoid this is to limit government's role.

The conservative also believes that paternalistic government cripples and stunts the individual. To the conservative, the inevitable result of government assuming more and more responsibility for taking care of the individual is to reduce that individual to a dependent and perpetually helpless child. At the root of this belief is the idea of Social Darwinism that to help people in the short run is to do them irreparable harm in the long run.* Moreover, in a fear that strikes a raw nerve of his deep-seated anti-Communism, the conservative sees the road to expanding welfarism as one that veers ever leftward towards socialism.

Finally, the conservative's most positive argument against the welfare state rests on his belief that it is both possible and more productive to rely on an independent sector composed of private charities, church groups, cooperatives and other such volunteer organizations to meet America's social welfare needs. The essence of the conservative's volunteerism is captured in these words of Ronald Reagan's favorite president, Herbert Hoover:

> *This is not an issue as to whether people shall go hungry or cold in the United States. It is solely a question of the best method by which hunger and cold shall be prevented. . . . if we break down the sense of responsibility of individual generosity to individual and mutual self-help in the country in times of national difficulty . . . we have not only impaired something infinitely valuable in the life of the American people, but have struck at the roots of self-government. . . . The basis of successful relief in national distress is to mobilize and organize the infinite number of agencies of self-help in the community.*[13]

2.   The Liberal's Welfare State.

> *Our object today should not be to weaken government . . . but rather strengthen it as the agency charged with the common good.*[14]
>
> ROBERT HUTCHINS

The liberal sees the government's role as extending far beyond the conservative's basic requirements of defense, law and order, and justice to ensuring that all citizens have jobs, food, clothing, shelter, education, and medical care.

One important pillar of the liberal's welfare state is the high value he places on the community. While the liberal regards the individual as important, he also believes that in an increasingly complex, crowded,

---

*The 1980s saw this idea popularized in George Gilder's controversial work *Wealth and Poverty.*

polluted, and technological society, it has become necessary to put the community's needs before those of the individual. As George Lodge has wryly observed: "City life has strained the traditional notions of individualism. It is, after all, impossible to stake out a land claim or build a beef herd in an apartment."[15]

Thus, in an urban, industrial society where "one man's ceiling is another man's floor,"[16] where the individual's right to burn wood in his fireplace interferes with the community's right to clean air, and where we are all dependent on one another for the basic necessities of life, the requirements and needs of the community now must come first.

A second important pillar of the welfare state is the liberal's more "positive" definition of liberty: Individuals must not only have the legal *right* to exercise their political, social, and economic freedoms, but also the *means.* To the liberal, the conservative's "negative liberty" where individuals merely are free to do as they please is a cruel hoax on the poor and disadvantaged who have neither the financial nor educational resources to enjoy such freedom. Positive liberty requires positive government, particularly where the disadvantaged are involved.

In this regard, the liberal believes that social welfare programs won't paternalistically imprison, but will rather eventually liberate the disadvantaged to a point where they can stand firmly on their own two feet. Indeed, government is the one hope the disadvantaged have of breaking out of a vicious cycle of poverty, ignorance, and disease. Nor does the liberal see government welfare programs as the camel's nose under the socialist tent. Rather, such programs are a legitimate function of a democratic government and compassionate society rightly committed to, as Harry Truman once put it, ensuring that everyone gets a Fair Deal.

Finally, while compassion drives much of the liberal's desire for social welfare programs, there also is a nagging fear that unless the deprivations of the disadvantaged are reduced, there will be violent upheaval in society. Indeed, any drastic cutback of America's social welfare programs will lead the nation down the road to more crime, social conflict, and ultimately, revolution. And no spontaneous "volunteerism" is likely to change that course.

3.   Minimal Versus Welfare-State Policy Games.   In erecting the policy scaffolding of the modern welfare state during the New Deal, Franklin Roosevelt ushered in a variety of government agencies, programs, and laws dedicated to promoting social welfare through government. Social security, the minimum wage, the right to unionize, public works projects, slum clearance and public housing, farm subsidies, as well as the first large-scale subsidization of the arts all had their genesis in New Deal legislation.

With Lyndon B. Johnson's Great Society, the American welfare state took another quantum leap. In the New Deal tradition, LBJ created the Job Corps, VISTA, and various community development projects; both public housing and the arts flourished anew from a massive infusion of federal subsidies; and bold new welfare programs like food stamps, aid to dependent children, and school lunch programs joined with an unprecedented national health care program for the aged (Medicare) to take their first significant bite out of the federal budget.

Today, the American government constitutes a rather well-developed welfare state and the policy battles over this phenomenon focus on both direct and indirect conservative efforts to dismantle it and liberal efforts to preserve or expand it. Indeed, the whole range of welfare programs, from food stamps and school lunches to job training programs faces constant conservative pressure for their reduction or elimination, while mass transit, farm, education, and housing subsidies are likewise subject to the conservative's budgeting knife. In no previous era since the New Deal has this pressure been more severe than during the reign of Ronald Reagan.

Besides this trench warfare over *specific* programs, the minimal versus welfare state controversy surfaces in a number of more general and indirect ways. For example, while conservative support for federal hiring freezes and tax cuts and such exotica as a gold standard for the dollar and a balanced budget amendment is steeped in the rhetoric of reducing budget deficits and runaway inflation, both conservatives and liberals are aware that any successful implementation of these measures means fewer dollars and resources for the functioning of the welfare state.

Let us turn now to our next policy game and see how the conservative–liberal splits over several of these principles underlie the public interest arguments for and against electric utility regulation.

8

The Dimming of America

THE ELECTRIC UTILITY POLICY GAME

How many times over your morning cornflakes and coffee have you noticed a story like this in the daily newspaper?

> *PUBLIC UTILITY COMMISSION AWARDS AMERICAN EDISON*
> *THE LARGEST RATE HIKE IN ITS HISTORY*
> *In a 3–2 vote, the state public utility commission (PUC) granted American Edison a $200 million rate increase. The 20 percent rate hike, the largest in Edison's history, will add roughly $12 per year to the average customer's electricity bill.*
>
> *John Jay, spokesperson for the Coalition Against Higher Rates, denounced the PUC's decision as a "bonanza for Edison's wealthy stockholders and an unconscionable rip-off of consumers." Jay predicted that the latest increase would leave many of the city's poor and elderly unable to light and heat their homes.*
>
> *Edison, which had asked the PUC for $400 million in rate increases, also condemned the PUC's decision. According to the company's Chief Executive Officer Chauncy Gerhardt, "This meager increase threatens both the future reliability of service and Edison's financial viability."*
>
> *Attorney General and gubernatorial candidate Ted Felloti joined the fray by describing the PUC as a "tool of Governor Bradford," who, Felloti pointed out, receives "large campaign contributions from utility interests." Felloti promised that his office would challenge the rate hike in the state supreme court.*
>
> *In a surprise statement, Governor Bradford also denounced the PUC's*

decision as "overly generous to the utility" and asked for the resignation of its chairman. Responding to the attorney general's attack, Bradford insisted that "Felloti's smears are typical election year posturings" and predicted that he would beat back Felloti's challenge in the upcoming primary election.

In an era of rising energy and capital costs, situations such as this have become an all too familiar part of the regulatory landscape. Caught in the middle of this rancorous dispute are the state PUCs that regulate electricity rates. These PUCs are the referees in an apparent "zero-sum" game, where the losses are exactly equal to the gains. In this case, every dollar of rate relief PUCs grant to utilities represents a transfer of income from the pockets of consumers to utility investors, while every dollar of rate relief they fail to give to utilities benefits consumers at the expense of investors.

But is this battle over electricity rates really a zero-sum game? That is, do consumers always win what their utility loses in a rate case? That is the paradoxical question posed by the electric utility policy game.

I. HISTORY AND BACKGROUND

State public utility commissions regulate the more than 100 large, private investor-owned utilities that supply America with over 80 percent of its electricity.* PUC regulation has its origin in the Populist and Progressive movements of the late 1800s and early 1900s.

During that era, robber barons like Jay Gould perpetrated multimillion-dollar stock swindles, while empire builders like John D. Rockefeller gobbled up smaller competitors to feed a burgeoning number of monopolistic corporate trusts. With such corporate abuses running rampant, the public's mistrust of the unbridled power of Big Business reached unprecedented heights. Out of this mistrust—skillfully transformed into political action by Populist and Progressive leaders—there emerged the most sweeping range of government interventions in the American economy ever witnessed.

---

*The remainder is supplied by federally owned utilities such as the Tennessee Valley Authority, rural cooperatives, and municipal utilities.

At the federal level, antitrust laws like the Sherman and Clayton Acts were passed to curb monopoly practices and to stem the tide of corporate mergers. At the same time, a veritable army of agencies was established to regulate industries where some of the worst abuses had been observed: among them, the Interstate Commerce Commission was formed to control the octopus railroad industry and the Commodities Exchange Commission was established to monitor that wild and woolly arena of speculation and fraud, the commodities market.[1]

At the state level, as part of this overall "trust busting" trend, the Progressives also put the growing water, gas, telephone, and electric utilities under government regulation. Such regulation likewise was in large part a response to growing abuses by rapidly growing public utilities. The New York Gas and Electric Light Company, for example, was discovered in 1905 selling electricity at about 8¢ per kilowatt hour, over twice the price it cost to generate it.[2] As a result of such abuses, in that same year, the legislature created a PUC to supervise the state's electric and gas utilities. Other states like Georgia and Progressive stronghold Wisconsin soon followed suit, and by 1930, most of the states had PUCs.

From among many proposed alternatives—including franchising, public ownership, and licensing—"rate of return regulation" typically was chosen by the states as the government mechanism to set utility prices. Under rate of return regulation, each utility is granted a monopoly in its particular service area, and for this exclusive right, the utility agrees to generate low cost, reliable service in whatever quantities consumers demand. In return, the PUC is legally obligated to set rates that are high enough to allow the utility the opportunity to earn a fair and reasonable return on its investment. As set forth in several important Supreme Court decisions, this "fair and reasonable doctrine" has been interpreted as a *capital attraction standard:* A utility must have the opportunity to earn its market cost of capital so that it is able to attract investors to buy its stocks and bonds at the same time that it maintains its financial integrity.[3]

For almost a hundred years, this regulatory arrangement worked extremely well for both ratepayers and utility investors. The electric utility industry provided its ratepayers with some of the safest and most reliable power in the world; at the same time, electricity prices steadily fell with improvements in technology and a continued increase in the size of power plants. For example, in 1900 a kilowatt hour of electricity cost about 5¢ while in 1967 it was only 2¢. Adjusted for inflation, this drop is even more striking: The real (that is, inflation-adjusted) price of a kilowatt hour in 1900 was over 20¢ while in 1967 it was less than a penny.

Throughout the 1960s and prior to the 1973 oil embargo, investors enjoyed the blue-chip status of their utilities' stocks and bonds, and the industry consistently earned a *real* rate of return* on its common equity of roughly 6 percent. This average return closely paralleled the return of other industrial stocks in the Fortune 500 and was at a level that likewise equaled its market cost of capital.[4]

Today, however, the regulatory arrangement between the PUCs and their utilities seems to have broken down, in large part due to dramatic rises in both energy and capital costs. These cost increases were precipitated by four major shocks to the U.S. economy and its utility industry.

The first came in the form of a general rise in the rate of inflation brought about primarily by Lyndon Johnson's refusal to cut back on social spending for his Great Society programs while at the same time defense spending for the Vietnam War was skyrocketing. This refusal sent the world inflation rate off on a roller coaster ride that still hasn't completely stopped. One of the first casualties of this inflation was the electric utility industry, which saw its capital costs begin to rise and its private investment get "crowded out" by large government budget deficits.

The second shock came in the wake of Rachel Carson's 1962 publication of *Silent Spring*. This book helped to raise the nation's consciousness about widespread environmental degradation, including the considerable pollution emitted by coal- and oil-fired utility power plants. One form this new awareness took was passage of a tough, new Clean Air Act in 1970; among other mandates, the act required the installation of sophisticated and expensive pollution-control technologies and forced utilities to burn cleaner and more expensive fuels. While these regulations succeeded in greatly reducing air pollution, they also raised the

---

*The real return is equal to the actual or "nominal" return minus the effects of inflation. In an inflationary economy such as ours, the real return is the best way to gauge a company's earnings. Suppose a firm earns a 15 percent nominal return; if inflation is 13 percent, its real return is only about 2 percent. On the other hand, if inflation is 5 percent, the company's real return is about 10 percent.

cost of building and operating a new power plant by as much as 25 percent.[5]

The third and most famous shock came in the form of the 1973–74 Arab oil embargo, with its consequent fourfold increase in petroleum prices. While the costs of all forms of energy rose with the OPEC price shock, petroleum-dependent utilities were particularly hard hit. (Ironically, just a few years earlier, many utilities had converted their coal plants to oil in order to comply with the Clean Air Act.)

Utilities that built nuclear power plants to avoid OPEC price hikes experienced the fourth major shock: In the wake of the 1979 incident at Three Mile Island, the Nuclear Regulatory Commission tightened safety standards for nuclear power plants. This tightening increased the investment and operating costs of existing nuclear plants as well as the costs of completing nuclear plants under construction.

The results of these shocks were immediate: Since the 1973 oil embargo, the electric utility industry has consistently earned a return well below its market cost of capital. According to economists Eugene Brigham and Dilip Shome, this earnings shortfall has been equivalent to about three percentage points below the industry's real (inflation-adjusted) market cost of capital.[6] Howard Thompson has similarly found the industry's average equity earnings to be about 40 percent "too low."[7]

At the root of these low utility earnings is a phenomenon that is widespread among the nation's PUCs, regulatory *rate suppression*. For a variety of political, institutional, and ideological reasons (which are explored below), electricity rates have not risen as fast as even more rapidly escalating energy and capital costs. As a result, for the last 10 years, electricity rates in most states have fallen short of the true market costs of generating electricity. While this failure of the regulatory process to keep pace with inflation has thus far kept consumers' rates lower than they otherwise would be, it has seriously impaired the financial health of the utility industry. The industry's ill health is evident in the decade-long deterioration of several of its financial "vital signs."

For example, during the 1960s and early 1970s, electric utilities consistently attained bond ratings of AAA and AA, showing the highest degree of credit-worthiness. But today, many utilities have fallen into the quicksand of A, BBB, and even lower ratings, indicating that they have become highly risky investments. As a result, credit is not only difficult to obtain, but it is also more expensive, since borrowing costs rise as bond ratings decline. For an industry that uses one-fifth of all the capital in the U.S. economy, this change in credit rating is indeed serious.

At the same time, there has been an equally dramatic drop in the "market-to-book" ratio of many utilities (the ratio of the market price of a utility's common stock to the book value of its assets). As the ratio falls, so too, does the real value of a shareholder's common stock. This sinking ratio thus provides a good measure of the underlying distributional struggle between utility stockholders and electricity consumers because the loss in stock value to shareholders represents, in a very real sense, a direct gain to ratepayers.

Note the subtlety, however, of this income transfer. On the one hand, electricity rates steadily rise so that increasingly angry consumers come to perceive that their utilities are gouging them. But at the same time, and to the distress of investors, the value of utility stocks and bonds declines because rates are not rising fast enough to meet even more rapidly escalating energy and capital costs.

Redistributive rate suppression is passive, then, in the sense that it prevents or blocks a large-scale transfer of wealth from ratepayers to shareholders that would have occurred if the regulatory process allowed utilities the opportunity to earn their market costs of providing electricity. From the standpoint of the politics of utility regulation, the interesting question is to what extent this redistributive rate suppression is attributable to "capture" of the regulatory process by angry ratepayers or to the good intentions of ideologically motivated regulators.

II. THE POLITICS OF ELECTRIC UTILITY REGULATION

A. The Public Interest View

As it has since been interpreted by economists, the Populist–Progressive rational for electric utility regulation represents a classic case of the "market failure" model of policy intervention (introduced in Chapter 1). Its interpretation runs as follows.

Electricity generation is characterized by "economies of scale" so that as the size of a power plant increases, the cost of generating a unit of electricity falls. Because of these economies of scale, an electric utility will tend toward "natural monopoly" in a free market. That is, a large utility with the cheapest costs will eventually drive out its smaller rivals; once its rivals are eliminated, ratepayers will be left at its mercy, and the utility will sell electricity at monopoly prices. Thus some form of government intervention is needed to prevent this inevitable market failure.

The choice of PUC regulation to correct the natural monopoly problem reflects a battle won long ago by the Progressive forebears of modern liberalism over the principle of a free market versus a regulated and planned economy; for, as mentioned earlier, there are other more market-oriented policy solutions to natural monopoly than the bureaucracy-laden regulatory approach of the PUCs. These options, typically preferred by conservatives, include such solutions as franchising and licensing, approaches that have been used with great success in areas such as cable television.

But while this free market-regulation split provides us with a plausible public interest explanation of the genesis of PUC regulation, it does little to explain why current PUC practices now result in redistributive rate suppression. Do we have here a case of a "government failure" where, despite their good intentions, PUC regulators are simply unable to provide efficient regulation? Or is redistributive rate suppression the intended result of well-meaning regulators intent on achieving some additional ideological goal?

The possibility of ideologically motivated rate suppression can be explained within the context of the second conservative–liberal split discussed in Chapter 7, that of property rights versus redistribution. For as we have seen, rate suppression transfers literally billions of dollars from utility shareholders to electricity consumers.* In doing so, such a large-scale transfer of income may in fact serve an important liberal goal: achieving a more equal, and therefore a more equitable, distribution of income. This will be true if one accepts the argument that utility shareholders are, on average, richer than electricity consumers.

In some sense, then, there is an analogy between rate suppression and the progressive income tax. In the taxation case, higher-income taxpayers bear a disproportionately higher share of the national tax burden than

---

*In a $280 billion industry that is roughly half financed by equity capital, rate suppression's three percentage point shortfall on the industry's annual real return on equity amounts to more than a $4 billion loss to shareholders. Much of this loss represents a direct gain to ratepayers.

lower-income taxpayers, while in the case of rate suppression, higher-income shareholders bear a disproportionately larger share of the rising cost of electricity generation than lower-income consumers.

Conservatives, for their part, challenge the use of regulation as a redistributive tool; as a matter of general principle, they see such a hidden transfer not as a fair redistribution, but rather, as an unfair confiscation of property. In this case, that confiscation comes in the form of a devaluation of a shareholder's utility stock.

While the property rights–redistribution split implies redistributive rate suppression is intentional, a perhaps equally strong case can be made that it is simply a bureaucratic accident. Massachusetts Institute of Technology economist Paul Joskow has provided the best application of this "government failure" explanation* to electric utility regulation.[8] According to Joskow, the institutional stage for rate suppression was set in the halcyon decades prior to the 1970s. During this period, consumers were content to watch their electricity bills steadily decrease even as utilities steadily increased their profits by building bigger, more technologically advanced power plants that steadily reduced the cost of generating electricity.

Thus, for the better part of half a century, utilities seldom filed for a new rate and when they did, it was for a rate *decrease*. Because of this low volume of rate cases, the PUCs enjoyed a relatively quiet life, and they tended to be sleepy little backwaters where few toiled and few tax dollars were spent.

As Joskow tells it, that PUC peace was broken in the 1970s when (because of the four shocks to the economy just described) energy and capital costs began to soar. With a half century of declining costs brought suddenly to an end, utilities began to file more and more frequently for rate increases—as often as once a year. However, the PUCs did not grow proportionately either in staffing or in resources to meet this new and heavy demand for their services. At the same time, many PUCs failed to embrace (or because of low budgets, could not afford) new technologies (e.g., computers) that would have greatly facilitated the processing of rate

---

*As discussed in Chapter 1, the government failure explanation accepts the basic premise that policymakers intend to serve the public interest, but, despite their good intentions, they sometimes fail to reach their objectives (in this case, fair and reasonable regulation) because of bureaucratic or institutional obstacles.

cases. Saddled with a regulatory formula now generally recognized as incapable of coping with inflation and with rate cases piling up in their in-boxes, these PUCs inevitably suppressed rates by their simple inability to process these cases in a swift and efficient manner.

We have then, two possible public interest explanations for rate suppression: one that it is an intentional redistribution on ideological grounds and one that it is an institutional accident. But what about the role of special interests; might they have something to do with it as well?

B.   Private Interest Capture

Viewed through the lens of private interest capture, electric utility regulation is primarily a distributional struggle between two major competing special interests: electricity consumers and utility shareholders. In this view, because each rate case is a zero-sum game, consumer groups try to suppress rate increases while utility management (which must protect shareholder interests), try to make them as large as possible. The presence of rate suppression, then, simply indicates that ratepayers are winning the lobbying war. An examination of who these ratepayer groups are and their strategies offers several reasons as to why this might be so.

Perhaps most important, electricity consumers vastly outnumber utility shareholders. This numerical superiority hardly ensures political success, however. As was demonstrated in our protectionism and farm policy games, large broad-based interest groups such as consumers and taxpayers are frequently on the losing end of public policy. The reason relates back to the problem of "concentrated benefits versus diffuse costs" and collateral disincentives for such groups to organize (discussed in Chapter 4).

In this instance, a utility that files for a $100 million rate hike has a considerable (or concentrated) amount of profits at stake for its relatively small number of shareholders. On the other hand, if the rate increase is granted, the millions of dollars that will accrue to shareholders will be spread out (or be diffused) over a much larger number of consumers who will pay a few more cents on their monthly utility bills.

Despite this apparent lack of incentive, consumers seem to have overcome these obstacles to organize. The major reason, no doubt, is that the rapid increases in electricity prices over the past decade have raised the consumer's stake in the rate-making game considerably—a "few more cents on the monthly bill" has become "many more dollars." With this increase—and increased anger—have come heightened incentives to organize. The result has been the rise of a number of powerful and vocal ratepayer groups.

At the same time, this remarkable rise in ratepayer resistance has been part of an overall trend towards increased consumer and citizen activism, a trend evident in the equally dramatic rise in a wide range of "public interest" groups. As discussed in Chapter 3, most of these groups are *oligarchical* in structure. That is, a large and largely passive membership is led by a small activist elite of political entrepreneurs such as Ralph Nader of Public Citizen and John Gardner of Common Cause. It is this oligarchical structure, coupled with the zeal of the groups' leaders, that has helped to overcome the well-known inertia of American consumers, taxpayers, and citizens.

This general description of public interest groups seems to fit the major consumer groups opposing rate hikes. Today, groups like Fair Share, Acorn, and Public Interest Research Groups (PIRGs) have chapters in many of the fifty states. Funded in part by member dues and contributions, in part by charitable trusts, and in part by federal funds, they typically are led by a small core of activists that represent literally thousands and thousands of financially contributing, but usually nonparticipating, members. To combat rate hikes, these consumer groups have at their disposal a variety of strategies and tactics, all of which are aimed at influencing or even controlling the PUCs.

The most direct and perhaps most effective tactic is to enlist the support of the politicians and bureaucrats in charge of the process through various direct and indirect lobbying techniques. In the 11 states where PUC commissioners are directly elected, consumers can exert control by electing only those candidates who promise to hold down rates. The classic case of a politician who championed ratepayer interests is that of Huey Long, who in the 1920s, rode consumer support all the way from the Louisiana PUC to the governorship. More recently, former race car driver Billy Lovett was elected as a commissioner to the Georgia PUC on a Populist platform of "no rate hikes," and he has consistently fought any rate increases, despite the fact that energy and capital costs are skyrocketing.

In the rest of the states were commissioners are appointed, consumer pressure can be directed toward the governor, who appoints the commissioners, and the legislature, which confirms those appointments. That this is sometimes an important and decisive election issue is evident in several cases, one of the most famous being the successful ascendancy to the governorship of Connecticut by the late Ella Grasso, who campaigned heavily against the utility industry. More recently, Mark White successfully challenged Bill Clements for the Texas governorship largely on the promise to hold rates down. The result has been several new appointments to the Texas PUC that have pushed it significantly toward the consumer position. (Interestingly, when a governor gets elected with considerable help from these ratepayer groups, often one or more of the group's leaders gets appointed to the commission. A case in point was the selection of consumer advocate Michael Love to chair the New Hampshire PUC in the wake of Meldrim Thomson's defeat for reelection on a pro-utility platform.)

A second important tactic that consumer groups have used with increasing success in recent years is litigation. This comes in the form of organized intervention in rate cases. The ratepayer group typically files a brief opposing the utility's rate hike, offers testimony in support of that brief, and engages in cross-examination of the utility's witnesses.

Such intervention can provide very useful information to help the PUC determine rates and in that sense is productive. However, such intervention also can delay the ratemaking process by increasing "regulatory lag." This tactic is of great strategic benefit to ratepayers because even if the utility "wins" the rate case, inflation will have eroded the value of the hike during the time the case is being heard. Thus it is often difficult to tell whether an intervention by a ratepayer group is designed to enhance the PUC's information (a public interest view of the process) or is merely a tactical weapon designed to postpone rate increases as long as possible (the capture view).

Regardless of which view one accepts, ratepayer intervention has increased dramatically in the last several decades. Today one or more ratepayer groups intervene in virtually every rate case that is heard before a PUC. At the same time, in response to political pressure, the federal government has facilitated such intervention by funding consumer groups. Similar pressures have led many state governments to establish their own offices of consumer representation or to use the attorney general's office to challenge rate increases by local utilities. For example, the attorney general's office in Massachusetts regularly intervenes on behalf of consumers, while the North Carolina and West Virginia PUCs have divisions that represent consumers, and states such as Maryland, Ohio, Connecticut, and Missouri have their own offices of consumers' counsel.

A third tactic that has gone hand in hand with increased rate case interventions is consumer groups' use of the media to generate grass-roots pressure on the PUCs. The fictitious newspaper story at the beginning of this chapter was intended to show that rate hikes are important news events, and it is an unfortunate fact of life that because of the large sums of money involved, they are very easy to sensationalize. However, while a headline that trumpets a $100 million rate increase is surely an eye-catcher, the accompanying story seldom says whether the increase is large (as it might be for a small utility) or small (as it might be for a large utility). This susceptibility of the rate-making process to such journalistic sensationalism can further skew the political pressures on the PUC toward holding down rates.

The utility industry—hardly an innocent bystander in this special interest battle—has sought to counter ratepayer pressure on the PUCs in a number of direct and indirect ways. Through its major trade association, the Edison Electric Institute, and through public relations offices within companies, the industry has launched multimillion-dollar public information and advertising programs to change its at times well-earned image from that of a greedy and mismanaged monopoly to that of a friend to consumers and a partner to national prosperity. These programs typically focus on the importance of the industry for national economic health and energy policy and suggest that rate hikes are necessary to promote economic growth and reduce oil imports. The argument that utility investors are suffering at the hands of ratepayers always remains elliptical.

At the same time, many utility companies have become more and more aggressive about seeking rate relief. In the face of rebuffs by the PUCs, they have quickly refiled for additional relief. Because the costs of a rate case are borne by ratepayers, there is little to lose in this strategy and much to gain; and as the PUC becomes overburdened, it is less likely to scrutinize the details of the utility's request. In a no doubt questionable practice, it thus becomes possible for the utility to overstate its expenses. This tactic of "padding" expenses, which some utilities have adopted in the guerrilla warfare of the rate case, is done in the hope that the gains from those expenses will offset whatever loss is imposed on the utility by the PUC's failure to grant it a higher return.

Utilities in some states have also pushed for more aboveboard and innovative rate-making reforms like the "future test year" to offset the effects of inflation in the rate-making process. In this effort as well as in rate cases, the industry uses a favorite tactic of business interests: It spends millions of dollars on consultants and academics, the so-called hired guns of the rate-making process. These paid experts offer testimony before the PUCs to extol the virtues of regulatory reform and to counter the arguments of hostile intervenors.

More subtly, through their extensive lobbying network, the utilities have sought changes in the rules of rate making that would work to their advantage. Virtually every major utility has one or more lobbyists who ply their trade not only on Capitol Hill, but also on the little "Capitol Hills" of the states in which the utilities do business. In some states, utilities have succeeded in instituting a mandatory time period within which a decision on rates must be reached; Massachusetts, for example, requires that a utility's rate request be adjudicated within six months.

Given the pervasiveness and degree of rate suppression over the last 10 years, it appears, however, that at least through the private interest lens, utility lobbyists are losing the battle over capture of the PUCs to a numerically superior and politically more powerful ratepayer lobby. The remaining question in the politics of electric utility regulation is to what extent this capture interpretation holds sway over the two alternative public interest views of rate suppression, liberal redistribution and government failure.

C. The Politics of Electric Utility Regulation: A Statistical Test

A variation on the capture-ideology framework's standard test was used to probe the relative roles of ratepayer capture, ideological redistribution, and government failure in explaining rate suppression.[9]

Four measures were chosen to gauge the susceptibility of each PUC to ratepayer capture; these were election of commissioners, length of commissioner terms, the PUC's funding mechanism, and the generation mix of the utility.

Following our preceding discussion, PUCs with elected (rather than appointed) commissioners were expected to be more rate suppressive under the assumption that because ratepayers are more numerous and vocal as a voting group than utility shareholders, candidates for elected

PUCs are more likely to run on platforms of rate reductions. Similarly, political pressure was expected to increase when commissioners' terms are relatively short because they must face reelection or reappointment and hence the pressure of the political process more frequently. Susceptibility to capture was likewise assumed to rise when the PUCs are funded from general revenue funds (rather than through assessments on utilities) and when there is a high percentage of oil in the generation mix. General revenue funding means that elected state legislators have greater leverage with the PUCs and thus bring more of their constituency pressure to bear on them. In states with heavy oil use and a fuel adjustment clause, ratepayers have been subjected to rapid and highly visible rate increases in the form of "fuel surcharges."* Following our discussion of the dynamics of consumer power earlier and in Chapter 4, these surcharges were assumed to heighten organized ratepayer awareness of and resistance to rate increases.

Three additional measures were constructed to gauge the susceptibility of each PUC to government failure on the assumption that a well-staffed and well-equipped PUC is more likely to process rate cases more quickly and correctly than a poorly organized or poorly equipped PUC. Accordingly, the odds that a PUC would suppress rates were expected to decline as salaries (adjusted for a state's cost of living) and budgets (adjusted for state size) rose. Similarly, the degree of rate suppression was expected to be less in states where PUCs were required by law to be trained professionals in disciplines such as law, economics, or engineering.

Finally, the susceptibility of each PUC to ideological arguments for redistributive regulation was measured by the percentage of Democratic commissioners on each PUC under the well-tested assumption that there is a high correlation between liberalism and membership in the Democratic party.

Table 8.1 ranks the various states and the District of Columbia by the degree of rate suppression that their PUCs are thought to practice. These rankings were statistically related to our various measures of capture,

---

*Most PUCs have some type of fuel adjustment clause that allows the utility to raise its rates by part or all of an increase in the price of fuel. In some states, utilities are required to list these adjustments separately as a fuel surcharge. The appearance of such surcharges has angered many consumers because, in some states whose oil use is heavy, they now comprise over *half* of the total monthly bill.

TABLE 8.1.   THE DEGREE OF RATE SUPPRESSION IN EACH STATE PUC[a]

Least Rate Suppression	Moderate Rate Suppression	Most Rate Suppression
Arizona	Arkansas	Alabama
Florida	Colorado	California
Hawaii	Delaware	Connecticut
Indiana	District of Columbia	Georgia
New Mexico	Idaho	Iowa
North Carolina	Illinois	Louisiana
Texas	Kansas	Maine
Utah	Kentucky	Massachusetts
Wisconsin	Maryland	Mississippi
	Michigan	Missouri
	Minnesota	Montana
	Nevada	North Dakota
	New Hampshire	Rhode Island
	New York	South Dakota
	Ohio	West Virginia
	Oklahoma	
	Oregon	
	Pennsylvania	
	South Carolina	
	Vermont	
	Virginia	
	Washington	
	Wyoming	

[a]This is a composite ranking developed from the rankings of Goldman Sachs, Merrill Lynch, Salomon Brothers, Valueline, and Duff and Phelps. Alaska, Tennessee, and Nebraska are typically not ranked.

government failures, and ideology within each state. The results of the test, presented in Table 8.2, confirm once again that both private and public interest motives are at work in public policy.* This table ranks each of the various measures according to their importance in explaining why a PUC is rate suppressive.

From the table, the capture measure of elected versus appointed PUCs appears to have the single most important effect. Moving from an appointed to an elected PUC significantly increases the odds that a PUC will be rate suppressive. This statistical conclusion is bolstered by the

*For complete results, see Appendix A.

TABLE 8.2.   THE INFLUENCE OF CAPTURE, IDEOLOGY, AND
GOVERNMENT FAILURE ON PUC RATE SUPPRESSION

Rank
1. Elected versus appointed commissioners (capture)
2. General revenue versus utility assessment funding of PUCs (capture)
3. Salary level (government failure)
4. Ideology
5. Longer versus shorter commissioner terms (capture)
6. Existence of a professional qualification requirement
   (government failure)
7. PUC budget (government failure)
8. Percentage of state oil dependence (capture)

observation that of the eleven states that elect commissioners, nine of them are ranked "most rate suppressive" in Table 8.1 and only one is in the least rate suppressive category. A second indicator of capture—general revenue funding—has an effect almost as large.

Despite the strength of these capture measures, public interest motives as an explanation of rate suppression are not far behind. In fact, the salary level indicator of government failure finishes in third place while ideology is close behind in fourth place. According to the test, salary level is 80 percent as powerful as the number one capture measure while ideology is almost half as powerful.

Thus all three explanations of rate suppression appear to have some grain of truth to them. The remaining question is whether such rate suppression is, in fact, in the public interest—or even in the interests of the ratepayers who would appear to gain the most from rate suppression.

III.   THE ECONOMICS OF RATE SUPPRESSION

The economic consequences of rate suppressive regulation are far reaching. They include higher consumer rates for less reliable service, a failure of national energy policy through increased dependence on foreign energy sources, and a failure of national economic policy in the form of reduced productivity, increased unemployment, and slower economic growth.

Rate suppression produces these consequences because it fundamentally alters the way electric utility executives plan their investments; these altered investment strategies in turn create three regulatory penalties that ultimately must be borne not by utility shareholders but by consumers and the nation. To understand why requires making a crucial distinction between the short- versus the longer-term effects of rate suppression.

A.   The Reverse AJ Effect and Capital Minimization

In the context of rate suppression, the short term is equivalent to the time it takes to process a single rate case. The decision a PUC renders in such a case is, as it was characterized earlier, quite literally a zero-sum transfer: Every dollar of rate relief the PUC refuses to grant the utility is a dollar off consumers' electricity bills.

However, neither the regulatory process nor the utility industry operates in the freeze frame of a single rate case. Instead, rate making occurs over time in an ongoing series of rate cases, and utility executives make their longer-term investment plans (e.g., how many power plants to build) in response to the regulatory treatment they expect to receive.

In the 1960s economists Harvey Averch and Leland Johnson formalized this temporal relationship between regulatory treatment and utility executive behavior in their famous "Averch–Johnson effect."[10] At that time, they predicted that if a utility is allowed to earn a return *higher* than its market cost of capital, it will tend to *overinvest* in new capacity.

The logic behind the so-called AJ effect is that a higher return provides an incentive for the utility to increase its use of capital; it thus tends to build more capacity than it needs to provide service at the lowest cost to consumers. The AJ effect was relevant during the 1960s when Averch and Johnson formulated their theory: Technological advances were making it possible for utilities to realize increasing economies of scale, inflation and energy prices were low and stable, and environmental and safety regulations imposed few costs. Their predictions seemed to be borne out when, during that decade, many utilities earned more than their regulators intended them to, and power-plant construction boomed.

Interestingly, the academic literature of that time assumed that if a utility earned a return *lower* than its market cost of capital, it would simply withdraw from the market. That assumption is now recognized as wrong because utilities are obligated by their legal mandate to provide service. Equally important, it is infeasible for a utility to simply leave its market and set up shop elsewhere because large, capital-intensive power plants have few alternative uses.

However, this situation has relevance for us today because rate suppression is, by definition, a reversal of the conditions that created the AJ effect and the collateral boom in power-plant construction. Today after a decade of rate suppression and earnings that are consistently less than the market cost of their capital, utility executives have put the AJ effect into reverse. Now we are witnessing a dramatic *underinvestment* in new power plants and economic projects such as coal conversion and conservation. Utility executives have adopted this "strategy of capital minimization" in order to minimize their firms' losses from rate suppression just as in previous decades they aggressively overinvested to maximize their profits.[11] But the results of this underinvestment are three regulatory penalties borne not by utilities but rather their ratepayers and the nation.

B. Regulatory Penalties

The *fuel penalty* arises when a utility fails to make otherwise economic investments in such options as coal conversion, conservation equipment, and the construction of new plants to replace existing plants that burn more expensive fuel (e.g., oil or natural gas). The New England Electric System, for example, has converted its oil plants at Brayton Point to coal, with reported savings to ratepayers of $110 million a year.[12] Consumers would not be reaping these benefits if the utility had refused to, or been deprived of the capital needed to, make the conversion. Nor would the nation be reducing its oil consumption and foreign imports by the 11 million barrels that this conversion annually saves.

Also included in the fuel penalty are the extra costs to the utility of operating old, inefficient plants and of buying power that is more expensive than the power that could be internally generated by new plants. Purchased electric power can be especially costly because its suppliers often link its price to the price of oil, regardless of how the electricity is actually generated.

For example, Canada supplies us with almost a billion dollars worth of electricity annually, and much of that is from cheap hydropower, which costs less than 1¢/kilowatt hour to generate. However, Canada's

National Energy Board has decreed that its selling price must be tied not to Canada's production costs but rather to the price of oil-fired generation. The result is a price tag upwards of 5¢/kilowatt hour. A fuel penalty results from such purchases when American utilities rely on them rather than building their own capacity that could deliver power more cheaply.*

The *cost-of-capital penalty* arises in two ways. First, as shown by economists such as Robert Trout and Stephen Archer, investors see rate-suppressed utilities as riskier than others and demand a one to two percentage point "risk premium" when buying the stocks and bonds of such utilities.[13] Thus, when a rate-suppressed utility sells bonds to build a new billion-dollar plant, it will pay $10 to $20 million more in annual interest costs than would a utility in a less rate suppressive state; these extra interest costs, however, are passed right through to consumers.

A second and more subtle way that the cost of capital penalty arises is in construction delays that result when rate suppression leaves a utility with a cash flow that is inadequate to complete a plant already under construction. The penalty results because the utility has to pay interest on the capital it has already invested in the plant for a longer period of time. These extra "carrying charges" can amount to millions of dollars: For example, a one-year delay on a half-completed two-billion-dollar plant means at least $100 million in extra interest charges with a 10 percent interest rate on bonds. In addition, since the real cost of building power plants has been steadily rising, these delays also increase the plant's total price tag in real dollars.

The *reliability penalty* arises most obviously when a utility fails to build enough new plants to meet its load growth and keep the lights on; this can happen when a utility expects such plants to earn inadequate investment returns under rate suppression. According to several studies by the Department of Energy, the utility industry has been canceling, delaying, and deferring new power-plant construction at a record pace; these studies also predict that because of such cutbacks, there will be serious electricity shortages in some regions during the 1980s and in other regions by the 1990s, with states like California, Texas, Arkansas, Louisiana, and the Dakotas particularly vulnerable.[14]

---

*A new coal-fired power plant can produce electricity 15 to 25 percent cheaper than the price stipulated in most Canadian contracts.

But the reliability penalty can be manifested in a more subtle way than simply by the existence of too few plants. When rate suppression squeezes a utility's earnings, it runs short of cash to pay expenses and shareholders' dividends. Its immediate response is a salutary one: It trims fat from its expense accounts by reducing personnel and cutting costs. But over time as this financial squeeze continues, it begins to cut into muscle and bone by skimping on its ordinary operations and maintenance expenses: Plant inspections and preventive repairs are made less often, old components are used longer, and fewer engineers are available to service the plants. As a result of this "O&M squeeze," plant reliability begins to deteriorate in exactly the same way as a different kind of "O&M squeeze" in Chapter 2 led to the deterioration of rent-controlled apartments. In turn, the probability of brownouts and black-outs rises and with it so does the reliability penalty—a particularly disturbing result for utilities with substantial nuclear capacity.[15]

Consumers bear this reliability penalty in several ways. Industrial or commercial consumers may respond to the prospect of electricity shortages either by shifting their production to less economic regions where electricity supply is more secure or by using capital they might have invested in modernization or expansion to build their own electrical generators. For residential customers, blackouts and brownouts mean tremendous inconvenience and discomfort, including the lack of air conditioning or heat in bad weather, refrigerator spoilage, crime in darkened streets, and even the loss of computer data.

C. Higher Consumer Rates for Less Reliable Service

Despite the fact that consumers are forced to bear these three regulatory penalties, it need not necessarily follow that they are worse off under rate suppression. After all, consumers realize substantial savings, at least in the short term. However, over the longer term, the reverse AJ effect begins to take its toll. For example, a rate-suppressed utility might forego converting several of its oil-burning plants to coal. As a result, its fuel expenses for those plants might be two or three times higher than if these plants had been converted.

Accordingly, at some point in time, there is a "crossover" whereby the consumer's electricity bill becomes higher under rate suppression because the utility's expenses are higher. The reason is that the costs of rate suppression in the form of higher expenses due to the regulatory penalties finally offset the benefits of rate suppression in the form of a lower rate of profit allowed to the utility.*

To find out whether consumers are better or worse off under rate suppression, it is necessary to evaluate the trade-off between lower electricity bills in the short term versus higher electricity bills in the longer term. This can be done using the concepts of net present value and the time value of money.

The "time value of money" simply means that a dollar today is worth more to us than a dollar a year from today. The reason is that if we had that dollar today, we could put it in the bank or otherwise invest it and earn interest on it so that a year from today we would have not only the original dollar but the interest as well.

The technique of "net present value" uses the concept of the time value of money to reduce a stream of payments (e.g., your annual electric utility bill) over a period of time (e.g., 20 years) to a single number. This single number indicates what that stream of payments over time would be worth in today's dollars, taking into account the opportunity to earn interest on it (i.e., taking into account the time value of money).†

Suppose, then, we are faced with the following choice. Under rate suppression, our utility bill at the end of this year will be $500 but, because of the regulatory penalties rate suppression imposes, it will be $1,000 next year. At an interest rate of 15 percent, the present value of these two payments today is $1,191.[16]

Alternatively, in the absence of rate suppression, our utility bill at the end of this year will be higher at $600 because our PUC has allowed the utility to earn its market cost of capital. But because our utility, in turn, has invested in an economic conservation project with some of these

*This trade-off can be a rather difficult concept to grasp. It helps to think of regulated electricity prices as consisting of two components: operating expenses *plus* the return on invested capital allowed by the regulators. Under rate suppression, the return on invested capital is lower (by definition), but over time, operating expenses are higher, primarily because of high fuel expenses due to a failure to undertake coal conversion and the like. Eventually, because of the three regulatory penalties, the low return on investment allowed by the PUC is offset by the higher expenses from the failure to undertake economic investment.

†The value of our dollar might be eroded by inflation, but inflation is usually built into the interest rate we can get on that invested dollar. Thus the present value procedure can also account for inflation.

earnings, next year, our bill will only be $700 (as opposed to the $1,000 under rate suppression). At the same interest rate of 15 percent, the present value of these two payments is only $1,051.[17]

In this example, at least, it is clear that the consumer is actually worse off under ostensibly beneficial rate suppression because he or she is forced to pay $140 more for electricity in today's dollars. To find out whether this result has any general application to today's situation of rate suppression and consumer welfare, I conducted a study for the U.S. Department of Energy that incorporated the net present value technique.[18]

My basic approach was to compute future electricity rates for a representative sample of electric utilities under two different scenarios— the status quo of rate suppression and capital minimization by utility executives versus a reformed regulatory climate in which utilities earned their market cost of capital and executives undertook all economic investments.

The results of that study confirmed that consumers will, as a rule, be worse off under rate suppression. For the six utilities examined, the per-utility costs of rate suppression ranged from a net present value of $242 million to a whopping $2.8 billion, while by the year 2000, electricity bills were projected to be 10 to 30 percent higher. Besides paying higher rates, consumers would have much less reliable service. Indeed, for some rate-suppressed utilities, available capacity to keep the lights on shrank to levels that virtually ensured brownouts and blackouts by the late 1990s. Unfortunately, the adverse effects of rate suppression do not stop with consumers; both national energy and economic policy goals are hurt as well.

D. Rate Suppression and National Energy Policy

Rate suppression hurts our national energy policy because it discourages utilities from investing in projects that would reduce the nation's consumption of foreign oil. As previously discussed, these projects range from energy conservation and the conversion of existing oil plants to coal to the construction of new, nonpetroleum power plants (using coal, wind, geothermal power, and the like) to replace existing, but noneconomic oil and natural gas plants.[19]

The importance of rate suppression to energy policy is evident in the fact that the electric utility industry is the single largest stationary source user of petroleum in the national economy, consuming well over one-half million barrels per day.* If the utility industry aggressively pursued all possible economic displacement of petroleum, the nation could cut its oil imports by a significant fraction. My DOE study confirmed this possibility: If rate suppression were eliminated, just the five petroleum-dependent utilities in the study sample could save enough oil to fill our entire Strategic Petroleum Reserve.

The desirability of such a reduction, after a decade of OPEC price shocks and heightened tensions in the Middle East, needs little elaboration. As history has painfully taught, heavy oil import dependence makes us vulnerable to inflation and worsens our trade balance at the same time that it heightens military tensions in an area of the world that furnishes a large share of oil to the United States and the industrialized democracies. The costs do not stop here, however. Today, as a result of the threat to national security that an oil import disruption implies, we spend roughly $5 billion annually on foreign aid and military construction to keep tankers moving in and out of the Persian Gulf region and Straits of Hormuz.

E. Rate Suppression and National Economic Policy

Rate suppression also hurts the goals of national economic policy—full employment, low inflation, increasing productivity, and steady growth.

At the "macro" level of the economy, there is a clearly established link between the rate of growth (as measured by the Gross National Product) and the growth in electricity demand.[20] In the context of rate suppression, this means that if the utility industry builds too few power plants to meet electricity demand—as current trends suggest it is doing—any sustained economic recovery in the 1980s and 1990s is likely to be jeopardized by an electricity shortage.[21] The result will be higher unemployment, lower real income, and a slower rate of growth (or possibly stagnation).

At the "micro" level of the economy where myriad business decisions are made, rate suppression likewise takes its toll because it affects key investment decisions by executives in other sectors of the economy. For

---

*The transportation sector is the largest nonstationary user.

example, one of the best ways for this nation to hold down inflation and stimulate growth is to invest in new productivity-enhancing technologies such as computers, robotics, and, in the steel industry, electric arc furnaces. However, executives who foresee a future of high-cost, unreliable electrical service due to rate suppression will be much more reluctant to invest in these time- and laborsaving electricity-intensive devices.[22]

Similarly, those executives who anticipate electricity shortages in a region may decide to relocate their plants or offices in regions where electricity supply is more secure but otherwise less economically attractive. Alternatively, they may use funds they might have otherwise invested in building more plants (and creating jobs) to build their own electricity supply. Even worse from the perspective of national employment, these executives may just opt to move their facilities to other countries where electricity supplies are cheaper and more secure, as the aluminum industry has begun to do.

In summary, the big losers from rate suppression include not only utility shareholders but consumers and national policy goals as well. What emerges from the economics of electric utility regulation, then, is a classic example of how playing the policy game better would make *everyone* better off. The remaining question is how to achieve this.

IV. POLICY REFORMS

As with previous cases, our analysis of the politics of rate suppression provides us with the key to developing constructive policy reforms.

To counter the political pressure on the PUCs and prevent them from being captured, PUC commissioners should be appointed rather than elected and their terms should be long enough to insulate them from the political clamor for lower rates. At the same time, the PUCs should be financed primarily through assessments on the utilities rather than from general tax revenues and the PUCs' budgets should to the greatest extent possible be out from under the control of state legislatures and their related constituency pressures.

To reduce the prospect of government failure, PUC budgets should be as large as the responsibilities that the PUCs face: PUC commissioners and their staffs should be paid salaries that are high enough to be competitive with those positions available in industry and the federal bureaucracy, and professional competency should be a legal requirement for the job. These reforms should help reduce the high turnover rates at the PUCs at the same time that they encourage the most highly qualified people to seek PUC positions.

Finally, the ideology of rate suppressive redistribution must be countered with information. One basic message that emerges from the economic analysis is that regardless of its intentions, rate suppression turns out to be a very counterproductive method of redistribution.

Liberals should not necessarily abandon their goals in this regard, however. If such redistribution is deemed desirable, there are other, more direct methods for achieving a more equal distribution. Options range from a general increase in the progressivity of the income tax to specific programs such as energy stamps or cash subsidies to lower-income electricity consumers. As with our rent control reforms, such programs would far more efficiently target benefits to those whom liberals intend to help.

The bulk of these policy reforms must necessarily be instituted at the state level, either through new legislation or public referenda. Whether such reforms will be embraced will depend on several important factors.

First, ratepayer groups must consider the possibility that their highly effective lobbying efforts ironically are working to defeat the very goals they pursue, the lowest possible rates for reliable service. Such a claim, of course, bears a suspicious resemblance to what the doctor sometimes tells us when we are sick: This is going to hurt, but it will make you better. One should rightly be skeptical of such reasoning, particularly when it involves paying higher prices to a business for its services. But in the case of electric utility regulation, rate suppression is arguably a virulent though subtle disease that afflicts ratepayers by raising rates higher than they otherwise would be. To avoid this affliction, ratepayers must be willing to pay slightly higher rates; such payments are, in fact, an investment in the nation's electricity future which promises a very real and substantial payback in the form of lower rates later, reduced foreign energy use, increased national security, and greater overall economic prosperity.

Second, in this new era of rising energy and capital costs and expanding technologies, states no longer can afford to lump their PUCs in with other state bureaucracies which, in today's world of government cutbacks, are subject to hiring freezes and budgeting caps. Instead, the states must invest in their PUCs as well to ensure against government failure; such an investment will likewise provide a big payback in the form of more jobs, more production, and ultimately, more tax revenues to finance necessary government services.

Finally, utility executives themselves have a responsibility to "clean up their act." The previous decades of prosperity and protective regulation did little to prepare these executives for the traumas and shocks of the 1970s and 1980s. In some cases, mismanagement has been the result of this complacency. Utility mistakes have, in turn, led to a collateral loss of faith by many consumers in their electric companies. This lost confidence has only made political matters worse for some utilities, never long on good reputation.

At the same time, some utility executives have had to be dragged kicking and screaming into the new era of high energy and capital costs. Rather than creatively embracing "soft path" options like energy conservation and a wider variety of electricity supply sources (wind, solar, geothermal), some of these executives have been content to merely follow the old "hard path" pattern of only building large central station power plants. The "smart path," however, is to embrace both hard and soft path approaches in a way that minimizes costs to customers.[23] A failure to do so only exacerbates the political and financial pressures now bearing down on the utility industry.

As a concluding comment, it must be noted that the implications of rate suppression for national energy and economic policies and national security far transcend the narrow distributional struggle being waged at the state level. Should the states fail to act on the preceding reforms, some federal solution to the problem of rate suppression may be desirable. The policy options range from a federalization or regionalization of PUC regulation to more Draconian solutions such as deregulation or nationalization of the industry.

Of these options, the most promising appears to be *regionalization*.[24] By setting up commissions on a regional basis but letting states have representation by allowing them to appoint their own commissioners, the government could preserve a degree of state control over state-based utilities that more closely parallels that of the regional electrical generation and delivery system. At present, most utilities provide electricity on an interstate basis and many are organized into sophisticated power pools that help minimize the cost of electricity through power sharing. In contrast, state PUCs rarely communicate or coordinate with one another. Accordingly, regional regulation would better mirror the organization of today's utility system. It would also provide a system better equipped to cope with the kinds of energy shortages that resulted from events during the last decade such as the oil embargo of 1973–74 and the 109-day coal strike of 1978.

Whether the states move to act or whether the federal government steps in must be settled soon, however. At least in the case of electric utility regulation, the long run is already here.

9
The Logic of Ideology

TRADITIONAL CONSERVATISM VERSUS MODERN LIBERALISM

In Chapter 7, we examined the logic of libertarian conservatism versus modern liberalism within the context of a set of three principles; the values, beliefs, and assumptions underlying those principles; and the policy preferences that those principles imply. Here we continue our examination of the logic of America's ideologies, this time by contrasting the four principles of traditional or Burkean conservatism with modern liberalism.

A. Traditionalism Versus Experimentalism

A resistance to change and respect for the status quo are themes that weave their way consistently through the four principles of Burkean conservatism. Nowhere are these precepts more evident than in the clash between traditionalism and experimentalism, a clash that marks the fourth major difference in principles between American conservatives and liberals.

1. Conservative Traditionalism

... I cannot see any better principle at present than to make as little innovation as possible; keep things going as well as we can in the present train.[1]

JOHN ADAMS

Broadly speaking, traditionalism refers to the tendency to rely on existing institutions, customs, traditions, and political, economic, and social arrangements to guide American society. The conservative's sacred trinity of the Church, the Family, and the Constitution, together with his embrace of basic American values such as the work ethic, constitute the bedrock of this traditionalist society.

The conservative's traditionalism begins in an essentially cynical view of man: The traditions and customs of society are necessary to help establish a set of rules that provide "checks upon man's anarchic impulses."[2] Religious tradition—in this case the values of Judeo-Christianity —plays a particularly crucial role here, providing man both with the proper guidelines for behavior and a powerful inducement to moral conduct.

This religious tradition is embodied in an important absolute—the Divine Law of God. Synonymous with the Ten Commandments and the Sermon on the Mount, this higher law means that there *are* objective standards of right and wrong. Thus, while mores may change, basic morals and ethics should not; and any such change is only symptomatic of the decay of society and its basic values. These beliefs give many in the conservative camp—particularly the far Right "moral majority"— their righteousness and fervor over social issues.

At the same time, the conservative embraces his intellectual forefather Edmund Burke's belief that the traditions of any society are both the transmitters and receptacles of knowledge. Because established governments, laws, customs, religions, and the like embody the accumulated wisdom of the past, they are worthy of respect and may be relied on for guidance.

In this regard, the conservative sees man as participating in the accumulated experience of his ancestors, a "partnership" as it were between "those who are living, those who are dead, and those who are to be born."[3] Through this Burkean lens, the conservative sees society as a fragile and delicate fabric woven through history. He fears that if we pull too hard at one or several of the delicate threads of tradition—by insisting on too rapid or radical change—the entire tapestry of society will unravel. Hence attacks on the family like "open marriage" and the sexual revolution have potentially grave consequences for social stability, as do other radical shifts in customs. Accordingly, the conservative resists change; if it must come, it should come slowly.

2. Liberal Experimentalism

The commitment of liberalism to experimental procedure carries with it the idea of continuous reconstruction of the ideas of individuality and of liberty in intimate connection with changes in social relations.[4]

JOHN DEWEY

The essence of liberal experimentalism is a willingness to alter, re-form, or abandon existing institutions, customs, traditions, and eco-nomic, political, and social arrangements. In the spirit of the doctrine's author, John Dewey, the liberal's intention is to improve society through such experimentation; his most prized contribution is positive and pro-gressive change.

This embrace of experimentalism begins in a skepticism, even a deep suspicion, about the role of existing traditions, institutions, and customs in society. In one sense, the liberal regards them not as Burke's embodi-ment of wisdom, but as "accidents of the past," sometimes useful but equally often, misleading. Thus there is no reason to favor ideas, institu-tions, or traditions merely because our ancestors have. Rather, a particu-lar idea or custom must prove its worth every day in the cauldron of changing circumstances. In this regard, John Stuart Mill's insistence that "the despotism of custom is everywhere the standing hindrance to hu-man advancement"[5] has far more appeal than the Burkean reverence for tradition.

In a more cynical way, the liberal also sees the yoke of tradition as a "delusory mysticism" propagated by the rich and powerful primarily to keep those on the lower rungs of society in their place. It is this attitude that makes the liberal the "enemy of authority, of prejudice, of the merely traditional, customary or habitual."[6] In this view, the ignorance and pov-erty of today are the products of the "errors and injustices of the past";[7] we should not cling to such a past, but rather be ready to throw off the yoke of tradition and undertake prompt, and even drastic revisions.

As a particular target, the liberal rejects religious tradition as a guide to secular politics, viewing the church as a primary progenitor of the delusory mysticism hindering progress. While the liberal may be deeply religious, he has a greater fear that without a clear separation of church and state, the church will unduly influence society and eventually corrupt government. Accordingly, he resists the encroachment of organized religion or any sectarian institution.

Nor does the liberal accept the conservative's religious absolutism. Instead, he prefers to "worship" the gods of relativism and reason, for to the liberal, "nothing is more certain in modern society than the principle that there are no absolutes."[8] Hence, truth, morality, and ethics need continual redefinition. And because the liberal "is confident that reason and rational science, without appeal to revelation, faith, custom, or intuition, can both comprehend the world and solve its problems,"[9] it follows that we should not hesitate to change our institutions and customs in seeking that better redefinition.

3. Traditionalist–Experimentalist Policy Games.   In the policy arena, the traditionalist–experimentalist clash is no more volatile than over social issues. To the conservative, legalized abortion, teenage birth control, homosexuality, premarital sex, pornography, and other such symptoms of the sexual revolution are dangerous solvents of basic American values. Accordingly, they are all targets of a traditionalist wrath that crystallizes in proposed or enacted laws, regulations, and even Constitutional amendments: Federal funds can't finance abortions, teenagers must get parental consent to buy birth control pills, gays can't teach in the public schools, and unmarried members of the opposite sex can't live together legally.

Similarly, the liberal has his hands full of traditionalist opposition when it comes to protecting and promoting women's rights through policies such as the "family wrecking" Equal Rights Amendment, the less heralded, but no less controversial Equal Pay Act, and other laws that facilitate single-parent families and accelerate divorce proceedings. On the religious front, the liberal also has to beat back the conservative's repeated efforts to bring church and state closer together through such policies as school prayer and subsidies to parochial schools.

Finally, the traditionalist–experimentalist split is also deeply embedded in several disputes over educational policy. While the liberal strongly supports widespread and well-funded public education as the best means to nurture man's intelligence and provide him with the reasoning powers to solve society's problems, the conservative sees in the experimentalist approach "a systematic attempt to undermine . . . society's traditions and beliefs."[10] At the same time, the conservative sees liberal educators creating a "mass adversary culture"[11] in which today's students seem "unable to distinguish between right and wrong."[12] He would reverse this trend by supporting higher academic standards and a more classical, religiously grounded curriculum rather than the liberal's avant garde, agnostic one. Tuition tax credits for parochial schools, cuts in federal aid to education, and dismantling the Department of Education all represent policy options in the conservative's arsenal to achieve these goals.

B. Law and Order Versus Due Process

Both the conservative and liberal recognize that law and order and due process are essential features of the American system. However, when these two requirements come into conflict—as they inevitably must— the conservative is more apt to lean toward law and order, while the liberal will be more concerned with due process. This conflict constitutes a fifth major battle in the ideology wars.

1. Conservative Law and Order

Repression is an unpleasant instrument, but it is absolutely necessary for civilizations that believe in order and human rights.[13]

WILLIAM BUCKLEY

To the conservative, law and order means that the police should have all the authority necessary to detect and apprehend criminals, that the courts should try people fairly but swiftly, that the guilty must face stiff and sure punishment, and that our jails are meant to punish, not "coddle," criminals.

At the same time, the conservative sees a much too liberal interpretation of the due process doctrine as thwarting law and order: The "exclusionary rule" is an "absurd proposition that a law-enforcement error, no matter how technical, can be used to justify throwing an entire case out of court, no matter how guilty the defendant or how heinous the crime."[14] Similarly, the Constitutional protection against cruel and unusual punishment has not only been used to prevent capital punishment (which the conservative favors), but has also been perverted to the point where it also lets prisoners demand "access to law libraries and color

TV,"[15] while legal loopholes such as the indiscriminate use of the Fifth Amendment and the insanity plea let villains walk away from their criminal deeds scot-free.

As with his traditionalism, the conservative's overriding concern for law and order is deeply rooted in his belief that there are "ineradicable limits, defects, evils and irrationalities in human nature."[16] Indeed, while man is basically good, he is also quite prone to evil[17] in the absence of any authority imposed upon him. Society must be protected from these "darker impulses of human nature"[18] through a strict system of law and order to hold back the Hobbesian jungle that would otherwise engulf us. Thus a strict system of law and order is an essential bulwark against anarchy and tyranny, and the liberal's contempt for law and order, coupled with a "permissive" attitude, has only paved the way for riots and social instability.

Finally, the conservative's insistence on swift and sure punishment is a logical extension of his belief that today's criminals "are not desperate men seeking bread for their families" but that "crime is the way they've chosen to live."[19] Accordingly, each individual—not his economic or social environment—must be held accountable for his actions and duly punished when he chooses a life of crime.

2. Liberal Due Process

No person shall be . . . deprived of life, liberty, or property, without due process of the law.

THE FIFTH AMENDMENT

To the liberal, due process means that police powers should be limited to those necessary to apprehend criminals, and law enforcement agencies should be closely monitored to ensure against any repressive practices. At the same time, criminal justice need not be so swift as to threaten the rights of the accused; the appeals process, no matter how lengthy, is an important insurance policy against convicting the innocent. While the guilty should be punished, the prisons administering that punishment also have an important responsibility to rehabilitate those who commit crimes.

At the same time, the liberal views the devices of due process such as the Fifth Amendment, the exclusionary rule, and the insanity plea as important safeguards of a free society founded on the law. While a few guilty individuals may abuse these safeguards and go free, the liberal sees this as a necessary price of freedom, for he would rather see one hundred men slip through Justice's grasp than have one innocent man go to jail.

At the heart of the liberal's concern for due process and his aversion to authoritarian cries for law and order is a much more optimistic view of human nature. To the liberal, human beings are naturally benevolent, generous, and good; when they do evil, it is because they have been forced to by the accident of their own unfortunate circumstances.

It is this belief that crime is rooted primarily in man's material environment, not human nature, that accounts for the liberal's more sympathetic and compassionate view toward the criminal: Robbery is often traceable to economic deprivation, violent crimes such as rape and murder are often rooted in a rage against social injustice or family abuse, and much revolution and social unrest begin in political repression.

Accordingly, while individuals must bear responsibility for their actions, society also must share much of the blame when man does evil. In this regard, the liberal sees the conservative's lust for law and order as a myopic attack on the symptoms of the disease rather than on the disease itself. Such an attack does not prevent anarchy; it encourages authoritarianism. Indeed, because the crime problem is largely traceable to economic, social, and political problems, expanding police powers and building more prisons is a "solution" that only worsens the problem and creates greater divisiveness in society.

Ultimately, the liberal's answer to the problems of crime and social unrest is not to destroy due process, but to eliminate crime's economic, political, and social causes. That means that government must shoulder the responsibility for achieving economic, political, and social reforms.

3. Law and Order–Due Process Policy Games. The high profile policy issues in this ideological conflict are the aforementioned capital punishment, which the conservative favors, and the exclusionary rule and insanity plea, which have come under constant conservative attack. But there also are a number of other policy issues that periodically take center stage.

Two well-known liberal bugaboos are "no-knock laws" (which permit police to forceably search the homes of suspected criminals without previously notifying them) and wiretapping—unpleasant activities that the conservative has supported or at least condoned as necessary to combat crime.

The conservative also has led the policy charge for an end to plea bargaining as well as bail reform, which would permit judges to keep repeat offenders "from using bail to return to the streets, never to be seen in court again until they are arrested for another crime,"[20] while one of the hottest new law-and-order issues supported by conservatives involves forcing criminals to pay restitution to their victims.

Finally, the prison system is an ongoing focus of ideological fireworks. On the one hand, the conservative wants to build more prisons to properly punish criminals with stiff sentences. On the other hand, the liberal laments this "Devil's Island mentality" and would rather use such government funds for more prisoner education and rehabilitation as well as for broader programs that attack the underlying economic, social, and political roots of crime.

C. Democratism Versus Republicanism

Stripped of their political party connotations, the "republican" and "democratic" labels convey a sixth conservative–liberal split. This split centers around a question the founding fathers first had to grapple with: To what extent should the American government be directly controlled *by* the people versus indirectly controlled *for* the people by their representatives?

1. Conservative Republicanism

We may appeal to every page of history . . . for proofs irrefragable, that the people, when they have been unchecked, have been as unjust, tyrannical, brutal, barbarous and cruel as any king or senate possessed of uncontrollable power.[21]

JOHN ADAMS

The essence of conservative republicanism is *indirect* control of the government by the American people through their elected representatives and appointed officials who rule for them in their best interests. While the upper echelons of government—the president, governors, legislators—may be chosen by popular vote, wherever possible, other offi-cials should be appointed on the basis of merit. Merit selection ensures that only individuals of talent are in positions to make policy choices, while the appointments process helps insulate these professionals (par-ticularly judges and regulators) from the sometimes misguiding pres-sures of the ballot box.

Thus, in the conservative's republic, government officials should lis-ten to the voice of the people, but they are to act more as "trustees" of the public interest than as delegates of the people; these highly qualified professionals should base their decisions on what they believe is good for the people, not necessarily on what the people clamor for. As Ed-mund Burke summarized this trustee responsibility: "While a member of the legislature ought to give great weight to the wishes of his constit-uents, he ought never sacrifice to them his unbiased opinion, his mature judgment, his enlightened conscience."[22]

At the same time, the republican system also features a number of "checks and balances" that make the policy process resistant to rapid change. For example, staggering the electoral terms of the president and Congress provides an imposing hurdle to rapid shifts in policy because it takes at least six years for the people to vote all of the members of an existing government out of office.

The cornerstone of the conservative's republicanism is his Madisonian fear of a tyranny of the majority: The clear danger of democracy is that it provides a powerful mechanism by which a majority can dictate policies to a minority. It was precisely this fear of "mob rule" that prompted the founding fathers to install various checks on majority rule: Equal repre-sentation in the Senate protects the smaller states from the larger ones, while the filibuster, presidential veto, and right of the Supreme Court to judicial review are all republican devices that a minority can use to thwart the majority's will.

The conservative's conception of the government official as trustee rather than delegate is likewise rooted in the belief that in a complex world where it is both difficult and expensive to be properly informed, the average American will have neither the information nor the training to make important policy decisions. Thus it is better to have a trained professional assume this role, and by appointing that official, the deci-sion process is insulated from the pressures of "popular sway" that can arise when the public is misinformed. The result is that republican government "refine(s) and enlarge(s) the public views by passing them through the medium of a chosen body of citizens . . . least likely to sacrifice it to temporary or partial considerations."[23] In contemporary terms, that means republican politicians will be less prone to sacrifice the long-run interests of the nation for short-run political expediency.

Finally, harking back to the logic of traditionalism, the features of republicanism that make the government resistant to rapid change—staggered terms, the filibuster, and other such devices—arise out of the conservative's belief that the American political system is the product of the wisdom of the Founding Fathers and, as a delicate yet enduring mechanism, it should not undergo any rapid or drastic alteration.

2.   Liberal Democratism

. . . it is necessary to introduce the people into every department of government as far as they are capable of exercising it . . . this is the only way to insure a long continued and honest administration of power.[24]

THOMAS JEFFERSON

In contrast, the essence of liberal democracy is *direct* popular control of the government by a voting majority. To achieve this goal, the people's representatives should be drawn from the whole spectrum of society rather than some elite pool of professional talent. Wherever possible, these officials should be elected rather than appointed to ensure that true representatives of the people are chosen, and any officials who shirk their responsibilities should be promptly subjected to the pressures of the ballot box. Thus government officials are expected to both listen to and obey the will of the people. As delegates, they are to serve their constituents, not necessarily their conscience.

At the same time, liberal democracy means that the government must be open and accessible to the people and readily responsive to public opinion. Democratic procedures such as the initiative, referendum, and recall provide the people with an ability to bring about changes more swiftly than they might otherwise achieve under a purely representative government.

The liberal's desire for an open and democratic, freely elected government begins in his Jeffersonian fear of any autocratic "ruling elite" entrenching itself in a professional bureaucracy dedicated to protecting the rich and powerful. In this sense, the electoral process, together with the "spoils system," which awards government jobs on the basis of political loyalties, are powerful cleansing agents and safeguards against attempts by elites to capture power and ensconce themselves.

At the same time, the liberal's conception of the government official as a delegate rather than a trustee is rooted in his faith that the American people are intelligent and informed enough to know what is good for them and that when they speak—through opinion polls, the ballot box, and other such conduits—their representatives should listen and obey.

Finally, democratic features such as the recall and referendum, which open the policy process up to popular and swift, rather than legislative and protracted, change hark back to the liberal's experimentalism. They are important instruments of progressive improvement in a government which, while established in the wisdom of one era, must necessarily adapt to changing conditions in a more modern era.

3. Republican–Democratic Policy Games. Practically speaking, the American system of representative democracy is a republican form of government. What distinguishes the conservative from the liberal in the policy wars over this principle is the *degree* of republicanism and democracy that each pursues. For example, in the past, women's suffrage, the adoption of direct referenda procedures, the direct election of senators, and the abolition of the poll tax were all post-Constitutional policy shifts that, with liberal support and despite conservative opposition, have pushed the American republic more toward the democratic end of the spectrum.

Today the conservative's policy preferences are largely reflected in a basic holding action against the seemingly inexorable liberal erosion of the republicanism written into the original Constitution. In recent years, this erosion has been evident in such liberal policy victories as the public financing of, and spending limits on, presidential and congressional elections; an end to the seniority system in Congress; "sunshine laws" opening up congressional hearings to the public; the increasing use of direct referenda; the move to elect, rather than appoint, state public utility commissioners; and such electoral reforms as lowering the voting age to 18 and the bilingual ballot.

Not satisfied with these victories, the liberal continues to press for further democratic reforms against stiff conservative opposition. Open voter and postcard registration remain at the top of the list of the liberal's preferred electoral changes, while turning the "cloture rule" in the Senate from a two-thirds to a simple majority vote is seen as essential to curb conservative abuse of the filibuster. And, of course, the age-old efforts of liberals to eliminate the electoral college's role in choosing the president are regularly reborn with each coming presidential election.

D. States' Rights Versus Federalism

From America's earliest days under the Articles of Confederation and its perhaps most difficult Civil War years to today's often vitriolic confrontations over issues ranging from desegregation to energy taxes, the banner of states' rights has periodically been raised by conservatives in defiance of attempts by the federal government to coordinate, and in some cases simply dictate, national policies to the states. This clash marks the seventh important battle in the ideology wars.

1. Conservative States' Rights

The powers not delegated to the United States by the Constitution . . . are reserved to the states.

THE TENTH AMENDMENT

The conservative favors the strong expression of states' rights within the context of a loose federal union and a strict construction of the Constitution and regards the right of the federal government to determine state policies as tightly constrained by the Tenth Amendment: All duties and responsibilities not explicitly set forth in the Constitution are the province of the states. Through this perspective of states' rights, the Constitution expressly forbids federal intrusion into a wide range of policy issues from school busing and public education to the control of local police and voter registration.

Harking back to his minimal state principle, the primary force behind the conservative's preference for states' rights is his "profound distrust of power in general and of centralized rulership in particular."[25] The Constitutional protection of states' rights is an important safeguard of freedom because it prevents "the accumulation of power in a central government that is remote from the people and relatively immune from popular restraints."[26]

At the same time, the states' rights principle is a natural extension of conservative republicanism because it prevents a different kind of "tyranny of the majority," that of one state or region over another state or region. In insisting on states' rights, the conservative thus may acknowledge the potential good of a coordinated federal policy, but he consciously elects to forego such federalist benefits because of a greater fear of the tyranny that might result.

Finally, as his most positive argument for states' rights, the conservative "recognizes the principle that essentially local problems are best dealt with by the people most directly concerned."[27] Thus, while the federal government has an important role to play in providing such things as national defense, the conservative believes that the states and local communities will perceive their problems more clearly and conceive better-tailored and infinitely wiser solutions to them.

2. Liberal Federalism

When the state governments fail to satisfy the needs of the people, the people appeal to the Federal Government.[28]

CHIEF JUSTICE EARL WARREN

In contrast, the liberal favors the strong expression of federal rights within the context of a loose construction of the Constitution. He prefers to read between the lines of that document for duties not explicitly stated, viewing federalism as a constructive means both to develop wise and prudent policies at the national level and then to assist (and if necessary, force) the states to adopt them.

While the conservative invokes the Tenth Amendment to argue for states' rights, the liberal finds his federalist license to challenge them in the "necessary and proper" clause that gives Congress a discretionary choice in making laws to carry out the spirit (as opposed to the mere letter) of the Constitution. This license allows the federal government to assume a wide range of responsibilities, from racial and educational policies to energy and environmental issues.

The liberal's federalist persuasion begins in his belief that if morality, ethics, economics, or just plain common sense make a public policy desirable (e.g., desegregation, environmental protection), then the policy should be adopted by the whole nation. But such a uniformity of result is impossible unless the federal government imposes it on the states;

some states will resist, either for fiscal or, more likely, philosophical reasons—a case in point being the Southern states' traditional ideological resistance to desegregation.

In one sense then, the liberal views states' rights not as a healthy buffer against a centralized government, but rather as a doctrinaire mask donned by reactionary minorities to thwart the democratic will of the people. Thus the liberal's embrace of federalism is merely a politically pragmatic response to pockets and enclaves of conservatism that would otherwise be immune to reform and change.

In another sense, the liberal is also aware of the financial obstacles that prevent the poorer states from adopting enlightened policies such as comprehensive public education and adequate sewage treatment without federal assistance. As an equally pragmatic redistributive tool then, the liberal also sees federalism not as a means by which some states or regions "beggar" others, but as a useful and equitable way to transfer income from the richer to the poorer states in the interests of the nation.

In justifying this response, the liberal argues that along with states' rights there are "corresponding states' responsibilities."[29] Thus, if some states fail to fulfill those responsibilities, the federal government has both a right and a duty to intervene.

Finally, the liberal invokes several economic arguments to counter conservative claims that state and local governments are better able to solve their problems. First, the federal government has the advantage of economies of scale: Because of its size, it has more expertise and resources to identify problems and develop policy responses. At the same time, it can implement many of those policies much more economically through its centralized bureaucracy, which can avoid the waste and inefficiency of duplicating the same policymaking apparatus in each of the 50 states.

Second, there is the familiar "free rider" problem that federalism can solve: the tendency of the states to enjoy the benefits of a public good like clean air and clean water without paying for them. For example, the liberal believes that the goal of cleaning up the environment is greatly enhanced by federalism. If a state such as Ohio were to enact lenient air pollution requirements while its neighbors in Indiana and Michigan were to enact strict laws, the result would be that industry would gravitate to Ohio to lower its costs and the pollution carried by winds would spill over the borders. Both Indiana and Michigan would lose not only clean air, but also jobs. Faced with such disincentives, the likely result is that states would compete for industry by abandoning strict environmental laws. Federalism eliminates this competition by imposing a uniform law on all the states.

3. States' Rights–Federalism Policy Games. While our ancestors fought over slavery and tariff issues, the most prominent modern states' rights policy issues include federally imposed school busing to achieve desegregation (which conservatives strongly oppose), the ongoing debate over whether public education should be funded by the federal government (as liberals favor) or by state and local governments (as conservatives insist), whether the states should ratify the Equal Rights Amendment, and the desirability of federal environmental regulations, which liberals have helped turn into legislation to fight air, water, and other forms of pollution.

The energy crisis of the 1970s has also given birth to several additional states' rights issues. For example, the conservative is in sympathy with the right of a state to impose severance taxes on the production of resources like coal and oil while, despite his desire to enhance competition in energy markets, he has resisted federal legislation that would grant coal slurry pipelines rights-of-way to compete with coal-carrying railroads by invoking eminent domain. In creating enormous pressures and strains on the state regulation of electric utilities, the energy crisis has also spawned a liberal vision of a regionalized or nationalized regulation of industry, a vision that the conservative would rather not see.

Finally, the states' rights issue is embedded in the more esoteric debate as to whether federal aid to the states should be earmarked by the federal government for specific purposes (e.g., sewage treatment) or, as conservatives prefer, offered in block grants to the states, which can then dispose of those funds at their own discretion. This debate has lain at the heart of the Reagan administration's attempt to introduce a "New Federalism" based on a greater fiscal responsibility of the states, both to raise funds to finance government and to distribute those funds. Given its conservative roots, the New Federalism might have been more aptly named a "new affirmation of states' rights."

Let us see, then, how several of these principles in the Burkean conservative–modern liberal split underlie the public interest arguments for and against the Equal Rights Amendment, which is the topic of our next policy game.

10

The 59¢ Gap

THE EQUAL RIGHTS
AMENDMENT POLICY GAME

It's time to set the record straight. The claim that American
women are downtrodden and unfairly treated is the fraud
of the century. The truth is that American women never
had it so good. Why should we lower ourselves to
"equal rights" when we already have the status of
special privilege?[1]

Thus spake Phyllis Schlafly—dar-
ling of the Right and bête noire of the feminist movement—and what
looked like a quick landslide victory for the Equal Rights Amendment in
1972 turned into a decade of frustration and, ultimately, bitter defeat for
feminists.* Today the seemingly endless struggle to ratify the amendment continues as once-spurned ERA supporters embark on yet another
ratification round and once-victorious ERA opponents again entrench
themselves for the latest onslaught.

In examining the politics and economics of this controversial issue

---

*Schlafly's opening gambit against the ERA in her monthly newsletter (epitomized in
the chapter opening quote) and the subsequent formation of STOP-ERA is generally
recognized as the major turning point in the 1970s' drive for ERA state ratification.

within the context of our capture-ideology framework, we will have the opportunity to showcase several of the principles dividing Burkean or traditional conservatives from modern liberals. At the same time, the ERA policy game will also demonstrate that, while it has great potential, economic analysis cannot always act as the final arbiter in a policy dispute. Indeed, on some issues like the ERA, one must go far beyond economics and sober cost-benefit analyses into the realm of wide-ranging and difficult to assess societal and religious impacts.

I.   HISTORY AND BACKGROUND

Equality of rights under the law shall not be denied or abridged by the United States or by any State on account of sex.

THE EQUAL RIGHTS AMENDMENT (SECTION 1)

This seemingly simple 24-word statement has one of the longest and most controversial histories of any piece of legislation ever proposed, a history that goes much further back than the early 1970s when the ERA first entered the consciousness and vocabulary of most Americans. In fact, the struggle for ERA ratification today is but an extension of a battle that began over 50 years ago in the wake of the debate over women's suffrage. If we were to travel back in time to that earlier era, here's what we would see.

The year is 1920. After decades of struggle, the women's movement in America has reached its zenith of political power with successful ratification of the Nineteenth Amendment, granting women the right to vote. Heady with victory and organized in a way that would make any army general envious, the successful suffragettes are, however, at a critical crossroads.

The more conservative members of the movement, led by the League of Women Voters, feel that the war for women's rights has been won. They now want to turn their attention to an array of broader social reforms, including child labor and wage-hour laws, social security and public health programs.

However, the more militant suffragettes, led by firebrand Alice Paul and the National Women's Party (NWP), see the Nineteenth Amendment not as an armistice, but as an intermediate stop on a still long march to full sexual equality. With the enemy of male supremacy on the run, they want to finish the war with total victory and they see equal rights legislation as the only way to end sexual discrimination once and for all.

In 1923, the NWP formally proposes the original ERA,[2] but as the amendment is introduced in Congress, it draws immediate opposition from the larger and more powerful League of Women Voters. And so the ERA struggle begins, with the battle lines clearly drawn between an earlier generation of radical feminists and conservative traditionalists.

The NWP ensconces itself in a large lobbying house on the edge of Congress. Primarily through its efforts, the ERA is introduced in varying forms in virtually every Congressional session for the next fifty-odd years. However, opposition from the League remains stiff and their ranks are joined by the National Women's Trade Union League, the American Association of University Women, and various other labor and civil rights organizations—all of which will in time switch sides.[3]

During most of the ensuing 40 years, the ERA lies buried deeply in committees. In the few years that the measure is seriously considered (1946, 1950, and 1953), it is soundly trounced. But with each defeat, the NWP, along with its major ally the National Federation of Business and Professional Women, gamely wipes the dust off and like Sisyphus, starts the ERA boulder rolling back up again.

Finally, in the 1960s, several events conspire to create a reemerged feminism. In 1963, the President's Commission on the Status of Women issues an eye-opening report that documents "just how thoroughly women are still denied rights and opportunities."[4] Besides alerting women to their own plight of discrimination, the report results in the formation of 50 state commissions to probe similar inequalities at the state level.

That same year, Betty Friedan publishes *The Feminine Mystique*, which documents the plight of overeducated women trapped in their roles of homemaker and mother. Books equally critical of woman's role as the "second sex"[5] by Kate Millett, Germaine Greer, and others soon follow. During a decade of social reform, these books arouse women to organize and speak out for their rights.[6]

In 1966, Friedan establishes what will soon become the largest pro-ERA lobby, the National Organization for Women (NOW). NOW helps organize a national women's strike in 1970 to commemorate the Nineteenth Amendment's fiftieth anniversary. The large numbers of supporters shock the country and, more important, the media, into recognizing the women's movement as a legitimate and potentially powerful force in American politics. The strike also helps NOW to expand its membership dramatically. The drive for the ERA once again begins in earnest.

On June 11, 1970, Representative Martha Griffins (D, Michigan) invokes the unusual tactic of a "discharge petition" to move the measure out of a House committee where arch-ERA foe Chairman Emanuel Celler (D, New York) has stalled it for 22 years. Ten days later, Griffins has enough signatures to liberate the ERA from committee and for the first time in history, the House passes the ERA by 325 to 15.

Two more years of procedural delays drag by before the full Congress approves the measure by a landslide, with the Senate vote 84 to 8 and the House vote 354 to 23. On March 22, 1972, the amendment is sent to the states for ratification by the required three-fourths majority.

At the crack of the Congressional starting gun, the ERA bursts out of the gate with all the style, strength, and speed of a Kentucky Derby thoroughbred headed for certain victory. Within hours, Hawaii grabs the honor of being the first state to ratify the ERA and in that year, 21 states follow suit.

But in that same year, traditionalist Phyllis Schlafly fires her first conservative broadside at the amendment in her monthly newsletter and announces the formation of STOP-ERA—to do just that. Joined by such acronymically creative groups as POW and HOTDOG (Protect Our Women and Humanitarians Opposed To Degrading Our Girls), Schlafly's anti-ERA forces begin to surface in the unratified states.

In 1973, the Georgia legislature soundly rejects ratification while Oklahoma, Nevada, and Virginia soon follow suit. To add insult to injury, Schlafly's armies launch a counteroffensive in several of the ratified states and pro-ERA forces watch in disbelief as three states that had voted favorably on the amendment—Tennessee, Nebraska, and Idaho— take the unprecedented (and possibly illegal)[7] step of rescinding their favorable vote, while the legislatures in Kentucky and South Dakota pass legislation that amounts to de facto rescission.[8]

In 1977, Indiana becomes the thirty-fifth and *last* state to ratify. With the clock ticking down to zero on their seven-year ratification deadline, ERA strategists write off the hard-core opponent states like Utah and Missouri and narrow their sights to North Carolina, Florida, Oklahoma, and Illinois, home base of Schlafly's organization and the only northern industrial state not to ratify.

The struggle is a protracted one in these four states, and a last-ditch effort is made to extend the ERA ratification drive. But while Congress grants ERA supporters an extension from March 22, 1979 to June 30, 1982—amidst cries of "foul" by the anti-ERA forces—this grace period is to no avail.

Despite a massive fund-raising and lobbying campaign, the ERA is dealt three crushing blows in the last month of its life as North Carolina, Florida, and Illinois all reject ratification. On June 30, 1982, the 10-year drive for the ERA is officially pronounced dead. In separate press conferences, pro-ERA forces issue a MacArthurian proclamation that "We Shall Return" and anti-ERA forces insist the coffin of the "unEqual Rights Amendment" is nailed shut forever. The map in Figure 10.1 shows the final tally: 30 states unequivocally for the ERA, 5 in the rescission or doubtful column, and 15 unalterably opposed.

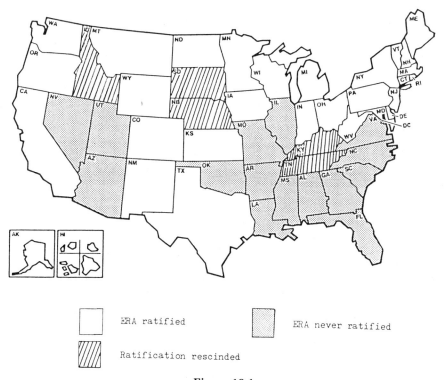

ERA ratified

ERA never ratified

Ratification rescinded

Figure 10.1.

It is against this historical backdrop—and cognizant that a new ERA is already trying to work its way through the ratification process—that we use our capture-ideology framework to analyze the politics of women's rights.

II. THE POLITICS OF THE ERA

Table 10.1 provides an overview of the major players in the ERA policy game. Let's introduce these players and then see how the goals of each group might fit into a capture versus an ideological interpretation of ERA lobbying.

A. ERA Supporters

Not surprisingly, women's groups represent the single largest lobbying force in support of the ERA; within the women's pro-ERA lobby, there are two basic divisions.

The most active and militant segment consists of a number of broad-based feminist organizations, the most important and politically potent being NOW, the National Women's Political Caucus (NWPC), and the Women's Equity Action League (WEAL).[9] NOW is the largest and most prominent feminist organization; its membership has steadily climbed throughout the ERA struggle, rising from 1,122 members and 14 chapters in 1962[10] to over 250,000 members and 800 chapters today.[11] Its budget has undergone an equally dramatic growth, rising from less than $7,000 in 1967[12] to over $6.5 million today.[13]

TABLE 10.1.   PLAYERS IN THE ERA POLICY GAME

ERA Supporters	ERA Opponents
The pro-ERA women's lobby	The anti-ERA women's lobby
The feminist movement	The business lobby
Traditional women's groups	The anti-ERA church lobby
The public interest lobby	The conservative lobby (and radical fringe)
The pro-ERA church lobby	
The government lobby	
The labor lobby	

A 1974 survey of NOW members provides an interesting profile of the "average" feminist: She is typically a young, highly educated, working woman earning substantially less than her husband and/or other males.[14] In the academic jargon of woman activist and scholar Jo Freeman, she is "experiencing the greatest amount of relative deprivation"[15] in the job market, an observation that supports the notion (discussed more fully later) that economic motives are an important force behind the women's movement.

The NWPC was established in 1971 at a Washington meeting arranged by a number of well-known feminist luminaries, including Bella Abzug, Shirley Chisholm, and Gloria Steinem. Its primary political task is getting more women elected and appointed. Structured on the "leadership" or "cadre" model of many lobbies, NWPC claims over 50,000 contributing members, but 80 percent of these members are merely "associates." Only 20 percent play an active participatory role.

WEAL is the smallest of the major feminist groups, with 3,500 members. The self-proclaimed "right wing" of the feminist movement, it was founded in 1968 by Ohio lawyer Dr. Elizabeth Boyer, who, while dedicated to the goal of equality for women and the ERA, found herself at loggerheads with NOW and its more radical stance on social issues such as abortion. WEAL purposely restricts its activities to "economic and educational discrimination and tax inequities"[16] and likewise purposely restricts its membership to a small core of professional and executive women in an attempt to "mobilize expertise rather than numbers."[17]

In addition to these feminist organizations, the other major segment of the women's pro-ERA lobby consists of a number of traditional women's groups. The most conspicuous is perhaps the League of Women Voters which, after 50 years of leading the ERA opposition, finally switched sides in 1972 when Congress passed the amendment. But the most active of these groups are the American Association of University Women and the General Federation of Women's Clubs.[18] Together these traditional groups can mobilize over 2.5 million members in the ERA battle.[19]

Joining these women's groups in the ERA drive is a coalition of public interest groups, a denominationally identifiable segment of the church lobby, various agencies and bureaucrats within the government lobby, and a large cross-section of labor unions.

Common Cause and the American Civil Liberties Union (ACLU) are the two most active of the public interest groups. While Common Cause focuses primarily on grass-roots organizational drives, the ACLU has spawned two very effective litigation and research groups. For example, the Women's Rights Project, which was founded with Ford Foundation assistance, litigates general women's rights issues, including issues of interpretation that have arisen from various states' passage of their own identically (or similarly worded) ERAs. Today, the ACLU assigns more legal staff to women's rights than to any other issue.[20]

The pro-ERA church lobby—which plays a rather meek role compared to its counterpart in the opposition forces—consists of a variety of denominations represented by groups like the American Jewish Congress,[21] the United Methodist and Presbyterian Churches, and the Unitarian Universalist Associations. These denominational groups, which unequivocally support the ERA, are joined by a number of Catholic organizations which, despite a division within the Catholic church, support the ERA.

Far more important than the Church in building support for the ERA is the government lobby. The "formal" segment of this lobby consists of a variety of agencies, commissions, and bureaus at both the state and federal levels that have issued statements, research documents, and legal opinions in support of the ERA. There are, for example, the State Commissions on the Status of Women (whose origins were discussed earlier). The first women's groups in government, they still operate in 49 states (excluding Texas), while some counties and cities have formed local commissions.

In addition, there are the Equal Employment Opportunity Commission, the Women's Bureau within the Department of Labor, and the United States Commission on Civil Rights. This latter commission first endorsed the ERA in 1973 and has published some of the more forceful government documents advocating and interpreting the ERA.

Besides this formal segment, there is an informal collection of bureaucrats who have, at various levels, helped to push the federal government out in front on the ERA. Dubbed "woodwork feminists,"[22] they are typically middle- and upper-level bureaucrats sympathetic to the goals of the women's movement. In the right place (a position of power) at the right time (during the rise of the women's movement), they have helped steer the policymaking apparatus of government towards equality for women.

Finally, rounding out the pro-ERA forces is a variety of labor groups, the most important of which is the AFL–CIO. Its importance derives not so much from the only moderately active lobbying role it has played, but rather from the fact that up until 1973, this largest of labor organizations actively opposed the ERA.

Depending on one's source, the AFL–CIO's opposition stemmed either malignantly from a male-dominated conservative leadership oblivious to the contradiction of opposing women's employment rights or more benignly from a genuine belief that the ERA would neutralize a whole set of laws protecting women in the workplace that the AFL–CIO had fought hard for. Regardless of the roots of the AFL–CIO's opposition, it, like the League of Women Voters, has switched sides and, along with other individual unions like the United Auto Workers and Teamsters, supports the amendment.

B. The ERA Opposition

The ERA opposition has its own versions of the women's and church lobbies. Joining these two important forces are a number of radical-fringe conservative groups and a segment of the business lobby.

Without question, STOP-ERA is the single most powerful and prominent organization, not only within the anti-ERA women's lobby, but also within the whole phalanx of ERA opponents.

While the pro-ERA women's groups typically offer a bureaucratic style of leadership, STOP-ERA is a paradigm of the "political entrepreneur" model of interest group politics. Just as Ralph Nader almost singlehandedly has organized and led a coalition of consumers and liberals, STOP-ERA's founder and president, Phyllis Schlafly, has attracted a faithful following of predominantly conservative housewives and mothers.

Schlafly's early training for her acknowledged role of commander-in-chief of the ERA opposition consisted of several unsuccessful bids for the U.S. Congress, a term as vice-president of the National Federation of Republican Women's Clubs (NFRWC), and the authoring of eight books, including Barry Goldwater's conservative campaign classic, *A Choice Not an Echo*.[23]

In 1968, Schlafly lost her bid for the NFRWC presidency and began to write, edit, and publish *The Phyllis Schlafly Report,* a monthly ultraconservative newsletter. As already discussed, she entered the ERA fray in February of 1972 with a *Report* broadside dedicated solely to criticism of the amendment. Shortly thereafter, she established STOP-ERA; by

January 1973, the organization had several thousand members. Active in 26 states, its strength initially lay in the South and Midwest, particularly in Schlafly's home state of Illinois.

When asked for information about their membership, STOP-ERA staff claim thousands of members, but give no exact figures, and report that their constituency of more than 50,000 members "comes from all walks of life."[24] Many observers believe, however, that the STOP-ERA membership is comprised primarily of housewives out of the job market who are generally older than their feminist counterparts.

The financing of STOP-ERA activities is likewise a mystery. While Schlafly claims that membership donations, speaking fees, and income and contributions generated by her newsletter pay her lobbying bills, she has not opened her books to the public. As a result, her critics often try to link her budget (as well as Schlafly) to the well-lined vaults of a number of radical-fringe conservative groups (discussed later).

In addition to this anti-ERA "mother ship," Schlafly also quickly formed several additional ad hoc anti-ERA satellite groups. One "blue ribbon" group—the National Committee of Endorsers Against ERA—included the wives of six congressmen. AWARE (American Women Already Richly Endowed) was also organized, primarily to launch letter-writing campaigns to legislators in unratified states, while Scratch Women's Lib was created with the help of STOP-ERA's legal advisor Evelyn Pitsch in response to requests from disenchanted members of some pro-ERA groups.

Besides the Schlafly groups, at least two other major women's opposition groups deserve mention: the venerable Daughters of the American Revolution, which helped to offset the power of the pro-ERA traditional women's groups like the League of Women Voters, and the ad hoc Happiness of Womanhood (HOW).

Joining these women's opposition groups are a number of right-wing radical-fringe groups. The most conspicuous, as well as the most active, is the John Birch Society. In 1972, shortly after congressional passage of the ERA, the society's members were urged by their founder and director, Robert Welch, "to plunge in and help relegate this subversive proposal to early and complete oblivion."[25]

The society kicked off its campaign by circulating a number of anti-ERA bulletins and, more important, by establishing a number of ad hoc groups once removed from the society to mobilize grass-roots opposition.

Out of this effort emerged organizations like POW (Protect our Women) and HOTDOG.*

Alongside the society, other radical-fringe groups that oppose ERA include the American Party, the National States' Rights Party, the Ku Klux Klan, the Christian Crusade, and the Manion Forum Trust Fund. The last organization is the creation of ultra conservative Clarence Manion. Together with the John Birch Society, the Fund is frequently linked to Schlafly's groups. It is "believed to be a major source of funding for the ERA opposition movement."[26]

Important though the right wing may be in bolstering the anti-ERA campaign, the church lobby, aided by its tax-exempt status, has played an even more formidable role, particularly in the key swing states and regions (primarily the South) where the first ratification drive ultimately stalled. For example, the Mormon church (formally known as the Church of Jesus Christ of Latter-Day Saints) must be given the most credit for mobilizing and coordinating the anti-ERA movement in three key unratified states: Utah, where the church is based, and Nevada and Arizona, which have sizable Mormon populations. In the close-knit Mormon community, pronouncements from the all-male hierarchy of the church are taken literally as gospel by most members and any formal public dissent constitutes grounds for excommunication.[27]

Similarly, in the Deep South where the majority of the unratified states lie, religious fundamentalists have fought openly against the amendment. The fundamentalist groups, which include the Church of Christ, Assembly of God, Pentecostal, and, numerically the largest, Southern Baptist denominations, believe very strongly in a literal interpretation of the Bible and that the ERA is fundamentally inconsistent with its teachings. Because "God clearly created male and female as different and distinct," the ERA represents "a denial of God, both as to His person and to His program and purposes for mankind."[28]

This religious fundamentalism acts in concert with the more secular and romantic traditions of the South where "the romantic southern ideal (is) that men are meant to wield power and women are to be protected

---

*The award for creative acronyms in the ERA struggle goes hands down to the opposition. Other eye-catchers include FOE (Females Opposed to Equality), HOME (Happiness of Motherhood Eternal), HA! (Home Administrators, Inc.), and HAM (Housewives and Motherhood Anti-Lib Movement).

and idolized."[29] This, together with the assertion that "girls in the South are more rigidly socialized into the traditional female role and, when married, show an unusually strong sense of duty to family,"[30] likewise help to lend the ERA opposition its distinctly regional flavor.

Besides the Mormons and fundamentalists, one other religious force has participated in the anti-ERA drive. While its "rank-and-file" priests, nuns, and lay members by and large appear to support the ERA, "the hierarchy of the Catholic Church has shown strong opposition to it."[31] The Church's primary worry appears to be that it would "pave the way for more abortions,"[32] a woman's right to which it is unequivocally opposed. However, like the Mormon church, the Catholic hierarchy may also worry about the effect of expanding women's equality on its basically all-male hierarchy.

Rounding out the ERA opposition forces are segments of a business lobby that have operated largely at the periphery of the debate. Helping to offset the labor lobby's influence, umbrella groups like the Chamber of Commerce, the National Association of Manufacturers, and the American Retail Federation, along with the trade associations and companies within the insurance industry, have waged a subtle war on the amendment.

On the whole, these groups have been more concerned with blocking specific pieces of women's legislation, ranging from equal pay to discrimination in credit extension. But these groups also have been cool to the ERA. This is particularly true of the insurance industry, which sees the ERA as a threat to practices such as higher disability premiums because of pregnancy and lower payoffs to women based on their longer life.

C. Private Interest Capture

Within the confines of the capture theory, it is possible to explain the activities of most, if not all, of the major players in the ERA policy game as a simple reflection of economic self-interest. Perhaps the easiest special interests to paint with the capture brush are the business versus labor lobbies.

The business lobby's opposition to the ERA first and foremost reflects a concern that the amendment will raise costs and thereby lower sales and profits. According to business, it would do so by adding to the already existing strong legislative pressures forcing companies to provide "equal pay for equal work."[33]

For corporations like AT&T, IBM, Xerox, and other members of the Fortune 500, which are heavily staffed with female clericals, the ramifications are far-reaching. By one estimate, the wage bill of the nation's largest employer of females, AT&T, would rise by $500 million annually.[34]

The ERA also poses a threat to the male-dominated executive hierarchy at the same time that it potentially interferes with management's (often discriminatory) hiring practices. For example, since legislation like the Civil Rights Act of 1964 led to a plethora of federal regulations regarding "minority hiring practices" (e.g., racial quotas), the business community has expressed a fear that the ERA would propagate similar regulations requiring that women be hired in the upper echelons of management where, at present, women are vastly underrepresented.

At the same time, the insurance industry has even more tangible concerns about the ERA. To the extent the amendment would preclude its charging women different premiums and paying different pensions, its profits and sales would likewise be affected.

The labor lobby's support for the ERA is equally clear: It is fighting for the higher wages and greater opportunities now denied to its female members.[35]

The major protagonists in the ERA policy game—the pro- and anti-women's lobbies—may likewise be portrayed in economic hues. For example, the pro-ERA women's lobby may be characterized as a special interest in pursuit of higher wages, greater opportunity for career advancement, and more access to a hitherto male-dominated corporate management structure.

By the same token, the anti-ERA women's lobby may be seen as a coalition of primarily unemployed and, on average, older housewives and mothers who are less concerned with discrimination in a labor market they do not participate in and more concerned with protecting what Phyllis Schlafly refers to as the "right not to take a job."[36] These women are also characterized as wanting to preserve a cultural and legal system that, at least according to the anti-ERA literature, provides such women protection from the economic hardships of divorce and widowhood through child support, alimony, and other laws favoring women.[37]

Nor are the various church lobbies "clean" when it comes to possible capture motives. Consider the Mormon, Fundamentalist, and Catholic opposition. To a greater or lesser degree, each of these churches is run by a basically all-male hierarchy that, since the advent of the women's movement, has come under increased scrutiny and attack. From pressure to allow women to be priests to opening the "elder hierarchy" to females, the women's movement, as symbolized by the ERA, cuts to the very core of this hierarchy's patriarchal underpinnings, threatening not only the stature of males within the church but their economic welfare as well.

In contrast, the pro-ERA churches—mostly Methodists, Presbyterians, and Unitarians—are already sexually integrated in the upper echelons and therefore have little or nothing to lose from passage of the amendment[38]—a fact which may account for their rather small supporting role.

Finally, there is the government lobby. Here the capture motives are more indirect: To the extent that sexual discrimination exists, various agencies and their bureaucrats are kept busy and well-budgeted to fight such discrimination. Moreover, as new laws like the ERA are passed, more jobs are created in the government in order to interpret and enforce the laws. Thus, in this admittedly cynical view of the nation's public servants, it is jobs and agency budgets that constitute the bureaucrat's economic stakes in the ERA.

D. The Public Interest View

Despite an arguable case for capture, there are, of course, equally powerful, and perhaps even more compelling, arguments in favor of a public interested, ideological interpretation of this issue. For one, several of the important interest groups participating in the debate—notably the conservative opposition and public interest group supporters—are very difficult to paint with the capture brush. For another, much of the rhetoric swirling around the debate has a distinctly ideological tinge to it. Keeping in mind the possibility that such rhetoric may merely be a cloak for special interests, let's examine some of the ideological arguments for keys to the content of the ERA debate.

1. Traditionalism Versus Experimentalism. Burning white-hot at the core of the ideological debate over the ERA is a classic confrontation between the Burkean conservative wing and modern liberals over traditionalism versus experimentalism. To the conservative, the ERA is nothing less than a total assault on the basic traditions, customs, and institutions that bind society together.

At greatest risk is the family. Within that institution, the conservative sees the primary role of women as obedient, loving wives to breadwinning husbands; industrious homemakers; and nurturing, teaching mothers to children who will eventually carry on society. For those within the religious Right, this role as "Adam's rib" is part of a "divine" plan that has as its blueprint an absolute natural order and as its ultimate aim, the stability, preservation, and perpetuation of a religious, God-fearing society.

At the same time, the more secular conservative sees another compelling argument for this traditional women's role. In George Gilder's contemporary tale of the function of the traditional patriarchal arrangement between men and women, the family unit not only provides stability to the society but also provides the major *economic* incentives for productive work: the need to support a wife and children spurs the *married* man to far greater levels of work and output than if he merely had to support himself.[39]

At the intellectual level, the ERA poses a grave threat to this patriarchal arrangement (and hence to social stability and economic prosperity) because it obliterates the key assumption that this arrangement is based on, which is that men are naturally different and thereby have naturally different roles in society. At the religious level, the amendment also is seen as an effort "to abolish the traditional Judeo-Christian code of morality upon which America was founded."[40] The fear is that it will "liberate" women but "from the cherished place they hold in the divine plan of God's universe, reduce them to physical and spiritual bondage, and destroy them as preservers of the heart of our society—the traditional American family."[41]

As a more practical matter, the conservative feels that the ERA also attacks this traditional arrangement by opening up opportunities to women that lure them to abandon their traditional role as wife, homemaker, and mother for the excitement, opportunity, and wealth of the working world. At the same time that it encourages this role change, the ERA also chips away at the foundation of financial security that women find within the home because, according to conservative interpretation, the amendment "will invalidate state laws which require a husband to support his wife and children." To the conservative, the implications are clear: ". . . since men would be relieved of the primary responsibility of supporting their families, it is entirely possible that the destruction of the conventional American family would follow."[42]

Besides this frontal assault on the family unit, the ERA also pulls hard at the delicate threads of a wide variety of traditional arrangements, morals, and mores that hold the social fabric together. The ultraconservative literature provides perhaps the most graphic—and to critics, alarmist—list of threats to the American social tapestry.

For example, the ERA is seen as eliminating all privacy between the sexes in public restrooms, prisons, reformatories, schools, and the military. The amendment will also put an end to sodomy, seduction, and rape laws and legitimize a proliferation of prostitution, obscene literature, and homosexual marriages. Besides finding such a unisexual, pornographic, and homosexual world disgusting and degrading, the conservative sees these changes as a catalyst to a rise in promiscuity and moral decay that will further threaten both the family and society.

The ERA also suffers from "guilt by association." Invariably, the amendment is linked in the minds of conservative opponents to their concerns about even more *specific* threats to society such as sex education and, perhaps the biggest bugaboo to the Moral Majority, abortion.

Through the conservative's traditionalist lens, the ultimate result of the ERA's pulling at the many threads of custom and tradition is the total unraveling of society. With greater sexual freedom, moral decay, and the demise of the family, comes "social disruption, unhappiness, and increasing rates of divorce and desertion. Weakening family ties may also lead to increased rates of alcoholism, suicide, and possibly sexual deviation."[43] At the same time that the family ebbs as a stabilizing force, Gilderian prosperity flies out the window. In the Far Right's worst case scenario, the ERA brings the nation nothing less than the total destruction of the economy and society.

To the liberal, this vision of the moral equivalent of Armageddon is simply unfounded reactionary alarmism based on a number of misguided assumptions. Rather than perceiving decay and decadence in the ERA's erosive effects on the patriarchal society, the liberal sees the ERA effect on marriage, for example, to be "the move from a patriarchal to a partnership model of marriage, in which women have full rights equal to those of men."[44] This move is viewed as a crucial, salutary, and necessary evolution of a modern American society committed to "honoring justice, equality, and equal protection for all."[45]

Furthermore, in their relativistic rejection of any immutable "divine" role for women, the liberal sees the ERA as "premised on the idea there is no absolute social order."[46] Rather, the liberal views society "as a natural and constant struggle of values"[47] and the evolutionary struggle for women's rights is but part of that larger struggle. By sanctioning the instinct to "move out of traditional roles," the amendment "reveals the possibility for change in both social values and the social structure."[48] Contrary to conservative claims, such changes are not threatening to the general social order; rather, they are a healthy, cleansing process that allows us to break from the "straitjacket of stereotypes and traditions."[49] Nor are specific institutions like the Church and family in any danger. Rather, the changes foreseen are on the whole positive and indeed necessary ones.

Finally, the liberal dismisses conservatives' claims that the legal system will interpret the ERA mandate in such a way as to create a unisex world where women and men share public restrooms and are left without any right to alimony and child support. Instead, the liberal sees the post-ERA judicial process as preserving privacy between the sexes, extending protection from sodomy, seduction, rape, and adultery to men, expanding the illegality of prostitution to men, and shoring up ambiguities in state alimony, child support, and property laws so that women will benefit.[50] At the same time, the extra income earned by females will provide the family with greater freedom from potentially divisive financial pressures, while greater involvement of fathers in child-rearing responsibilities would bring families closer together.

2. States' Rights Versus Federalism, the Minimal Versus the Welfare State. A second important area of ideological dispute centers around the states' rights versus federalism split and, to a lesser extent, the minimal versus the welfare state. The conservative sees the ERA as "a power grab by Washington" and fears that "state's rights pertaining to women will go to the national government."[51] As evidence of this federalist conspiracy, the conservative is quick to point out that Section 2 of the ERA resolution debated in the Ninety-first Congress (1969–70) originally read:

> *Congress and the several States shall have power, within their respective jurisdictions, to enforce this article by appropriate legislation. [emphasis added]*

However, all references to the states have been subsequently deleted in the resolutions[52] which have passed Congress and been sent to the states for ratification. The conservative has interpreted this omission as a clear "shift away from local autonomy and towards a centralized government."[53]

The primary danger of this shift, as it pertains to the ERA, is found in this variation on the conservative's familiar "shoe-pinching" argument that local problems are best solved locally:

> *Although the Congress is popularly elected, it is but a single legislature. It is not able to provide the flexibility and accountability of the fifty State legislatures, not to mention the countless local ordinance-passing bodies. The deletion of State authority means the wholesale elimination of the careful network of State laws worked out to promote and protect stable family and personal relationships.*[54]

Accordingly, the conservative would prefer to continue to rely on state interpretations of Constitutional sanctions against sexual discrimination as embodied in the equal protection clauses of the Fifth and Fourteenth Amendments.

Such a view is consistent with the conservative's preference for a minimal state because it avoids the possible creation of any additional (particularly federal) bureaucracy to administer the new federal law. At the same time, keeping the ERA genie in the bottle also prevents more specific expansions of the welfare state, the most likely being "taxpayer-financed child-care centers for all children, regardless of needs,"[55] federal funding of abortion,[56] and an increase in government spending associated with changing facilities such as military barracks to a unisex standard.[57]

The liberal, on the other hand, sees the ERA as a necessary federalist response both to a bloc of recalcitrant states that systematically have denied equal protection and rights to women and to the fact that sexual discrimination is "deeply entrenched in our laws and persistently reflected in governmental action."[58] In this regard, the Fifth and Fourteenth Amendments have proven to be totally inadequate in providing equal protection to women because, historically, these provisions have "never been interpreted to prohibit all discrimination against women as a class."[59] The result is an unfair "patchwork quilt" of literally thousands of laws and regulations that typecast and discriminate against women.

Such discriminatory laws exist in all areas of women's lives—criminal law, domestic relations, employment, and civil rights. To name just a few in the area of employment, five states (Arkansas, Connecticut, Illinois, Louisiana, and Rhode Island) still prohibit women from holding jobs in mines or establishments selling alcoholic beverages, while 15 states have some form of law prohibiting women cosmetologists from serving men.[60]

The ERA is necessary to redress these historical oversights and, through the federalist vehicle, will provide a uniform and durable guarantee of equal status to women. Thus, rather than a Washington "power grab," the amendment is merely an equitable means of ensuring that the states meet their responsibilities to provide equal protection to women; in their previous failures to meet these responsibilities, the states have forfeited any "rights" in the matter.

3. Nationalistic Anti-Communism Versus International Globalism.* Finally, the ideological debate over the ERA has spilled over into what at first glance might seem to be the rather remote realm of the conservative's staunch anti-Communism. However, even as domestic an issue as the ERA has been associated with what some conservatives see as an orchestrated "Communist conspiracy."

This linkage to Communism, which at once galls and baffles both liberals and feminists alike, has, like several other of the more polemic charges against the ERA, been most frequently made by ultraconservative groups. The basic argument for a conspiracy is summarized in this John Birch Society article, which describes the purpose of "Women's Lib" in general and the ERA in particular as: ". . . to take women out of the home, restructure their thinking in favor of an atheistic, Socialist ideology, and mobilize them into a powerful political lobby that can be used for Communist revolutionary purposes."[61]

The major pieces of evidence presented in support of this socialist plot are a number of oft-cited quotes and comments from communist leaders. These range from the historical denunciation of the institute of the family by Marx and Engels and Lenin's dictum that women must be drawn out of the "deadening atmosphere of household and kitchen"[62] into public, military, and political life in order to build socialism to the more contemporary strategic declaration of the U.S. Communist party

---

*This principle is discussed in more detail in Appendix B and Chapter 11 on the defense policy game.

secretary that the struggle for communism rests on establishing "the tie-in between the forces of women's liberation and the working class."[63]

E. The Politics of the ERA: A Statistical Test

To measure the relative importance of special interests versus ideology in influencing the outcome of the ERA debate, the capture-ideology framework was used to examine the voting patterns of the 50 state legislatures during the 1972–82 ERA ratification drive. The expectation was that the outcome of the ratification vote in each state would hinge on the relative political strengths of the major special interest and ideological forces, with the pro-ERA women's and church lobbies joining hands with labor, public interest groups, and ideological liberals to oppose the coalition between the anti-ERA women's and church lobbies and ideological conservatives.

Following our standard procedure, a number of measures were constructed to reflect the political pressures exerted by these major special interest and ideological players.

For example, the power of the "traditional segment" of the pro-ERA women's lobby was reflected in the total number of members by state in several of the larger women's organizations (as a percentage of state population), while the anti-ERA church lobby was measured by the total number of Mormons and fundamentalists by state (as a percentage of state population). Similarly, the power of the public interest lobby was measured by the total members in the lobby's most active ERA participant, Common Cause, while the labor lobby was reflected in the number of members in the AFL–CIO, Teamsters, and United Auto Workers.

At the same time, the general ideological orientation of a state was reflected by the percentage of votes for Ronald Reagan in the 1980 presidential election, with a high percentage reflecting a high degree of conservatism.

These measures of special interests and ideology were related to the voting records of each of the state legislatures on ERA ratification through the use of a common statistical procedure. The results of this test are displayed in Table 10.2 which ranks each of the various measures by their statistical importance.*

*The full test results are reported in Appendix B.

TABLE 10.2.   THE INFLUENCE OF
SPECIAL INTERESTS AND IDEOLOGY IN
THE ERA RATIFICATION DRIVE

Rank[a]
1. Ideology
2. Feminist segment of pro-ERA women's lobby
3. Traditional segment of pro-ERA women's lobby
4. Labor lobby
5. Public interest lobby
6. Anti-ERA church lobby
7. Pro-ERA church lobby
8. Anti-ERA women's lobby

[a] No suitable measures for the business and government lobbies could be found in this case, so their effect must remain conjectural.

Perhaps not surprisingly, given the tenor of the ERA debate, ideology turns out to be the single most important predictor of whether a state voted for or against the ERA. This statistical conclusion is reinforced by a reportage of the legislative votes by some notably liberal and conservative states. For example, bastions of liberalism such as Delaware, Massachusetts, and Wisconsin overwhelmingly approved ERA ratification while conservative strongholds such as Arizona, Oklahoma, and Virginia soundly rejected it.

However, very close on the heels of ideology are the two segments of the pro-ERA women's lobby. As the second and third ranked measures in the test, the feminist and traditional groups showed a statistical importance that individually closely rivaled that of ideology; and (although the results are not strictly additive due to statistical reasons), one can conjecture that the combined effect of the two segments of the pro-ERA women's lobby might even outweigh ideology as an explanatory force. In any case, this result lends strong support to the view (further discussed in our economics section) that the ERA is as much an issue of bread and butter for women as it is an ideological one of social justice versus societal decay.

The results of the test confirm that both labor interests and the public interest groups (ranked fourth and fifth) played important supporting roles in the drive for ratification just as they reinforce the claim that the anti-ERA church lobby was a more potent lobbying force than the pro-ERA church lobby.

The only anomalous result of the test would appear to be the last place finish for the vaunted anti-ERA women's lobby. There are, however, several plausible explanations for this.

First, and perhaps most important, Phyllis Schlafly personally refused to provide any information on either the memberships in her organizations or their campaign contributions to state legislators. Thus the test was left with only a weak proxy for the Schlafly forces (state membership in the venerable but politically much less active Daughters of the American Revolution).

Second, in considering the effect of both the anti-ERA women's lobby and the anti-ERA church lobby, it is important to remember the "rules of the ratification game." In particular, two-thirds of the states had to ratify for the amendment to pass. This provided an opportunity for the Schlafly forces to muster in just a few states to wage an effective battle; this leverage is not reflected in the statistical test. This also helps to explain what appears to be only a moderate influence by the anti-ERA church lobby. In fact, this lobby can legitimately share the major responsibility with Schlafly for scuttling the amendment. The reason: the anti-ERA church lobby needed to pressure only a few states to block ratification so that the Mormons in Utah, Arizona, and Nevada together with Fundamentalists in states like Georgia were likewise very effective, despite their lack of a national power base.

In summary, both special interests and ideology seem to have played a major role in determining the outcome of the first ERA ratification drive. Before going on to examine the economic issues pertaining to the amendment, one piece of unfinished political business remains that will provide insight into the potential success or failure of any second ERA ratification drive, that is, examining the various strategies and tactics that led to the ERA's 1982 defeat.

F.   Strategies and Tactics of the ERA Combatants

How did the ERA opposition bring a runaway ratification drive to a screeching halt? Delving into the differing strategies and tactics of those on both sides of the ERA during the various stages of the political struggle sheds light on this question.

1. The Supporters' ERA Offensive. The early success of the pro-ERA forces in the late 1960s and early 1970s lay in three important functions that the newly formed feminist groups served.

First and foremost, these groups finally provided a vehicle for the grass-roots mobilization of a long-latent movement for women's rights. Through conventional grass-roots lobbying techniques such as newsletters, alerts, and newspapers, as well as through more creative activities like "consciousness raising sessions," and educational "kits" exposing credit discrimination, NOW and NWPC in particular provided oppressed women with a flag to rally around.

Second, the feminist groups provided a key ingredient lacking in previous ERA campaigns: a substantial lobbying war chest. Through membership dues, solicitations, fairs, and benefits, feminists raised hundreds of thousands of dollars to promote the ERA. At the same time, several traditional women's groups, spurred on by the fund-raising efforts of the feminist organizations, launched their own highly successful drives. The Business and Professional Women's Club, which at a crucial moment in the congressional lobbying drive made thousands of telephone calls to Congressmen, raised several hundred thousand dollars through special assessments of its members, while the more entrepreneurial League of Women Voters hawked ERA bracelets to raise a similar amount.[64]

Third, the feminist groups acted as a very powerful catalyst for an emerging pro-ERA coalition that drew into its activist fold not only the traditional (and traditionally lukewarm) women's groups but also Common Cause, the ACLU, and various church organizations. In this way, these groups provided an essential "critical mass" for a national chain reaction of public opinion mobilized in favor of the amendment. That chain reaction was the result of well-orchestrated, and by and large very traditional, direct and grass-roots lobbying strategies, planned and implemented by the pro-ERA coalition.

Perhaps the most powerful of the grass-roots tactics was a public relations campaign that, at least at the outset, created an image of the ERA as a long-overdue fair solution to a perennial problem in *role equity*. According to supporters, in one fell swoop, the amendment would wipe out all the sex discrimination women ritually encountered not only in the job market but also in their marriage contracts and other places. Through pamphlets and programs aimed at associating women's equality with the broader goals of social justice and democracy, this narrow image of the ERA gave no hint of any radical social upheaval that opponents would later skillfully project.

In creating this image of the ERA as a rectifier of social injustice, the government lobby was extremely effective: Reports issued by the State Commissions on Women's Rights, the Equal Employment Opportunity Commission, and the U.S. Civil Rights Commission argued for passage of the ERA on the basis of economic discrimination against women at the same time that any broader social implications were heavily discounted.[65]

Meanwhile, research departments within several of the women's groups worked hard at unearthing and disseminating data documenting the extent of economic discrimination. One particularly effective evocation of the role equity issue was NOW's publicity on the famous "59¢ gap": for every dollar men earn, women only earn 59 cents. This "59¢ gap" became a very powerful symbol of sex discrimination that supporters effectively exploited, not only through their own publications but also through the free media publicity that their press releases and public demonstrations were generating.

In this regard, the tactic of public demonstrations in the form of parades, rallies, picketing, sit-ins, street theater, and pray-ins were extremely effective in attracting media attention. As previously discussed, the massive 1970 public strike organized by NOW proved to be a watershed, not only for the organization's membership (which soon after tripled) but also for public attention, as the media thereafter began to treat women's rights less as a curiosity and more as a legitimate movement.

Similarly, feminists demonstrating during a Senate Judiciary Committee on lowering the voting age to 18 were instrumental not only in forcing ERA hearings but also in helping to break the congressional committee logjam holding up approval of the amendment. ERA supporters also made very effective use of public opinion polls which, beginning in the early 1970s, had "discovered" women's rights as an important new survey subject. The results of these polls suggested that in broad terms, a majority of Americans—both men and women—favored "equal rights for women."[66] The touting of these results on Capitol Hill, in particular, had a major effect on a Congress ever sensitive to seismic shifts in public opinion.

2. The Opposition's Counteroffensive. However, even as the ERA was breezing through Congress and gaining easy ratification in the first 30 states, the seeds of its defeat were being sown by an effective grass-roots opposition campaign. The primary tools in the opposition's lobbying effort were a battery of newsletters, alerts, and public speeches that formed the core of a propaganda campaign aimed at shifting the ERA issue from the firm, narrow, and comfortingly liberal confines of a role equity issue into the broader, more threatening, conservative quicksand of a *role change*.

From Phyllis Schlafly's monthly attacks on the amendment to the John Birch Society's weekly *Review of the News* polemics, opposition leaders played on a latent fear and discontent with "women's lib" and thus mobilized a small army of housewives, mothers, and religious fundamentalists.

The genius of this grass-roots campaign lay in its ability to transform the perception of the ERA from a fair-minded and simple solution to sexual discrimination into a trap door through which virtually the whole of American values would fall.

The opposition's basic recipe for what symbolically amounted to cooking the ERA's goose was one part bold accusations; one part bold assertions; a two-part appeal to home, family, and patriotism; a liberal (actually, a conservative) dose of religious censure; and more than an occasional dash of unbridled demagoguery.

The accusations were generally in the form of direct attacks on the women's movement. Its leaders were portrayed as castrating, radical, lesbian, atheist bitches[67] unable to keep a house and unwilling to make a home. The movement itself was frequently tarred with the brush of socialism, while its members were depicted as "sharp-tongued, high-pitched" unmarried whiners.[68]

The assertions lay in the sweeping ramifications that the ERA would have on society, the economy, and even national security. In Phyllis Schlafly's post-ERA world of chaos, drafted women would pull down their army fatigues and urinate side by side with men in the trenches; lazy and idolatrous husbands would sit home fat, dumb, and happy, drinking beer and watching the tube while their beast-of-burden wives scratched and scraped as waitresses and secretaries to support them; children would turn into robots under the communal (and communistic) influence of federal day care centers; the public restrooms would be transformed into unisex horror chambers where all forms of abuse—from simple embarrassment to forcible rape—were likely to occur.

Nor did the opposition always restrict itself to the merits and demerits of the ERA itself. Instead, they effectively linked the amendment to other, even more controversial issues, particularly abortion. In this propaganda campaign, many of the caricatures contained kernels of truth. For example, even some supporters admitted that the ERA would make women eligible for the draft and combat duty.[69] But always, the potential effects of the ERA were cloaked in a gut-wrenching passionate rhetoric that was meant to startle and scare. Moreover, these accusations and assertions always ended with an appeal to home, hearth, and basic American values. It was this apple pie and motherhood association with the ERA's defeat, coupled with the amendment's image as a role-changing home- and family-wrecking law, that constituted the most powerful message of the opposition's ERA symbology.

At the same time, the opposition skillfully attacked the weak underbelly of public opinion polls supporting the amendment. As supporters were touting a general majority support for the broad question of "equality for women," Senator Sam Ervin was reading into the *Congressional Record* results of similar polls indicating that on more specific questions, a majority of Americans did *not* think that women should share the responsibility of child support, be drafted, be admitted to private men's clubs, or play football on sex-integrated teams—events which the opposition led many Americans to believe would result if the ERA were passed.

On the mobilization front, this war of words served to stir up a small but vocal army ready to march in step with charismatic leaders of the ad hoc anti-ERA groups to which they flocked. Perhaps the most powerful deployment of these forces was in the opposition's well-orchestrated direct mail campaign against the amendment.

The anti-ERA mail campaign was particularly potent because many of the letters were handwritten, passionate epistles reflecting the fears and emotions that the opposition's rhetoric had stirred up.* This "letter

---

*Interestingly, while the opposition managed to "outwrite" ERA supporters at the state level, letter writing had been an extremely effective tool for supporters during the congressional campaign. According to Joan Freeman, "some Congressmen received as many as 1,500 a month and Congressperson Tip O'Neill of Massachusetts was quoted as saying that the ERA had generated more mail than the Vietnam War."[71]

to a legislator" tactic was perfect because it could be "done in the home at one's discretion—ideal conditions for the housewife antagonistic to the ERA who wants to 'do something.' "[70]

This success on the mail front was further enhanced by several questionable practices.* The first, and more benign, involved letters written to legislators in other states, a traditional "no-no" in American politics. More perniciously, many legislators received anti-ERA mail from fictitious persons—a ruse uncovered when answers to these letters were returned marked "no such person at this address."[72]

This grass-roots campaign was further augmented by several equally effective direct lobbying tactics. Schlafly, for example, drew kudos from admirers and grudging respect from ERA supporters for her role as the perfect witness against the ERA at legislative hearings.[73]

And while Schlafly maintained a high profile in the capitols of the unratified states, shaking hands with and twisting the arms of legislators, her lieutenants stalked the halls and offices of these legislatures, seeking meetings and distributing literature. In some very effective public demonstration tactics, they also staged skits satirizing the ERA, baked bread and cookies to pass out as mock "bribes" for legislators, sent flowers to their supporters, and showed up at the steps of state capitols with their daughters wearing Don't Draft Me signs.

At the same time, church leaders spread the anti-ERA gospel from the pulpit on Sundays and through the week in meetings, phone calls, and by word of mouth. In the Mormon states of Utah and, to a lesser extent, Arizona and Nevada, such proselytizing was particularly effective given the church's close-knit community network and the respect for church authority instilled in the congregation. Nor did the Mormon leaders limit themselves to proselytizing. For at least one woman member who publicly disagreed with the church's ERA stand, the result was excommunication.[74]

At the same time, in the Southern cradle of fundamentalism, religious censure, primarily among the Southern Baptist and Pentecostal denominations, took its toll on ERA supporters. How, after all, does a devout

---

*While mail campaigns are notoriously ineffective as political persuaders, this criticism more generally applies to computer-generated "mass mail" than the letters that numerically small but sophisticated lobbying organizations often use to bombard legislators.

"believer" reconcile statements like this with any secular preference for women's equality:

> God clearly created male and female as different and distinct, though both are equally human. Thus, to deny the difference is to deny reality, but, more than that, to deny the Word of God. (I would point out here that I believe this is the essence of ERA. It is a denial of God, both as to His person and to His program and purposes for mankind).[75]

The end result of this lobbying counteroffensive was first to reduce the number of states ratifying the ERA to a trickle by 1975 and, shortly after Indiana's 1977 yes vote, to run the ratification drive completely dry.

3. Mistakes and Miscues. Given that both sides used very similar strategies, why was the opposition's seemingly more effective? The answer can be found in three basic mistakes committed by ERA supporters.

The first blunder was that the women's movement had no charismatic leader waiting in the wings who could match Schlafly's ability to convince and coerce, either in the public or political arenas. This was basically an organizational problem within the feminist bureaucracy. Early on, the major groups in the movement (including NOW and NWPC) had developed an aversion to what was known in the 1960's radical vernacular as the "cult of personality."

Practically speaking, this meant that the feminist organizations, by and large, developed collective decision-making bureaucracies that actively discouraged the emergence of charismatic spokespersons. Moreover, within the movement, "seeking fame" at the expense of other women was actively discouraged. Thus, despite the availability of such political talent as Gloria Steinem and Betty Friedan, none of these women were groomed for, and given free rein to be, the leader of the organization.

When lobbying at the national level, little price was paid for this collectivist* strategy. However, supporters paid dearly for this lack at the state and local levels where the ratification drive was waged and where segments of the political populace thrive on charisma. The result was

---

*This term, as used here, is devoid of any association with socialism. It refers to the collective decision-making process within the feminist organization.

that no one was waiting in the wings to slug it out toe-to-toe in the ratification trenches with Schlafly when she burst on the scene.

The second mistake ERA supporters made was to commit the cardinal political sin of overconfidence. In the first stampede of states to ratify the amendment in 1972, supporters were lulled into thinking that victory was immediately at hand.

One result of this overconfidence was that the feminist organization did not build up its state and local organization muscle with the same unwavering intensity that had made the federal congressional campaign such a success. Nowhere was this complacency more evident than in the battle plan devised by the ERA Ratification Council, an umbrella group of about 30 support organizations. According to that plan:

> The National Women's Political Caucus, for example, was to identify those legislators opposed to ERA who could be defeated for reelection and run candidates against them. The National Organization for Women would analyze the records and political-economic alliances of legislative opponents to determine what groups or individuals might bring pressure on them to change their viewpoint. NOW members were also to see to it the subject of ERA was raised wherever the legislator appeared while seeking reelection. The Common Cause research staff was to analyze opposition arguments and prepare rebuttals. The League of Women Voters was to train lobbyists, particularly in smaller urban areas, where its constituency is far stronger than that of other proponent groups.[76]

But the plan was never implemented, largely because there was no specter of defeat to propel the coalition into action. Precious years were lost, and by the time such activities were implemented, it was too late.

The final and most serious error of ERA supporters lay in their lack of a strategic response to the opposition's strident propaganda onslaught. Rather than respond in kind to the impassioned war of words waged by Schlafly and company, the ERA leadership at first refused to even take the opposition's accusations and assertions seriously; as one leader of the Business and Professional Women's Club explained: "I assumed there couldn't be a woman living who was against the ERA. And when this opposition developed, we just didn't have time to carry on the opposition we should have."[77]

Thus, while Schlafly argued from the gut and aroused hot passions and deep fears about the ERA, feminists—largely well-educated, working women who prided themselves on their rationalism—refused to stoop to that level. Far worse, seeing the opposition's accusations and assertions as baldly ludicrous, they made the egregious error of assuming that such demagoguery would have no appeal to housewives, mothers, and religious fundamentalists who felt genuinely threatened by "women's lib," the sexual revolution, and other symptoms of "moral decay" ushered in by the war-torn, drug-crazed 1960s.

So it was that, at least at the outset, cooler-headed feminists fought these impassioned pleas of the heart with rational denials and a logical defense. The result, however, was that when the hard-hitting attacks obviously began to fall on responsive ears, supporters found themselves forced into a defensive posture. As one feminist leader remarked, "We've found ourselves arguing about women being drafted and losing custody of their children, instead of discussing discrimination in housing, insurance and credit."[78]

These three major errors—a lack of charismatic leadership, overconfidence, and a weak rationalism—characterized the crucial early years of the ERA ratification drive. It was during that period that supporters lost what presidential hopeful George Bush once affectionately referred to as "Big Mo" or political momentum. In doing so, they lost any hope of ratifying the amendment, a reality that hit with final brute force when the sun set on the first ratification drive of June 1982.

4. Lessons Learned. Despite the ERA's defeat, feminists appear to have learned from their mistakes and, to complete this discussion of strategies and tactics, it is useful to point out the strategic adaptations the movement has made, adaptations that will likely bear fruit on the next ratification round.

First and foremost, the defeat has served as a warning against complacency and overconfidence as well as a catalyst to a better organized, more muscular women's movement. Today, both the traditional and feminist women's rights groups are more organized, vocal, and powerful than a decade ago. While the "gender gap" hangs like Damocles' sword over the heads of conservative presidential and congressional aspirants, this organizational muscle is also filtering down deep into the grass roots so that the next round of letter writing, phone calls, legislative lobbying, and demonstrations is likely to be the equal to that mounted by Schlafly's forces.

Moreover, in exercising this new-found political strength, the women's movement is no longer content to cajole predominantly male legislators. Instead, its new strategy is literally to avoid the "middle man" and elect state legislators (primarily women) who are sympathetic to their views.

This commitment to playing hardball election politics, begun in the later stages of the first ratification drive, was formalized by former NOW President Eleanor Smeal who, at a press conference called on the 1982 deathday of the first drive, announced a "hit list" of over 100 legislators the movement has targeted for electoral defeat.

Nor is this an empty threat since NOW and other organizations have already been instrumental in turning anti-ERA legislators out of office. For example, in their "We'll Remember in November" campaign, they claimed at least partial responsibility for replacing six anti-ERA men in the Florida state legislature with women, and likewise, for doubling the number of women in the New Jersey legislature.[79] Thus it is a threat being taken seriously, not only among state legislators but also members of Congress and occupants of the Oval Office, who, besides worrying about the attitudes of labor, business, minorities, and the like, must worry about women and a "gender gap."

Second, ERA supporters have finally learned to fight fire with fire: When the opposition uses McCarthyesque tactics to portray the amendment as a radical, lesbian, Communist plot, supporters rebut by linking that opposition to a reactionary, ultraconservative "lunatic" fringe. While at times, the result has been to drag the debate down into the mud, this "guilt by association" tactic has helped to discredit the opposition.

Finally, the women's movement is pressing ahead with an economic boycott that is wreaking havoc among convention cities in the unratified states. Begun in 1979, this boycott is now supported by the Democratic National Committee, the League of Women Voters, the National Council of Churches, the National Education Association, and the United Auto Workers. Hardest hit are cities like Miami, Atlanta, New Orleans, Kansas City, and Chicago, which, according to one estimate, have lost millions of dollars.[80]

Thus, as the latest ERA ratification drive rolls along, the prognosis for eventual passage is good. The remaining question is whether such passage is indeed desirable. A look at the economics and (straying a bit beyond our usual borders) the sociology of the ERA should help us decide.

III.   THE ECONOMICS OF THE ERA

Economics is 99.9% of the ERA.[81]

CONGRESSPERSON PATRICIA SCHROEDER
(D, COLO.)

Given our previous examination of the ideological arguments against, and sociological implications of, the ERA, Congressperson Schroeder's weighing of the economic stakes in the ERA policy game may be somewhat exaggerated. But unquestionably, the amendment would have very significant economic effects.

For the most part, these effects are redistributional in nature and occur in the microeconomy. That is, by eliminating sex discrimination in areas such as wages, job and educational opportunities, social security and private pensions, and marital property, the ERA will transfer billions of dollars to women from employers, insurers, the government, and most of all, men.

In producing these redistributional results, the ERA's economic effects will also include several important macroeconomic impacts, including inflation, unemployment, effects on economic growth and productivity, and a rise in the size of federal, state, and local government budgets.

Surprisingly, despite the duration and intensity of the ERA debate, no systematic assessment of these effects exists. Instead, when one looks beyond the well-publicized 59¢ gap, there is precious little quantitative analysis of most of the redistributional effects by either side. Within the context of this dearth of "hard numbers," let us move with some trepidation to try and put our own price tags on the ERA's economic effects.

A.   Wage Discrimination

The feminist claim—which is well documented by government statistics—that the average woman only earns 59¢ for every dollar earned by the average man is often cited as evidence of wage discrimination against American women. However, this claim might appear to exaggerate the true discriminatory wage differentials because it does not compare the wages of men and women working in the *same* jobs.

Table 10.3 provides such a comparison by listing the wage gap for the eight occupations in which 92 percent of all women toil. Note that for

TABLE 10.3.   WAGE GAP BY FULL-TIME OCCUPATIONS AND JOBS

Occupation	Men	Women	Women's Pay to $1 for Men
Clerical workers	$16,503	$ 9,855	60¢
Service workers	11,925	7,319	61¢
Professional	21,310	13,701	64¢
Operatives	14,921	8,562	57¢
Sales workers	17,084	8,880	52¢
Managers	21,835	11,705	54¢
Laborers (except farm)	11,974	8,985	75¢
Craft workers	17,106	10,585	62¢

most of these occupations, the gap is somewhat less than 59¢ ranging from 60¢ for clerical workers to 75¢ for laborers. However, note also that for some occupations like sales workers and managers, the wage gap is as much as 52¢. Averaging for these eight occupations, women earn 60¢ for every dollar earned by men.

There are several reasons aside from discrimination that such gaps might exist. The most commonly cited is the generally greater work experience and continuity of service that men have because their careers tend to be interrupted less by family matters such as pregnancy. However, these factors explain only a small portion of the wage gap—which, as the table indicates, is still undeniably large and systematic across occupations.

What would be the economic consequences of closing this gap? As a first approximation, let's assume that upon passage of the ERA, the wage gap disappeared overnight as women's wages rise to equal those of men. In just these 18 occupations, the wage bill of American business would rise by $277 billion annually.[82]

Like the 59¢ symbol, this estimate both simplifies and exaggerates the effect, however. On closer inspection, we might expect much more complex adjustments in both the labor market and economy overall. For example, the first consequence of a rise in women's wages would be a cutback in employment by the simple law of supply and demand. At the same time, the increased wage bill would likely stimulate more automation as employers substituted machines for labor. More robots, word processors, and the like would in turn mean even fewer laborers, clericals, and so on. This rising pool of unemployed workers, together with more automation, would in turn exert *downward* pressure on wages paid to men by now "sex blind" employers.

How these effects would ultimately sort out is difficult to determine. Both the initial increases in unemployment and inflation from raising women's wages might be totally offset by the increase in employment due to a lowering of men's wages (again by the laws of supply and demand),* while automation might actually improve productivity to the point where growth in the economy stimulates even more jobs. On the other hand, the total number of jobs may actually decrease and inflation may permanently inch up another notch.

The only unequivocable statement one can make about rectifying wage discrimination is that it will involve a redistribution of wealth from men and employers to women who do not become unemployed with the rise in wages and automation.

B.   Job and Educational Opportunities

Properly construed, the 59¢ gap is more indicative of systematic sex discrimination in the realm of job opportunities and the educational background required for career advancement than in actual wages. The facts speak for themselves.

Today, over 50 percent of employed women are clustered in just 21 occupations, while working men are distributed uniformly across 250 occupations. Moreover, 60 percent of women are employed in just three kinds of jobs: clericals, saleswomen, and service workers (e.g., waitresses).[83]

The starkest contrast occurs in the executive and professional worlds. No chief executive officer of any company in the Fortune 500 is a woman, 70 percent of the top 1,300 companies have no women on their boards of directors, and women represent only 2 percent of corporate directors of the top companies.[84] Furthermore, only 1 percent of women have penetrated the upper echelons of management.[85]

Similarly, in the professions, women comprise just 15 percent of doctors (and most are in fields such as gynecology), 16 percent of lawyers, and 9 percent of architects.[86] At the same time, women are only 36

---

*If men's wages are lowered, then employers will be willing to hire more men.

percent of securities and commodity brokers and 33 percent of accountants, but represent 93 percent of bank tellers and bookkeepers, and 99 percent of secretaries.[87]

The educational opportunities that would help break down the doors of corporate capitalism and the "male professions" are likewise scant: While the total number of undergraduate and master's degrees are distributed fairly evenly among men and women, women represent just 31 percent of graduating Ph.D.'s. Moreover, the master's degrees women do receive are similarly skewed towards traditional female occupations.

For example, 60 percent of women's master's degrees are in just three areas—education, health services, and library sciences—while in the more lucrative and upwardly mobile, traditionally male occupations, women account for just 34 percent of math degrees, 24 percent of business degrees, and a mere 8 percent of engineering degrees.[88] The problem not only lies in the admissions process but also in the well-publicized problem of "role education," which discourages women—at the earliest age—from studying subjects like mathematics and science and instead channels them into typing, teaching, and home economics.

At the vocational level, women also have been denied training by restrictions and quotas placed on them in military service. Indeed, the military is the "largest single vocational training institution in the Nation," offering not only "job training at full pay but also lifelong post service benefits as well."[89] Historically, women have been denied access to this important route of upward mobility because of recruitment goals that operate as quotas, differential entrance requirements, and other factors.

Rectifying these forms of discrimination would be relatively costless for the economy and may, in fact, lead to the most positive and tangible benefits from ERA ratification. Specifically, training, encouraging, and allowing women to compete for America's higher-paying jobs would increase the pool of qualified applicants. This, together with the unleashing of women's hitherto constrained creative and intellectual potential, would produce greater competition in these portions of the economy and likely lead to higher levels of production, innovation, and growth.

C. Social Security, Private Pensions, and Life Insurance

Current practices in the Social Security, private pension, military retirement pay, and life insurance system round out a literally cradle-to-grave sex discrimination that begins in limited educational and job opportunities, manifests itself as an earnings gap, and ends in what is, for many American women, an old age of grinding poverty. Indeed, "current trends suggest that by 2000 almost all the U.S. poor will be female—primarily single mothers and elderly widows."[90]

In the realm of Social Security, sex discrimination arises because the system does not grant women the same status as men. This happens in two ways. The first is undeniably discriminatory: The contributions of married working women into the Social Security fund are given less weight than those of married men. The result is a "retrogressive" payout scale in which a two-earner couple receives *lower* monthly benefits than a one-earner couple with the same income.

The second way is more controversial. Advocating the concept of "marital income," feminists argue that married women, and particularly full-time homemakers, should be accorded equal economic status with their husbands. In this view, total "marital income" consists of the wages brought home by the working male as well as the housekeeping and mothering services women provide. The argument ends in the assertion that since women provide an equal (albeit nondollar) contribution to marital income, they establish, and are entitled to a *full* claim on all the assets of the marriage, including Social Security (as well as private pensions, retirement pay, and life insurance). Through this lens, Social Security further discriminates by limiting a divorcee's Social Security claim to one-third of total benefits (the "dependent's benefits") and a widow's to two-thirds.

The counterargument, of course, is that Social Security is a mandatory pension plan, not welfare. In the extreme view, this means that only those who pay into the system should get anything out—not anything, but exactly what they put in plus interest—and women who did not contribute to the system are lucky to get even a one- or two-thirds share.

Regardless of which view one accepts, reforming Social Security according to the feminist formula would entail some rather large costs. Providing widows and divorcees with 100 percent of benefits alone would swell an already strained Social Security budget by millions of dollars annually, and the amount would escalate dramatically with the coming "geriatrification" of American society. Raising benefits to two-earner couples would have a similar effect.

Patterns of discrimination likewise exist in private pension plans and military retirement pay. For example, under current federal law, a home-maker may find that she has no claim to any portion of her husband's pension. Similarly, the legal system has denied wives any right to their husband's government pensions, including military retirement pay. According to feminists, "The ERA will strengthen the view of pensions as marital property to which the homemaker spouse made a nonfinancial but nonetheless valuable contribution."[91]

As with Social Security, conforming pension practices to the concept of "marital income" will entail both redistributive and inflationary effects. In particular, a redistribution of pension income will flow from divorced men to their estranged spouses, while overall premiums for private pensions as well as the budget for funding government pensions may rise if it is determined that payments must continue to be made to widows.

D. Marital Property

In many states, the laws determining property rights in marriage are based on the traditional "patriarchal," rather than the "partnership," view of marriage. As a result, in these states husbands have greater control over, and rights to, the ownership and possession of marital property. For example, in some states, household goods that are purchased during marriage belong to the husband while real estate held jointly by husband and wife is controlled only by the husband so that no rents or profits produced by the property accrue to the wife.[92]

Adopting a state's legal system to the partnership view would entail some legal costs, but the primary effect of rectifying this form of discrimination would be redistributional, with a transfer of wealth flowing once again from men to women.

E. Macroeconomic Effects

We have already alluded to several likely "macroeconomic" consequences of the ERA associated with rectifying sex discrimination in the microeconomy. For example, closing the wage gap will involve, at least in the short run, a likely rise in unemployment and inflation; opening up job opportunities to women would likely enhance economic growth;

and feminist Social Security and pensions reforms will raise the federal budget.

Similarly, revising the rules on women's pension rights (or, for that matter, Social Security) would likewise entail legal, regulatory, and administrative costs which, in turn, would be reflected in larger government budgets. On this issue of implementation costs, more must be said. Both ERA supporters and their opposition agree that making the ERA work would entail substantial legal, regulatory, and bureaucratic costs.

Indeed, the preceding discussion should have removed any remaining doubt that the 24 words of the ERA are merely symbolic. Feminist legal experts have written tomes on the far-reaching legal and judicial ramifications of an implementation process projected to take over 10 years while ERA critics have asserted, no doubt correctly, that those seemingly simple 24 words will engender over 24,000 new complex rules, regulations, and laws.

All of this implementation will, of course, cost money; and the redistributive effects won't be just from men to women, but from taxpayers to lawyers and bureaucrats. Just how much it will cost no one knows. Surely, it will run into the millions of dollars and, for the entire American legal system, it may reach the billion-dollar mark or more.

Given these implementation costs and the other economic effects discussed above, the ultimate question is "What price social justice?" Let us move to our concluding section on policy reforms to suggest several possible answers to that question.

IV. POLICY REFORMS

A central tenet of this book is that economic analysis can serve as the final arbiter of many policy disputes among special interests and ideologues. But while the economic analyses of our previous cases have, by and large, implied concrete policy reforms that could make all (or at least most) of us better off, the ERA analysis lacks such a virtue.

One major reason is that the ERA is more of a zero-sum issue than any of our previous policy games. That is, its economic effects are basically redistributive; and where possible gains to the economy exist (e.g., through increased productivity), these gains are likely to be offset totally or in part by the very real legal and other costs associated with implementing the amendment.

But a second major reason is that some of the most important effects of the ERA fall well outside the scope of economic analysis and are more properly in the domain of sociologists. The most obvious of these effects are embedded in the conservative's claim that passage of the ERA will precipitate the entire moral collapse of the society and in the liberal's/ feminist's counterclaim that it will give us a stronger, more equitable society. Ultimately, then, the policy implications of our economic analysis can only be assessed within the context of one's own ideology, and in particular, one's view of social justice versus the prospects of societal decay.

On the one hand, those who believe the dire warnings of conservatives that the home, family, and ultimately, the entire social fabric will unravel in a post-ERA holocaust should follow the advice of John Adams and resist any such change with all possible force.[93] For those who believe that social justice requires equal treatment for all Americans regardless of race, color, creed, and in this case, sex, the only policy option is to pass the ERA as quickly as possible and then help ensure that the amendment is implemented with all due speed in the workplace, the courts, the university, government agencies, and every other nook and cranny of the economy and society where sex discrimination persists.

Yes, such passage will entail costs and yes, it will involve a massive redistribution of wealth from businesses and men to women. But if one unequivocable point emerges from the economic analysis, it is that women have suffered more systematic discrimination in more areas than any other interest group in America.

11

The Weapons Sweepstakes

THE DEFENSE POLICY GAME

By all means follow your lines of hope and your paths of peace, but do not close your eyes to the fact that we are entering a corridor of deepening and darkening danger, and that we shall have to move along it for many months and possibly for years to come.[1]

Sir Winston Churchill

These words on the Nazi re-armament of the 1930s have an all too eerie resemblance to the 1980s' rhetoric warning of a massive Soviet arms escalation, rhetoric that has been used to justify and accelerate the largest peacetime military buildup in America's history.

Unfortunately, because defense issues are so complex, it is very difficult to sort out reality from alarmist cant. Are we being prudent, as the words of Sir Winston seem to suggest, in racing to match the Soviets missile for missile, bomb for bomb, laser beam for laser beam? Or are we merely being paranoid and, worse, provocative?

On the one hand, America has been caught unawares once, and few Americans who remember Pearl Harbor want to risk exposing this nation to a second "day of infamy," particularly in a nuclear age. On the other hand, more recent history has also taught us to be wary of dire warnings about Soviet military might. Since the end of World War II, the American public has been fooled repeatedly by a number of false "gaps" between the U.S. and the Soviet Union.

For example, in 1960 Americans were whipped up into near hysteria by the prospect of a large Russian missile arsenal to be built within a few years. As a result, we rapidly accelerated the development of a huge strategic "triad" of land-based missiles, submarine-launched missiles, and manned nuclear bombers. But the alleged "missile gap" never materialized; by 1963, the Russians had built a mere 3 percent of the missiles predicted.

Shortly thereafter, the Counsels of Fear warned that the Russians were erecting an impenetrable anti-ballistic missile (ABM) shield over their entire country. This spurred a fivefold increase in our warheads targeted at the Soviet Union and the development of deadly multiple-targeted independent reentry vehicles (MIRVs) designed to overwhelm this shield. But the truth of the "ABM gap" later turned out to be a small and now obsolescent system around Moscow.

Similar real and imagined bomber, megatonnage, and antisubmarine gaps in the 1970s likewise facilitated American weapons development. However, the Soviets in turn have responded by accelerating their own pace of weapons development so that the previous false gaps have almost become self-fulfilling prophecies. As a result, we are seeing a drastic acceleration of the arms race and heightened world tension.

Today, we are being warned of a "throw weight gap" (the Soviets have bigger missiles to handle bigger warheads), another bomber gap (the Soviet Backfire bomber allegedly flies rings around our B-52s), a "star wars" gap (Soviet laser beams are going to zap our satellites and control outer space), and a "window of vulnerability" (the Soviets may attack before we modernize our defenses).

Is the wolf—or Russian bear—really here this time? Further, do our massive expenditures guarantee that we will be safe from the Soviet threat, or do they merely increase the probability of war and encourage inefficiency and waste? When every dollar of the $2 trillion defense budget projected for the 1980s represents a dollar that will not be spent on hospitals, schools, or more productive endeavors, can we afford all these "guns" at the expense of badly needed "butter"? Finally, what is the cost of our persistent failure to negotiate successfully with the Soviets? Is ideological blindness closing off pragmatic avenues of negotiation that would decrease both the need for huge defense expenditures and the prospect of war? In this policy game, we examine these questions within the context of the politics and economics of the defense budget.

I.   HISTORY AND BACKGROUND

. . . standing armies in times of peace are inconsistent with the principles of republican government, dangerous to the liberties of a free people, and generally converted into destructive engines for establishing despotism.[2]

GEORGE WASHINGTON

From the days of George Washington until World War II, the United States advocated an antimilitarism that was reflected in its stiff opposition to a large standing army and a permanent military establishment. After the Revolution, Washington completely disbanded his army and left America's defenses to ragged and inept state militias. When, as president, he later asked for a small regular army, his request was denied. By 1845, on the eve of the war with Mexico, we had only 9,000 soldiers, while by 1904 there were just over 50,000. Even on the eve of World War II, our troops numbered barely 140,000.[3]

However, under the threatening spurs of Hitler and Tojo, the military establishment mushroomed. With the coming of peace, it was not dismantled; and today, we have over two million military personnel stationed in over 8,500 bases, camps, and installations worldwide. At the same time, in the decades after Hiroshima, the American nuclear arsenal has mushroomed to over 25,000 warheads and missiles, enough explosive power to destroy the Soviet Union—and the world—many times over.

To support defense efforts, the U.S. spends over $200 billion annually, a full 25 percent of the total budget. More important from the standpoint of balancing that budget, defense spending is the single largest item in the "discretionary" budget: that part other than entitlement programs like Social Security that the Congress has the full power to control.

Roughly 10 percent of the defense budget is devoted to maintaining and expanding our *strategic* umbrella of nuclear deterrence. These strategic forces are embodied in the aforementioned triad of land-based intercontinental ballistic missiles, submarine-launched missiles, and a bomber force capable of delivering nuclear warheads. Another 40 percent is devoted to maintaining a conventional combat force while the remainder is spread among basic support services, from intelligence gathering to retirement pay.

Figure 11.1 charts past and projected future defense spending as a percentage of Gross National Product (GNP) in the post-World War II period.* From the figure, an interesting trend is evident. The rollercoaster line indicates that defense expenditures have been *highly cyclical*. During the Korean War, the defense budget consumed up to 13 percent of GNP, while during the height of the Vietnam War, the figure was 9 percent. As one would expect with a return to peacetime, both of these buildups were followed by sharp and steady declines in defense spending. However, the post-Vietnam decline in the 1970s—characterized by some as a decade of defense neglect—was particularly steep and prolonged. Thus, even while we were spending more and more on defense in *nominal* (inflated) dollars during the 1970s, defense spending both in *real* dollars (adjusted for inflation) and as a percentage of GNP was actually sinking to levels well below those during the peacetime eras of the 1950s and 1960s.

Today defense expenditures are once again on the rise. As Figure 11.1 indicates, expenditures are projected to once again reach as high as 8 percent of GNP. While this is a significant fraction of the nation's GNP, it is interesting to note that it is still slightly below the fraction of GNP devoted to defense during the peacetime years of the Eisenhower administration.

A closer look at the defense budget reveals two additional trends. First, the per-unit cost of weaponry has been rising dramatically in real terms. But because our budget dollars for weapons procurement have not risen commensurately, the quantity of weapons available to our combat forces has been dramatically reduced. This trend is evident in Figure 11.2,

*Relating defense spending to the yardstick of GNP is the best way of thinking about the relative size of the defense budget compared to our other spending. Simply stating defense expenditures in nominal dollars (unadjusted for inflation) overstates the growth in defense spending, while stating defense dollars as a percentage of the total budget understates that growth because of the rapid growth in the nondefense portion of the budget since the 1960s.

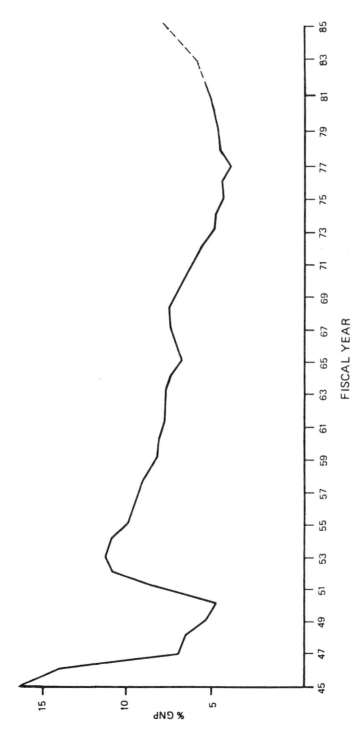

Figure 11.1. Defense expenditures as a percentage of gross national product.

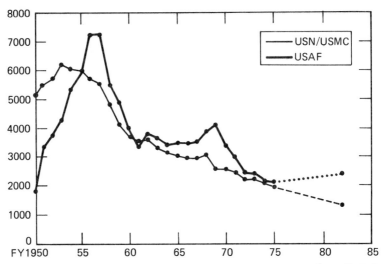

Figure 11.2. Fighter/attack aircraft inventory. Source: Inventories from DoD Defense Management Summary (U), FY50-75, FY82 from Secretary's FY83 *Annual Report*; procurement from DoD comptroller (U), FY71-82, and as projected in FY83-87 Five Year Defense Program.[5]

which charts the inventory of a typical weapon, fighter/attack aircraft; this trend has been wryly characterized as the "curve of unilateral disarmament" and humorously captured in Augustine's Final Law of Economic Disarmament, which states: "In the year 2054, the defense budget will purchase one tactical aircraft."[4]

Second, not only is the defense budget buying fewer and fewer conventional weapons for more and more dollars, but a very small number of strategic weapons programs—the MX missile, the B-1 bomber, and the Trident submarine—are consuming more and more of the share of that budget. In the mid-1980s, we will spend over $55 billion on these three weapons programs alone, or one-fifth of U.S. weapons procurement dollars. This means that defense contractors, who are primary players in the defense policy game, are fighting for fewer and fewer, albeit larger, shares of the defense pie. Such competition intensifies both political pressure on the budgetary process and economic pressure on what is, in many of its subsectors, an ailing industry.

Let's examine this pressure within the context of the politics of the defense budget. Then, economic analysis in Section III illustrates how the patterns of cyclical defense spending, rising weapons costs, and fewer weapons systems are taking bigger chunks out of the defense budget and have dramatically reduced both the combat and strategic readiness of our military forces.

II. THE POLITICS OF DEFENSE POLICY

A.   Private Interest Capture

Under the spur of profit potential, powerful lobbies spring up to argue for ever larger munitions expenditures. And the web of special interest grows.[6]

DWIGHT EISENHOWER

In perhaps his most famous presidential utterance, Eisenhower coined the term "military-industrial complex" (MIC) to warn of the growing power of special interests in shaping defense policy.* At the same time, Ike also innocently created one of the great misconceptions of our time, that the MIC is a monolithic prime mover behind all defense policy decisions. Rather, as Senator William Proxmire has observed: The MIC "has more tentacles than an octopus. Its dimensions are almost infinite. It is a military-industrial-bureaucratic-trade-association-labor-union-intellectual-technical-service-club-political complex whose pervasiveness touches nearly every citizen."[7]

To see if this "octopus" has captured defense policy, let us probe its many tentacles: the corporate defense contractors doing considerable business with the Pentagon; the labor movement that fills those contractors' factories; the universities and think tanks that plot strategy and help conceive new weapons; the vast government lobby that includes civilian bureaucrats, their military counterparts, and Congress; the strong state and regional interests that vie both for military bases and production facilities, and finally, the many veterans' organizations and their service liaisons.

1. The Defense Contractors.   Weapons research, development, and procurement is unquestionably the largest government sweepstakes that American industry plays. Each year, over 20,000 contractors win a

---

*The man responsible was actually Malcolm Moos, Ike's speechwriter, who went on to become president of the University of Minnesota.

share of the more than $100 billion that the military awards for defense and aerospace research, development, and production programs. These "prime" contractors in turn select over 100,000 subcontractors that share roughly half of every contract dollar. Together, they build the weapons, fabricate mechanical parts and electronic components, and provide materials ranging from aluminum and steel to the exotica of titanium sponge and beryllium.

The giants of U.S. defense production are familiar names: Boeing, General Dynamics, Grumman, McDonnell Douglas, Northrop, Rockwell, United Technologies. These firms have been among the top 12 recipients of defense contracts for nearly a decade: Between 1970 and 1980 they received a total of more than $100 billion from the Pentagon (25 percent of all its business) and $11 billion from the National Aeronautics and Space Administration (NASA).

The best guide to the distribution of the spoils of the procurement process is the Department of Defense (DoD) list, which ranks its 100 largest contractors by total dollars received; these contractors garner roughly two-thirds of all awards while the top 12 contractors, which are arrayed in Table 11.1, account for almost 40 percent of DoD's procurement dollars.

The firms listed in Table 11.1 diverge widely in their degree of reliance on defense business. For example, while General Electric and Boeing have over half of their business in civilian enterprises, Northrop and Grumman are almost totally dependent on weapons dollars. Accordingly, with their very survival at stake, these more DoD-dependent firms are likely to exert greater political pressure during the procurement process.

At the same time, the table indicates that each firm tends to specialize in a few weapons or weapons systems. United Technologies is, for example, primarily in military aircraft engine and helicopter manufacturing, while Raytheon specializes in missiles and electronics. Similarly, General Dynamics makes the F-16 and F-111 jet fighters, while McDonnell Douglas makes the F-15 and F-18. Thus, while there would appear to be enormous competition for shares of the overall defense budget, many firms have carved out a comfortable niche in the market where they bid, often with very little or no competition.

2. Labor's Defense Lobby.   One out of every 10 Americans is employed in a defense or defense-related white- or blue-collar job. Accord-

TABLE 11.1.   TOP U.S. PRIME DEFENSE CONTRACTORS

Company	DoD Contract Dollars	Major Work
	(000)	
1. General Dynamics Corporation	5,891,101	F-16 and F-111 aircraft Nuclear submarines
2. McDonnell Douglas Corporation	5,630,104	Fighter aircraft Missile systems
3. United Technologies Corporation	4,208,293	Aircraft engines Helicopters
4. General Electric Company	3,654,097	Nuclear reactors for submarines and aircraft carriers Minuteman Missile Space vehicle components
5. Lockheed Corporation	3,498,550	Trident and Aegis missile systems Space vehicles Amphibious assault ships
6. Boeing Company	3,238,796	AWACs Radio and TV equipment Various aircraft
7. Hughes Company	3,140,735	TOW, Maverick, Phoenix and Trident missile systems Electronics and communications equipment
8. Rockwell International Corporation	2,690,518	Aircraft, missile and space systems B-1 bomber
9. Raytheon Company	2,262,290	Missile systems Electronics and communications equipment
10. Martin Marietta Corporation	2,008,354	Pershing and Titan missile systems Guided missile launchers
11. Grumman Corporation	1,900,489	F-14 Tomcat and other aircraft
12. Northrop Corporation	1,598,194	F-5 Freedom Fighter aircraft Missile and space systems

Source: Directorate for Information Operations and Reports. *The One Hundred Companies Receiving the Largest Dollar Volume of Prime Contract Awards for Fiscal Year 1982.* (Washington, D.C.: Office of Secretary of Defense, 1984).

ingly, a variety of labor organizations take an active interest in both the size and dispensation of the annual defense budget.

Chief among these organizations is the AFL–CIO. With its over 10 million members and 121 affiliated unions, this organization has not only supported a high level of defense spending but also, in different periods of its history, has taken an active role in American foreign policy—partly to promote trade unionism abroad and partly to protect the lucrative foreign markets for arms sales. For example, during the reign of George Meany, the AFL–CIO was involved in a wide range of activities, including the CIA-funded training of foreign unionists to help overthrow governments in Brazil, the Dominican Republic, and British Guiana; intelligence gathering; and using strikebreakers to facilitate the unloading of American arms in European ports.[8]

Closer to home, labor leaders and their union journals carefully monitor the defense budget sweepstakes and its implications for employment opportunities. In this effort, labor interests are aided greatly by the Pentagon, which regularly supplies press releases and bulletins documenting in excruciating detail the number of carpenters, electricians, metalworkers, and the like that a new weapons system will employ.

3. Universities and Think Tanks. All told, the academic and intellectual community receives over 1.5 billion defense dollars per year, a sum that constitutes over 20 percent of all research spending by American universities. Heading the beneficiary list of the MIC's "brain lobby" with over $200 million is the Aerospace Group, a think tank with headquarters in California. Close behind are a number of prestigious institutions, including Johns Hopkins University with $235 million, and the Massachusetts Institute of Technology with $216 million. Other major recipients include the MITRE Corporation, Draper Labs, the University of California, and Stanford University.

The harnessing of America's academic community for defense purposes is a relatively new phenomenon. Before WWII, weaponry was sufficiently simple that the government and private industry had little need to go on campus for help. But with the splitting of the atom in 1937 and the rise of sophisticated electronics, a qualitative change took place in the American arsenal and in the relationship of the military and academia. After the war, universities were confronted with a choice of whether to continue their defense-related research, and the lure of millions of dollars of grant money was too much for most to spurn.

Today, the DoD, NASA, and similar agencies provide universities with funds, new classrooms, libraries, and laboratories. These resources allow professors and their graduate students to perform research, bring prestige to the universities, and lend power to university presidents. They also provide numerous contacts and nonuniversity consulting opportunities that can earn professors healthy supplemental incomes. As Clark Kerr has observed: "intellect has also become an instrument of national purpose, a component part of the 'military-industrial complex'."[9]

Joining their academic brethren are those intellectuals ensconced in private research and educational think tanks. Their ranks include the Hoover Institution on War, Revolution, and Peace, the American Security Council, the Center for Strategic Studies, and the American Enterprise Institute. While these think tanks are no doubt dedicated to the advancement of public knowledge, it also is true that the funds, facilities, and prestige of these institutions are often dependent on the size of the defense budget.

4. The Government Lobby.   Nowhere is the government lobby of more size and importance than in defense policy. Conceptually, this lobby consists of three major segments: bureaucrats within the DoD, the CIA, NASA, and other defense-related agencies; members of the military services; and the Congress itself.

Far and away the largest bastion of bureaucratic players in the defense policy game, the DoD owns over $400 billion worth of property, holdings that dwarf even those of the largest American corporations. It populates this considerable real estate with some one million civilians and two million military personnel.

The size and dispensation of the defense budget provides these bureaucrats with employment, power, and opportunities for advancement. Their interaction with the private defense industry also creates opportunities for more lucrative employment beyond the department's constrictive government pay-scale walls.

To plead its cases, the DoD maintains over 300 lobbyists within the Pentagon, more than one for every two members of Congress. Moreover, its lobbying budget exceeds the expenditures of virtually all other government and most private lobbying efforts.

Besides the DoD, various segments of other administrative agencies also have a large stake in the defense budget. These include the Department of State and clandestine CIA, the money faucet OMB, foreign aid funnel Agency for International Development, and the Department of Energy, which makes all our nuclear warheads.

Historically, each of the major military services has sought to maintain its autonomy by maintaining separate budgets and lobbying organizations, unique weapons systems, and to some extent, preferred contractors. One result of pressure from the military lobby has been a vast overlapping and duplication among the supply systems for the military and massive collateral waste and inefficiency.

Despite repeated efforts to reduce this "interservice rivalry," the problems persist. For example, critics of the land, sea, and air-based strategic triad attribute its existence more to the unholy army–navy–air force trinity than any strategic imperative; efforts to abandon the triad concept (e.g., by foregoing the MX missile or the B-1 bomber and instead relying on one or two of the triad's legs) provoke great howls of protest from the service branch affected.

According to Senator William Proxmire, almost 25 percent of the 435 House members and almost 40 percent of Senators hold officer ranks in the reserve, some as high as major general.[10] These and other members of Congress also have large economic interests to protect, with almost 1,000 major defense plants and military installations located in 363 of the 435 congressional districts.

While a military background does not ensure a pro-military bias, it can create a sympathetic environment for defense lobbyists. At the same time, the dispersion of defense-related facilities creates pressures on congressmen hostile to defense budget interests and a natural constituency for pro-defense candidates.

Enormous competition exists among congressmen over defense dollars for their districts. One of the premier procurers of such dollars was Mendel Rivers, longtime chairman of the House Armed Services Committee. The legendary South Carolinian's campaign slogan was "Rivers delivers," and deliver he did: His Charleston area district is literally crammed with military installations: an air force base, an army depot, a navy shipyard, a marine air station and training base, two navy hospitals, a submarine training center, and more.

Similarly, Georgia Senator Richard Russell was so effective in luring air force dollars to the Peach State that one general commented: "One more base would sink it."[11] Today, senators like John Tower and John Stennis carry on in the Rivers–Russell tradition. But the military machinations within the Congress are hardly confined to hawks; loud protests are ritually heard from liberal doves like Edward Kennedy, Alan Cranston, and William Cohen whenever whispers are heard about shutting down the Boston Navy Yard, curtailing the California production of the B-1, or cutting shipbuilding dollars for Maine's boat works.

5.   Regional Interests.   While defense plants and military bases blanket the country, the bulk of these facilities is concentrated geographically, both by function (e.g., weapons factories and military bases) and weapons system (e.g., missiles and ships).

California is by far the largest beneficiary of the defense budget, with mini–military–industrial complexes located both in Los Angeles and the San Francisco Bay Area. Besides being a leading supplier of electronics and ammunition, it, together with Massachusetts, receives more than half of all "high tech" missile and space contracts.

By the same token, Texas and New York receive over half of the air force and air assembly contracts while Virginia, Mississippi, and, to a lesser extent, coastal Maine, capture the lion's share of shipbuilding contracts. Only heavy hardware such as tanks continues to be produced in the Midwest, where Michigan and Ohio receive over half of the combat vehicle appropriations.

While high tech production concentrates in the higher-income metropolitan areas of California, Massachusetts, and New York, a large portion of our military bases is located in Sun Belt and other lower-income states such as Arizona, Nevada, Florida, Georgia, and New Mexico.

These geographical concentrations have important implications for the politics of defense spending, intensifying rivalry among the defense haves and have-nots for tax dollars. They also create opportunities for logrolling among both production and military base states. Thus, a senator from Washington might be willing to support a bill to keep open a base in South Carolina if he knows the quid pro quo is the Southern senator's vote for a Boeing weapon like the B-1 bomber.

6.   Veterans and Service Organizations.   Rounding out the cast of the MIC, a plethora of veterans and service organizations function both as a political mouthpiece for defense interests and as a liaison between the civilian and military components of the other defense lobbies.[12] Perhaps the two most famous of the veterans' groups are the

Veterans of Foreign Wars (VFW) and the American Legion (AL), boasting over one and two million members, respectively. Both organizations are highly supportive of a strong defense, and presidents frequently find their meetings to be favorable forums to make a pitch for a bigger defense budget or more weaponry.

Although less visible, the various service organizations likewise have a formidable membership and raise millions to defend the defense budget. For example, the Association of the United States Army has about 100,000 members and a budget of over $1 million. The Air Force Association, Navy League of the United States, and the National Guard Association of the United States provide similar muscle for their respective services, while the American Ordinance Association (AOA) is one of the most effective liaison groups between "science, industry, and the armed forces in the research, development, and production of superior weapons."[13]

7. The Peace Lobby.   For its part, the peace lobby is loosely and weakly organized. Its most vocal components are consumer-oriented think tanks and citizen groups concerned about the arms race and prospects of nuclear war.

Organizations like the Council on Economic Priorities and the Center for Defense Information are largely concerned with waste and mismanagement at the Pentagon. However, the pamphlets and reports that they publish serve only as a weak countervailing force to the profusion of documents generated annually by pro-defense forces.

On a more grass-roots level, church groups such as the American Friends Service Committee and Clergy and Laity Concerned, citizen groups like SANE (Citizens Committee for a Sane Nuclear Policy) and the Council for a Livable World, and recently, academic and professional groups such as the Physicians for Social Responsibility and the Union of Concerned Scientists lobby against escalations in the arms race and for a nuclear weapons freeze.

Despite these groups' recent successes on issues like the nuclear freeze, continued congressional support for a large strategic weapons buildup makes it clear that the peace lobby is still dwarfed by the overwhelming force of defense proponents.

B.   Strategies and Tactics of the Defense Lobby

The methods of pressure employed by the players in the defense policy game mirror the breadth and power of these groups and run virtually the entire gamut of our basic strategies and tactics.

   1.   Direct Lobbying.   Most of the larger defense contractors maintain lobbying offices in Washington from which they sally forth with technical reports and other information to shake the hands and twist the arms of their audience. According to Ronald Fox, the "contractor representatives assigned to these offices are supposed to develop and maintain working relationships with government personnel. They are selected on the basis of their personal qualities, the ability to meet and converse with people, rather than their technical skills."[14] Many of these firms also maintain centers of operation near military buying facilities; Fox, for instance, found one typical firm setting up such offices in at least nine states.

   While the defense bureaucrats and military bear the brunt of much of the industry's direct lobbying, these government groups are no slouches when it comes time to apply their own pressure on Capitol Hill and the administration. The Pentagon's lobbyists, euphemistically called congressional liaison specialists, "woo Congress as ardently as Romeo wooed Juliet."[15]

   Academics and think tank intellectuals (often under the sponsorship of the defense budget) present their research results in reports and testimony. Frequently, this information provides "erudite rationales" for new exotic weaponry or warns of the adverse economic consequences of shutting down military installations in a state.

   2.   Indirect Lobbying.   Because of the number of defense related jobs and military base and defense plant sitings in congressional districts, indirect lobbying can be an even more important source of influence for the defense lobby.

   Perhaps the most ubiquitous of the grass-roots lobbying tools is the letter-writing campaign. To stir up congressional support for contract awards, upper echelon executives typically issue announcements in company newsletters exhorting employees to write their congressmen about an upcoming piece of legislation. While letter writing is not as a rule particularly effective, it often carries more weight for defense interests because the letters are not spewed out by a computer, but are the actual concerns of a congressman's constitutents. Also, with one of ten U.S. jobs being defense-related, the election of many congressmen is heavily dependent on defense budget dollars for their districts.

The flurry of letters to Capitol Hill during the B-1 bomber debate is but one small illustration of the pervasiveness of letter writing. Representative Les Aspin, for example, received hundreds of letters from Rockwell employees in a plant bordering his district. This is all the more interesting since, while Rockwell is one of the prime contractors for the B-1, the employees actually made televisions in a Rockwell subsidiary.

A second tactic of the defense contractors is advocacy ads, where trade journals, newspapers, and even television and radio bombard the public with images of patriotism, U.S. military might, and dire Soviet threats. While most of these ads traffic in patriotic propaganda, some are not always aboveboard. An oft-cited example is the pro-ABM spread that appeared in publications across the country. The "spontaneous grassroots" organization that published it, the Citizen's Committee for Peace and Security, proclaimed that "84 percent of all Americans say the United States should have an ABM system." While the poll turned out to be a gross misrepresentation, even more damning was the fact that among the signers of the ad "were 11 key officials of eight companies which held more than $150 million in ABM contracts."[16]

In rationalizing their use of advocacy ads, defense contractors claim that the military "often ask(s) us to help sell the project to the administration and Congress through advertising."[17] This is hardly surprising since both the military services and the DoD expend even more energy and dollars promoting the defense budget through propaganda, persuasion, and public relations. The Pentagon spends over $25 million on public relations while the navy, air force, and army spend another $25 million. Over 200 military and civilian personnel staff the Public Affairs office at DoD alone, while a staff of over 50 at the Directorate for Information generates all of DoD's news releases, and its Defense Information School graduates over 2,000 students each year.

Another office in the Pentagon is responsible for the approval and release of all television, movie, radio, and other audiovisual material provided by the DoD. It also approves and coordinates cooperation and funding between the DoD and private filmmakers—but only for those films that glorify war. A famous example of this bias is that of the Vietnam War–vintage John Wayne epic *The Green Berets*. According to Congressman Benjamin Rosenthal (D., N.Y.), the Army billed Wayne's film company less than $20,000 for over 100 days of filming at Fort Benning, Georgia, while the true cost to the army was a million dollars or more.[18] In contrast, more controversial films like *Fail-Safe*, *The Deerhunter*, and *Apocalypse Now* were denied Pentagon cooperation; the investigative reporting teams of CBS's *60 Minutes* likewise are regularly denied Pentagon help.

Perhaps the most revealing incident of the Pentagon's orchestrated efforts to persuade is the so-called Starbird scandal. In a now-classic memo outlining the strategy to sell the public the ABM, General Alfred D. Starbird called for a "public relations public affairs program on a country-wide basis," ordering that "magazine articles will be prepared by Army staff members . . . for submission to military, scientific, and professional journals." In a coopting tactic, the general also commanded his staff to "encourage and assist in the preparation of magazine articles . . . by *civilian* scientific or technical writers of national stature."[19] When this memo and an only slightly less damaging one by Secretary of the Army Stanley R. Resor were intercepted by the *Washington Post*, the ensuing publicity forced Resor and Starbird to withdraw their memos and conduct their campaign "in more circumspect and more restrained forms."[20]

Finally, the academic and think-tank wings of the defense lobby perform an important grass-roots lobbying function. Missile gaps, domino theories, containment policies, limited nuclear war doctrines, and the like all have their origins as articles in prestigious journals or as documents or technical reports, eventually filtering down to become what John Kenneth Galbraith has called a "conventional wisdom."

In their dissemination of defense doctrine, various members of the intellectual defense lobby also play important roles. Hard-line groups like the American Security Council and the Center for International Studies aggressively spread information through educational programs, seminars, and media programs, while more subtle and sophisticated conservative groups like the Hoover Institution at Stanford, the Center for Strategic and International Studies at Georgetown, and the Foreign Policy Research Institute of Pennsylvania publish their own materials but rely more on third parties to promote their point of view.

3. Dollar Lobbying. The strategy of dollar lobbying is primarily the preserve of the defense contractors and, to a lesser extent, of some of the veterans and trade organizations. The principal conduits for both campaign contributions and in-kind services are the numerous defense lobby PACs. Table 11.2 compares the ranks of the top 12 prime contractors listed in Table 11.1 with their ranks by defense PAC contributions. Note the high correlation between contract awards and PAC contributions. For example, United Technologies ranks third in both contract dollars and PAC contributions, while Lockheed holds the fifth spot in both categories. All 12 contractors have PACs that rank within the top 20 defense contributors.

The primary beneficiaries of these contributions are the members of key defense budget committees and the congressmen and senators in whose jurisdiction the PAC's corporation has facilities or does business. Like most PACs, they typically spread their largess in a nonideological and nonpartisan manner: Liberals as well as conservatives benefit. For instance, in the early 1980s when the debate over the B-1 bomber was particularly intense, Rockwell's Good Government PAC provided over $50,000 in campaign contributions to members of two key committees: the Armed Services Committee and defense and military construction subcommittee of the Appropriations Committee. The Senate Armed Services committee chairman, John Tower, received over $3,000 and the

TABLE 11.2. RANK OF TOP PRIME CONTRACTORS
BY DEFENSE PAC CONTRIBUTIONS

Company	Rank by Defense Contract Dollars	Rank by Defense PAC Contributions
General Dynamics	1	7
McDonnell Douglas	2	10
United Technologies	3	3
General Electric	4	9
Lockheed	5	5
Boeing	6	15
Hughes Aircraft	7	11
Rockwell International	8	6
Raytheon	9	16
Martin Marietta	10	14
Grumman	11	4
Northrop	12	19

House Military Construction Subcommittee chairman received $1,100. Similarly, Democratic members like Howard Cannon received $5,000, while Republicans like Lowell Weicker and Robert Badham received $5,000 and $1,000, respectively.

At the same time, Rockwell was very generous to those congressmen and senators in whose states the B-1 was to be built. For example, Bill Dannemeyer, representative of the home of Rockwell's Autonetics Division, received $1,250, while Daniel Patrick Moynihan, senator from the state of the B-1's associate contractor, AIL, received $1,000. All told, Rockwell's PAC devoted over 57 percent of its campaign contributions to these two targets: committee members and home representatives.

4. Questionable Practices. Historically, the most headline-grabbing of the questionable practices has been the defense contractor's penchant for entertaining congressmen and their staffs and defense department bureaucrats. In the heyday of this tactic, contractors flew key policymakers to golf links, testing facilities, and the like, and rented out large hotels, cozy hunting lodges, and banquet rooms to throw parties.

Today, public scrutiny of these practices has sharply reduced their incidence. DoD officials, for example, are now forbidden to accept gifts or trips from defense contractors, while congressmen are certainly more wary. Nonetheless, other questionable practices go on, perhaps the most important of which is the cooptation of military and civilian bureaucrats through employment opportunities. This tactic was first brought to the public spotlight by Senator William Proxmire in 1960 when he reported that over 2,000 former high-ranking military officers worked for the 100 largest defense contractors. Lockheed alone harbored over 200, including 22 generals and admirals, while Boeing (with 15 generals and admirals), McDonnell Douglas, General Dynamics, and Rockwell had over 100 ex-officers on their payrolls.[21] Although there is no doubt some benefit in having knowledgeable retired military officers help private industry on technical matters, such a freely swinging revolving door

> . . . can have a subtle, but debilitating effect on an officer's performance . . . in a procurement management assignment. If he takes too strong a hand in controlling contractor activity, he might be damaging his opportunity for a second career following retirement. Positions are offered to officers who have demonstrated their appreciation for industry's particular problems and commitments."[22]

The flow of ex-military officers and civilian bureaucrats into private industry is not the only problem, however. Former top executives in the defense contractor's pool often wind up in upper echelon civilian posts in the DoD, CIA, and other defense-related agencies. For example, a number of former secretaries and undersecretaries of defense have come from the contractors' ranks, among them Robert McNamara of Ford Motor Company (at that time, one of the top 10 largest defense contractors), David Packard of Hewlett-Packard Corporation, and, more recently, Caspar Weinberger of Bechtel Corporation.

For its part, the government lobby, and particularly the Pentagon, is guilty of several other questionable practices. Two familiar tactics often used with potentially hostile inquiring congressmen are that of *delay* and *inundation*. In response to an information request, the DoD can either drag its heels in providing the data or "present the Congressman with so much detail that he will never figure out what is happening."[23] Another familiar gambit is lying with statistics. In cataloguing the "games" DoD plays, Ronald Fox is instructive on this: "Be selective with statistics that will support arguments for increased spending. If we want more ships, indicate that a potential enemy has more ships than the United States. Don't mention that U.S. ships are larger or have greater firepower."[24]

5. Questionable Payments.   The propensity to bribe is no doubt the greatest among those contractors who do considerable business beyond our borders where "side payments" appear to be a more prevalent fact of political life.

Perhaps the most blundering was Lockheed's attempt to sell its Starfighter plane—the so-called flying-coffin or widow-maker—to NATO forces, particularly to West Germany. During its multiyear sales campaign, Lockheed paid out millions of dollars in bribes to influential Europeans, often to discreet-sounding front organizations like the Temperate Zone Research Foundation (headquartered in Panama). A raft of memos was subsequently discovered, exposing Lockheed to public ridicule and the governments involved to heavy criticism.[25]

Similarly, Northrop, which is perhaps the most dependent on foreign arms sales of the large defense contractors, was involved in numerous covert transfers to influence peddlers in Japan, Italy, and the Netherlands. The revelation of these transfers badly shook all three governments.

C.   The Public Interest View

While special interests and their strategies and tactics abound in the defense policy game, it is also an unquestionable truth that a strong national defense is in the public interest. That is, of course, not a matter of ideological dispute. But where conservatives and liberals disagree is over the thorny questions of how big the defense budget should be, how these defense dollars should be spent, and how the United States should relate, economically and militarily, to the rest of the world. This disagreement may be illustrated through a discussion of the eighth and final principle in the logic of the American ideologies. In this particular context, the "fusionist" conservative's *nationalistic anti-communism* is contrasted with the modern liberal's more *international* and *global* approach to defense policy.*

1.   Conservative Defense Policy

In the last 15 years or more, the Soviet Union has engaged in a relentless military buildup, overtaking and surpassing the United States in major categories of military power, acquiring what can only be considered an offensive military capability. All the moral values that this country cherishes—freedom; democracy; the right of peoples and nations to determine their own destiny, to speak and write, to live and worship as they choose—all these basic rights are fundamentally challenged by a powerful adversary which does not wish these values to survive.[26]

RONALD REAGAN

From his nationalistic perspective, the conservative sees the United States locked in a deadly duel with Soviet conspirators who are skillfully orchestrating and financing phony "wars of national liberation" around the globe. Such revolutions are not the expression of oppressed majorities, but rather, the machinations of extremist minorities indoctrinated and heavily armed by Soviet masters or their puppets.

---

*As discussed in the introduction to Part III, "fusionist conservatism" refers to the observed convergent views of libertarian and traditional conservatives on the general issues of foreign and defense policies and on the particular issue of the nature and extent of the Soviet threat. Appendix B provides a fuller treatment of the eighth fusionist principle and its relationship to modern liberalism and thereby completes the theoretical discussion of the logic of ideology.

In successfully fomenting Communist revolutions, the Soviets are steadily encircling the nations of the free world. To the conservative, the "domino" pattern of these conquests is ominous: North Vietnam gobbles up first South Vietnam and then Laos and Cambodia in Southeast Asia, Communist beachheads are established in Angola and Mozambique by Cuban and North Korean mercenaries, and revolutions in Nicaragua, El Salvador, and of course Cuba, spread the Soviet gospel to our hemisphere.

At stake in this battle is not only American survival, but also the preservation of the values and legacies of Western civilization. Particularly to the traditional conservative, the struggle for world domination between a democratic, free America and a Communistic, totalitarian Russia is but a proxy religious war between basic Judeo-Christian values and a messianic Marxist–Leninist communism. Given the high stakes in this struggle and the conviction that the Soviets do indeed intend to "bury us," it becomes impossible for the conservative to trust them. Every conciliatory Soviet statement is designed to lower America's guard and weaken her will to resist; the rhetoric of détente is but a smokescreen for a secret Soviet drive to arms superiority.

From these values, beliefs, and assumptions naturally flow the conservative's more hawkish policy preferences. Most important, he presses for a bigger defense budget to counter a massive Soviet arms buildup. These additional defense dollars must be devoted to producing the latest (and typically largest) weapons in order to maintain America's perceived military superiority. That means we must proceed not only with projects such as the B-1 bomber, and the MX and Cruise missiles, but also rush to develop more sophisticated weaponry such as particle beam weapons and killer satellites in order to be ready for the inevitable next war front: space.

At the same time, the conservative is more willing to cut social spending to fund defense. This is not only because of his overriding concern for national security, but also because such a cutback of government welfare programs dovetails nicely with his minimal state principle.

The basic mistrust of the Soviets likewise makes the conservative less willing to negotiate with them. Because they are out to "bury" us, such negotiations can only be a ruse. If we are to negotiate, it must be from a standpoint of military superiority, not of weakness or even parity. Again, that means a sustained commitment to more defense spending.

To stem the Communist tide, we also must provide strong support to any country that opposes the Soviets, regardless of its internal policies on matters such as human rights or land reform; and we must be prepared to provide substantial military aid to our allies under the siege of internal, Soviet-inspired revolutions and, where our interests dictate, be willing to intervene militarily in these nations—either through limited covert operations or explicit military action. Since much of the internal strife abroad is propagated by guerrillas supplied with weapons from the Communist bloc, we must counter that military aid with our own military assistance—and a bigger defense budget.

2. Liberal Defense Policy

. . . the "Economy of Life" in America has been starved in order to feed the "Economy of Death."[27]

RICHARD BARNET

While sharing the conservative's anti-Communist sentiment, the liberal's more internationalist perspective gives him a different perception of the communist threat. Rather than seeing a Kremlin-orchestrated conspiracy, the liberal views the many revolutions around the globe as legitimate expressions of oppressed people—the inevitable response of the lower ranges of society to stark poverty, dramatically unequal income distributions, and authoritarian control by small wealthy minorities. These revolutions are not part of any pattern; rather, they are random, if expected, events. Accordingly, the liberal believes we should support such revolutions, or at least not interfere with their natural course, for they are much akin to America's own shedding of the British yoke over 200 years ago. And once these revolutions are consummated, we should lend our strong economic support to raising a stable, more equal, and more democratic society.

Indeed, the best antidote to the spread of socialism is economic, not military, aid. For a prosperous society is the poorest of soils for social unrest and Communist revolution. Further, by providing arms to authoritarian regimes, particularly those that violate human rights, we only help sow the seeds of socialist revolution.

At the same time, the liberal also sees an internal threat perhaps more dangerous than an external Communism, that of our own social unrest.

The sources of this threat are poverty within our own borders, limited employment opportunities, and an income distribution unacceptably skewed to the richer end of the spectrum. Such conditions breed crime and ultimately, revolution. It follows that while we must buy some guns, we must be careful not to divert too many dollars to this "economy of death" at the expense of social welfare programs that are the "butter" of the "economy of life."

In the same vein, the liberal views the drive for U.S. military superiority as a reckless race towards world destruction. To the liberal, there already exist sufficient nuclear arsenals on both sides to destroy the planet many times over and any bid to beat the Russians in the nuclear race only whips up the winds of war.

A better solution to the arms race is negotiation. The liberal believes that the same economic pressures created by an arms race also buffet the Russians. Since they, too, are rational people, it should be possible to negotiate an arms reduction, one that will not only increase the prospects for peace, but also lead to more economic prosperity worldwide.

Thus, in contrast to the conservative, the liberal favors a relatively lower level of defense spending (and a correspondingly higher level of social spending), is more willing to accept weapons parity and negotiate from that premise with the Soviets, prefers economic to military aid, and is far less willing to intervene militarily in the internal affairs of other nations plagued by revolution.

D.   The Politics of Defense: A Statistical Test

To resolve this private versus public interest debate over defense policy with some "hard numbers," the capture-ideology framework was used to analyze Senate voting on the defense budget. The expectation was that special interest members of the defense lobby, together with ideological conservatives, would tend to support a relatively higher defense budget, while members of the peace lobby together with ideological liberals would tend to oppose higher defense spending.

Following the framework's standard approach, a number of measures were constructed to reflect the degree of political or economic pressure that the major players in the defense policy game are likely to exert on a senator's voting behavior.

For example, the political influence or constituency pressure of defense contractors and labor interests was measured by the dollar value of defense contracts awarded to each state as a percentage of state personal income. At the same time, the economic influence of defense contractor dollar lobbying was measured by PAC contributions to each senator over the last three electoral cycles by the top 40 contractors.

Similarly, the political clout of the "brain lobby" was measured by the dollar value of DoD contracts awarded to each state's educational and nonprofit institutions, while the power of the peace lobby was proxied by contributions by state to a major segment of that lobby, the American Friends Service Committee. Other measures were similarly constructed for the various segments of the government lobby, and the veterans and service organizations.

Besides these special interest measures, the ideology of each senator was measured by his or her rating (on a 0–100 scale) by the liberal Americans for Democratic Action, with a high rating indicating a liberal and a low rating indicating a conservative.

These special interest and ideological measures were fed into a computer and a common statistical procedure was used to determine their relative importance in influencing senate voting on legislation to raise the defense budget.

In a world of "pure ideology" in which U.S. senators act to promote their differing conceptions of the public interest, liberal senators would consistently vote against higher defense spending, regardless of the number of defense plants or military installations in their state and irrespective of any large defense PAC contributions. Conservative senators, on the other hand, would consistently vote for higher defense spending, even if relatively few defense dollars are spent in their state and even if their defense PAC contributions are small.

Conversely, in a world of "pure capture," liberal senators from defense production states (e.g., California, Connecticut, and Massachusetts) and military base states (e.g., Hawaii) would abandon their ideology and vote for higher defense spending, as would liberal senators receiving large defense PAC contributions.

The results of the test, presented in Table 11.3, once again confirm that neither pure capture nor pure ideology sufficiently explains the politics of policy issues such as defense spending. This table ranks each

TABLE 11.3.   RANKING THE INFLUENCE OF SPECIAL INTERESTS AND
IDEOLOGY ON THE SIZE OF THE DEFENSE BUDGET[a]

Rank
1. Ideology
2. Defense contractors and labor's defense lobby
3. The brain lobby (universities and think tanks)
4. The peace lobby
5. Defense PACs
6. The government lobby
7. Veterans and service organizations

[a]The regional flavor of the politics of defense spending is embedded in the "defense contractor and
labor defense lobby" measure.

of the special interest and ideology measures according to its statistical
importance in explaining Senate voting on the defense budget.*

From the table, it appears that ideology is the strongest predictor of a
senator's vote; its influence is more powerful than in any of our previous
tests—more than *three times* as great as any other special interest variable. Nor is it difficult to find strong supportive evidence for this statistical conclusion in the voting behavior of some of the Senate's premier
ideologues.

In the realm of pure conservatism, senators like John Stennis of Mississippi, Strom Thurmond of South Carolina, and John Tower of Texas
all consistently and predictably vote for higher defense spending, although this "evidence" of public-interested behavior is somewhat tainted
by the fact that these conservatives each have a significant defense lobby
constituency: Stennis and Tower each received over $50,000 in defense
PAC contributions while Thurmond received over $30,000. More con-
vincing perhaps are the voting records of senators like James McClure of
Idaho, Paul Laxalt of Nevada, New Right-sponsored Gordon Humphrey
of New Hampshire, and North Carolina's ultraconservatives John East
and Jesse Helms; these gentlemen consistently supported a higher defense budget in the absence of any significant defense spending in their
states while receiving defense PAC contributions well below those provided to the average senator.

*The full statistical results are reported in Appendix A along with a description of the
measures and votes analyzed.

But the real acid test of ideological purity in defense issues comes on the liberal end of the spectrum, where many senators face not only significant defense lobby constituencies but also the temptation of large PAC contributions. Despite these pressures, we find liberal senators from states responsible for much of America's high tech weaponry like Alan Cranston of California, Paul Tsongas of Massachusetts, and Lowell Weicker of Connecticut regularly opposing increases in the defense budget, while Hawaii's Spark Matsanuga has likewise gone against the grain of a large military installation constituency to vote the liberal position.*

This ideological voting is, however, in sharp contrast to the voting behavior of a number of other senators who appear to have been captured either by their constituencies or "PAC power." For example, as counterpoint to the ideological purity of the Connecticut–Hawaii duo of Weicker and Matsanuga, there is Connecticut's junior senator, Christopher Dodd, and Hawaii's senior senator, Daniel Inouye. Dodd regularly scores at or near a perfect 100 on the ADA's liberalness scale and is generally recognized as one of the most outspoken critics of conservative defense policy, particularly in Latin America. However, Dodd also represents a state with the largest dependency on defense contracts in the nation and has also been the recipient of large PAC contributions, particularly from Connecticut-based companies such as United Technologies. Perhaps not surprisingly, Dodd has voted for a higher defense budget the majority of the time, as has Inouye, perhaps serving Hawaii's military base constituency.

Similarly, 1984 presidential aspirants Gary Hart of Colorado and Ohio's John Glenn both regularly score in the 80s on the ADA liberalness scale. Hart, however, is from a key missile-producing and military base state while Glenn, who is well known for his dependency on PAC money, has received over $20,000 in defense PAC contributions; both have consistently voted for a higher defense budget.

Given these observations, it is hardly surprising that in our table of results the three capture measures of defense contractors, military installations, and PAC power all show at least a moderate statistical influence on Senate voting. Nor is it surprising given the discussion in an earlier

---

*Interestingly, Cranston has consistently voted for increased spending on the B-1 bomber, which is in large part made in California. This flipflop exposed him to frequent accusations of special interest capture during his ill-fated 1984 run for the presidency.

section of this chapter that the peace lobby ranks rather low on the totem pole of political influence.

The only really anomalous result of the test involves the brain lobby: While it ranks third in importance in the test, its influence is actually negative (see Appendix A). That is, the more defense dollars that universities and think tanks in a state receive, the more these interests are likely to *oppose* higher defense spending. However, given the reticence and nervousness with which universities in particular often exhibit when accepting the "tainted" money of the Pentagon, this "bite the hand that feeds them" conclusion for the brain lobby may not be so anomalous after all.

In summary, the politics of the defense budget indicate that public-interested ideological behavior is the predominant force determining the size of America's military shield. This conclusion is somewhat at odds with that of preceding chapters, where ideology seemed to play no more than a roughly equal role to special-interest capture. However, it is a very logical conclusion given the extreme complexities of defense issues and the fact that, more than any previous issue, national security is synonymous with the national interest.

Nonetheless, in what should be the apotheosis of a public interest issue, the special-interest players in the defense policy game *still* manage to exert at least a moderately important influence on its outcome, so that one may correctly conclude that the military industrial complex is more reality than myth. The remaining questions are what are the economic consequences of defense budget politics and what can be done to prevent some of these consequences?

III.   THE ECONOMICS OF DEFENSE POLICY

The economics of the defense policy game are at the center of a dangerous paradox: we are spending more and more dollars for less and less defense, while efforts to reduce this trend only exacerbate it. The basic problem underlying this paradox—dubbed the Spinney syndrome after its primary theoretician, Pentagon analyst F. C. Spinney[28]—is the steady rise both in the real (inflation-adjusted) cost of the *procurement* of new weapons and in the O&M portion of the budget, which pays for personnel and the operation and maintenance of military facilities.

For example, after adjustments for inflation, the army is now spending roughly the same amount on new tanks as it did during the Korean War. But that amount buys one-tenth the tanks it used to—700 today compared to almost 7,000 in 1953. Similarly, we built over 6,000 fighter planes in 1951 with $7 billion, but can build only about 300 with $11 billion today.[29]

Because the defense budget has not risen in real terms to meet procurement cost growth, we now have far less hardware with which to defend ourselves. Witness to this fact is the dramatic drop in inventory of many of our major weapons. For example, the number of active ships in the navy's fleet has declined from 800 to 500 since 1960, while fighter aircraft inventories were halved in a similar time period. Thus because of procurement cost growth, our materiel readiness has fallen.

At the same time, personnel costs have been steadily rising because of such factors as the shift to a volunteer army and an explosion in retirement pay. But because the defense budget has not risen in real terms to match the personnel portion of O&M cost growth, we have less purchasing power to pay and train our military forces. One result of this "cost growth squeeze" is a reduced level of skill and, in some branches of the service, fewer troops, which reduces our combat readiness. For example, since the Vietnam War, the opportunity for pilots to train has declined; pilots are flying less and sorties per aircraft are down. Similarly, the number of servicemen in uniform has fallen from 3.5 million in 1968 to 2.4 million in 1973 to 2.1 million today.

The cost growth squeeze has also reduced the operations and maintenance of military equipment and facilities. Because troops are less well trained to operate and maintain equipment, the probability of equipment failure is increased and equipment reliability is lowered. Again, the result is lower combat readiness.

During the periodic downward swings in the defense budget, we have reacted in ways that have further steepened that spiral. For one, we have simply extended, or "stretched out" the development and production periods of some weapons systems. Spinney counts no less than 43 major weapons systems undergoing the procurement stretch-out. This stretch-out has not only increased the overall cost of the weapons, but also slowed the pace of their modernization. More perniciously, in some circumstances, we have borrowed heavily from the O&M portion of the budget to keep procurement on track. But this borrowing from Peter to pay Paul has only further accentuated the cost growth squeeze on O&M and personnel, further reducing our combat readiness.

Moreover, during periods of upswings in the budget cycle, we have tended to favor procurement expenditures in an attempt to catch up with modernization. Nonetheless, these budget hikes have still not kept pace with procurement cost growth.

In summary, our defense umbrella, as measured in materiel and troop readiness, has been steadily declining and efforts to reverse that decline have only worsened the situation. Thus a bigger defense budget paradoxically has not meant more defense. Nor does it follow that even greater levels of spending will halt this downward spiral if a bigger procurement budget means a tighter squeeze on the O&M and personnel budget. This dangerous situation is the result of the complex interactions among the strategic foundations of defense policy, the market structure of the defense industry, the institutional structure of the defense agencies and defense lobby political pressures, and traditional ideological conflicts.

A. Strategic Foundations of U.S. Defense Policy

Underlying America's entire defense effort is a basic strategy of using our superior technology as the decisive edge in confrontations.[30]

SENATOR SAM NUNN

The U.S. policy reliance on a "quality edge" to offset the superior quantities of weapons and troops enjoyed by our enemies, particularly the Soviets, is embodied in what James Fallows describes as "the pursuit of the magic weapon." Such weapons range from computerized tanks and planes that can run rings around the more plodding hardware of our adversaries to more visionary "star wars" weapons that will be able to zap an entire missile arsenal from outer space.

Underlying this quest for technological superiority is an institutional mindset that conceives of weapons procurement not as a budgeting problem in economics, but as an engineering problem in maximizing technical performance. But from the standpoint of economics, the basic "optimization problem" of defense policy is to "maximize deterrence of enemy attack" by "combining limited quantities of missiles, crews, bases, and maintenance facilities."[31] In order to solve this problem within the constraints of a budget, it is necessary to look at the trade-offs between the *quality* of high tech weapons and the *quantity* of more conventional and simpler systems.

First and foremost, more technology has typically meant more *complexity* in weapons systems, which in some instances, has been a natural progression. But in many cases, we have ignored the maxim that technology should be employed to make weapons "elegantly simple," not "simply elegant,"[32] an oversight duly satirized in this passage from *Through the Looking Glass:*

> "I was wondering what the mouse-trap was for," said Alice. "It isn't very likely there would be any mice on the horse's back."
> "Not very likely, perhaps," said the Knight, "but if they do come, I don't choose to have them running all about." "You see," he went on after a pause, "it's as well to be provided for everything. That's the reason the horse has all those anklets around his feet . . . to guard against the bites of sharks."[33]

Complexity, however, greatly increases the costs of weapons. Most obviously, it increases *direct* costs simply because all the big and little gadgets that are added to a weapon are expensive. For example, the General Dynamics F-16 was a lightweight and simple fighter plane at its fly-off test. Cheap and effective, it was believed to be one of the greatest fighters ever built. However, the air force decided to have it undergo "full scale engineering development" before it went into production. They added complex radar and avionics, structural reinforcement, and nuclear equipment. The result was a fighter plane with greater weight, reduced acceleration and maneuverability, and difficult-to-maintain electronics. With its added baggage, it cost 118 percent more than the original model. It was an aircraft that was "so much less than it might have been" yet cost so much more.[34]

Another case of cost and technical escalation involves the army's Viper antitank weapon. The original design was for a cheap and light antitank bazooka, with an estimated cost of $75 apiece. Yet once again, the original blueprints were modified. The Viper now costs 10 times as much and can no longer penetrate the front armor of modern tanks. (The army, rarely willing to drop a project, instead has redefined its mission. The Viper now fulfills the dubious task of sniping at tanks from the side or the rear.)

At the same time, complexity *indirectly* raises procurement costs because complex equipment has lower, and therefore less economic, production rates. Instead of big assembly lines churning out fighter after fighter, tank after tank, the production process is highly specialized; many parts are hand-crafted and many weapons are individually assembled.

Adding insult to injury, the wonder weapons don't even seem to work as well as the less sophisticated designs they replaced. Indeed, "the more complex (so-called higher performance) weapons suffer from markedly lower kill-rates in actual combat than weapons with simpler applications of the same advanced technology."[35]

Finally, complexity also eats away at the O&M budget. Once built, oversophisticated weapons break down more often than their simpler counterparts. Fixing them requires equally sophisticated and expensive diagnostic testing equipment, more highly trained and skilled repair personnel, and a more expensive inventory of spare parts. But this only exacerbates the squeeze on O&M and lowers the reliability and readiness of the wonder weapon arsenal. It is not surprising then that "Our strategy of pursuing ever increasing technical complexity and sophistication has made high technology solutions and combat readiness mutually exclusive."[36]

B. Market and Institutional Sources of U.S. Defense Policy

Within each of the major segments of the defense market, sometimes one and often only two or three firms supply a major weapons system. In addition to this tendency towards a *monopolistic* or, at best, oligopolistic market structure, many of these suppliers are *vertically integrated*, performing not only the research and development (R&D) for a weapon, but also producing it.

These two market characteristics interact with certain institutional practices and features of the defense agencies and Congress in a way that only reinforces the Spinney syndrome. This can be seen in three major areas: Pentagon procurement practices, interservice rivalry, and the congressional appropriations process.

1. Procurement Practices. *The* major procurement problem is simply a lack of competition: Less than 10 percent of all contract dollars are awarded through open, formally advertised price competitions. A full 40 percent are negotiated noncompetitively with a *single* contractor, while another 20 percent consist of noncompetitive negotiations for follow-on business. Part of the problem is that once the R&D phase of procurement is completed, production contract awards are often "sole sourced," that is, only one firm "competes" for the government's business. For example, only General Dynamics makes Trident submarines and tanks, only FMC makes armored personnel carriers, and only the Newport News shipyard can build aircraft carriers. Consequently, the difference between the prices for weapons charged by a monopoly and by competitors can be staggering: Jacques Gansler estimates that the Pentagon could reduce procurement costs by as much as 30 percent on many weapons if it had a second company produce the items now made by one.[37]

Another procurement practice that follows from the basic strategy of U.S. defense policy is to award contracts on the basis of technical performance rather than lowest bid. Thus the limited competition among the defense firms occurs not in the dimension of price cutting, but rather, in adding the most state-of-the-art "bells and whistles," again raising costs by increasing complexity. This problem is compounded by weapons testing that is corrupt in the sense that the Pentagon office monitoring the contract, the armed services involved, and the firm itself often collaborate in the test. All have a special interest in seeing the weapon pass with flying colors, frequently not only overlooking minor flaws, but also creating ideal—as opposed to real battlefield—test conditions.

Similarly, there appears to be an institutional assumption that the firm awarded the R&D contract will also get the often more lucrative rights to produce. This vertically integrated procurement practice reinforces vertical integration in the industry, a tendency that is further strengthened through the practice of "concurrency": very often, firms are allowed to begin producing a weapon before it has been fully tested. This raises costs when weapons must be recalled for modification or repair, and reduces competition by eliminating the possibility that the Pentagon will cancel a project that fails to meet performance or cost specifications and seek a new contractor.

But all of these practices merely set the stage for perhaps the most pernicious interaction between the market and the defense institutions— the "buy-in," where firms make unrealistically low initial cost estimates in order to win a contract. After the buy-in, in the later stages of both R&D and production, the Pentagon allows substantial changes in the contract so that the contractor can recover the costs that he originally underbid. Although these changes are often used to swell contractor profits, they are sanctioned for an important political reason: While the Pentagon is often aware that the original cost estimates were too low, it accepts them because the low estimates make it easier to forge the consensus needed to build the weapon, within both the agency and Congress. Once the project is started, it then is easier to force Congress to up the ante.

2. Interservice Rivalry. The interaction of interservice rivalry and market forces is a further spur to the Spinney syndrome. Perhaps the worst aspect of this rivalry is the tendency of each of the services to adopt its own "pet" contractors. For example, while McDonnell Douglas and General Dynamics are the main manufacturers of fighter planes for the air force, the navy prefers to deal with Grumman for its aircraft. This practice reinforces the monopolistic character of the industry and further weakens the Pentagon's bargaining position.

A second aspect is the overlap in the supply lines and weaponry of each service, as each strives not only for more high tech equipment than the Russians, but also its rival branches—a problem borne out by this briefing chart presented by an air force colonel to (successfully) argue for funding for a fighter aircraft development program to compete with one of the Navy's:

> Unless the U.S. Air Force thoroughly studies high performance austere fighters and is prepared to consider them as a necessary complement to other air superiority aircraft, the U.S. Air Force may be:
> A. Outgamed by the Navy (Again)
> and/or
> B. Outfought by the Russians[38]

3. Congressional Appropriations. Perhaps the most damaging role of Congress in the Spinney syndrome is its propensity for cyclical defense appropriations. From the post-Vietnam defense drought to the Reagan-inspired splurge, it has sanctioned such cycles through its appropriations process.

At the same time, Congress has also been a "victim" of the market and the institutional forces that buffet it. For example, the fact that "in each area there is only a single weapon system available to modernize the forces . . . means that Congress is faced with the decision of approving the procurement of that sole sourced system or denying modern weapons to our armed forces."[39] This all-or-nothing situation leaves Congress with no bargaining room. Similarly, the domestic economic pressures that perennially weigh on Congress can create an environment for overstating the case within the Pentagon: "If we told the truth to Congress, we would never get our program approved. So we have to understate the cost and overstate the performance. . . . Our military bias is to get as much as we can get—after all, we don't know who the future enemy is or what he will have in the way of weapons."[40]

C. Ideological Interactions

Thus far, this economic analysis has been limited to considering how U.S. defense dollars are being spent. In turning to the ideological interactions underpinning the Spinney syndrome, it is time to ask *why* there is a need to spend such vast sums—25 percent of our budget—on building weaponry.

In considering this question, the concept of "opportunity cost" is extremely useful. Its essence is captured in these words of Dwight Eisenhower:

> The cost of one modern heavy bomber is this: a modern brick school in more than 30 cities.
> It is two electric power plants, each serving a town of 60,000 population.
> It is two fine, fully equipped hospitals.
> It is some 50 miles of concrete highway.[41]

More broadly, the opportunity costs of defense are not measurable in the dollars we spend, but rather, in the thousands of Americans pulled away from civilian occupations and put into uniform; the hospitals, highways, and schools that aren't built; the consumer goods our various factories don't produce; and the square miles of America filled with bases, missiles, and nuclear test sites instead of homes, cars, and factories. These costs also include the smaller number of jobs that defense expenditures yield relative to private investment, the accelerated effect on inflation that defense spending can exert under certain conditions, and the drain on our balance of payments.

Reducing the defense budget by reducing the need for defense through arms control and lowered East–West tension would save the nation these opportunity costs. Thus, while special interests play an important role in driving defense expenditures, much of the blame for the ever escalating arms race must be laid at the doorstep of America's ideological conflict.

In this regard, conservatism is perhaps the most responsible. Ever since the dawning of the Cold War in the late 1940s, theologians of the Right have consistently played on American fears of the Soviets. From the rhetoric of John Foster Dulles and the sharp warnings of Henry Kissinger to the polemical attacks of Zbigniew Brzezinski and the dire cautions of Caspar Weinberger, the conservative conception of the Soviet Union has held sway in American foreign policy.

This ideologically propagated climate of fear and mistrust has made it impossible, except for brief periods like the détente-SALT interlude, to undertake serious arms control negotiations with the Soviet Union. Conservative rhetoric has likewise provoked equally shrill outbursts from the Soviets and spurred their weapons production. The results have been a heightening of tension, an escalation of the arms race, and a swelling of the defense budget.

Similarly, by perennially insisting on an American nuclear superiority, conservatives have made the US–USSR relationship a spending contest between superpowers, ignoring legitimate Soviet fears about their own vulnerability to a first strike: While we have Pearl Harbor to remember, indelibly etched into the minds of the Russian people is the surprise Nazi invasion that took over 20 million Soviet lives and laid waste their cities and countryside. Conservatives also fail to recognize that the United States has actually considered nuclear first strikes against the Soviets on a number of occasions, the most serious being that after World War II when Churchill urged America to use its then nuclear monopoly to "strangle the Soviet baby in its crib."[42]

Liberals, too, have contributed to the arms race by erring on the other side of conflict resolution. Too often, with liberals at the negotiating table, America has not only left itself in a weaker strategic position, but also backed off on the one condition—verifying that agreements are being kept—that would most assuage and soothe their conservative counterparts' fears. In so doing, they have left negotiations vulnerable to the criticism that they don't work to strengthen prospects for peace, but rather, to weaken us strategically. Thus is the arms race further escalated.

Between these two ideological poles lies a pragmatic road to peace that alleviates both the Spinney syndrome and the opportunity costs of a burgeoning defense budget. How to reach that goal most rapidly is discussed in the next section.

IV. POLICY REFORMS

The politics of the defense policy game suggest that the weapons procurement process is quite vulnerable to private interest pressures. It likewise appears that the historically cyclical and economically unhealthy swings in the overall defense budget are largely the result of unresolved ideological conflicts. At the same time, the economics of defense indicate that political and ideological pressures, together with market failures within the defense industry, institutional failures within the defense agencies, and questionable defense strategies, have created a dangerous situation in which the nation is spending more and more defense dollars for less and less defense. The policy prescriptions to address these market, institutional, strategic, and political problems are listed in Table 11.4.[43]

1. Improving the Market. Because it is still possible in many segments of the market to stimulate competition, all new weapons and equipment systems should be developed under a prototype program in which there are two or more competing contractors. This will ensure an oligopolistic rivalry that many economists argue is just as effective as pure competition. These contractors should compete to produce the best possible design for a clearly defined mission or task.

The competing designs should be pitted against each other in rigorous contests. To avoid corrupt testing, these "fly-offs," "shoot-offs," and the like should be overseen by a testing group that is separate from the contractors, the Pentagon office monitoring the R&D design, and the military branch involved. In judging these competitions, economic as well as performance criteria should be the determining factors. The most

TABLE 11.4.   DEFENSE POLICY PRESCRIPTIONS

Improving the Market	Improving the Institutions	Abandoning Questionable Strategies
Dual sourcing, competitive bidding	Accurate cost estimates	"Hi-Lo" procurement/ evaluation
Independent monitoring of design contests	Discourage "buy-in"/ discourage contract changes	Diversification into civilian products by defense contractors
Adopt economic as well as performance criteria	Balance O&M and procurement budgets	Negotiations based on verification
Judge whether a weapon is necessary before producing it	De-emphasize complexity	
Separate R&D from testing and production	Consolidate and centralize the services	
Multiyear procurement, multiyear budgets		

technologically advanced weapon need not necessarily win if a less sophisticated weapon can be produced at substantially lower costs. In this vein, each weapon should be compared with the full range of alternatives, including *existing* weapons. Thus, for example, the performance of *one* new aircraft that costs 10 times as much as an existing one should be compared with the performance of 10 of the existing planes.

Nor does there need to be any "winner" in these contests. If all weapons fail to meet the test, the contractors should be sent back to the drawing board. To prevent any production *fait accompli*, it is also important that a weapon be judged both necessary and effective *before* it goes into production. Accordingly, "concurrency" should not occur, and unworkable systems should be canceled.

Once a design is chosen, the winner should be paid for the R&D phase, but the *production* of the design should be put up for bids from the winner as well as other firms. Thus a vertical integration of R&D with production should not be assumed. In most cases, the production should also be dual-sourced to maintain competition as well as ensure against any efforts to alter the contract by a firm put in a monopoly position, thereby countering any "buy-in" tendencies. This separation of R&D from production will also encourage the growth of R&D firms.

Finally, the Congress should consider switching to a multiyear defense budget—say three or five years—to avoid cyclical swings in defense spending. This will save defense dollars by reducing contractors' risks and hence their capital costs. It will also encourage more private, rather than government, investment in the industry. In the same vein, the DoD should continue to expand its system of multiyear procurement to ensure a steady flow of dollars to a developing system, thereby preventing stretch-out.

2. Improving the Institutions. The wisdom of the government failure model is that no matter how dedicated to promoting the public interest government bureaucrats might be, they are still prone to mistakes. The bureaucracies as mammoth as those encompassing defense are no exception, but there are steps these agencies can take to reduce the incidence of government failure.

Perhaps most important, defense bureaucrats must insist on, and seek to determine, accurate, realistic cost estimates. They must also hold the line on extensive contract changes that contractors typically use after the "buy-in" to boost their projections. In this regard, it may be useful to impose additional restrictions on the revolving door between the defense agencies and their contractors to minimize the "job-opportunity" cooptation that is at least partly responsible for the pliability of some defense bureaucrats.

In a similar vein, the Pentagon must strike a better balance between today's combat readiness (i.e., its O&M expenses) and tomorrow's weapons procurement, ending the situation in which we have had to "borrow" from the O&M portion of the defense budget to pay for cost overruns in procurement. The defense agencies must learn to live within their budget if the United States is to maintain readiness. This means penalizing contractors for cost overruns, ending the shift of funds from O&M to procurement, and canceling ineffective projects.

Curbing cost growth also means that complexity must assume less importance within the defense agencies and services, for if higher quality means less quantity and lower reliability, the best defense will not be ensured.

As a final institutional change, the consolidation of command and centralization of the services that began with Harry Truman[44] must be pursued to curb the perennial parochial tendency of each service to cultivate and protect its own elaborate weapons and supply systems. This step involves a radical reform of the Joint Chiefs of Staff.

Currently, the chairman of the Joint Chiefs acts not as a leader, but as a mediator, between the service branches. That means when the air force and army disagree, the dispute is often left unsettled. One radical solution to this problem, made by Army Chief of Staff General Edward Meyer, is to give the chairman the power to rule. At the same time, he would remove his "dual hat" as both Joint Chiefs chairman and head of his respective service, and serve only the president and the military as a whole. To consolidate this power, his 400-member staff would wear "purple uniforms, meaning that they would not owe their allegiance to their respective service branches."[45] The result of these reforms would be a strong chairman and an independent staff capable of settling interservice disputes and driving a powerful wedge into an entrenched segment of the bureaucracy.*

3. Abandoning Questionable Strategies. Most important from a strategic viewpoint, the defense agencies and military should abandon their singular quest for the *revolutionary* "wonder weapon" and instead adopt a more *evolutionary* approach to weapons development and a more diversified weapons arsenal.

One positive step would be to replace the strategy based on American technical superiority with a "hi-lo" strategy that balances high tech with hardware, quality with quantity, and complexity with reliability. The essence of "hi-lo" is to build a mix of state-of-the-art and conventional weaponry.† For example, the navy plans to build over 10 nuclear attack submarines in the 1980s at a cost of $700 million each. A better approach, which would help overcome the Soviets' three-to-one advantage in this area, would be to build a few of these nuclear Rolls Royces and

---

*The obvious danger is a consolidated, all-powerful military. While such a danger cannot be completely dismissed, the strength of American democracy should be such as to contain the coup d'état problem.

†A Leading advocate of the hi-lo strategy is Senator (and 1984 presidential aspirant) Gary Hart of Colorado.

devote the remaining funds to a companion fleet of conventional diesel subs, which can be bought for as low as $100 million. Similarly, fewer Nimitz-class aircraft carriers could be built in favor of smaller, less expensive carriers, while funds diverted from the sophisticated M-1 tank would buy three times the more reliable M-60s. Such a strategy will result in a more diversified, and ultimately, more potent and reliable arsenal. It will also give us a greater combat readiness, and, as a bonus, more economic production rates for the conventional weapons constructed.

A second strategic shift would be for the government to encourage more diversification into civilian products by defense contractors. This would allow civilian businesses to absorb the cyclical ups and downs of defense spending, reduce the current heavy dependence of some military-only firms on foreign arms sales, and perhaps most important, raise the nation's overall productivity because the diversified firm could share some of its defense plant equipment in producing civilian goods. There are a number of ways to encourage diversification, such as tax credits and the allowance of some of the firm's civilian plant charges on military contracts, but it may be that, following the Swedish example, Congress will want to legislate that defense firms have at least a certain percentage of their business in civilian products.

The remaining sources of political and economic problems are perhaps less tractable. In the ideological realm, the issue of negotiations deserves particular attention. A successfully negotiated end to the arms race—a goal dear to liberal hearts—is undoubtedly in the nation's best interest. But conservatives will never sign any such agreement unless it contains an ironclad clause for verification. The obvious ideological compromise is to negotiate *openly* and *seriously* with the Soviets, stipulating that verification is the first priority of any new treaty.

In considering the preceding reforms, it is perhaps appropriate to end this policy game with some words of advice from defense expert Jacques Gansler:

> The great difficulty of making even small structural changes in the defense industry must be recognized. Some changes will be perceived as threatening by the powerful vested interests involved (the industrial giants, the labor unions, the military services, or the Congress). To "sell" such changes, each of these groups must be made aware of the broader advantages to them and to the nation.[46]

Summary and Conclusions

By playing the policy game in a variety of local, state, and federal political arenas, this book has illustrated the diversity of the capture-ideology framework as a way of thinking about and improving the performance of America's political system and its economy. Across cases ranging from rent control, protectionism, and farm subsidies to electric utility regulation, the Equal Rights Amendment, and defense spending, the basic insight of the framework appears to hold. That is, both private and public interest motives are necessary to explain any given public policy. This means we can reject both the cynical myth of an American government totally corrupted by special interests and its competing pie-in-the-sky presumption that all government policies are in the "public interest" in favor of a more realistic and ultimately more powerful way of thinking out the myriad policy games that go on around us.

By way of summary, let us recap the basic capture-ideology approach and, in so doing, illustrate the powerful levers the framework provides for playing the policy game better.

The first step is to understand the politics of an issue in all its rich interest group and ideological diversity. This means identifying the special-interest players in the game together with their lobbying strategies and tactics. It also means examining the various public-interested rationales of well-intentioned conservatives and liberals; this entails using the "logic of ideology" not only to identify the contrasting ideological principles but also to probe the underlying values, beliefs, and assumptions that so often put well-meaning liberals and conservatives on opposite sides of the policy fence.

The second step is to analyze the economics of the issue to determine what selfish special interests and perhaps misguided ideologues have wrought. This step, in essence, measures the penalties for misplaying the policy game at the same time that it reveals who in the economy must pay those penalties.

Such an economic analysis sets the stage for the third step, which is to construct useful policy reforms that will make most (if perhaps not all of) the players in the game—as well as the nation—better off. It is in this final step that our political and economic analyses swing back into action by giving us several important levers for change.

On those issues where narrow special interests are important, the perennial losers in the policy game—taxpayers, consumers, and the average voting citizen—must become more politically involved. The capture-ideology framework spurs such involvement in several ways.

By identifying both the special interests and their lobbying strategies and tactics, the framework's political analysis alerts us to just who has captured our government and just how they are doing it. At the same time, by providing us with a price tag and catalog of abuses, the framework's economic analysis provides us with the necessary information and incentives to speak up. The message must be loud and clear: We, the general public, will no longer tolerate selfish raids either on the treasury or on our pocketbooks. This message can be sent individually through the ballot box and through letters to our political representatives. It can also be sent collectively through membership and participation in, and financial support of taxpayer, consumer, and other such broad-based organizations formed to offset the power of narrow special interests. The high economic costs of special-interest greed that we have uncovered in each of our policy games—on the order of tens of billions of dollars— make such increased political activism a crucial part of any continued national prosperity.

On those issues where public-interested ideological motives are important, the capture-ideology framework provides us with a number of levers for constructive change.

First, by uncovering a "logic of ideology," the framework emphasizes that the conservative–liberal debate is as much a debate over a differing set of values, beliefs, and assumptions as it is about policy choices themselves. Acknowledging this deeper dimension to the "ideology wars" should help the nation avoid the pitfalls of "knee jerk" and irreconcilable positioning at the policy level in favor of a more informed discussion of the underlying forces that cause conservatives and liberals to disagree. While there may not always be room for movement, conducting the policy debate at this deeper level—which recognizes the legitimate concerns of opposing ideologues—should provide the possibility for more political compromise.

For example, in the defense policy game, we saw that the conservative's intense mistrust of the Soviet Union leads to the insistence that verification must be the linchpin of any strategic arms limitation agreement. If liberals recognize this stipulation as an ironclad condition for negotiations—rather than as hostility to the process of negotiating itself—then it may be easier for conservatives and liberals to agree on a negotiating strategy and posture.

Similarly, liberals may accept the more market-oriented price support system advocated by conservatives out to reform farm policy if it can be shown—as Chapter 6 did—that this type of system will better achieve liberal goals such as a fair level of income for farmers.

Second, by exposing instances of government failure, the capture-ideology framework emphasizes that it is the policy goals that are of paramount interest to conservatives and liberals, not necessarily the means to achieve those goals. Thus, if a policy is found not to work, it need not follow that its ideological goal be abandoned but merely the particular means to achieve it. This was the lesson, for example, of our rent control case where controls were failing to achieve their liberal goals of affordable housing for, and income redistribution to, lower income groups. But we also saw that liberals need not abandon these goals but rather may find different ways, such as public housing or "rent stamps," to better target benefits. At the same time, conservatives may agree to such a policy shift if they can be convinced that the new policies will at least be less costly and more efficient than the old ones.

In conclusion, the capture-ideology framework vividly demonstrates that we, as a nation, can learn to play the policy game much better. To counter the power of special interests, we must become more informed and involved. To counter the problems created by well-intentioned ideologues, we must learn to be more pragmatic. In this pragmatism, it is not necessary to compromise one's principles but merely recognize that

there are better ways to achieve their ultimate goals. Accordingly, special-interest politics must fall before the force of a well-informed and
better-organized citizenry, and blind ideology must yield to more pragmatic solutions, solutions that begin with the basic insight that constructive policy reforms can make us all better off. The time for such
participation in the policy game is now. We can no longer sit on the
sidelines while the prosperity and promise of our nation slips away. This
book provides you with the information you need to participate effectively in the myriad policy games going on around you, serious and
important games that ultimately affect not only the national welfare but
your personal welfare as well.*

---

*Any questions, comments, or requests can be directed to: *The Policy Game*, P.O. Box
803, Cambridge, MA 02238.

APPENDIX **A**

The Politics of the Policy Game

A SUMMARY OF STATISTICAL RESULTS

This appendix presents the statistical results of applying the capture-ideology framework to the issues of rent control, protectionism, farm subsidies, utility regulation, the Equal Rights Amendment, and defense spending. As explained in Chapter 2, the basic approach of the framework is to statistically explain a policy choice such as rent control or farm subsidies on the basis of various measures of special-interest pressures and public-interested, ideological behavior.

The "functional form" of such a test is:

$$\text{Policy Choice} = f(\text{special interests, ideology}) \qquad (1)$$

where the observed policy choice is determined by, or "is a function of," special interests and ideology. In the case of, say, rent control, this general functional form becomes testable in the specific statistical equation form of

$$\text{RENTCONTROL} = b_0 + b_1 \text{ TENANTS} + b_2 \text{ IDEOLOGY} + E_1 \quad (2)$$

where RENTCONTROL is the "dependent variable" to be statistically explained by the "explanatory" variables TENANTS and IDEOLOGY; b_0 is a constant term, b_1 and b_2 are the parameter estimates, and E_1 is an "error term" typically placed in such an equation.

This equation can be tested using any one of a number of common statistical procedures. In the six applications below, either linear regression or the logit technique was used, with the choice depending on how the policy choice was specified. Regression analysis was typically used except in cases where the policy choice was specified as a binomial or trinomial choice. For example, in the utility regulation test, the degree of rate suppression was measured trinomially, with 1 being least rate suppressive, 2 being moderately rate suppressive, and 3 being very rate suppressive. In that case, regression analysis was augmented by the logit technique.

The results of such a test yield a set of parameter estimates represented by b_1 and b_2 in Equation 2 along with other measures of statistical significance, the most important of which are the "t-statistics" and the R^2. These parameter estimates can, in turn, be transformed into a set of standardized estimates or "beta coefficients," which essentially rank the relative influence of each of the explanatory variables.* These beta coefficients are reported below along with their t-statistics and the R^2 of the model. Descriptions of each of the variables in the tests and a statement of the statistical procedure used are also reported.†

CHAPTER 2 RESULTS: THE POLITICS OF RENT CONTROL

In this case, the policy choice examined was voting by the Cambridge electorate for a pro-rent control city council. Because of Cambridge's unique system of proportional voting, the number of "first place" votes by precinct for the titular head of the Cambridge rent control movement, Councilor David Sullivan, was chosen as the most suitable proxy for rent control sentiment.† Tenant pressure was reflected in an explanatory variable measuring the number of rent-controlled units in Cambridge by

*This ranking is achieved by expressing the original parameter estimates in units of standard deviation. That is, the estimated slope parameters are adjusted by the ratios of the standard deviations of the independent variables to the standard deviation of the dependent variable. These standardized beta coefficients show the relative sensitivity of the dependent variable to each of the explanatory variables.
†An excellent source on statistical procedures used in economics is Pindyck, R., and Rubinfeld, D. *Econometric Models and Economic Forecast* (New York: McGraw-Hill, 1981).
†Similar results were obtained when voting for the entire pro-rent control slate, the Cambridge Civic Association candidates, was examined. For further details on Cambridge's system of proportional voting and testing of a more complex model, see my paper "The Politics of Rent Control: Capture and Ideology in Cambridge" (available on request).

TABLE A.1.   STATISTICAL RESULTS OF THE POLITICS
OF RENT CONTROL^a

Ranked Explanatory Variables	Beta Coefficients (t-statistics in parentheses)
1. Ideology	0.49
	(4.85)
2. Rent-control tenants' lobby	0.41
	(4.08)

$^a R^2 = 0.57$.

precinct. Ideology was measured by the number of votes against the death penalty (Question 2, Cambridge, November 2, 1982), as a percentage of the total number of votes on the question by precinct, with the degree of liberalism rising with the percentage. (Similar results were obtained with two alternative measures of ideology, voting on a nuclear freeze and a bottle bill.) Regression analysis yielded the results presented in Table A.1.

CHAPTER 4 RESULTS: THE POLITICS OF PROTECTIONISM

In this case, the policy choice examined was congressional voting patterns on the 1982 Fair Practices in Automotive Products Act in the House of Representatives (HR 5133), which would have established domestic content requirements for the automobile industry.

Each of the various jobs-at-stake explanatory variables were calculated according to industry employment as a percentage of employment in a congressman's district. The measures included steel interests and auto workers along with the import-beleaguered industries (apparel, footwear, TV and radios, motorcycles and bicycles) and the export-dependent industries (aircraft, computers, logging, and construction and related machinery).

PAC contributions by the four automakers were calculated on the basis of Federal Election Commission data over the 1977–78, 1979–80, and 1981–82 election cycles, consumer interests were reflected in total car registrations per capita, and, ideology was measured by the four-year average of each representative's liberalness rating by the ADA.

TABLE A.2.   STATISTICAL RESULTS FOR THE
POLITICS OF PROTECTIONISM[a]

Ranked Explanatory Variables	Beta Coefficients (t-statistic in parentheses)
Ideology	.45
	(8.91)
Steel interests	.19
	(4.98)
Autoworkers PAC contributions	.17
	(3.05)
The import-beleaguered industries	.12
	(2.97)
Auto-worker jobs at stake	.10
	(2.57)
Chrysler PAC contributions	.09
	(1.93)
Auto consumers	−.09
	(−1.53)
General Motors PAC contributions	−.08
	(−1.57)
Ford PAC contributions	.04
	(0.91)
American Motors PAC contributions	−.04
	(−1.93)
The export-dependent industries	−.03
	(−0.74)
AFL–CIO PAC contributions	.02
	(0.31)

[a]$R^2 = .44$.

Regression analysis was used to relate these explanatory variables to a two-vote logit index of congressional voting on the domestic content bill. Table A.2 ranks each of the explanatory variables by the absolute value of their beta coefficients and reports other summary statistics.

CHAPTER 6 RESULTS: THE POLITICS OF FARM POLICY

The policy choice examined was U.S. Senate voting on grain and dairy price support and supply control programs during debate on the 1981 Agricultural and Food Act. As indexed by the Congressional Quarterly system, the grain votes examined were CQ262, CQ263, and CQ264. The dairy votes included CQ251, CQ252, CQ258, CQ33, and CQ34.

The grain and dairy producer explanatory variables were measured by the ratio of commodity value to total state personal income (based on a three-year average). The logroll measure is total value of agricultural output in a state minus the commodity being tested for divided by state personal income, the food stamp lobby is reflected in food stamp expenditures per capita, the PAC variables represent the total amount of funds contributed by the relevant producer interests to the senator over the years 1977–82, and ideology is reflected in a four-year average of the senators' liberalness rating by the ADA.

TABLE A.3.   STATISTICAL RESULTS FOR THE POLITICS OF FARM POLICY

Ranked Explanatory Variables	Beta Coefficients (t-statistics in parentheses)
Grain Votes[a]	
Ideology	.61
	(6.60)
Grain producers	.38
	(1.94)
Food stamp lobby	.22
	(2.18)
Grain PACs	.12
	(1.34)
Logrolling	.05
	(0.27)
Dairy Votes[b]	
Ideology	.60
	(6.31)
Dairy producers	.30
	(3.38)
Food stamp lobby	.25
	(2.36)
Logrolling	.25
	(2.82)
Dairy PACs	.19
	(2.32)

[a]$R^2 = .44$ for grain votes.
[b]$R^2 = .47$ for dairy votes.

Regression analysis was used to relate these explanatory variables to the grain and dairy vote logit indices. The results are reported in Table A.3.

CHAPTER 8 RESULTS: THE POLITICS OF ELECTRIC UTILITY RATES

The policy choice examined was the degree of rate suppression practiced by each of the state PUCs. Rate suppression was reflected in a composite ranking by five major investment and research firms: Goldman Sachs, Merrill Lynch, Salomon Brothers, Valueline, and Duff and Phelps.

The salary explanatory variable was measured by state commissioner salaries (adjusted by a cost-of-living index), PUC budgets were weighted by state population, the method of PUC funding was reflected in the percentage of PUC expenditures raised through appropriations from the general tax fund, the tenure variable was simply the length of the commissioners' terms, and the oil dependence variable was measured by the state's percent of oil use in electricity generation (interacted with a variable indicating the presence or absence of an automatic fuel adjustment clause).

Several "indicator variables" were likewise used: the method of selection of commissioners equaled one if commissioners were appointed and zero if directly elected, while the professional qualifications variable equaled one if the state had a statute specifying a professional requirement and zero otherwise.

Finally, ideology was measured by the percentage of Democrat commissioners on a PUC under the well-tested assumption that there is a high correlation between liberalness and Democrats. (A regional indicator variable was also included to sort out the effect of Southern Democrat conservatives.)

Table A.4 reports the results of an "average commission analysis" derived from logit estimates for each of the explanatory variables.* This average commission analysis measures the effect that each of the explan-

*These coefficients are reported in my *Energy Journal* article "Public Utility Commission Regulation: Performance, Determinants, and Energy Policy Impacts," Vol. 3, No. 2, 1982, p. 132.

TABLE A.4.   STATISTICAL RESULTS OF THE POLITICS OF ELECTRIC
UTILITY RATES: THE AVERAGE COMMISSION ANALYSIS

Ranked Explanatory Variables	Effect on the Probability of Rate Suppression
1. Elected versus appointed commissioners	.48
2. General revenue versus assessment funding	.40
3. Salary level	.39
4. Ideology	.19
5. Longer versus shorter terms	.11
6. Existence of professional requirement	.11
7. PUC budget	.09
8. Consumer pressure (state oil dependence)	.07

atory variables will have on the probability or "odds" that a PUC will be rate suppressive. These probabilities form the basis of the rankings reported in the table: The higher the probability, the more important the variable is in creating the rate suppression syndrome. (This procedure differs slightly from our usual beta coefficient approach. Probabilities are used here because the test is somewhat different from the voting study method adopted in the other cases. Also, this approach emphasizes that there are other ways besides the use of beta coefficients to rank private and public interest motives.)

CHAPTER 10 RESULTS: THE POLITICS OF THE EQUAL RIGHTS AMENDMENT

The policy choice examined was the voting patterns of the 50 state legislatures during the 1972–82 ERA ratification drive. Support for the ERA on a state-by-state basis was reflected in a dependent variable measuring the percentage of votes for ERA ratification within each state legislature (typically the House). In the event of multiple voting, the latest recorded vote was used.

The traditional segment of the pro-ERA women's lobby was measured by the combined number of members in the two most important traditional women's group supporting the ERA, the League of Women Voters, and the Business and Professional Women's Club while the feminist

TABLE A.5.   STATISTICAL RESULTS FOR THE POLITICS
OF THE EQUAL RIGHTS AMENDMENT[a]

Ranked Explanatory Variables	Beta Coefficients (t-statistics in parentheses)
Ideology	−.56
	(−1.18)
Feminist segment of pro-ERA women's lobby	.44
	(1.14)
Traditional segment of pro-ERA women's lobby	.31
	(1.03)
Labor lobby	.30
	(1.55)
Public interest lobby	.22
	(1.09)
Anti-ERA church lobby	−.15
	(−0.75)
Pro-ERA church lobby	.10
	(0.53)
Anti-ERA women's lobby	−.10
	(−0.39)

[a] $R^2 = .60.$

segment was measured by the number of subscribers to *Ms.* magazine within each state.* The public interest lobby was measured by the number of members by state in the public interest organization most actively supporting the ERA, Common Cause. The labor lobby was reflected in the combined membership of the AFL–CIO, United Auto Workers, and the Teamsters.† The pro-ERA church lobby was reflected in the number of church members by state in the Episcopalian, Unitarian, and Friends denominations while the anti-ERA church lobby was indicated by the number of Mormons and fundamentalists by state. Finally, the anti-ERA women's lobby was measured by state membership in the Daughters of the American Revolution while ideology was reflected by the percentage of votes for Ronald Reagan in the 1980 election by state. All variables

*The ideal measure would have been membership by state in the National Organization for Women but, like the Phyllis Schlafly forces, NOW leaders refused to provide the necessary data.
†The UAW is now part of the AFL-CIO.

TABLE A.6.   STATISTICAL RESULTS OF THE POLITICS
OF THE DEFENSE BUDGET[a]

Ranked Explanatory Variables	Beta Coefficients (t-statistics in parentheses)
1. Ideology	−.56
	(−5.38)
2. Defense contractors and labor's defense lobby	.16
	(1.65)
3. The brain lobby (universities and think tanks)	−.12
	(−1.38)
4. The peace lobby	−.10
	(−1.04)
5. Defense PACs	.07
	(0.79)
6. The government lobby	.07
	(0.84)
7. Service and veterans organizations	.01
	(0.14)

[a]$R^2 = .39$.

(except ideology) were adjusted by state population. Table A.5 presents the regression results.

CHAPTER 11 RESULTS: THE POLITICS OF THE DEFENSE BUDGET

The policy choice examined was U.S. Senate voting on the defense budget between 1980 and 1982. As indexed by the Congressional Quarterly system, the votes examined were CQ100 (1980), CQ101 (1980), CQ435 (1981), CQ125 (1982), and CQ435 (1982).

The defense PAC explanatory variable was measured by the sum of PAC contributions by the top 40 largest contractors to each senator over three election cycles (1977–78, 1979–80, 1981–82), as reported by the Federal Election Commission. The brain lobby was measured by the dollar value of Department of Defense contracts to educational and non-profit institutions in each state divided by state personal income while the combined defense contractor and defense labor lobby measure equaled Pentagon expenditures less funds to the brain lobby also normalized by state personal income.

The congressional government lobby measure was based on the number of years each senator served in the military and is reported in Table A.6 while the military segment of that lobby is indirectly indicated in the defense contractor measure, which is based on Pentagon expenditures. Veterans and service organization pressure was measured by the combined membership in four service organizations: the Navy League, and the Air Force, Army, and Coast Guard Associations. (Because of a high degree of correlation between these groups and veteran groups such as the Veterans of Foreign Wars and American Legion, this variable was deemed a suitable proxy for both interests.)

Finally, the peace lobby was reflected in the percentage of households per state contributing to the American Friends Service Committee while ideology was reflected in a three-year average of each senator's liberalness rating by the American's for Democratic Action. Table A.6 reports the results of the regression analysis of the five-vote logit index.

APPENDIX B

The Logic of Ideology

FUSIONIST CONSERVATISM VERSUS MODERN LIBERALISM

Guns or butter, hard lines or soft lines, cold wars or détente, arms races or nuclear freezes? These code words are but a drop in the doctrinarial bucket of foreign policy and national defense differences that help to delineate the final major area of ideological disagreement between American conservatives and liberals.

1. Conservative Nationalistic Anti-Communism

The principal purpose of the foreign policy of the United States is to maintain the liberty of our people. Its purpose is not to reform the entire world or spread sweetness and light and economic prosperity to peoples who have lived and worked out their own solution for centuries, according to their customs, and to the best of their ability.[1]

"MR. REPUBLICAN," ROBERT TAFT

The conservative embraces a distinctly nationalistic, staunchly anti-Communist perspective on foreign affairs. A patriot, he is in sympathy with such vintage slogans as "America—Love It or Leave It" and "Our Country—Right or Wrong." A "realist," he is deeply suspicious of the spread of Communism, particularly Soviet communism—a suspicion that leads him to want to build American foreign policy around "factors of national power and self-interest."[2]

At the epicenter of the conservative's nationalism is a distinctly Hobbesian view of international relations that is strongly suggestive of the organic theory of the state: America is engaged in a power struggle among competing countries; in that struggle, we compete economically against allies like Germany and Japan and both politically and militarily against "enemies" like the Soviet Union and its clients. As a matter of national pride, economic self-interest, and strategic survival, it is important that America first and foremost look out for its own interests and maintain its world supremacy in all areas—economic, political, and military.

Similarly, the seed of the conservative's staunch anti-Communism is his belief in a Soviet-inspired communist conspiracy: Russian strategists are plotting, orchestrating, and financing a coordinated effort to encircle America in a sea of socialism by sponsoring phony wars of national liberation, often with alarming success. It is this view of the Soviet Union as "master puppeteer" that constitutes the biggest difference between the American conservative and his liberal counterpart.

To the conservative, the conspiratorial pattern is clear: Dominoes are threatening to fall everywhere the Soviet Union and its client Cuban and North Korean mercenaries dare to tread: in Southeast Asia, Africa, and most dangerously close to home, Central and South America. Accordingly, this conspiracy represents the single greatest threat to world peace and American freedom. In his more hawkish moments, the conservative admits to wanting nothing more or less than "the destruction of the power of Soviet-based Communism."[3]

This "mortal enemy" mistrust of the Soviet Union likewise combines with the conservative's more generally pessimistic view of human nature to warn him against any hope of successful peace negotiations with the Soviets. Because of man's tendency towards evil and his thirst for power, international conflict is inevitable; the only realistic foreign policy to prevent such conflict is to maintain a supremacy based on an American arms superiority and a mutual fear or "balance of terror."

To the conservative, America has been far too optimistic and idealistic in its dealing with the Soviets. Where the liberal sees the potential for good faith, the conservative is convinced that the Soviets will agree only to that which will give them an advantage. As an historical fact, he believes "that in every negotiation ever conducted . . . the majority and often the entirety of concessions have always come from" the American side while "the net political and strategic profit has always gone to the Communists."[4]

A final source of the conservative's nationalistic anti-Communism is his deeply religious nature. America is locked not only in a secular struggle between democratic freedom and Soviet totalitarianism, but is also in a religious struggle between the "two irreconcilable faiths"[5] of Christianity and a Messianic, atheistic Communism. From this crusade against Communism emerges the conservative's hard line: the Soviet Union must constantly be confronted to prevent the triumph of Eastern Communism over the Judeo-Christian values of the West. This belief is the capstone to the conservative's vision of foreign affairs as a bipolar struggle between East and West, Christianity and Communism, and the two standard bearer superpowers, America and Russia.

2. Liberal International Globalism

It is a legitimate American national objective to see removed from all nations—including the United States—the right to use substantial military force to pursue their own interests. Since this residual right is the root of national sovereignty and the basis for the existence of an international arena of power, it is, therefore, an American interest to see the end of nationhood as it has been historically defined.[6]

W. W. ROSTOW

The liberal is more internationalist in his outlook on foreign affairs than his conservative counterpart. While respectful of America and its values, he views expressions of patriotism and nationalism as dangerous, parochial sentiments that, by dividing nation from nation, provoke conflict and confrontation. While also "anti-Communist," he is nonetheless less hostile to, and fearful of, the Soviet Union, favoring discussion, negotiation, and compromise over coercion and confrontation. An "idealist," he insists that American foreign policy be built around "concepts of morality": Its purpose should be to promote "freedom, justice, and human dignity."[7]

The liberal's internationalism begins in his view that foreign affairs should be more a cooperative global effort to achieve world prosperity and peace than a power struggle for economic or military advantage. In this effort, America has a moral obligation to share its wealth, knowledge, and institutions with the world. A pragmatist as well, he is convinced that promoting world prosperity is the best strategy to combat Communism and achieve world peace. This global view is reinforced by the liberal's optimism about the ability and desire of the civilized peoples of the world to cooperate with one another and to plan and coordinate activities, which make it possible to transcend national and doctrinal differences in the interests of world peace.

At the same time, the source of the liberal's less hawkish sentiments toward the Soviet Union is a markedly different view of revolutions around the world. Rather than accept the theory of a "Communist conspiracy" orchestrated by the Soviet Union, the liberal sees these insurgencies as rooted in the social injustices of corrupt regimes or oppressive colonialists. For example, the socialist turmoil in Central America is more the result of mistreatment of the people by feudalistic landholding oligarchies than the diabolical work of a Cuban client working the Soviet Union's will. Accordingly, the biggest threat to world peace is not an encroaching Communist tide, but an arms race that may result in a nuclear war triggered by the mistaken presumption that the Soviets are successfully plotting every Marxist takeover in the Third World.

But even if the liberal accepts that in some places the Soviet Union has been responsible for Communist takeovers, he refuses to see an ominous pattern of dominoes falling around the globe. Instead, he observes a more random series of indigenous wars in which he believes America has no right to interfere. In this regard, collective self-determinism by the people is more important than the system they choose, even if the choice is socialism. Thus, while the conservative worries about nationalized businesses and the loss of strategic ports and air bases when revolutions occur, the liberal sees in the upheavals a victory for freedom and the popular will of the people.

Ultimately, the modern liberal's internationalism rests on his faith that since all people are rational, they must share his desire for peace. All conflicts should therefore be resolvable through rational discussion rather than a resort to force: War is "irrational and destructive of the human values he cherishes; war is a last resort to be considered only after the failure of every constructive and nonviolent effort at solving diplomatic problems."[8]

Thus the liberal believes that America "must be willing to talk to the Russians wherever and whenever there seems to be the faintest hope."[9]

Because both Americans and the Russians are rational, such negotiations can be undertaken in good faith and in a spirit of mutual trust and mutual interest. In this regard, his aim is to coexist peacefully with and contain Communism rather than crush it. Through this détente, he believes that Communism will soften: That is, through its contact with the West, it will converge towards Western values.

3. Nationalism–Internationalism Policy Game. In the policy arena, America's defense and foreign policies form the focus of the nationalism–internationalism ideological split. The most important disputes involve the "guns versus butter tradeoff," the desirability of an arms buildup versus an arms reduction, the appropriate strategy to combat the spread of Communism, and the role of the U.S. in international organizations like the United Nations.

The sine qua non of the conservative's nationalism is a strong national defense. To achieve that goal, he favors a policy of sustained higher levels of defense spending and, in a budgetary move that coincides with his minimal state principles, a corresponding lower level of social spending. In striving to maintain an essential military superiority over the Russians, he supports the development of such strategic weapons systems as the B-1 bomber and MX missile as well as the beefing up of our conventional forces, believing that such superiority is a safer course than the dicey game of negotiations.

The liberal likewise is concerned about a strong defense, but is less willing to trade off guns for butter to achieve that goal. Viewing domestic poverty as an internal threat to American stability on par with the external Soviet threat, he is much more insistent that any continued U.S. military buildup be accompanied by sincere attempts to negotiate an arms reduction with the Soviets. Moreover, he is far more willing to accept arms parity as a negotiation principle and decries conservative insistences upon U.S. arms superiority.

To counter the spread of Communism abroad, the conservative seeks to arm our allies to resist Soviet attempts at subversion. Accordingly, he favors foreign aid packages more heavily weighted towards military than economic aid, and is much more willing to provide such aid even to authoritarian regimes if American strategic concerns dictate it.

At the same time, because Soviet, Cuban, and North Korean advisers are at the cutting edge of the Communists' subversive activities, the conservative feels that U.S. military advisers are needed as a counter-weight. Accordingly, U.S. covert activities on the part of the U.S. government are unpleasant but necessary.

In contrast, the primary thrust of the liberal strategy for the containment of Communism is world economic development. To create prosperity—a poor soil for the spread of socialism—foreign aid should be primarily for economic development, not weapons. To remove the political sources of revolution, the liberal also seeks to tie such aid to democratic reforms and expanded human rights: authoritarian regimes like Argentina, Chile, and the Phillipines thus would receive less. Far less interventionist since the days of Vietnam, the liberal likewise wants neither U.S. advisors nor CIA agents secretly plotting the overthrow of unfriendly governments, regardless of Soviet activities.

Finally, the conservative supports a "get tough" policy with international organizations like the U.N. and World Bank, which he views as leftist fronts attempting to bully America and further the Communist conspiracy. Accordingly, he insists that America's political power in these forums must reflect the fact that the United States is the single largest source of their financial support.

The liberal, on the other hand, sees the U.N. and other such agencies as vital forums for fostering and promoting global cooperation. Reluctant to reinforce America's image as the plundering imperialist, he is more willing to abide by the democratic decisions of the many participating nations than play America's economic trump card by reducing its financial contributions.

Notes

Preface

1. Thurow, Lester, C., *The Zero Sum Society: Distribution and the Possibilities for Economic Change* (New York: Basic Books, 1980).

PART 1

Chapter 1

1. Gardner, Bruce, *Food and Agricultural Policy* (Washington, D.C.: American Enterprise Institute for Policy Research, 1977), p. 6.

2. The best-known, and perhaps best-argued, application of the Marxian framework to the American experience is Charles Beard's book, *An Economic Interpretation of the Constitution of the United States* (New York: MacMillan, 1913). In his controversial volume, Beard claims that the Constitution was designed by a coalition of propertied classes—merchants, money lenders, security holders, manufacturers, shippers, capitalists, and financiers—and implemented to protect them from the attack of relatively unpropertied classes (non–slave-holding farmers and a large class of debtors). See also Mills, C. Wright, *The Power Elite* (New York: Oxford University Press, 1959).

3. Two well-known Nader exposes are found in: Cox, E., *The Nader Report on the Federal Trade Commission* (New York: Grove Press, 1970) and Fellmeth, Robert, *The Interstate Commerce Omission: The Public Interest and the ICC* (New York: Grossman, 1970).

4. See Bentley, Arthur F., *The Process of Government*, 1908, rpt. (Cambridge, Mass.: Harvard University Press, Belknap Press, 1967).

5. Truman, David B., *The Governmental Process: Political Interests and Public Opinion*, 2nd ed. (New York: Alfred A. Knopf, 1971), p. 514.

6. Bentley, Arthur F., *The Process of Government,* 1908, rpt. (Cambridge, Mass.: Harvard University Press, Belknap Press, 1967), pp. 226–227.

7. The antipluralist critics include Henry Kariel, Grant McConnell, and Theodore Lowi. For a discussion see McCraw, Thomas K., "Regulation in America: A review Article," *Business History Review* **49** (Summer 1975), pp. 159–83. One of the most cogent discussions of pluralism's flaws is found in Olson, Mancur Jr., *The Logic of Collective Action: Public Goods and the Theory of Groups* (New York: Harvard University Press and Schocken Books, 1965), p. 121.

8. McCraw, Thomas K., "Regulation in America: A Review Article," *Business History Review* **49** (Summer 1975), p. 178.

9. Kolko, Gabriel, *Railroads and Regulation, 1877–1916* (Princeton, N.J.: Princeton University Press, 1965).

10. Stigler, George J., "The Theory of Economic Regulation," *Bell Journal of Economics and Management Science,* **2** (Spring 1971), pp. 3–21.

11. The *externalities problem* arises when the public costs or benefits of a good diverge from the private costs or benefits to the good's producer. For example, a factory not only produces steel but it also emits air pollution. If the producer makes no effort to reduce that pollution (e.g., by buying pollution control technology), the private cost of production will be less than the public cost, because the latter also takes into account the damage pollution does to lungs and property. The result will be an overproduction of both steel and pollution.

12. The developers of this model include Kalt, Joseph P., *The Economics and Politics of Oil Price Regulation: Federal Policy in the Post-Embargo Era* (Cambridge, Massachusetts: MIT Press, 1981); Kau, James B. and Paul H. Rubin, "Self-Interest, Ideology, and Log-rolling in Congressional Voting," *Journal of Law and Economics* **22** (October 1979), pp. 365–384; Lopreato, Sally C. and Smoller, Fred. "Explaining Energy Votes in the Ninety-Fourth Congress." Center for Energy Studies, University of Texas at Austin, June 1978, discussion paper; and Mitchell, Edward J., *Energy and Ideology* (Washington, D.C.: American Enterprise Institute, October 1977).

Chapter 2

1. This historical description draws heavily on Monica Lett's fine volume *Rent Control: Concepts, Realities and Mechanisms* (New Brunswick, N.J.: Center for Urban Policy Research, 1976), Chapter 1.

2. Drellich, Edith Berger and Andree Emery, *Rent Control in War and Peace* (New York: National Municipal League, 1939), p. 11.

3. Lett, Monica, *Rent Control: Concepts, Realities and Mechanisms* (New Brunswick, N.J.: Center for Urban Policy Research, 1976), p. 2.

4. Massachusetts General Laws, Ch. 842, 1970.

5. The relevant Supreme Court Cases are *Block* v. *Hirsh,* 256 U.S. 135(1921) and *Marcus Brown Holding Co.* v. *Feldman,* 256 U.S. (1921). For a discussion, see Lett, Monica, *Rent Control: Concepts, Realities and Mechanisms* (New Brunswick, N.J.: Center for Urban Policy Research, 1976), p. 2.

6. Lett, Monica, *Rent Control: Concepts, Realities and Mechanisms* (New Brunswick, N.J.: Center for Urban Policy Research, 1976), pp. 32–34.

7. For a discussion of the relationship of vacancy rates to shortages, see Lett, Monica, *Rent Control: Concepts, Realities and Mechanisms* (New Brunswick, N.J.: Center for Urban Policy Research, 1976), pp. 37 and 39. As Lett observes: "Vacancy rates are traditionally viewed as crucial in explaining housing shortages, since rents and vacancy rates vary inversely within a critical zone of occupancy." (Lett, p. 37)

8. For example, Lett observes that "the existence of a housing shortage" is usually equated with the declaration of an emergency, while the assertion that rent increases can adversely affect or threaten the health, safety, and general welfare "is generally included to justify the use of police power." Lett, Monica, *Rent Control: Concepts, Realities and Mechanisms* (New Brunswick, N.J.: Center for Urban Policy Research, 1976), p. 35.

9. According to one member of the Rent Control Board, there are about 90 individuals who are active participants in the hearings.

10. The fifth member is Alfred Velluci. According to one political analyst, Velluci has regularly sided with the CCA in exchange for the tacit agreement of that organization not to campaign heavily in Velluci's ethnic strongholds.

11. *The Cambridge Express*, December 18, 1982, p. 3.

12. For a detailed example of how the capture-ideology framework may be applied, the interested reader can refer to the work of one of the pioneers of its development, for example, Kalt, Joseph P., *The Economics and Politics of Oil Price Regulation: Federal Policy in the Post Embargo Era* (Cambridge, Mass.: MIT Press, 1981).

13. This ranking is achieved by converting the initial parameter estimates (e.g., regression coefficients) into a set of *standardized* estimates or "beta coefficients." These beta coefficients adjust the estimated slope parameters of, say, the regression coefficients by the ratio of the standard deviation of the independent or explanatory variables in the test to the standard deviation of the policy choice or dependent variable in the test. Standardizing the parameter estimates in this way allows us to see the relative strength of each explanatory variable in influencing the dependent variable or policy choice. (For further discussion, see Appendix A.)

14. 1981 Campaign Finance Report filed by Walter Sullivan and submitted to the city clerk of Cambridge, and discussions with William Walsh, Esq.

15. Pennance, F. G., in Institute of Economic Affairs, *Verdict on Rent Control,* Readings No. 7 (Sussex, England: I.E.A., 1972), p. xi.

16. Lett, Monica, *Rent Control: Concepts, Realities and Mechanisms* (New Brunswick, N.J.: Center for Urban Policy Research, 1976), p. 92.

17. Ault, Richard W., in Block, Walter and Edgar Olsen, eds., *Rent Control: Myths and Realities* (Vancouver, Canada: The Fraser Institute, 1981), p. 67.

18. Navarro, P., "Rent Control and the Landlord's Loophole: Condominium Conversions in Cambridge," *Urban Land*, **39,** No. 10 (November 1980), pp. 6–9.

19. Between 1971 and 1979, over 2,000 apartment units (the vast majority of which were under rent control) were converted to condominiums. That represents roughly 10% of the 20,000-plus units that were first placed under controls.

20. City of Cambridge Community Development, Cambridge Housing Data, 1980 and 1975 Mid Decade Census Housing Summary.

21. See, for example, "Cambridge Bars Condo Exception," *Boston Globe,* **20** (October 1981, Metro Region Section), pp. 21 and 23.

22. Cheung, Steven N. S., "Roofs or Stars: The Stated Intents and Actual Effects of a Rents Ordinance," *Economic Inquiry* **XIII** (March 1975), pp. 1–21.

23. Lett, Monica, *Rent Control: Concepts, Realities and Mechanisms* (New Brunswick, N.J.: Center for Urban Policy Research, 1976), p. 151.

24. Leonard, Herman B., *Regulation of the Cambridge Housing Market: Its Goals and Effects,* a report prepared for the Cambridge Chamber of Commerce, 1981, p. 55.

25. Ault, Richard W., in Block, Walter and Edgar Olsen (eds.), *Rent Control: Myths and Realities* (Vancouver, Canada: The Fraser Institute, 1981), p. 68.

26. Lett, Monica, *Rent Control: Concepts, Realities and Mechanisms* (New Brunswick, N.J.: Center for Urban Policy Research, 1976), p. 136.

27. Leonard, Herman B., *Regulation of the Cambridge Housing Market: Its Goals and Effects,* a report prepared for the Cambridge Chamber of Commerce, 1981, p. 81.

28. Leonard, Herman B., *Regulation of the Cambridge Housing Market: Its Goals and Effects,* a report prepared for the Cambridge Chamber of Commerce, 1981, p. 81.

29. This example is taken from Lett, Monica, *Rent Control: Concepts, Realities and Mechanisms* (New Brunswick, N.J.: Center for Urban Policy Research, 1976), pp. 152–53.

30. Ault, Richard W., in Block, Walter and Edgar Olsen (eds.), *Rent Control: Myths and Realities* (Vancouver, Canada: The Fraser Institute, 1981), p. 109.

31. Leonard, Herman B., *Regulation of the Cambridge Housing Market: Its Goals and Effects,* a report prepared for the Cambridge Chamber of Commerce, 1981, p. 86.

32. City of Cambridge, Massachusetts, *Annual Budget, 1983–1984.*

33. Rydell, Peter C. et al., *The Impact of Rent Control on the Los Angeles Housing Market* (Santa Monica, Calif: The Rand Corporation, 1981), p. 27.

34. F. A. Hayek, in Ault, Richard W., in Walter Block, and Edgar Olsen (eds.), *Rent Control: Myths and Realities* (Vancouver, Canada: The Fraser Institute, 1981), p. 44.

35. Leonard, Herman B., *Regulation of the Cambridge Housing Market: Its Goals and Effects,* a report prepared for the Cambridge Chamber of Commerce, 1981, p. 74.

36. Jeffrey Sterns, quoted in Leonard, Herman B., *Regulation of the Cambridge Housing Market: Its Goals and Effects,* a report prepared for the Cambridge Chamber of Commerce, 1981, p. 224.

37. Baird, Charles W., *Rent Control: The Perennial Folly* (San Francisco: CATO Institute, 1980), p. 58.

38. For a discussion of the various abuses that have occurred under rent control, see State of New York, Temporary State House Rent Commission, *Report on Rent Control in New York State,* 1955, pp. 16–18.

39. Rydell, Peter C. et al., *The Impact of Rent Control on the Los Angeles Housing Market* (Santa Monica, Calif.: The Rand Corporation, 1981), p. 59.

40. Rydell, Peter C. et al., *The Impact of Rent Control on the Los Angeles Housing Market* (Santa Monica, Calif.: The Rand Corporation, 1981), p. 60.

41. McClure, cited in Leonard, Herman B., *Regulation of the Cambridge Housing Market: Its Goals and Effects,* a report prepared for the Cambridge Chamber of Commerce, 1981, p. 18.

42. Leonard, Herman B., *Regulation of the Cambridge Housing Market: Its Goals and Effects*, a report prepared for the Cambridge Chamber of Commerce, 1981, generally Chapter 3 and p. 23.

43. Ault, Richard W., in Block, Walter and Edgar Olsen (eds.), *Rent Control: Myths and Realities* (Vancouver, Canada: The Fraser Institute, 1981), p. 57.

44. Rydell, Peter C. et al. *The Impact of Rent Control on the Los Angeles Housing Market* (Santa Monica, Calif.: The Rand Corporation, 1981), p. 13.

45. Leonard, Herman B., *Regulation of the Cambridge Housing Market: Its Goals and Effects*, a report prepared for the Cambridge Chamber of Commerce, 1981, p. 21.

46. Leonard, Herman B., *Regulation of the Cambridge Housing Market: Its Goals and Effects*, a report prepared for the Cambridge Chamber of Commerce, 1981, p. 28.

47. Leonard, Herman B., *Regulation of the Cambridge Housing Market: Its Goals and Effects*, a report prepared for the Cambridge Chamber of Commerce, 1981, p. 39–41.

48. Leonard, Herman B., *Regulation of the Cambridge Housing Market: Its Goals and Effects*, a report prepared for the Cambridge Chamber of Commerce, 1981, p. 42.

PART 2

Chapter 3

1. *Congressional Record*, 97th Congress, Second Session (Washington, D.C., August 1982).

2. William P. Browne in Hadwiger, Don F. and Ross B. Talbot (eds.), *Food Policy and Farm Programs* (New York: The Academy of Political Science, 1982), p. 203.

3. Haider, Donald H., *When Governments Come to Washington: Governors, Mayors, and Intergovernmental Lobbying* (New York: The Free Press, 1974), Preface, p. x.

4. Bilmes, Linda, "Congress Doesn't Live Here Anymore," *Harvard Political Review* (Spring 1979), p. 26.

5. The "noneconomic" distinction is hardly clear-cut. For example, black groups that pursue affirmative action programs implicitly seek higher incomes and environmentalists benefit not only from the psychic satisfaction of a cleaner earth, but also from the material enjoyment of protected parks and forests. See Zeigler, L. Harmon and Wayne G. Peak, *Interest Groups in American Society*, 2nd ed. (Englewood Cliffs, N.J.: Prentice Hall, 1972).

6. Berry, Jeffrey, *Lobbying for the People* (Princeton, N.J.: Princeton University Press, 1977), p. 292.

7. Berry, Jeffrey, *Lobbying for the People* (Princeton, N.J.: Princeton University Press, 1977), pp. 27–28.

8. Judge John Sirica, quoted in Guither, Harold, *The Food Lobbyists* (Lexington, Mass.: Lexington Books, 1980), p. 100.

9. While a discussion of the various ideological pressure groups also fits into the discussion of ideology in Part 3 of this book, some of the major groups are listed

here since the pursuit of ideological goals, broadly construed, represents a special interest, albeit one more altruistically motivated.

10. Deakin, James, *The Lobbyists* (Washington, D.C.: Public Affairs Press, 1966), p. 34.

Chapter 4

1. McConnell, Grant, *Private Power and American Democracy* (New York: Alfred A. Knopf, 1970), p. 30.

2. Hamilton, Alexander, Report on Manufactures (Secretary of Treasury to the House of Representatives, December 5, 1791) in Cooke, Jacob E. (ed.), *The Reports of Alexander Hamilton* (New York: Harper and Row, 1964).

3. Joseph M. Jones has observed: "As a score of writers have pointed out, the world depression and the Hawley–Smoot tariff are inextricably bound up one with the other, the latter being not only the first manifestation of, but a principal cause of, the deepening and aggravating of the former." Jones, Joseph M., *Tariff Retaliation: Repercussions of the Hawley–Smoot Bill* (Philadelphia: University of Pennsylvania Press, 1934), p. 2.

4. Pastor, Robert A., *Congress and the Politics of U.S. Foreign Economic Policy 1929–1976* (Berkeley and Los Angeles: University of California Press, 1982), p. 27. (For a more detailed discussion of the history of trade policy, see this excellent book.)

5. Pastor, Robert A., *Congress and the Politics of U.S. Foreign Economic Policy 1929–1976* (Berkeley and Los Angeles: University of California Press, 1982), p. 27. The decline is for the time period 1929 to 1933.

6. For a discussion of this shift, see Pastor, Robert A., *Congress and the Politics of U.S. Foreign Economic Policy* (Berkeley and Los Angeles: University of California Press, 1982), p. 110.

7. Caves, Richard E. and Jones, Ronald W., *World Trade and Payments*, 2nd ed. (Boston: Little Brown and Company, 1973), p. 215.

8. For a discussion, see Reich, Robert B., *The Next American Frontier* (New York: Times Books, 1983), pp. 180–186.

9. Cline, William as quoted in Murray, Alan, "Congress and the GATT: Free Trade Under Fire," *Congressional Quarterly Weekly Report* (November 20, 1982) p. 2889.

10. Tasca, Henry J., *The Reciprocal Trade Policy of the United States* (Philadelphia: University of Pennsylvania Press, 1938), p. 1.

11. Bureau of Labor Statistics, *Directory of National Unions and Employee Associations, 1979* (Bulletin 2079) (Washington, D.C.: GPO, 1980) pp. 55 and 62.

12. See, for example, Pastor, Robert A., *Congress and the Politics of U.S. Foreign Economic Policy* (Berkeley and Los Angeles: University of California Press), p. 139.

13. The role of state and other government agencies is discussed in Pastor, Robert A., *Congress and the Politics of U.S. Foreign Economic Policy 1929–1976* (Berkeley and Los Angeles: University of California Press, 1982), pp. 140–141.

14. Consumers for World Trade, "Protection," 1983 pamphlet, Washington D.C., p. 5.

15. Munger, Michael C., "The Costs of Protectionism: Estimates of the Hidden Tax of Trade Restraint." (St. Louis: Center for the Study of American Business, Washington University, 1983) Working Paper Number 80, for apparel, textiles, shoes, pp. 9–10,

14–15. For auto costs, Consumers for World Trade, "How Much Do Consumers Pay for U.S. Trade Barriers?" (Washington, D.C.: CWT Information Paper, Winter 1984), p. 2.

16. This example is drawn from Magaziner, Ira and Reich, Robert, *Minding America's Business* (New York: Harcourt, Brace and Jovanovich, 1982) pp. 205–6.

17. For an elaboration of this problem, see generally Olson, Mancur, *The Logic of Collective Action* (New York: Harvard University Press and Schocken Books, 1965) and more specifically, Wilson, James Q., "The Politics of Regulation," in *Social Responsibility and the Business Predicament*, edited by James W. McKie (Washington D.C.: Brookings Institution, 1974) pp. 141–142.

18. Weidenbaum, Murray L., "The Drift to Protectionism." *Challenge* (March–April 1983), p. 45.

19. See, for example, H.R. 5133 "The Fair Practices in Automotive Products Act" proposed in the 97th Congress. It specified a 90% requirement in 1985 for manufacturers selling more than 500,000 vehicles per year.

20. The use of ADA ratings as a proxy for ideology is not without controversy. Chicago economist and capture theorist Sam Peltzman, for example, has argued that these ratings do not represent public-interested motives but merely reflect the explanatory power of private interests left out of the test. However, in a seminal article in the *American Economic Review*, Joseph Kalt of Harvard and Mark Zupan of the Massachusetts Institute of Technology have presented the results of exhaustive tests on the purity of the ADA ratings; they leave little doubt that they are an excellent and accurate measure of ideological behavior. On this controversy and its resolution, see Kalt, Joseph P. and Mark A. Zupan, "Capture and Ideology in the Economic Theory of Politics" *American Economic Review*, **74** (June 1984).

21. Barone, Michael and Grant, Ujifusa, *The Almanac of American Politics 1984* (Washington, D.C.: National Journal, 1984), p. 204.

22. Lowry's Seattle district is a hub of aircraft production while McHugh's is a major center of office and computing machines manufacture.

23. With 10 percent of his district's employment dependent on steel, Wilson is the only one of the three with even a marginal amount of probable interest in his district.

24. A source at Ford, who requested anonymity, said Ford supported DCL as "a message to the Japanese."

25. For a more detailed treatment, see Caves, Richard E. and Ronald W. Jones. *World Trade and Payments*, 2nd ed. (Boston: Little Brown and Company, 1973), p. 199.

26. The original voluntary export restraint (VER) called for a 1.68 million car ceiling. The latest (1984) VER is slightly higher at 1.85 million.

27. The Department of Commerce's Auto Trade Force concluded that under assumptions that U.S. auto manufacturers responded to DCL by increasing prices and volume, employment would increase about 62,900 in the auto industry. The UAW, using *average* employment per auto (in both auto and auto supplier industries) estimated that 941,000 jobs would be created. The Congressional Budget Office's report criticized the UAW methodology as inappropriate and provided an estimate set (optimistically) at 90,000. See U.S. Congress House of Representatives Committee on Ways and Means Subcommittee on Trade, *Domestic Content Legislation and*

the U.S. Automobile Industry: Analyses of HR5133, The Fair Practices in Automotive Products Act, WMCP: 97-33 (Washington, DC: U.S. GPO, 1982).

28. For stockholder median income, New York Stock Exchange, Fact Book 1982 (New York: New York Stock Exchange, 1982), p. 47. For median income of all Americans, Statistical Abstract of the United States, 103rd ed. (Washington, D.C: U.S. G.P.O., 1982), pp. 430–431.

29. For textiles and shoeworker income, Bureau of Labor Statistics, Employment and Earnings, October 1982 (Washington, D.C.: U.S. G.P.O., 1982), pp. 106 and 110.

30. Bureau of Labor Statistics, Employment and Earnings, October 1982 (Washington, D.C.: U.S. GPO, 1982), pp. 102 and 104.

31. In the case of a quota, it is the foreign importer who captures this revenue in the form of a "scarcity rent." It is this windfall that often makes it politically easier for a foreign country to accept quotas or voluntary restraints. For details, see the Federal Trade Commission. "Staff Report on Effects of Restrictions on United States Imports" (Washington, D.C.: U.S. GPO, June 1980), p. 9.

32. For a summary of deadweight loss estimates, see Kindleberger, C. P. and P. H. Lindert. International Economics (Homewood, Ill.: Richard D. Irwin, 1978), p. 120.

33. Munger, Michael C., "The Costs of Protectionism: Estimates of the Hidden Tax of Trade Restraint" (St. Louis, Missouri: Center for the Study of American Business, Working Paper Number 80, July 1983).

34. Congressional Quarterly, February 19, 1983, p. 375.

35. U.S. News and World Report, March 1, 1982, p. 57.

36. Magaziner, Ira and Robert Reich, Minding America's Business (New York: Harcourt, Brace and Jovanovich, 1982) p. 155.

37. Between 1979 and 1982, employment in production of motor vehicle and equipment manufacturing (SIC 371) fell about 28%. Sources: Bureau of Labor Statistics, as cited in MVMA Motor Vehicle Facts and Figures '83 (Detroit: MVMA, 1983).

38. Magaziner, Ira and Robert Reich, Minding America's Business (New York: Harcourt, Brace and Jovanovich, 1982) p. 206–207.

39. Harvey Leibenstein discusses this theoretical concept in Beyond Economic Man: A New Foundation for Microeconomics (Cambridge: Harvard University Press, 1976). W. M. Corden places the approach explicitly into the context of international trade in Trade Policy and Economic Welfare (Oxford, England: Oxford University Press, 1974).

40. Noting that allocational losses seldom exceeded $\frac{1}{10}$ percent, Leibenstein observes that intrafactory productivity rates often diverge by much larger magnitudes, even given identical capital and technological endowments. See Leibenstein, Harvey, Beyond Economic Man: A New Foundation for Microeconomics (Cambridge: Harvard University Press, 1976) pp. 34–44.

41. This quote as well as the preceding example are drawn from Reich, Robert B., The Next American Frontier (New York: Times Books, 1983), p. 183.

42. Kuczynski, Pedro-Pablo, "Latin American Debt: Act Two," Foreign Affairs, Fall 1983, p. 27 and staff writers, "The International Debt Threat: A Way to Avoid a Crash," The Economist, April 30, 1983, p. 11. Kuczynski estimates a $330 billion debt burden alone for Latin America.

43. For a discussion of the close macroeconomic interdependence of the developing countries and the industrialized democracies, see "The Third World Threat to the West's Recovery," *Business Week*, February 7, 1983, pp. 48 ff. In 1982, 28 percent of all OECD country exports were destined for the Third World. See also, Chinn, Menzie, "Protectionism: The Rising Tide," *Harvard International Review*, January/February 1984, pp. 34–36.

44. This scenario is firmly rooted in reality. As an article in the April 30, 1983 issue of *The Economist*, "The International Debt Threat: A Way to Avoid a Crash," April 30, 1983, points out, "10 large American banks have outstanding loans which by far exceed their total equity" and these loans are just to Brazil, Mexico, and Venezuela (p. 13). At the same time, the way international debt is currently structured implies "if the foreign banks cannot meet their liabilities to the American banks the Federal Reserve will have to provide the shortfall" (p. 12). Moreover, if the Federal Reserve were not to step in to bail out the American banks, the results would be worse from the standpoint of our scenario: a collapse of the domestic banking system and a bailout to bank investors by another federal agency, the Federal Depositors Insurance Corporation.

45. At present, funds available for job search are limited to $600. More generous is the government's promise to pay 90 percent of relocation expenses should a job be found. However, it is currently taking up to six months rather than the stipulated 60 days for the Department of Labor to decide if workers in a firm or industry qualify for adjustment assistance. Personal communication, James Turner, Department of Labor, February 13, 1984.

46. As reported in *Consumers for World Trade*, "Protection from imports will cost you, the American consumer this year $15,000,000,000 in inflated prices," 1983 pamphlet (no page numbers).

Chapter 5

1. Adams, Henry, *The Education of Henry Adams* (Boston: Houghton Mifflin Company, 1961), p. 261.

2. Milbrath, Lester, W., *The Washington Lobbyists* (Chicago: Rand McNally & Co., 1963), p. 212.

3. Milbrath, Lester, W., *The Washington Lobbyists* (Chicago: Rand McNally & Co., 1963), pp. 227–28.

4. Jacob Viner, quoted in Guither, Harold D., *The Food Lobbyists* (Lexington, Mass.: Lexington Books, 1980), p. 159.

5. Abraham Lincoln, quoted in Milbrath, Lester W., *The Washington Lobbyists* (Chicago: Rand McNally & Co., 1963), p. 250.

6. Richard Berman, quoted in Fraser Associates, *The PAC Handbook* (Cambridge: Ballinger Publishing Co., 1980), p. 51.

7. This anecdote was related to me by a Washington lobbyist under condition the Congressman go unnamed.

8. Berry, Jeffrey, *Lobbying for the People* (Princeton, N.J.: Princeton University Press, 1971), p. 222.

9. Cameron, Simon, quoted in Bilmes, Linda, "Congress Doesn't Live Here Anymore," *Harvard Political Review,* Spring 1979, p. 27.

10. For details, see Murphy, Thomas P., *Pressures Upon Congress: Legislation by Lobby* (Woodbury, N.Y.: Barron's Educational Series, Inc., 1974), pp. 23–24.

11. Wertheimer, quoted in Adams, Gordon, *The Iron Triangle: The Politics of Defense Contracting* (New York: Council on Economic Priorities, 1981), p. 112.

12. Green, Mark, and Andrew Buchsbaum, *The Corporate Lobbies: Political Profiles of the Roundtable and the Chamber of Commerce* (Washington, D.C.: Public Citizen, 1980), p. 99.

13. D. Craig Yesse, quoted in Fraser Associates, *The PAC Handbook* (Cambridge, Mass.: Ballinger Publishing Co., 1980), p. 81.

14. *U.S. News and World Report,* 12 September, 1977, pp. 39–41.

15. Fox, Ronald J., *Arming America: How the U.S. Buys Weapons* (Boston: Division of Research, Graduate School of Business Administration, Harvard University, 1974), p. 137.

16. Ziegler, L. Harmon, and Wayne G. Peak, *Interest Groups in American Society,* 2nd ed. (Englewood Cliffs, N.J.: Prentice-Hall, 1972), p. 116.

17. Ziegler, L. Harmon, and Wayne G. Peak, *Interest Groups in American Society,* 2nd ed. (Englewood Cliffs, N.J.: Prentice-Hall, 1972), p. 256.

18. Andrew Biemiller, lobbyist for American Federation of Labor, p. 271, "Lobbying Activities."

19. Ervin, Sam J. Jr., *The Whole Truth: The Watergate Conspiracy* (New York: Random House, 1980), p. 7.

20. Ziegler, L. Harmon, and Wayne G. Peak, *Interest Groups in American Society,* 2nd ed. (Englewood Cliffs, N.J.: Prentice-Hall, 1972).

21. Bromley, quoted in Green, Mark J., *The Other Government: The Unseen Power of Washington Lawyers* (New York: Grossman Publishers, 1975), p. 125.

22. For a breezy account of the phenomenon, see *People* magazine, February 14, 1983, pp. 35–37.

23. Green, Mark J., *The Other Government: The Unseen Power of Washington Lawyers* (New York, Grossman Publishers, 1975), p. 153.

24. For details, see Navarro, P., "The Politics of Air Pollution," *The Public Interest,* Spring 1980, pp. 36–44.

Chapter 6

1. Franklin D. Roosevelt, quoted in Eberling, Walter, *The Fruited Plain: The Story of American Agriculture* (Berkeley and Los Angeles: University of California Press, 1979) p. 259.

2. Executive Office of the President, Office of Management and Budget, *The U.S. Budget in Brief, FY 1984* (Washington, D.C.: U.S. GPO, 1983), pp. 8, 40, and 41. Until FY 1982, outlays for farm income stabilization and support ran at about $4 billion per annum. But with the deterioration of demand for farm goods overseas and record crop production at home, market prices plummeted. As a result, esti-

mated budget outlays for farm support were about $13 billion for FY 1982 and an unprecedented $19.4 billion for FY 1983.

3. Cox, Meg, "Farm Protest Movement Spreads as New Groups Spring Up in Several States to Fight Foreclosures," *Wall Street Journal*, February 16, 1983, p. 56. In 1982, an admittedly very poor year for farmers, who had just suffered two years of depressed markets, 25% of the Farmer's Home Administration's (FHA) 270,000 loans were declared delinquent. Eight thousand borrowers went out of business, while 844 experienced forced foreclosures. No figures on forced foreclosures were kept for 1981.

4. This coinage dates back to the 1930s and is a common fixture in academic farm literature. As Earl Heady has observed: "Overcapacity and low incomes in agriculture have been a major problem in the United States since 1933." Heady, Earl O. et al. (eds.), *Food Goals, Future Structural Changes and Agricultural Policy: A National Base Book* (Ames, Ia.: Iowa State University Press, 1965), p. 3.

5. U.S. Department of Commerce, Bureau of the Census, *Abstract of the Fifteenth Census of the U.S., 1930* (Washington, D.C.: U.S. DoC, 1933) pp. 9 and 19, and U.S. Department of Commerce, Bureau of the Census, *1978 Census of Agriculture*, Vol. 1, Pt. 51 (AC 78-A-51), (Washington, D.C.: U.S. GPO, 1979), p. 1.

6. Johnson, Glenn, and C. Leroy Quance, *The Overproduction Trap in U.S. Agriculture* (Baltimore: Johns Hopkins University Press, 1972), p. 160.

7. The use of import restrictions and export subsidies is a third important component of farm policy, but a discussion of these devices is omitted here because they are, in effect, the *result* of price supports. Specifically, price supports have stimulated (and implicitly, subsidized) surpluses; the federal government has then sold these surpluses on foreign markets at world market prices or given them away. To prevent the reentry of these crops into the American domestic market, it has then had to impose import quotas.

8. Benedict, Murray R., *Farm Policies of the United States, 1790–1950* (New York: America Book–Stratford Press, 1953), p. 414. For more on the programs of the war years, see pp. 408–450.

9. Congressional Quarterly, *Congress and the Nation 1945–64*, (Washington, D.C.: Congressional Quarterly, 1965). In 1958 Eisenhower again attempted to implement drastic reforms after years of attempting to deal with excess production on a piece-meal basis. The president proposed moving to a flexible support of 60 to 90 percent of parity, in an attempt to adjust supply to demand. Both chambers attempted a freeze at the 1958 level, but the president vetoed the bill (SJ Res 162). After additional negotiations, the bill passed in a form that allowed for supports to be gradually lowered over time.

10. Dwight Eisenhower, quoted in Ed Edwin, *Feast or Famine: Food, Farming, and Farm Politics in America* (New York: Charterhouse, 1974), p. 313.

11. For a detailed discussion of what a "market oriented" approach to farm policy entails, see Paarlberg, Don, in American Enterprise Institute, *Food and Agricultural Policy* (Washington, D.C.: American Enterprise Institute for Public Policy Research, 1977), pp. 197–203.

12. Because it is such an important component of farm policy, it is worthwhile to illustrate the three steps of a sample parity calculation for milk prices. First, the

DOA determines the average price of milk during the base period of 1910–1914 to be $1.58 per hundredweight.

Second, an index is calculated for the prices farmers currently pay for both production items like tractors and plows and consumption items like food, clothing, and furniture. For example, in the fall of 1982, this index equaled 1075, meaning that the price of milk would have to be 10.75 times the base price of $1.58 per hundredweight to yield the farmer the same purchasing power for his products as in the base period.

Third, the parity price is calculated by simply multiplying the base price times the index. In our example, the parity price for milk would then be 10.75 times $1.58, or $16.99.

It is important to differentiate between these parity prices and other more obscure variants. Crop prices as a percentage of parity are defined as already described. "Parity income" is the ratio between the purchasing power of farmers' net income and nonfarmers' net income (1909–1914). This concept was soon dropped as impractical. A third measure is the "parity ratio," which compares prices paid to prices received by farmers. However, despite the title employed, parity price, insofar as it attempts to establish "fair" prices, is an income-based concept, as much as any of the other two measures are.

13.   The federal government has typically based support prices at something less than 100 percent of parity. During the New Deal, FDR's flexible supports ranged from 52 to 75 percent of parity, while after World War II, fixed supports were pegged at 90 percent for wheat, upland cotton, peanuts, rice, tobacco, and milk. Today no major farm product's price supports are set by the parity formula. The *1981 Act* provides *actual* supports or targets in dollar terms, while lower and upper bounds may be established on the basis of price parity (as they are for milk). However, the demise of parity has not meant a similar fate for supports through nonrecourse loans. Such loan rates are modified by changes in the DOA's estimates of "costs-of-production" for that crop, or some arbitrarily legislated formula.

However, farmers have traditionally pressed for a 100 percent parity standard, particularly during periods of badly depressed farm prices. At times, this peaceful political demand has been transformed into a battle cry to revive the parity formula for all crops and commodities, as was the case when farmers surrounded Capitol Hill with the tractorcade of 1978 and chanted "100 percent parity, 100 percent parity."

14.   Hardin, Charles M., *The Politics of Agriculture* (Glencoe, Ill.: The Free Press, 1952), p. 105.

15.   Reported in McCune, Wesley, *The Farm Bloc* (New York: Greenwood Press, 1968), p. 64.

16.   This illustration draws heavily on examples in: U.S. Department of Agriculture, Economic Research Service, *Commodity Program Provisions Under the Food and Agriculture Act of 1977* (Washington, D. C.: DoC/NTIS, October 1977), p. 10.

The actual calculation can be much more complex. For example, payments may be made at a lower rate on bushels not planted, even though the full allotment was not used (e.g., out of a 100 acres, only 60 were planted). Assuming 30 bushels are harvested per acre and a target price of $2.47, deficiency payments equal $0.22/bushel times 30 bushels/acre times 40 acres = $263.00.

17. Gardner, Bruce, *The Governing of Agriculture* (Lawrence, Kansas: The Regents Press of Kansas, 1981), p. 17.

18. The classic statement on the farm bloc is found in McCune, Wesley, *The Farm Bloc* (New York: Greenwood Press, 1968), p. 64.

19. Edwin, Ed, *Feast or Famine: Food, Farming, and Farm Politics in America* (New York: Charterhouse, 1974), p. 293.

20. Edwin, Ed, *Feast or Famine: Food, Farming, and Farm Politics in America* (New York: Charterhouse, 1974), p. 294.

21. For an interesting empirical investigation of the farm lobby's support for its clientele agencies, see Kenneth Meier in Hadwiger, Don F. and William P. Browne, *The New Politics of Food* (Lexington, Mass.: Lexington Books, 1978), pp. 57–66.

22. McCune, Wesley, *The Farm Bloc* (New York: Greenwood Press, 1968), p. 262.

23. Figures for ASCS are FY 1983 budget amounts. U.S. Office of the President and Office of Management and Budget, *Budget of the Government, FY 1983* (Washington, D.C.: U.S. GPO, 1983), Appendix.

24. Alex McCalla, in Hadwiger, Don F., and William P. Browne, *The New Politics of Food* (Lexington, Mass.: Lexington Books, 1978), p. 77.

25. Alex McCalla, in Hadwiger, Don F., and William P. Browne, *The New Politics of Food* (Lexington, Mass.: Lexington Books, 1978), pp. 78–89.

26. U.S. Department of Commerce, Bureau of Economic Analysis, *Local Area Personal Income 1974–1979*, Vol. 1, Summary (Washington, D.C.: U.S. GPO, June 1981). The definition of a farm-state was any state with more than two percent of personal income originating in the farm sector. Such calculations are misleading, as they omit from the farm-state category states like Illinois, Ohio, and Montana. It also underestimates the impact of farming by omitting industries that produce agricultural inputs, like fertilizer, tractors and combines.

27. Edwin, Ed, *Feast or Famine: Food, Farming, and Farm Politics in America* (New York: Charterhouse, 1974), p. 294.

28. Edwin, Ed, *Feast or Famine: Food, Farming, and Farm Politics in America* (New York: Charterhouse, 1974), pp. 294–95.

29. In Illinois, hard hit by both low farm prices and depressed markets for agricultural machinery, the Democrats picked up two seats, while in the Peoria-based Eighteenth District, Robert Michel, for whom Reagan had personally campaigned, nearly lost his 26-year incumbency. Minnesota in turn saw conservative Tom Hagedorn ousted.

30. Common Cause, *A Common Cause Guide to Money, Power, & Politics* (Washington, D.C.: Common Cause, 1981), pp. 1 and 19.

31. McCune, Wesley, *The Farm Bloc* (New York: Greenwood Press, 1968), p. 91.

32. Brooks, Jackson, "The Problem with PACs," *Wall Street Journal*, **17** (November 1982), p. 30.

33. Edwin, Ed, *Feast or Famine: Food, Farming, and Farm Politics in America* (New York: Charterhouse, 1974), p. 326. The Nixon administration admitted to receiving $427,000, but emphasized that there was no link between these contributions and the decisions concerning milk supports.

34. Edwin, Ed, *Feast or Famine: Food, Farming, and Farm Politics in America* (New York: Charterhouse, 1974), p. 293.

35. McCune, Wesley, *The Farm Bloc* (New York: Greenwood Press, 1968), p. 1.

36. Attributed to Hyde H. Murray, Counsel, House Committee on Agriculture, by Paarlberg, Don, in American Enterprise Institute, *Food and Agricultural Policy* (Washington, D.C.: American Enterprise Institute for Public Policy Research, 1977) p. 6. See also his comments on pp. 211–217.

37. John G. Peters, in Hadwiger, Don F., and William P. Browne, *The New Politics of Food* (Lexington, Mass.: Lexington Books, 1978), pp. 24–25.

38. John G. Peters, in Hadwiger, Don F., and William P. Browne, *The New Politics of Food* (Lexington, Mass.: Lexington Books, 1978), pp. 24–25. Even with this link between farm programs and the repealing of right-to-work laws, the vote was close—221 to 172.

39. Pizza Hut also testified extensively before both the House and Senate Agriculture Committees. See U.S. Senate, Committee on Agriculture, Nutrition, and Forestry, *Semiannual Milk Price Adjustments*, February 15, 1981 (Washington, D.C.: U.S. GPO, 1981) and U.S. House, Committee on Agriculture, *Milk Support Price Adjustment*, March 12, 17, 1981 (Washington, D.C.: U.S. GPO, 1981).

40. Patton notes that: "A family farm is one on which the management decisions are made by the family and the bulk of labor is done by the family, preferably as owners as well as operators." Patton, James G., *The Case for Farmers* (Washington, D.C.: Public Affairs Press, 1959), p. 1.

41. This summary is based on my unpublished paper with Menzie D. Chinn, "Capture and Ideology in American Farm Policy."

42. Zorinsky and Pressler voted for supports on 3 of the 3 votes examined, while Abdnor and Andrews voted 2 of 3 times for supports.

43. The spread in numbers is due mainly to the extremely poor markets for agricultural goods over the past few years. Until FY 1982, the figure had been about $4 billion. See footnote 2.

44. Figures are for FY 1981, admittedly a poor year for farmers, but not the worst. U.S. Department of Agriculture, Commodity Credit Corporation, *Report of Financial Conditions and Operations of the CCC* (Washington, D.C.: USDA, 1981).

45. The best-known estimate is Charles Schultze's: While taxpayers' costs amounted to about $5 billion annually, consumers' costs were an additional $4.5 billion, as cited in *The Distribution of Farm Subsidies: Who Gets the Benefits?* (Washington, D.C.: The Brookings Institution, 1971), p. 1. In D. Gale Johnson's article "Where U.S. Agricultural Comparative Advantage Lies," in Johnson, D. Gale, and John A. Schnittker (eds.) *U.S. Agriculture in a World Context: Policies and Approaches for the Next Decade* (New York: Praeger, 1974), pp. 55–56, figures of $4.7333 billion and $4.83 billion, respectively, are cited. Bruce Gardner's estimates in *The Governing of Agriculture* (Lawrence, Kan.: The Regents Press of Kansas, 1981), p. 73, indicate $1.44 billion in taxpayers' costs (after taking into account tariff revenues) and $5.85 billion for consumers in the 1978–79 period.

46. In addition to this "static" inefficiency of too much capital in the farm sector, some economists argue that a "dynamic" inefficiency is also present. This argument, as set forth by Glenn Johnson, runs that price supports extend the economic life of

investment in old technologies at the same time that they stimulate overinvestments in technologies that were available at the inception of price support programs. *The result is an oversized, aging capital stock that imposes higher production costs on and reduces the competitiveness of U.S. farmers.* Thus, in reducing the rate of technical change in parts of the farm sector, dynamic inefficiency is "partially responsible for the obsolete nature of many of our farms." Glenn Johnson in Johnson, Glenn and C. Leroy Quance, *The Overproduction Trap in U.S. Agriculture* (Baltimore: Johns Hopkins University Press, 1972), p. 175.

47. In the USDA's *A Time to Choose* (Washington, D.C.: U.S. GPO, 1981), pp. 81–82, these 1977 estimates are cited: Each year 4.044 billion tons of soil are lost to water runoff, 1.462 billion tons to wind erosion, and yet another 298.3 million to gully erosion. Thus our total soil losses per year amount to almost six billion tons.

48. This calculation involves Standard International Trade Classification (SITC) codes 0, 1, 22, 263, and 4, for a combined export figure for farm products of $44 billion for 1981. Total U.S. exports of goods (excluding services) were $237 billion. The only larger one-digit SITC component of exports is SITC 7—machinery, transport, and equipment—at almost $49 billion. Source: United Nations, Statistical Office, *Commodity Trade Statistics* (New York: United Nations, 1982).

49. For a discussion, see Johnson, D. Gale, *Farm Commodity Programs: An Opportunity for Change* (Washington, D.C.: American Enterprise Institute for Public Policy Research, 1973), pp. 45–48.

50. As Luther Tweeten has observed:

> *Empirical evidence of capitalization of farm benefits into land values has been found for virtually all controlled commodities, but has been particularly pronounced for tobacco. Allotment values for tobacco have been estimated to be as high as $3,000 per acre—the difference between the land value with and without the tobacco allotments.*

In Tweeten, *AEI, Food and Agricultural Policy* (Washington, D.C.: American Enterprise Institute for Public Policy Research, 1977), p. 49.

51. Calculated from Gardner's estimate of $1.20/lb rental, and a per acre yield between 1600 and 2500 pounds. Gardner, Bruce, *The Governing of Agriculture* (Lawrence, Kans.: The Regents Press of Kansas, 1981), p. 78.

52. *AEI, Food and Agricultural Policy* (Washington, D.C.: American Enterprise Institute for Public Policy Research, 1977), p. 74.

53. U.S. Department of Agriculture, Economics, Statistics and Cooperatives, *Monitoring Foreign Ownership of U.S. Real Estate: A Report to Congress* (Washington, D.C.: USDA, 1980).

54. Howard Hjort in *AEI, Food and Agricultural Policy* (Washington, D.C.: American Enterprise Institute for Public Policy Research, 1977), p. 4.

55. On this point, see Brandow, George, in *AEI, Food and Agricultural Policy* (Washington, D.C.: American Enterprise Institute for Public Policy Research, 1977), p. 79.

56. Hamilton, W. E., in *AEI, Food and Agricultural Policy* (Washington, D.C.: American Enterprise Institute for Public Policy Research, 1977), p. 147.

57. Johnson, D. Gale, *Farm Commodity Programs: An Opportunity for Change* (Wash-

ington, D.C.: American Enterprise Institute for Public Policy Research, 1973), pp. 65–66.

58. Johnson, D. Gale, *Farm Commodity Programs: An Opportunity for Change* (Washington, D.C.: American Enterprise Institute for Public Policy Research, 1973), pp. 66–67.

59. See Schultze, Charles L., *The Distribution of Farm Subsidies: Who Gets the Benefits* (Washington, D.C.: The Brookings Institution, 1971), pp. 15–30.

60. *AEI, Food and Agricultural Policy* (Washington, D.C.: American Enterprise Institute for Public Policy Research, 1977), p. 2.

61. Tweeten, Luther, in *AEI, Food and Agricultural Policy* (Washington, D.C.: American Enterprise Institute for Public Policy Research, 1977), p. 44. Details of this evidence are likewise presented.

62. According to Luther Tweeten:

> In the absence of farm programs since 1954 the level of prices received by farmers would have been 28 percent higher in the 1968–72 period and total net income 40.3 percent higher in the same period. The reason for these results is that the absence of farm programs would have reduced gains in productivity and agricultural investment, eventually driving prices and incomes to higher levels under a free market according to the Nelson–Cochrane results.

In Tweeten, Luther, *Food and Agricultural Policy* (Washington, D.C.: American Enterprise Institute for Public Policy Research, 1977), p. 48.

63. For a discussion of the Brannan Plan, see Christenson, Leo, in Edwin, Ed, *Feast or Famine: Food, Farming, and Farm Politics in America* (New York: Charterhouse, 1974), p. 310.

64. Chowdhury, Ashok, and Earl O. Heady, *An Analysis of American Agriculture Under Various Policy Alternatives for 1980* (Ames, Ia.: Center for Agriculture and Rural Development, 1979), p. 54. One problem with this approach is that it would concentrate diversions in certain regions such as the Great Plains, Appalachia, and the Northwest. The idling of land would, in turn, hurt these local economies because of the reduced trade in such farm goods as tractors, fuel, and seeds. Chowdhury and Heady recommend using some of the savings from the reform to stimulate economic activity in the affected areas.

65. Tweeten, Luther, *AEI, Food and Agricultural Policy* (Washington, D.C.: American Enterprise Institute for Public Policy Research, 1977), p. 53.

66. Hedrick, J. L., "Factor Returns Under the Tobacco Program," in George S. Tolley (ed.), *Study of U.S. Agricultural Adjustments* (Raleigh: State University of North Carolina, 1970) pp. 261 and 165.

67. Johnson, D. Gale, *Farm Commodity Programs: An Opportunity for Change* (Washington, D.C.: American Enterprise Institute for Public Policy Research, 1973), p. 62.

68. Johnson, D. Gale, *Farm Commodity Programs: An Opportunity for Change* (Washington, D.C.: American Enterprise Institute for Public Policy Research, 1973), p. 63.

69. Johnson, Glenn L., in Johnson, Glenn and C. Leroy Quance, *The Overproduction Trap in U.S. Agriculture* (Baltimore: Johns Hopkins University Press, 1972), p. 182.

PART 3

Chapter 7

1. For discussion, see Krauss, Melvyn B, *The New Protectionism: The Welfare State and International Trade* (New York: New York University Press, 1978), p. xx.

2. This tension is evident in the efforts of traditional conservative Peter Viereck to disassociate himself from his libertarian conservative cousins:

    > A distinction between rooted (traditional) conservatives and rootless, counter-revolutionary (libertarian) doctrinaires is the measure of the difference between two different groups in contemporary America: the humanistic value-conservers and the materialistic, old-guard Republicans. The latter are what a wrong and temporary journalistic usage often calls "conservative." It is more accurate to call them nineteenth-century Manchester liberals with roots no deeper than the relatively recent post–Civil War "Gilded Age."

    Dolbeare, Kenneth M., and Patricia Dolbeare, *American Ideologies: The Competing Political Beliefs of the 1970s*, 3rd ed. (Chicago: Rand McNally College Publishing Co., 1976), p. 65.

3. For a discussion of fusionism, see Nash, George, *The Conservative Intellectual Movement in America since 1945* (New York: Basic Books, 1976), Chapter 6.

4. William F. Buckley, quoted in Nash, George, *The Conservative Intellectual Movement in America since 1945* (New York: Basic Books, 1976), p. 125.

5. Mill, John Stuart, *Principles of Political Economy, Book V* (Toronto: University of Toronto Press, 1965), p. 945.

6. Milton Friedman, quoted in Hayek, Friedrich A., *The Road to Serfdom* (Chicago: University of Chicago Press, 1944), p. 204.

7. Ralph Nader, quoted in Lodge, George C., *The New American Ideology* (New York: Alfred A. Knopf, 1975), p. 86.

8. John Locke, quoted in Baradat, Leon P., *Political Ideologies: Their Origins and Impact* (Englewood Cliffs, N.J.: Prentice-Hall, Inc., 1979), p. 63.

9. Goldwater, Barry, *The Conscience of a Conservative* (Shepardsville, Ky.: Victor, 1960), p. 59.

10. David Buel, Jr., quoted in Volkomer, Walter E., *The Liberal Tradition in American Thought* (New York: Capricorn Books, 1970), p. 147.

11. Richard Nixon, quoted in Reichley, James, *Conservatives in an Age of Change* (Washington, D.C.: Brookings Institution, 1981), p. 19.

12. Goldwater, Barry, *The Conscience of a Conservative* (Shephardsville, Ky.: Victor, 1960), p. 16.

13. Herbert Hoover, quoted in Sigler, J. A. (ed.), *The Conservative Tradition in American Thought* (New York: Capricorn Books, 1970), p. 320. Hoover went on to read the following pledge, a pledge which the election of Roosevelt never allowed him to fulfill:

> *I am willing to pledge myself that if the time should ever come that the voluntary agencies of the country together with the local and state governments are unable to find resources with which to prevent hunger and suffering in my country, I will ask the aid of every resource of the federal government because I would no more see starvation amongst our countrymen than would any Senator or Congressman (p. 323).*

14. Robert Hutchins, quoted in Burnham, James, *Suicide of the West: An Essay on the Meaning and Destiny of Liberalism* (New Rochelle, N.Y.: Arlington House, 1964), p. 90.
15. Lodge, George C., *The New American Ideology* (New York: Alfred A. Knopf, 1975), p. 125.
16. From the song of the same name by Paul Simon.

Chapter 8

1. As Chapter 1 discussed, some scholars have explained the rise of federal regulatory agencies during this period through the capture lens. For example, Gabriel Kolko has argued that the ICC was in fact a creation of the railroad monopoly rather than a public interest tool to correct monopoly abuses. See Kolko, Gabriel, *Railroads and Regulation, 1877–1916* (Princeton, N.J.: Princeton University Press, 1965).
2. Anderson, Douglas, *Regulatory Policies and Electric Utilities* (Boston: Auburn House, 1981), pp. 48–51.
3. The relevant decisions are *Bluefield Co., v. Public Service Commission,* 262 U.S. 679 (1922) and *Federal Power Commission v. Hope Natural Gas Co.,* 320 U.S. 591 (1944).
4. For bonds or "debt capital," a utility's market cost of capital is basically the interest rate that must be paid to the bond holders. The market cost of equity capital (stocks) is more complex: It equals the total return investors expect to earn on their investment where the return comes in the form of *both* dividends and stock appreciation.
5. For discussion, see Navarro, P., "The Politics of Air Pollution," *The Public Interest* No. 59 (Spring 1980), pp. 36–44.
6. Brigham, Eugene, and Dilip, Shome, "Equity Risk Premiums in the 1980s" (University of Florida, Working Paper No. 58, 1982).
7. Thompson, Howard, "Estimating Return Deficiencies of Electric Utilities 1963–1981" (Madison: University of Wisconsin Graduate School of Business, Working Paper 8-83-15, 1983).
8. See Joskow, Paul L., "Inflation and Environmental Concern: Structural Change in the Process of Public Utility Price Regulation," *Journal of Law and Economics,* October 1974, pp. 291–311.
9. The technical article on which this section is based is Navarro, P., "Public Utility Commission Regulation: Performance, Determinants, and Energy Policy Impacts," *Energy Journal,* March/April 1982, pp. 119–139.
10. Averch, Harvey, and Johnson, Leland, "Behavior of the Firm under Regulatory Constraint," *American Economic Review,* **LII** (December 1962), pp. 1052–69.

11. This problem is discussed in great detail in my book, *The Dimming of America* (Cambridge: Ballinger Publishing, 1984).

12. New England Electric Service Research Department.

13. See Trout, R. R., "The Regulatory Factor and Electric Utility Common Stock Investment Values," *Public Utilities Fortnightly*, November 22, 1979, pp. 28–31; and Archer, S. H., "The Regulatory Effects of Cost of Capital in Electric Utilities," *Public Utilities Fortnightly*, February 26, 1981, pp. 36–39. See also Dubin, Jeffrey A. and Navarro, Peter, "Regulatory Climate and the Cost of Capital," in *Issues in Utility Economics*, edited by Michael Crew (Lexington, Mass.: Lexington Books, Fall 1982).

14. The relevant studies by the U.S. Department of Energy are: *The National Electric Reliability Study: Final Report* (Washington, D.C.: April 1981) and *The Nation's Energy Future* (Washington, D.C.: 1983).

15. Economist Marie Corio has found that the availability of generating capacity falls sharply as rate suppression increases. As Corio commented, "If a utility's earnings are squeezed, poor unit power-plant performance follows—although it takes a couple of years for this to become apparent in lower equipment availability and . . . higher costs to the ratepayer." Corio, Marie R., "Why Is the Performance of Electric Generating Units Declining?" *Public Utilities Fortnightly*, April 29, 1982, pp. 25–301.

16. The calculation is $(500/1.15) + (1000/1.15^2) = \$1,191$.

17. The calculation is $(600/1.15) + (700/1.15^2) = \$1,051$.

18. U.S. Department of Energy, *Long Term Consumer Impacts of Electricity Rate Regulatory Policies*, January 1983, Office of Policy, Planning and Analysis.

19. For a discussion of the economics of oil displacement, see Navarro, P., "Oil Conservation," *Wall Street Journal*, March 11, 1981.

20. For a discussion, see Navarro, P., "Generating Real GNP Growth," *Business Week*, March 22, 1982, p. 17.

21. Ibid.

22. For further discussion, see Navarro, P., "Our Stake in the Electric Utility Executive's Dilemma," *Harvard Business Review*, May/June 1982.

23. Navarro, P., "The Soft, Hard, or Smart Path: Charting the Electric Utility Industry's Future," *Public Utilities Fortnightly*, June 18, 1981, pp. 25–30.

24. For a fuller discussion of these options, see my book *The Dimming of America* (Cambridge: Ballinger Publishing, 1984), Chapter 9.

Chapter 9

1. John Adams, quoted in Kirk, Russell, *The Conservative Mind: From Burke to Eliot* (Chicago: H. Regnery, 1960), p. 78.

2. Kirk, Russell, *The Conservative Mind: From Burke to Eliot* (Chicago: H. Regnery, 1960), p. 8.

3. Edmund Burke, quoted in Kirk, Russell, *The Conservative Mind: From Burke to Eliot* (Chicago: H. Regnery, 1960), pp. 15–16.

4. Dewey, John, *Liberalism and Social Action* (New York: Capricorn Books, 1965), p. 39.

5. Mill, John Stuart, "On Liberty," *The Essential Works of John Stuart Mill* (New York: Bantam Books, 1961), p. 318.

6. Oakshott, Michael, *Rationalism and Politics* (New York: Basic Books, 1962), pp. 1–2.

7. Schapiro, J. Salwyn, *Liberalism: Its Meaning and History* (Princeton: D. Van Nostrand Co., 1958), pp. 12–13.

8. Fred A. Vinson, quoted in Nash, George, *The Conservative Intellectual Movement in America Since 1945* (New York: Basic Books, 1976), p. 44.

9. Burnham, James, *Suicide of the West: An Essay on the Meaning and Destiny of Liberalism* (New Rochelle, N.Y.: Arlington House, 1964), p. 53.

10. Weaver, Richard M., *Visions of Order: The Cultural Crisis of Our Time* (Baton Rouge: 1964), pp. 114 and 116.

11. Jeffrey Hart, quoted in Nash, George, *The Conservative Intellectual Movement in America since 1945* (New York: Basic Books, 1976), p. 300.

12. Gerhart Niemeyer, interpreted and quoted in Nash, George, *The Conservative Intellectual Movement in America since 1945* (New York: Basic Books, 1976), p. 300.

13. William F. Buckley, quoted in Nash, George, *The Conservative Intellectual Movement in America since 1945* (New York: Basic Books, 1976), p. 281.

14. Reagan, Ronald, "Address to the International Association of Chiefs of Police," New Orleans, September 28, 1981, *The New York Times*, September 29, 1981, p. A18.

15. Harlan, Doug, "Hinckley Case Should Focus Attention on Penal System," *The Dallas Morning News*, April 13, 1982.

16. Burnham, James, *Suicide of the West: An Essay on the Meaning and Destiny of Liberalism* (New Rochelle, N.Y.: Arlington House, 1964), p. 293.

17. Reagan, Ronald, "Address to the International Association of Chiefs of Police," New Orleans, September 28, 1981, *The New York Times*, September 29, 1981, p. A18.

18. Reagan, Ronald, "Address to the International Association of Chiefs of Police," New Orleans, September 28, 1981, *The New York Times*, September 29, 1981, p. A18.

19. Burnham, James, *Suicide of the West: An Essay on the Meaning and Destiny of Liberalism* (New Rochelle, N.Y.: Arlington House, 1964), p. 293.

20. Reagan, Ronald, "Address to the International Association of Chiefs of Police," New Orleans, September 28, 1981, *The New York Times*, September 29, 1981, p. A18.

21. John Adams, quoted in Rossiter, Clinton, *Conservatism in America: The Thankless Persuasion*, 2nd ed. (New York: Alfred A. Knopf, 1962), p. 114.

22. Edmund Burke, quoted in Baradat, Leon, *Political Ideologies: Their Origins and Impact* (Englewood Cliffs, N.J.: Prentice-Hall, 1979), p. 76.

23. James Madison, quoted in Baradat, Leon, *Political Ideologies: Their Origins and Impact* (Englewood Cliffs, N.J.: Prentice-Hall, 1979), p. 85.

24. Jefferson, Thomas, letter to the Abbé Arnoud, Paris, July 19, 1789, quoted in McKenna, George, *American Populism* (New York: Capricorn Books, 1974).

25. Mason, Alpheus T., *The States Rights Debate: Anti-Federalism and the Constitution* (Englewood Cliffs, N.J.: Prentice-Hall, 1964), p. 8.

26. Mason, Alpheus T., *The States Rights Debate: Anti-Federalism and the Constitution* (Englewood Cliffs, N.J.: Prentice-Hall, 1964), p. 8.

27. Goldwater, Barry, *The Conscience of a Conservative* (Shepardsville, Ky.: Victor Publishing Co., 1960), p. 29.

28. Mason, Alpheus T., *The States Rights Debate: Anti-Federalism and the Constitution* (Englewood Cliffs, N.J.: Prentice-Hall, 1964), p. 195.

29. Mason, Alpheus T., *The States Rights Debate: Anti-Federalism and the Constitution* (Englewood Cliffs, N.J.: Prentice-Hall, 1964), p. 195.

Chapter 10

1. *The Phyllis Schlafly Report* (Alton, Ill.: The Eagle Trust Fund, February 1972), pp. 2–3.

2. The original 1923 version stated, "Men and women shall have equal rights throughout the United States and every place subject to its jurisdiction." This was revised in 1943 by the Senate Judiciary Committee to its current form.

3. *Editorial Research Reports*, "The Women's Movement: Agenda for the 80s," (Washington, D.C.: Congressional Quarterly, 1981), p. 188.

4. Freeman, Jo, *The Politics of Women's Liberation* (New York and London: Longman Press, 1975), p. 52.

5. See, for example, the forerunner of this genre: Beauvoir, Simone de. *The Second Sex*, translated and edited by H. M. Parshley (New York: Alfred A. Knopf, 1953).

6. This point is made in Gelb, Joyce and Palley, Marian L., *Women and Public Policies* (Princeton, N.J.: Princeton University Press, 1982, p. 19).

7. The rescission drive opened yet another can of legal worms: while pro-ERA forces insisted that recision was unconstitutional, anti-ERA forces vowed to press the rescission in the courts if the amendment were ratified.

8. The Kentucky legislature voted to rescind in 1978 but the Lieutenant Governor, acting as governor, vetoed the bill. South Dakota passed a resolution in 1979 declaring its earlier vote null and void if the ERA was not approved by its original March 22, 1979 deadline.

9. The National Women's Party (NWP) which originally sponsored the ERA remains very active but operates as a relative unknown. "It has been harassing Congress for half a century with a small, tightly knit lobbying organization whose members have grown old with the organization." Freeman, Jo, *The Politics of Women's Liberation* (New York and London: Longman Press, 1975), p. 64.

10. Gladstone, Leslie, *Equal Rights Amendment (Proposed).* Issue Brief IB74122. Washington, D.C.: Government Division, Library of Congress, Congressional Research Service, Major Issues System, January 29, 1982.

11. National Organization for Women, Alice Chapman, Treasurer. Personal communication, November 1983.

12. Freeman, Jo, *The Politics of Women's Liberation* (New York and London: Longman Press, 1975), p. 90.

13. National Organization for Women, Alice Chapman, Treasurer. Personal communication, November 1983.

14. Freeman, Jo, *The Politics of Women's Liberation* (New York and London: Longman Press, 1975), p. 92.

15. Freeman, Jo, *The Politics of Women's Liberation* (New York and London: Longman Press, 1975), p. 92.

16. Freeman, Jo, *The Politics of Women's Liberation* (New York and London: Longman Press, 1975), p. 152.

17. Gelb, Joyce and Palley, Marian L., *Women and Public Policies* (Princeton, N.J.: Princeton University Press, 1982), p. 31.

18. The other major groups include B'nai Brith Women, National Federation of Professional Women's Clubs, the National Council of Jewish Women, and the United Methodist Women.

19. Gelb, Joyce and Palley, Marian L., *Women and Public Policies* (Princeton, N.J.: Princeton University Press, 1982), p. 26.

20. One critic has charged that, in doing so, feminists have "coopted" the ACLU. Gelb, Joyce and Palley, Marian L., *Women and Public Policies* (Princeton, N.J.: Princeton University Press, 1982), p. 34.

21. Jewish support excludes Orthodox and Hasidic Jews.

22. Freeman, Jo, *The Politics of Women's Liberation* (New York and London: Longman Press, 1975), p. 228.

23. For further details, see Boles, Janet K., *The Politics of the Equal Rights Amendment* (New York and London: Longman Press, 1979), p. 68, from which this description is taken.

24. STOP-ERA. Personal communication, November, 1983.

25. In Boles, Janet K., *The Politics of the Equal Rights Amendment* (New York and London: Longman Press, 1979), p. 67.

26. Boles, Janet K., *The Politics of the Equal Rights Amendment* (New York and London: Longman Press, 1979), p. 67.

27. For example, in 1979, Sonia Johnson, then president of Mormons for ERA (MERA), was formally excommunicated by the Church for her support of the Amendment. *Encyclopedia of Associations.* "National Organizations of the U.S." (Detroit, Michigan: Gale Research Co., 1983), Vol. 1, p. 9323.

28. A Georgian Baptist minister in Boles, Janet K., *The Politics of the Equal Rights Amendment* (New York and London: Longman Press, 1979), p. 109.

29. Boles, Janet K., *The Politics of the Equal Rights Amendment* (New York and London: Longman Press, 1979), p. 168.

30. Boles, Janet K., *The Politics of the Equal Rights Amendment* (New York and London: Longman Press, 1979), p. 168.

31. *Editorial Research Reports.* "The Women's Movement: Agenda for the 80s." (Washington, D.C.: Congressional Quarterly, 1981), p. 182.

32. *Editorial Research Reports.* "The Women's Movement: Agenda for the 80s." (Washington, D.C.: Congressional Quarterly, 1981), p. 182.

33. The Equal Pay Act of 1963, for example, is supposed to ensure equal pay for equal work, but as we shall see in the discussion of the economics of the ERA, considerable wage differentials exist among women and men in the same occupations.

34. Freeman, Jo, *The Politics of Women's Liberation* (New York and London: Longman Press, 1975), p. 190. Note that this figure refers to a 1972 assessment at 1972 prices.

35. Of course, the existence of a male hierarchy in many of the unions, as well as the fact that female advancement will tend to take place at the expense of some male union members, suggests an internal conflict within labor—as witnessed by the waffling of the AFL–CIO over ERA support.

36. *The Phyllis Schlafly Report* (Alton, Ill.: The Eagle Trust Fund, February 1973), p. 3.

37. This claim is hotly disputed by pro-ERA forces that maintain that married women will be much better off with the uniform protection of the ERA since it will ensure them a rightful claim to their husband's property and will only create a child support or alimony obligation for a woman if she earns more than her husband.

38. This observation on asymmetrical motives may help explain the asymmetrical efforts of the church lobby. While the anti-ERA denominations fought very hard against the amendment, the pro-ERA denominations have lent it only moderate support.

39. See Gilder, George, *Wealth and Poverty* (New York: Basic Books, 1981).

40. John Birch Society, *The Review of the News*, November 12, 1975, p. 4.

41. John Birch Society, *The Review of the News*, November 12, 1975, p. 6.

42. John Birch Society, *The Review of the News*, November 12, 1975, pp. 3 and 4.

43. Davison, Jacquie, in Boles, Janet K., *The Politics of the Equal Rights Amendment* (New York and London: Longman Press, 1979), p. 5.

44. Brown, Barbara A., Ann E. Freedman, Harriet N. Katz, and Alice M. Price, *Women's Rights and the Law* (New York: Praeger Publishers, 1977), p. 97.

45. Brown, Barbara A., Ann E. Freedman, Harriet N. Katz, and Alice M. Price, *Women's Rights and the Law* (New York: Praeger Publishers, 1977), p. 10.

46. Brown, Barbara A., Ann E. Freedman, Harriet N. Katz, and Alice M. Price, *Women's Rights and the Law* (New York: Praeger Publishers, 1977), p. 9.

47. Brown, Barbara A., Ann E. Freedman, Harriet N. Katz, and Alice M. Price, *Women's Rights and the Law* (New York: Praeger Publishers, 1977), p. 10.

48. Brown, Barbara A., Ann E. Freedman, Harriet N. Katz, and Alice M. Price, *Women's Rights and the Law* (New York: Praeger Publishers, 1977), p. 10.

49. Brown, Barbara A., Ann E. Freedman, Harriet N. Katz, and Alice M. Price, *Women's Rights and the Law* (New York: Praeger Publishers, 1977), p. 10.

50. For a very detailed description of the likely legal interpretation of the ERA, see Brown, Barbara A., Ann E. Freedman, Harriet N. Katz, and Alice M. Price, *Women's Rights and the Law* (New York: Praeger Publishers, 1977).

51. Boles, Janet K., *The Politics of the Equal Rights Amendment* (New York and London: Longman Press, 1979), p. 120, quoting Georgia opponents.

52. One explanation for this that falls outside the "federalist conspiracy" notion is offered by Janet Boles: "The deletion was made to conform to the almost identical language found in the 13th, 14th, 15th, 19th, 23rd, 24th, and 26th amendments." Boles, Janet K., *The Politics of the Equal Rights Amendment* (New York and London: Longman Press, 1979), p. 36.

53. United Families of America, "Equality Yes! ERA No!" Concern Sheet No. 1 (Arlington, Va.: United Families of America, 19), p. 1.

54. United Families of America, "Equality Yes! ERA No!" Concern Sheet No. 1 (Arlington, Va.: United Families of America, 19), p. 1.

55. John Birch Society, *The Review of the News*, August 11, 1976, p. 6.

56. *The Phyllis Schlafly Report* (Alton, Illinois: The Eagle Trust Fund, June 1983), p. 1.

57. Boles, Janet K., *The Politics of the Equal Rights Amendment* (New York and London: Longman Press, 1979), p. 171.

58. Brown, Barbara A., Ann E. Freedman, Harriet N. Katz, and Alice M. Price, *Women's Rights and the Law* (New York: Praeger Publishers, 1977), p. 5.

59. Brown, Barbara A., Ann E. Freedman, Harriet N. Katz, and Alice M. Price, *Women's Rights and the Law* (New York: Praeger Publishers, 1977), p. 1.

60. Brown, Barbara A., Ann E. Freedman, Harriet N. Katz, and Alice M. Price, *Women's Rights and the Law* (New York: Praeger Publishers, 1977), pp. 218–219 and 234.

61. John Birch Society, *The Review of the News*, November 12, 1975, p. 6.

62. John Birch Society, *The Review of the News*, November 12, 1975, p. 5.

63. John Birch Society, *The Review of the News*, November 12, 1975, p. 5.

64. In an increasingly common, but arguably questionable practice, much of the ERA lobbying money has been "laundered" through arm's-length tax-exempt trust funds loosely affiliated with the mother organizations.

65. For instance, United States Commission on Civil Rights, "Sex Bias in the U.S. Code" (Washington, D.C.: U.S. GPO, April 1977), and Equal Employment Opportunity Commission, "Hearings on Job Segregation and Wage Discrimination" (Washington, D.C.: U.S. GPO, 1980).

66. Boles, Janet K., *The Politics of the Equal Rights Amendment* (New York and London: Longman Press, 1979), pp. 103–4.

67. Pejoratives included "hairy-chested and braless," "women but not ladies," and "nihilistic versions of T. S. Eliot's Hollow Man." See Boles, Janet K., *The Politics of the Equal Rights Amendment* (New York and London: Longman Press, 1979), p. 88.

68. *The Phyllis Schlafly Report* (Alton, Ill.: The Eagle Trust Fund, February 1972), p. 3.

69. Delsman, Mary A., *Everything You Need to Know About ERA* (Riverside, Calif.: Merganza Press, 1975), p. 224.

70. Boles, Janet K., *The Politics of the Equal Rights Amendment* (New York and London: Longman Press, 1979), p. 115.

71. Freeman, Jo, *The Politics of Women's Liberation* (New York and London: Longman Press, 1975), p. 218.

72. For details, see Boles, Janet K., *The Politics of the Equal Rights Amendment* (New York and London: Longman Press, 1979), p. 116.

73. Personal Communication. The Eagle Forum, Washington, D.C. December 1, 1983.

74. See the aforementioned excommunication of Sonia Johnson.

75. Boles, Janet K., *The Politics of the Equal Rights Amendment* (New York and London: Longman Press, 1979), p. 109.

76. In Boles, Janet K., *The Politics of the Equal Rights Amendment* (New York and London: Longman Press, 1979), p. 62–63.

77. In Boles, Janet K., *The Politics of the Equal Rights Amendment* (New York and London: Longman Press, 1979), p. 104.

78. Brenda Fasteau, quoted in *Editorial Research Reports*, "The Women's Movement: Agenda for the 80s" (Washington, D.C.: Congressional Quarterly, 1981), p. 181.

79. Alice Chapman, treasurer, National Organization for Women, personal communication.

80. *Editorial Research Reports,* "The Women's Movement: Agenda for the 80s" (Washington, D.C.: Congressional Quarterly, 1981), p. 185. The legality of this boycott was unsuccessfully challenged in an antitrust suit filed by Missouri against NOW.

81. Business Week, "ERA Round 2: Now the Issues are Economic." Industrial Edition Number 2801, August 1, 1983. (New York: McGraw-Hill, 1983), p. 92.

82. A concrete example of the magnitude of the sums involved is found in the court dockets of a suit against the largest employer of women, AT&T. It was estimated that women were due $3.5 billion in back pay. Freeman, Jo, *The Politics of Women's Liberation* (New York and London: Longman Press, 1975), p. 150.

83. These 1975 statistics are taken from Freeman, Jo, *The Politics of Women's Liberation* (New York and London: Longman Press, 1975).

84. NOW Fact Sheet, "ERA and Money," 1981, p. 1.

85. A 1975 statistic reported by Business Week, as cited in *Editorial Research Reports, The Women's Movement Agenda for the '80s* (Washington, D.C.: Congressional Quarterly, 1981), p. 48.

86. U.S. Department of Labor—Bureau of Labor Statistics, *Employment and Earnings January 1983* (Washington, D.C.: GPO, 1983).

87. NOW Fact Sheet, "ERA and Money," 1981, p. 1.

88. Unpublished 1982 data from Survey of Earned Degrees Conferred, National Center for Education Statistics, Washington, D.C.

89. United Commission on Civil Rights, the Equal Rights Amendment: Guaranteeing Equal Rights for Women under the Constitution, Clearing House Publication 65 (Washington, D.C.: U.S. GPO, 1981), p. 20.

90. *Business Week,* as cited in *Editorial Research Reports, The Women's Movement Agenda for the '80s* (Washington, D.C.: Congressional Quarterly, 1981), p. 92.

91. Brown, Barbara A., Ann E. Freedman, Harriet N. Katz, and Alice M. Price, *Women's Rights and the Law* (New York: Praeger Publishers, 1977), p. 17.

92. For example, Massachusetts, Michigan, and North Carolina have a common-law rule that the husband manages and controls the entire property assets of his wife. He may deplete her assets without her consent, and her rights to one-half of the property upon divorce or all of it upon her husband's death may be nullified. In Louisiana, the husband has the sole rights to manage, sell, or give away his and his wife's community property, including his wife's wages. Brown, Barbara A., Ann E. Freedman, Harriet N. Katz, and Alice M. Price, *Women's Rights and the Law* (New York: Praeger Publishers, 1977), pp. 162–163.

93. ". . . I cannot see any better principle at present than to make as little innovation as possible; keep things going as well as we can in the present train." John Adams, quoted in Kirk, Russell, *The Conservative Mind: From Burke to Eliot* (Chicago: H. Regnery, 1960), p. 78.

Chapter 11

1. Winston Churchill, quoted in James, Robert Rhodes (ed.), *Winston Churchill: His Complete Speeches, 1897–1963* (New York: Chelsea House Publishers, 1947), p. 5627.

2. George Washington, quoted in Fox, Ronald J., *Arming America: How the U.S. Buys Weapons* (Boston: Harvard Graduate School of Administration, 1974), p. 26.

3. Lens, Sidney, *The Military-Industrial Complex* (Philadelphia: Pilgrim Press and Kansas City: The National Catholic Reporter, 1970), p. 18.

4. Augustine, Norman R. *Augustine's Laws* (New York: American Institute of Aeronautics and Astronautics, 1982), p. 48.

5. Holwill, Richard N., (ed.), *Agenda '83* (Washington: D.C.: The Heritage Foundation, 1983), p. 75.

6. Dwight Eisenhower, *Waging Peace* (New York: Doubleday, 1965), p. 615.

7. Proxmire, William, *Report from Wasteland* (New York: Praeger Publishers, 1970), p. 9.

8. For details, see Lens, Sidney, *The Military-Industrial Complex* (Philadelphia: Pilgrim Press and Kansas City: The National Catholic Reporter, 1970), p. 102.

9. Clark Kerr, quoted in Lens, Sidney, *The Military-Industrial Complex* (Philadelphia: Pilgrim Press and Kansas City: The National Catholic Reporter, 1970), p. 126.

10. Proxmire, William, *Report from Wasteland* (New York: Praeger Publishers, 1970), p. 110.

11. Proxmire, William, *Report from Wasteland* (New York: Praeger Publishers, 1970), p. 100.

12. The discussion on veterans' and service organizations draws heavily on Yarmolinsky, Adam, *The Military Establishment: Its Impact on American Society* (New York: Harper & Row, 1971), pp. 207–209, which the reader may want to consult for further details.

13. Lens, Sidney, *The Military-Industrial Complex* (Philadelphia: Pilgrim Press and Kansas City: The National Catholic Reporter, 1970), p. 48.

14. Fox, Ronald J., *Arming America: How the U.S. Buys Weapons* (Boston: Harvard Graduate School of Business Administration, 1974), p. 29.

15. Lens, Sidney, *The Military-Industrial Complex* (Philadelphia: Pilgrim Press and Kansas City: The National Catholic Reporter, 1970), p. 42.

16. For details, see Lens, Sidney, *The Military-Industrial Complex* (Philadelphia: Pilgrim Press and Kansas City: The National Catholic Reporter, 1970), pp. 51–52.

17. A defense contractor, quoted in Fallows, James, *National Defense* (New York: Random House, 1981), p. 73.

18. Lens, Sidney, *The Military-Industrial Complex* (Philadelphia: Pilgrim Press and Kansas City: The National Catholic Reporter, 1970), p. 52.

19. Proxmire, William, *Report from Wasteland* (New York: Praeger Publishers, 1970), p. 21.

20. Yarmolinsky, Adam, *The Military Establishment: Its Impact on American Society* (New York: Harper & Row, 1971), p. 194.

21. Proxmire, William, *Report from Wasteland* (New York: Praeger Publishers, 1970), pp. 153–154.

22. Ronald J. Fox, quoted in Fallows, James, *National Defense* (New York: Random House, 1981), p. 66.

23. Fox, Ronald J., *Arming America: How the U.S. Buys Weapons* (Boston: Harvard Graduate School of Business Administration, 1974), p. 137.

24. Fox, Ronald J., *Arming America: How the U.S. Buys Weapons* (Boston: Harvard Graduate School of Business Administration, 1974), p. 137.

25. For details, see Sampson, Anthony, *The Arms Bazaar* (New York: Bantam Books, 1977), pp. 147–148.

26. Ronald Reagan, quoted in "Reducing the Danger of Nuclear Weapons," *U.S. Department of State Bulletin*, **83**, No. 2074 (May 1983), p. 1.

27. Barnet, in Weidenbaum, Murray L., *The Economics of Peacetime Defense* (New York: Praeger Publishers, 1974), p. 151.

28. Franklin C. Spinney's works include: *The Plans/Reality Mismatch* (Washington, D.C.: U.S. GPO, 1982), and "Defense Facts of Life," in U.S. Congress, Senate, Committee on Armed Services, Subcommittee on Manpower and Personnel, *Hearings, Impact of Technology on Military Manpower Requirements, Readiness, and Operations* (Washington, D.C.: U.S. GPO, 1981).

29. Isaacson, Walter, in "The Winds of Reform," reported by Bruce W. Nelan et. al. *Time*, March 7, 1983, pp. 12–30.

30. Nunn, quoted in U.S. Congress, Senate, Committee on Armed Services, Subcommittee on Manpower and Personnel, *Hearings, Impact of Technology on Military Manpower Requirements, Readiness and Operations* (Washington, D.C.: U.S. GPO, 1981), p. 1.

31. Hitch, Charles J. and Ronald N. McKean, *The Economics of Defense in the Nuclear Age* (Cambridge, Mass.: Harvard University Press, 1960), p. 2.

32. Perry, William J., under secretary of defense for research and engineering, in U.S. Congress, quoted in U.S. Congress, Senate, Committee on Armed Services, Subcommittee on Manpower and Personnel, *Hearings, Impact of Technology on Military Manpower Requirements, Readiness and Operations* (Washington, D.C.: U.S. GPO, 1981), p. 5.

33. Lewis Carroll, quoted in Weidenbaum, Murray L., *The Economics of Peacetime Defense* (New York: Praeger Publishers, 1974), p. 26.

34. This example and quote are from Fallows, James, *National Defense* (New York: Random House, 1981), p. 106.

35. Kuhn, quoted in Holwill, Richard N., (ed.), *Agenda '83* (Washington, D.C.: The Heritage Foundation, 1983), p. 70.

36. Spinney, "Defense Facts of Life," in U.S. Congress, Senate, Committee on Armed Services, Subcommittee on Manpower and Personnel, Hearings, Impact of Technology on Military Manpower Requirements, Readiness, and Operations (Washington, D.C.: U.S. GPO, 1981), p. 196.

37. For this and a summary of other savings totaling $4.5 billion a year, see Gansler, S. Jacques, *The Defense Industry* (Cambridge, Mass.: MIT Press, 1980), pp. 220–223.

38. Fallows, James, *National Defense* (New York: Random House, 1981), p. 102.

39. Fox, Ronald J., *Arming America: How the U.S. Buys Weapons* (Boston: Harvard Graduate School of Business Administration, 1974), p. 48.

40. Fox, Ronald J., *Arming America: How the U.S. Buys Weapons* (Boston: Harvard Graduate School of Business Administration, 1974), p. 138.

41. Dwight Eisenhower, quoted in Hitch, Charles J. and Ronald N. McKean, *The Eco-

nomics of Defense in the Nuclear Age (Cambridge, Mass.: Harvard University Press, 1960), p. 600.

42. Winston Churchill, quoted in Lens, Sidney, *The Military-Industrial Complex* (Philadelphia: Pilgrim Press and Kansas City: The National Catholic Reporter, 1970), p. 9.

43. In framing these recommendations, the papers of Franklin C. Spinney, *The Plans/ Reality Mismatch* (Washington, D.C.: U.S. GPO, 1982), and "Defense Facts of Life," in U.S. Congress, Senate, Committee on Armed Services, Subcommittee on Manpower and Personnel, *Hearings, Impact of Technology on Military Manpower Requirements, Readiness, and Operations* (Washington, D.C.: U.S. GPO, 1981); the work of Jacques S. Gansler, *The Defense Industry* (Cambridge, Mass.: MIT Press, 1980); George Kuhn's article in Holwill, Richard N. (ed.), *Agenda '83* (Washington, D.C.: The Heritage Foundation, 1983); and the excellent article, Isaacson, Walter, "The Winds of Reform," reported by Bruce W. Nelan et al., *Time*, March 7, 1983, pp. 12–30, were particularly helpful.

44. The first attempt was made by President Truman, who created a unified DoD in 1947 to replace the old cabinet posts of secretary of war and secretary of the navy and gave legal status to the joint chiefs of staff. The next attempt at reform was made by DoD Secretary Robert McNamara during the Kennedy and Johnson years. McNamara tried—with only partial success—to centralize DoD and force the services to share materials.

45. Isaacson, Walter, "The Winds of Reform," reported by Bruce W. Nelan et al., *Time*, March 7, 1983, p. 30.

46. Gansler, Jacques, S., *The Defense Industry* (Cambridge, Mass.: MIT Press, 1980), p. 259.

Appendix B

1. Robert Taft, quoted in Sigler, Jay (ed.), *The Conservative Tradition in American Thought* (New York: Capricorn Books, 1970), p. 343.

2. Larson, Arthur, *A Republican Looks at his Party* (New York: Harper Brothers, 1956), p. 13.

3. Burnham, James, *The Coming Defeat of Communism* (New York: 1950), p. 137.

4. Burnham, James, *Suicide of the West: An Essay on the Meaning and Destiny of Liberalism* (New Rochelle, N.Y.: Arlington House, 1964), p. 291.

5. Whittaker Chambers, quoted in Nash, George, *The Conservative Intellectual Movement in America since 1945* (New York: Basic Books, 1976), p. 104.

6. Rostow, W. W., quoted in Burnham, James, *Suicide of the West: An Essay on the Meaning and Destiny of Liberalism* (New Rochelle, N.Y.: Arlington House, 1964), p. 177. (Ironically, Rostow went on to become one of the chief architects of the bombing of Hanoi during the Vietnam War.)

7. Hamby, Alonzo, *Beyond the New Deal: Harry S. Truman and American Liberalism* (New York: Columbia University Press, 1973), p. 13.

8. Hamby, Alonzo, *Beyond the New Deal: Harry S. Truman and American Liberalism* (New York: Columbia University Press, 1973), p. xvii.

9. Hubert Humphrey, quoted in Burnham, James, *Suicide of the West: An Essay on the Meaning and Destiny of Liberalism* (New Rochelle, N.Y.: Arlington House, 1964), p. 89.

Index